Risk Management in Banking, Insurance
and Financial Services

Published by
ACADEMIC FOUNDATION
in association with

Institute of Public Enterprise

Risk Management in Banking, Insurance and Financial Services

Editors

R.K. Mishra, Inder Sekhar Yadav,
A. Pawan Kumar, Swayam Prava Mishra
and J. Kiranmai

ACADEMIC FOUNDATION
NEW DELHI

www.academicfoundation.com

First published in 2014
by

ACADEMIC FOUNDATION
4772-73 / 23 Bharat Ram Road, (23 Ansari Road),
Darya Ganj, New Delhi - 110 002 (India).
Phones : 23245001 / 02 / 03 / 04.
Fax : +91-11-23245005.
E-mail : books@academicfoundation.com
www.academicfoundation.com

in association with

Institute of Public Enterprise, Hyderabad

Disclaimer:
The findings/views/opinions expressed in this book are solely those of the author and do not necessarily reflect the views of the publisher.

Cataloging in Publication Data--DK

Courtesy: D.K. Agencies (P) Ltd. <docinfo@dkagencies.com>

Risk management in banking, insurance and financial services / editors, R.K. Mishra ... [et al.].
p. cm.
Contributed articles.
ISBN 9789332701397

1. Banks and banking--Risk management--India. 2. Insurance--Risk management--India. 3. Financial services industry--Risk management--India. I. Mishra, R. K., 1948- II. Institute of Public Enterprise (Hyderabad, India)

DDC 332.10954 23

Typeset by Italics India, New Delhi.

Printed and bound by The Book Mint, New Delhi.
www.thebookmint.in

Contents

Section IV

Risk Management and Hedging

Section V

Non-Financial Institutions and Risk Management

List of Tables, Figures and Annexures

Tables

Figures

Annexures

About the Editors/ Contributors

Editors:

R.K. Mishra, Sr. Professor and Director, Institute of Public Enterprise (IPE), Hyderabad, India, is a graduate of International Management Program, SDA Boccioni, Milan. He has been a Fellow of British Council and Commonwealth Secretariat and a Task Force Member on Memorandum of Understanding (MoU) by Department of Public Enterprises (DPE) for Corporate Social Responsibility (CSR) and Sustainable Development. He is a member of the UN Task Force on International Task Force on Standards of Excellence in Public Administration and Education and is associated with the United Nations Development Programme (UNDP) project on 'Macro-Economics of Poverty Reduction' carried out by RBI's Indira Gandhi Institute of Development Research (IGIDR). He has handled assignments for the Union Ministries of Finance, Power, Heavy Industries, Trade and Commerce, Heavy Industry and Public Enterprises, and Disinvestment. He has prolifically published many articles and books and conducted several training programmes in this area.

Inder Sekhar Yadav, Assistant Professor, IPE, Hyderabad, India, holds a Masters, MPhil and PhD degree in Economics from University of Hyderabad. He has taken over as the Coordinator of the Risk Management Cell of the institute and is working on identified thrust areas of research. He has conducted a number of management development programmes on enterprise risk management. His teaching and research interests include: financial risk management, banking, macroeconomics and industrial economics. He has published several articles in reputed national and international journals. He has also presented research papers in several national and international conferences.

A. Pawan Kumar, Assistant Professor, IPE, Hyderabad, India, holds Masters in Commerce and has PhD degree in Economics from University of Hyderabad. His research interests include international business and international financial management. He has published several articles in reputed national and international journals. He has also presented his work in several national and international conferences.

Swayam Prava Mishra, Assistant Professor, IPE, Hyderabad, India, holds a Masters and PhD degree in Economics from University of Hyderabad. For her doctoral degree, she has worked in the area of corporate credit risk. She specialises in financial economics, macroeconomics, econometrics and time series. She has publications in international and national journals and has also presented papers in several national and international conferences.

J. Kiranmai, Assistant Professor, IPE, Hyderabad, India, holds Masters in Commerce and an MPhil in Management. She specialises in the areas of accounting and finance. Her areas of interest include corporate governance, public enterprise management and restructuring. She is the joint coordinator, Post Graduate Diploma in Management (PGDM)-Banking, Insurance and Finance, at the institute. She has undertaken many research and consultancy assignments apart from organising management development programmes at the institute. She has attended and presented research papers in national and international conferences, and published in many national and international journals.

Contributors:

Debashis Acharya, Associate Professor, School of Economics, University of Hyderabad, Hyderabad, Andhra Pradesh, India.

Shardul Admane, Sr. Assistant Director, Insurance Regulatory and Development Authority, Hyderabad, Andhra Pradesh, India.

Ruchi Agarwal, Doctoral Fellow, University of Edinburgh Business School, Edinburgh, United Kingdom.

Jake Ansell, Professor, University of Edinburgh Business School, Edinburgh, United Kingdom.

Karthik Athelli, Student, IBS (Indian School of Business) Hyderabad, Hyderabad, Andhra Pradesh, India.

Mohammed Kasim C., Assistant Professor, Department of Economics, Farook College, Kozhikode, Kerala, India.

Biswajit Chakraborty, Doctoral Fellow, Department of Computer Applications, Techno India College of Technology (TICT), Kolkata, West Bengal, India.

Phanindra Goyari, Associate Professor, School of Economics, University of Hyderabad, Hyderabad, Andhra Pradesh, India.

Nitin Hande, Doctoral Fellow, Department of Economics, Swami Ramanand Teerth Marathwada (SRTM) University, Nanded, Maharashtra, India.

R. Hariharan, Doctoral Fellow, Department of Banking Technology, Pondicherry University, Puducherry, India.

V. Jayalakshmi, Assistant Professor, Siva Sivani Institute of Management, Secunderabad, Andhra Pradesh, India.

Pratap Kumar Jena, Doctoral Fellow, School of Economics, University of Hyderabad, Hyderabad, Andhra Pradesh, India.

Aathira K., Doctoral Fellow, Department of Commerce, University of Madras, Tamil Nadu, India.

A.S. Kalyana Kumar, Assistant Professor, Institute of Public Enterprise, Osmania University Campus, Hyderabad, Andhra Pradesh, India.

R.V. Kulkarni, Head, Department of Computer Studies, Chhatrapati Shahu Institute of Business Education & Research (CSIBER), Kolhapur, Maharashtra, India.

M.A. Lagesh, Doctoral Fellow, School of Economics, University of Hyderabad, Hyderabad, Andhra Pradesh, India.

Pardhasaradhi Madasu, Associate Professor, Siva Sivani Institute of Management, Secunderabad, Andhra Pradesh, India.

Laila Memdani, Faculty, IBS Hyderabad, Hyderabad, Andhra Pradesh, India.

Amit B. Mirji, Lecturer, Department of Management, Institute of Excellence in Management Science, Hubli, Karnataka, India.

Tuhin Mukherjee, Assistant Professor, Department of Business Administration, University of Kalyani, Kalyani, West Bengal, India.

S. Sudalai Muthu, Associate Professor, Department of Banking Technology, Pondicherry University, Puducherry, India.

Kesseven Padachi, Associate Professor, Department of Accounting and Finance, University of Technology, Mauritius.

M. Padmavathi, Assistant Professor, School of Management, Sri Krishna College of Technology, Coimbatore, Tamil Nadu, India.

Savita S. Patil, Assistant Manager, State Bank of India, Bijapur, Karnataka, India.

P.S. Subha Prada, Doctoral Fellow, School of Management Studies, University of Hyderabad, Hyderabad, Andhra Pradesh, India.

Sudha Rajagopal, Doctoral Fellow, Jain University, Bangalore, Karnataka, India.

Vanarase Shilpa Satish, Assistant, Defence Institute of Advanced Technology, Pune, Maharashtra, India.

R. Shanthi, Assistant Professor, Department of Commerce, University of Madras, Tamil Nadu, India.

D.K. Sreekantha, Coordinator, PG Department of Computer Science, Basaveshwar Science College, Bagalkot, Karnataka, India.

Padma Srinivasan, Professor, R.V. Institute of Management, Bengaluru, Karnataka, India.

Vikas Srivastava, Associate Professor and Chairperson (Post Graduate Programme for Executives; PGPEX), Indian Institute of Management (IIM) Ranchi, Ranchi, Jharkhand, India.

Thirumalvalavan, Professor, Bharathiar School of Management and Entrepreneur Development, Bharathiar University, Coimbatore, Tamil Nadu, India.

Veenapani, Faculty, Department of Management, Sarojini Naidu Vanita Mahavidyalaya, Hyderabad, Andhra Pradesh, India.

Polodoo Virendra, Researcher, IFS School of Finance, University of Mauritius, Mauritius.

Preface

Risk management is an increasingly important business driver and stakeholders have become much more concerned about risk. Risk may be a driver of strategic decisions, it may be a cause of uncertainty in the company or it may simply be embedded in the activities of the company. An enterprise-wide approach to risk management enables a company to consider the potential impact of all types of risks on all processes, activities, stakeholders, products and services. Implementing a comprehensive approach will result in companies benefiting from what is often referred to as the upside of risk.

This book consists of blind refereed articles related to risk management in banking, insurance, financial services and other allied areas divided into five different sections. The first section is on enterprise risk management which mainly discusses the necessary framework, approach and process of risk management in an enterprise. This section also provides a brief overview on advances on credit risk management. The second section attempts to study and examine various issues related to risk management in banks with focus on Basel norms. The next section provides comprehensive issues related to risks in insurance industry and the risk mitigation thereof. Section four examines various techniques of hedging as a tool of risk management. The last section is devoted on risk management in non-financial institutions and issues thereof.

R.K. Mishra, Inder Sekhar Yadav, A. Pawan Kumar,
Swayam Prava Mishra and J. Kiranmai

Acknowledgements

We offer our sincere gratitude to every person who supported our endeavour in bringing out this book. We are thankful to all the members of our advisory board, programme committee and review committee members for their consent, valuable suggestions and guidance. We wish to express our heartfelt thanks to all the authors whose contributions made this book possible. We also take this opportunity to thank our publishers who have taken great pains in publishing this book.

SECTION I

Enterprise Risk Management

1 Enterprise Risk Management

The Approach, Framework and Process

R.K. Mishra and Inder Sekhar Yadav

Introduction

Risk is an indispensable element of any business enterprise. If a given foreseen or unforeseen risk is properly identified, examined, measured and managed, it would bring and augment growth and opportunity of the enterprise. Charles Tremper[1] said, "The first step in the risk management process is to acknowledge the reality of risk. Denial is a common tactic that substitutes deliberate ignorance for thoughtful planning." The business enterprise risk management is the process of recognising or identifying various associated risk, assessing or evaluating the impact and probability of risk and prioritising the various issues of potential risk. Once the risk issues are identified and the impact and probability are assessed, the enterprise needs to effectively coordinate and economically strategise in order to mitigate or hedge the relevant risks to the organisation. This is effectively done by minimising, monitoring and controlling the probability and impact of occurrence of adverse events. If this is done with responsibility and effectively, business enterprises can guard and generate value for their owners, employees, customers, regulators and the economy as a whole.

In the context of globalisation, a modern day business enterprise functions in an intricate, dynamic and multi-faceted environment where every decision of management is reflected and affected by various types of relevant risk and uncertainty. This risk and uncertainty faced by the enterprise can be internal as well as external. For example, the various

1. Director of Strategic Planning and Partner Relations for the Center for Digital Innovation.

kinds of internal risks pertaining to a business enterprise can broadly be identified as operational risk, hazard risk, financial risk, strategic risk, technology risk, reputational risk, marketing risk, human resource risk, ethics risk and so on. The external risk associated with business enterprise can be market risk, economic risk, political risk, credit risk, environmental risk, social risk, legal risk and so on. More importantly, the adoption of enterprise expansion plans like mergers and acquisition, investment in emerging markets, major organisational restructuring, outsourcing key processes, major capital investment projects and developing significant new process and products, can all increase enterprise's risk exposure.

Further, risks can arise from uncertainty in domestic and global financial and capital markets, project failures, legal liabilities, industrial accident and natural disasters as well as conscious and intentional assault from an opponent or events of uncertain root-cause. Moreover, there are specific and unique risks associated with specific corporations and/or industry. Sometimes a given risk has both internal and external drivers and most of the risks are inter-related.

Perceptibly, if these risks and uncertainties are left unidentified, unmeasured and unaddressed, these can adversely impact profits of the enterprise and lead to irreversible cost. Therefore, in order to maximise the shareholders wealth and growth of the enterprise, it is understood that there is an enormous need to mitigate the different levels of perceived risks pertaining to a business enterprise. In this regard, the International Organisation for Standardization (ISO) has noted that enterprise risk management is an integral part of organisational process which creates value not only for the enterprise but also for the consumers. Further, it notes that risk management is an essential part of decision making which implicitly and explicitly addresses the problem of risk and uncertainty.

Further, the risk management standard developed by the team drawn from the major risk management organisations in the UK namely The Institute of Risk Management (IRM), The Association of Insurance and Risk Managers (AIRMIC) and ALARM: The National Forum for Risk Management in the Public Sector in 2002 have stated that "Risk management is a central part of any organisation's strategic management. It is the process whereby organisations methodically address the risks attaching to their activities with the goal of achieving sustained benefit within each activity and across the portfolio of all activities."

Thus, in view of the inherent potential risks and uncertainties, the business enterprises are expected to have a systematic and structured risks and uncertainties identifying, measuring and mitigating strategies based on the best available information which can be tailored as per the need of the enterprise. The risk mitigating strategies should be dynamic, iterative and responsive enough to absorb the relevant and perceived shock.

Depending up on the need, several risk mitigating strategies have been designed from time to time. For example, we have price and credit risk transferring vehicles. Basically, these strategies use instruments which reallocate financial risks to those who are less averse to them or who have offsetting exposure, and who are presumably better able to shoulder them. However, some features of many risk management vehicles/strategies have come under severe criticism mainly for imposing heavy cost on the insurer and for having no measurable improvement on risk. This warrants risk transferring and risk mitigating innovations in the area of enterprise risk management.

Approach to Risk Management

Due to the diversity of risk, management of risk requires a broader and an integrated approach. The Economist Intelligence Unit (EIU) (2001) survey "Enterprise Risk Management, Implementing New Solutions" highlighted: "Many companies perceive a rise in the number and severity of the risks they face. Some industries confront unfamiliar risks stemming from deregulation. Others worry about increasing dependence on business-to-business information systems and just-in-time supply/inventory systems. And everyone is concerned about emerging risks of e-business—from online security to customer privacy." Therefore, all regulators and stakeholders are pressing boards of directors to have a broader, systematic and integrated risk management approach so that the enterprise can manage risk more comprehensively, rigorously and systematically. In this regard, Pattie Dunn, Vice-Chairman of Barclays Global Investors and a member of the board of Hewlett-Packard, said: "I think what Boards tend to miss and what management tends to overlook is the need to address risk holistically. They overlook the areas that connect the dots because risk is defined so 'atomistically' and we don't have the perspective and the instrument panel that allows us to see risk in a 360 degree way" (McCarthy and Flynn, 2004).

The process of risk management is undergoing a fundamental sea change with the discipline of risk management converging at the top of the organisation and being more openly discussed in the same breath as strategy and protection of shareholders wealth. Assuming bigger risk requires more attention and control. In the approach of risk management, risk control is viewed as essential and important to maintain stability and continuity in the running of enterprises. However, in the aftermath of a series of unexpected risk management failures leading to company collapses and other corporate scandals particularly in the US, UK and other parts of Europe and Asia, stakeholders at large have expressed concerns about the low level of confidence in board oversight of corporate operations, in financial reporting, in the safeguards provided by external auditors and in the degree of risk management control. These concerns led to a cry for greater corporate governance, which led to a series of reports on corporate governance such as Kumar Mangalam Birla Committee (1999) and N.R. Narayana Murthy (2002) to name a few in India.

In early 1999, Securities and Exchange Board of India (SEBI) had set up a committee under Kumar Mangalam Birla to promote and raise the standards of good corporate governance. Similarly, with the belief that the efforts to improve corporate governance standards in India must continue because these standards themselves were evolving in keeping with the market dynamics, SEBI again constituted a committee under the chairmanship of N.R. Narayana Murthy on Corporate Governance in 2002, in order to evaluate the adequacy of existing corporate governance practices and further improve these practices. In this regard, considering the significance of risk management in the scheme of corporate management strategies, the Department of Public Enterprises (DPE), Government of India, has issued guidelines on corporate governance for central public sector enterprises. As per DPE guidelines on enterprise risk management (ERM) strategies, its oversight should be one of the main responsibilities of the board and the management. Further, the board should ensure the integration and alignment of the risk management system with the corporate and operational objectives and also that risk management should be undertaken as a part of normal business practice and not as a separate task at set times.

The Role of the Board

It has been highlighted that due to the massive failures of many corporate giants in the last two decades or so, board members can no longer claim impunity from a lack of knowledge about business risks. Now the rules of the game are very simple which state that when something goes wrong as inevitably it does, board members will be held accountable. Thus, the most proactive and appropriate solution is for board members to learn of the potential for adverse events and be sufficiently aware of the sources of risk within the area of business that they are operating in, to be afforded the opportunity to take pre-emptive action (McCarthy and Flynn, 2004). Moreover, the task for boards is to ensure the effective and timely implementation of their risk management policies. As part of strategic risk management, the boards can appoint a C-level risk officer empowered not only with the responsibility, but with the authority to act on all risk management matters. The boards can also ensure that this risk officer is independent and can work objectively with the company's external advisers (external audit, legal) and the governing decision maker. The boards must be satisfied as to the adequacy of the depth of current risk analysis actions, from an identification, assessment and mitigation standpoint. They should be confident that the risk management information that board members receive is accurate, timely, clear and relevant.

Often boards can actively participate in regular dialogue with key stakeholders to understand if their objectives have been captured, debated and aligned, are being met and whether stakeholders may derail current initiatives. Boards can strive to build a culture where risk management and strategic planning are a joint exercise. Further they can ensure that risk management remains focused on the most serious issues.

Enterprise Risk Management (ERM): The Framework

ERM is all about protecting and enhancing share value to satisfy the primary business goal of shareholder wealth maximisation. All enterprises face risks and uncertainties and the challenge for management is to determine how much risk and uncertainty to accept as it strives to maximise stakeholder value.

The ERM framework in an organisation supports the risk management process for decision making in the organisation. The framework also aggregates information on risks, risk management, and performance of risk controls in the organisation. The risk management process (RMP) is the key element of the ERM framework. The RMP ensures that risk management and the operation of risk controls will increase good consequences and reduce bad consequences within a continuous improvement cycle. The framework has to be practical. Managers are usually overworked and one extra responsibility for which they are accountable is need to be manageable if it is to be done effectively. Overly prescriptive approaches, while comprehensive and detailed, may be too onerous and counterproductive. Therefore, a principle-based approach is used and adopted to the circumstances. Successful frameworks are usually simple to understand and to implement yet allow for sophistication and subtlety in their application and continuous improvement. As a general rule, efforts in risk management should be proportional to the magnitude of the risk and/or the benefits of the risk controls including impacts on stakeholders.

The first step to implementing ERM is to have a list of components that provide a comprehensive specification for the framework. Then these components must be designed and the associated implementation plan developed. Most ERM frameworks, including ISO 31000, do not specify these components but rather give conceptual guidance on the framework and its relational structure. In general the framework of ERM is composed of five elements. First, corporate governance is required to ensure that the board of directors and management have established the appropriate organisational processes and corporate controls to measure and manage risk across the business. Second, the creation and maintenance of a sound system of internal control is required to safeguard shareholder's investment and a business's assets. Third, a specific resource must be identified to implement the internal controls with sufficient knowledge and experience to derive the maximum benefit from the process. Fourth, a clear risk management process is required which sets out the individual processes, their inputs, outputs, constraints and enablers. Fifth, the value of a risk management process is reduced without a clear understanding of the sources of risk and how they should be responded to. The framework breaks down the source of risk down into two key elements labelled as internal processes and the business operating environment.

According to the Committee of Sponsoring Organisations of the Treadway Commission (COSO) (2004), the framework of ERM consists of aligning entity's risk appetite and strategy, enhancing risk response decisions, reducing operational surprises and losses, identifying and managing multiple and cross-enterprise risks, seizing opportunities and improving deployment of capital.

COSO (2004) defined ERM as, "a systematic process, effected by an entity's board of directors, management and other personnel, applied in strategy setting and across the enterprise, designed to identify potential events that may affect the entity, and manage risk to be within its risk appetite, to provide reasonable assurance regarding the achievement of entity objectives."

Therefore, ERM is a comprehensive and integrated framework for managing company-wide risk in order to maximise an enterprises value. According to COSO (2004), ERM framework is geared to achieve an entity's objectives, set forth in four categories *viz.*, (i) strategic objectives ensuring high-level goals are aligned and support its vision and mission, (ii) operations objectives ensuring effective and efficient use of its resources, (iii) reporting objectives ensuring reliability of reporting and (iv) compliance objectives ensuring compliance with applicable rules and regulations and laws.

In order to achieve success in each of these four ERM objectives, COSO (2004) has formulated eight interrelated components which are derived from the way management runs an enterprise and are integrated with the management process. These components are:

1. *Internal Environment:* The internal environment encompasses the tone of an organisation, and sets the basis for how risk is viewed and addressed by an entity's people, including risk management philosophy and risk appetite, integrity and ethical values, and the environment in which they operate.

2. *Objective Setting:* Objectives must exist before management can identify potential events affecting their achievement. Enterprise risk management ensures that management has in place a process to set objectives and that the chosen objectives support and align with the entity's mission and are consistent with its risk appetite.

3. *Event Identification:* Internal and external events affecting achievement of an entity's objectives must be identified, distinguishing between risks and opportunities. Opportunities are channeled back to management's strategy or objective-setting processes.

4. *Risk Assessment*: Risks are analysed, considering likelihood and impact, as a basis for determining how they should be managed. Risks are assessed on an inherent and a residual basis.

5. *Risk Response:* Management selects risk responses—avoiding, accepting, reducing, or sharing risk—developing a set of actions to align risks with the entity's risk tolerances and risk appetite.

6. *Control Activities*: Policies and procedures are established and implemented to help ensure the risk responses are effectively carried out.

7. *Information and Communication*: Relevant information is identified, captured and communicated in a form and timeframe that enable people to carry out their responsibilities. Effective communication also occurs in a broader sense, flowing down, across and up the entity.

8. *Monitoring:* The entirety of enterprise risk management is monitored and modifications made as necessary. Monitoring is accomplished through ongoing management activities, separate evaluations or both.

The ISO 31000[2] framework is the current best practice for risk management frameworks. It incorporates best practice from COSO, PMI (Project Management Institute), the Australian and New Zealand Standard

2. ISO 31000 was published in 2009 as an internationally agreed standard for the implementation of risk management principles.

(AS/NZS 4360:2004) and other leading international risk management standards. The ISO framework of ERM is principle-based rather than prescriptive. It gives a general framework for ERM with the expectation that individual economies, industrial sectors and companies will craft their own detailed and specific frameworks to their own unique situations. The important aspect of ISO ERM principle is that risk management should have net value to the company where essentially it should make money, enhance reputation, contribute to public safety, improve sustainability, generally enhance benefits and reduce harm.

The comprehensive concept of the ISO ERM framework is that the risk management in an organisation is fully integrated into the management and direction of the organisation. Importantly, risk management is not an add-on step but rather is fully integrated and embedded in all decision processes. The ERM framework is integrated into the organisation's overall strategic and operational policies and practices. The ISO (2009a) definition of a risk management framework, and thus an ERM framework, is: set of components that provide the foundations and organisational arrangements for designing, implementing, monitoring, reviewing and continually improving risk management throughout the organisation. An organisation's risk management framework exists only to facilitate the risk management process, which should be used for any decision in the organisation.

ISO describes the components of a risk management implementation framework. Figure 1.1 provides a simplified version of this implementation framework. It includes the essential steps in the implementation and ongoing support of the risk management process. The initial component of the ISO 31000 framework is 'mandate and commitment' by the Board and this is followed by: design of framework, implement risk management, monitor and review framework and improve framework.

The ISO standard's risk management process can be applied to the whole organisation, to part of the organisation, to particular types of risk in isolation, or to a specific asset, project, or activity. The standard recognises that management of risk is more effective if it is conducted in a consistent manner across an organisation as defined by the ERM framework.

Figure 1.1

ISO 31000 Framework for Managing Risk

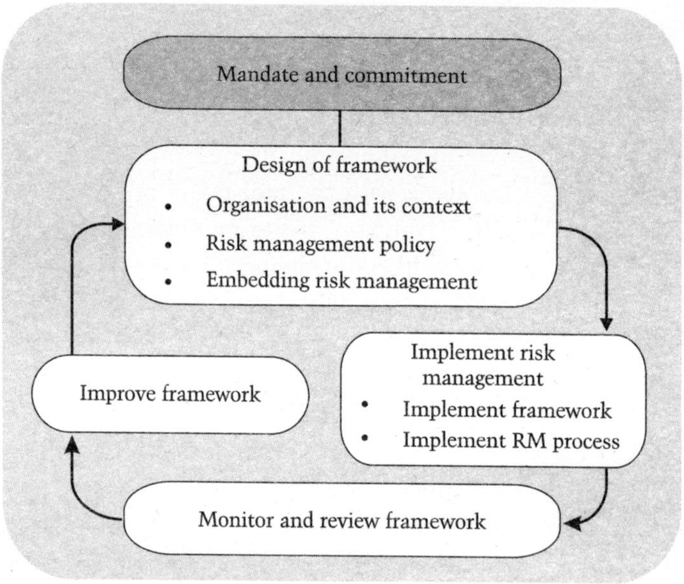

Source: IRM (2010). *A Structured Approach to ERM and the Requirements of ISO 31000*.

ERM: The Process

ERM is a logical and systematic process or method of identifying, analysing or measuring or assessing, treating or mitigating, monitoring and reporting the risks involved in any activity, operation or process of a given enterprise. ISO 31000 defines ERM as, "the identification, assessment and prioritisation of risks followed by coordinated and economical application of resources to minimise, monitor, and control the probability and/or impact of unfortunate events or to maximise the realisation of opportunities." The risk management process can be presented as a list of coordinated activities. There are alternative descriptions of this process, but the components listed below are usually present. This list represents the 7Rs and 4Ts of risk, management: (i) recognition or identification of risks, (ii) ranking or evaluation of risks, (iii) responding to significant risks (4Ts—tolerate, treat, transfer, terminate), (iv) resourcing controls, (v) reaction planning, (vi) reporting and monitoring risk performance, and (vii) reviewing the risk management framework.

In brief, keeping in view the company's objectives, it first examines the external and internal environment in which it is operating and identifies internal and external risks (financial and non-financial risks) faced by the company. Second, the company measures the extent or the impact of risks on losses along with the probability of occurrence of the identified risks. Third, the company treats or mitigates the identified risks. This mainly includes a decision whether to accept, avoid, reduce or transfer the identified risks. Fourth, the company continuously monitors the success and failures of the entire process of risk management. Finally, the company reports the same internally and externally to all the important stakeholders.

Concluding Observations

All the companies in a free market are exposed to several types of risks. This risk exposure exists from their inception. In the last two decades or so, it has been said that risk is now more complex, diverse and dynamic. In particular, the source of risk is broader and the rate of change of the sources of risk has dramatically increased. The emergence of enterprise risk management has come about from the desire and need to move away from managing risk in silos and identifying and managing risk interdependencies. It has been noted that board members believe that ERM is essential to business growth. Experience suggests that many corporates have failed and collapsed across the world because boards of directors are under constant and greater scrutiny and expectations of corporate governance have significantly increased. In the present dynamic economic environment which is confronted with several foreseen and unforeseen risks, the board members cannot distance themselves anymore from risk management or believe that they will not be held to accountable. Therefore, the need of the hour is risk management should be integrated with the primary activities of the board. More importantly, whatever the approach companies adopt and implement, risk management should strike a judicious balance between risk and opportunity.

References

COSO (2004). *Enterprise Risk Management: Integrated Framework*. Committee of Sponsoring Organisations of the Treadway Commission. September.

Chapman, R.J. (2006). *Simple Tools and Techniques for Enterprise Risk Management*. England: John Wiley & Sons Ltd.

Economist Intelligence Unit (2001). *Enterprise Risk Management: Implementing New Solutions*.

Hunt, B. (2001). "Issue of the Moment: The Rise and Rise of Risk Management", in James Pickford (ed.), *Mastering Risk—Volume 1: Concepts*. UK: Pearson Education Ltd.

ISO (2009). *ISO 31000: Risk Management: Principles and Guidelines*. Geneva.

———. (2009a). *ISO/IEC: Guide 73, Risk Management—Vocabulary*. Geneva.

IRM (2010). *A Structured Approach to Enterprise Risk Management (ERM) and the Requirements of ISO 31000*.

McCarthy, M.P. and T.P. Flynn (2004). *Risk from the CEO and Board Perspective*. New York: McGraw Hill.

Standards Australia (2005). *HB 254. Governance, Risk Management and Control Assurance*. Sydney, Australia.

2 Advances in Credit Risk Management

R.K. Mishra and
Swayam Prava Mishra

Introduction

The financial institutions (FIs) and banks in the process of financial intermediation face a lot of risks like market risk, credit risk, operational risk, currency risk, commodity risk, interest rate risk, liquidity risk, etc. Therefore, it is the responsibility of top management and bank officials to carefully identify, measure, monitor and mitigate the risks. The need for an effective risk management set-up is called for. All the three Basel accords have stressed upon the credit risk as an important element for the financial sector. The Basel committee which is set by the Bank for International Settlements (BIS) advocated the sound principles for credit risk management.

Effective credit risk management is required to deal with many aspects of credit risk such as concentration risk, loan migration, collateral, recovery rate, credit review, counterparty and country risk. Traditionally most Indian banks have relied on policies and procedures as a tool for credit risk management. In contrast, the portfolio approach to credit risk management combines the credit risk in an individual account along with the other quantified measures pertaining to concentration risk, risk of slippage, loan facility related risks, etc.

The recent crisis also made the financial institutions, banks and nations as a whole to give due relevance to credit risk management. We need to know both the credit risk of the company we've extended credit to, and we need to know our own credit risk, in order to make the buy and sell transactions that make sense for the shareholder.

Credit risk is a combination of default risk, exposure risk and recovery risk. Default risk is the probability of default. The outstanding balances at the time of default are not known in advance particularly under facilities like committed lines of credit, project financing, etc., and these come under exposure risk. Recovery risk relates to the uncertainty over the likely recovery of outstanding amounts due.

Measurement of Credit Risk

There are mainly two facets of credit risk measurement in banks:

1. To identify the unit level credit risk: it is related to each loan/borrower emanating from the ability of a borrower to repay the loan. It is affected by counterparty risk and business risks.
2. Portfolio risk (concentration risk): it is the aggregation of individual transaction-related risks. Portfolio risk results out of poor quality credit policies, loan approval process, credit risk systems, loan monitoring and comprehensive credit information system which is internal to an entity. The government policies, investment climate, state of economy, natural calamities, industrial recession and market play a crucial role in affecting portfolio risk.
3. There are various models used by banks, financial institutions, corporations and credit rating agencies to predict the credit risk involved in the loans given to the counterparties. The next section gives a concise review on these credit risk models.

Credit Risk Models

Selection of appropriate credit risk model is an important aspect of credit risk management, as inappropriate model contains model error and the model error introduces risk into the credit risk management process. For example in the case of J.P. Morgan, the model error was that the bank was not using a credit model which linked the key macro factor driving the pay-off on the transaction, the Thai baht, with the default probability of the counterparty, even though the link was very direct and recognised at the time the transaction was originated.

The first class of credit risk models adopted was the 'structural' models which include the original Merton model (1974) and the extension of this model to random interest rates by Shimko, Tejima and Van Deventer (1993). This class of models imposes assumptions on the evolution of the firm's underlying assets. The recent kind of models were the reduced form models that impose their assumptions directly on the prices of the firms' traded liabilities, primarily its debt, and on the default free-term structure of interest rates.

First Generation Models

The first generation models, largely developed in the 1960s and 1970s, were based on a number of assumptions that were sophisticated in nature. Examples of first generation models include: the Black-Scholes options model (1973); single factor term structure models of interest rate movements; Jamshidian (1989) option model and trinomial lattice based American options models. Each of these models made a powerful assumption that the counterparty making the promise to pay was either default free or the amount and timing of the amount of loss from default was known with certainty. For examples, the Black-Scholes options model implicitly assumes that the payer on a put or call option on common stock will pay with certainty. The only uncertainty is the value of the common stock, from which we can then derive the value of the put or call.

Second Generation Models

Second generation models seek to maximise the insights in credit risk derived from first generation models with little or no modification. Examples of second generation models include: the Merton model of risky debt and Monte Carlo simulation of portfolio value. The Merton model of risky debt assumes that equity is a Black-Scholes call option on the value of assets of the firm. In this model, there is one risky variable, the market value of the assets of the firm. Interest rates are assumed constant as in the Black-Scholes option model. Monte Carlo simulation of portfolio value approach assumes that the default probability of the payer is known from some external source, that the default probability is uncorrelated with any of the factors or micro factors that may drive the market value of the underlying instruments, that models which assume the payer is risk free can be used for valuation and that default probabilities are constant over time.

Third Generation Models

Third generation models have two common characteristics: they include at least two random factors, not one, and they make an explicit assumption about the potential default of the counterparty and carry that in a consistent way through the calculation used to value all related instruments. There are a number of models of this type. For example, the Jarrow-Turnbull model (1995) assumed that default was a random statistical process and interest rates were random, arriving at valuation formulas for a number of 'defaultable' security types. The Jarrow-Lando–Turnbull (1997) model allowed for random evolution of default probabilities according to a rating transition matrix. The Shimko-Tejima-Van-Deventer (1993) credit model allowed for random interest rates in the Merton model framework. The Jarrow model (2001) greatly expands the default intensity framework to allow for interest rate driven and market index driven default probabilities.

Various Models used by Credit Rating Agencies

Many of the international banks like Swiss Bank Corporation, Union Bank of Switzerland, Bank of America, Industrial Bank of Japan, etc., have adopted credit risk models for evaluation of credit portfolio. These models offer banks framework for examining credit risk exposures, across geographical locations and product lines in a timely manner, centralising data and analysing risks. Some of these models are given below.

Altman's Z Score Model

It uses the multiple discriminant analysis (MDA) technique to forecast the probability of a company entering bankruptcy. It uses 5 financial ratios and calculates the Z score. It was initially used for predicting US bankruptcy using a sample of 33 bankrupt and 33 non-bankrupt firms.

J.P. Morgan's Credit Metrics

It focuses on estimating the volatility in the value of assets caused by variations in the quality of assets. The J.P. Morgan's goal is to establish an accessible benchmark to measure and manage credit risk across an institutional balance sheet and create integrated value at risk (VaR) statements for creditors that seek to capture the cost of concentration risks and the benefit of diversification. It incorporates a multistate view of the credit risk.

Credit Suisse Financial Products 'Credit Risk+ Model'

This model is based on actuarial calculation of expected default rates and unexpected losses from default. It has four types of model inputs like credit exposures, obligor default rates, default rate volatility numbers and recovery rates. Credit Risk + Model suggests using a one year horizon. It was developed mostly for non-rates loans held in a 'hold to maturity' account.

KMV Portfolio Manager Model

KMV (Kealhofer, McQuown and Vasicek) measures credit risk through expected default frequencies (EDFs), a measure that is derived through firm value. The underlying theory is that equity is a call option on a firm's assets and the firm will remain solvent till the value of the assets of the firm is greater than the value of its liabilities.

Credit Risk Response Strategy

The credit risk response strategies include risk removal, risk transfer, risk acceptance and risk reduction. In recent times, a lot of strategies have come into existence to transfer the credit risk to other parties. Broadly these fall under three types.

Asset Securitisation

This involves creating suitable instruments to pass on or transfer the credit risk. For example, mortgage-backed securities (MBS) and Collateralised Debt Obligations (CDO) are instruments through which illiquid assets or debts are packaged, converted into tradable securities and sold to third party investors. A CDO is a financial tool that bundles individual loans into a product that can be sold on the secondary market (those who purchase an interest in a loan from an original lender, such as banks or institutional investors). The product is called an 'asset-backed security' if the loans are corporate debt and 'MBS' if they are mortgages.

Rediscounting

The central banks rediscount credit given to certain priority sectors. This is to act as an initiative for banks to lend to these sectors. The rate of rediscounting is less than the rate of issuing loan, enabling the banks to earn a spread to cover their operational costs. Similarly, whenever the lending to a single business group or industry is high, the banks invite other banks to participate in sharing a part of the total loan amount.

Credit Default Swap

A credit default swap (CDS) provides insurance like protection against the possibility of a default. It is a contract through which a buyer pays money (a premium) to a seller who agrees to pay the buyer a certain amount (a settlement) if a specified event occurs (e.g., a financial instrument defaults). The contracts can be traded, or swapped, between investors. Both buyers and sellers can trade their CDS contracts to others. The regulators need to be vigilant in reporting and monitoring these credit derivatives.

Now we turn to discuss on the issues related to credit risk management in India.

Issues in Credit Risk Management in India: A Brief Note

In India, the problem of risk modeling is more accentuated due to a lot of reasons. Some of these issues are discussed below.

Prudential Limits

In order to limit the magnitude of credit risk, prudential limits should be laid down on various aspects of credit:

1. Stipulate benchmark current/debt equity and profitability ratios, debt service coverage ratio or other ratios, with flexibility for deviations. The conditions subject to which deviations are permitted and the authority therefore should also be clearly spelt out in the loan policy;

2. Single/group borrower limits, which may be lower than the limits prescribed by the Reserve Bank of India (RBI) to provide a filtering mechanism;
3. Substantial exposure limit i.e., sum total of exposures assumed in respect of those single borrowers enjoying credit facilities in excess of a threshold limit, say 10 per cent or 15 per cent of capital funds. The substantial exposure limit may be fixed at 600 per cent or 800 per cent of capital funds, depending upon the degree of concentration risk the bank is exposed;
4. Maximum exposure limits to industry, sector, etc., should be set up. There must also be systems in place to evaluate the exposures at reasonable intervals and the limits should be adjusted especially when a particular sector or industry faces slowdown or other sector-/industry-specific problems. The exposure limits to sensitive sectors, such as, advances against equity shares, real estate, etc., which are subject to a high degree of asset price volatility and to specific industries, which are subject to frequent business cycles, may necessarily be restricted. Similarly, high-risk industries, as perceived by the bank, should also be placed under lower portfolio limit. Any excess exposure should be fully backed by adequate collaterals or strategic considerations; and
5. Banks may consider maturity profile of the loan book, keeping in view the market risks inherent in the balance sheet, risk evaluation capability, liquidity, etc.

Risk Rating

Banks should have a comprehensive risk scoring/rating system that serves as a single point indicator of diverse risk factors of counterparty and for taking credit decisions in a consistent manner. To facilitate this, a substantial degree of standardisation is required in ratings across borrowers. The risk rating system should be designed to reveal the overall risk of lending, critical input for setting pricing and non-price terms of loans as also present meaningful information for review and management of loan portfolio. The risk rating, in short, should reflect the underlying credit risk of the loan book. The rating exercise should also facilitate the credit granting authorities some comfort in its knowledge of loan quality at any moment of time.

The risk rating system should be drawn up in a structured manner, incorporating, *inter alia*, financial analysis, projections and sensitivity, industrial and management risks. The banks may use any number of financial ratios and operational parameters and collaterals as also qualitative aspects of management and industry characteristics that have bearings on the creditworthiness of borrowers. Banks can also weigh the ratios on the basis of the years to which they represent for giving importance to near term developments. Within the rating framework, banks can also prescribe certain level of standards or critical parameters, beyond which no proposals should be entertained. Banks may also consider separate rating framework for large corporate/small borrowers, traders, etc., that exhibit varying nature and degree of risk. The updating of the credit ratings should be undertaken normally at quarterly intervals or at least at half-yearly intervals, in order to gauge the quality of the portfolio at periodic intervals. Variations in the ratings of borrowers over time indicate changes in credit quality and expected loan losses from the credit portfolio. Thus, if the rating system is to be meaningful, the credit quality reports should signal changes in expected loan losses.

Risk Pricing

Risk-return pricing is a fundamental tenet of risk management. In a risk-return setting, borrowers with weak financial position and hence placed in high credit risk category should be priced high. Thus, banks should evolve scientific systems to price the credit risk, which should have a bearing on the expected probability of default. The pricing of loans normally should be linked to risk rating or credit quality. The probability of default could be derived from the past behaviour of the loan portfolio, which is the function of loan loss provision/charge-offs for the last five years or so. Banks should build historical database on the portfolio quality and provisioning/charge-off to equip themselves to price the risk. But value of collateral, market forces, perceived value of accounts, future business potential, portfolio/industry exposure and strategic reasons may also play an important role in pricing. Flexibility should also be made for revising the price (risk premia) due to changes in rating/value of collaterals over time.

Portfolio Management

The existing framework of tracking the non-performing loans around the balance sheet date does not signal the quality of the entire loan book. Banks should evolve proper systems for the identification of credit weaknesses well in advance. Most of international banks have adopted various portfolio management techniques for gauging asset quality. The Credit Risk Data Mart (CRMD), set up at Head Office, should be assigned the responsibility of periodic monitoring of the portfolio. The portfolio quality could be evaluated by tracking the migration (upward or downward) of borrowers from one rating scale to another. This process would be meaningful only if the borrower-wise ratings are updated at quarterly/half-yearly intervals. Data on movements within grading categories provide a useful insight into the nature and composition of loan book.

The banks may evaluate the utility of the credit risk models with suitable modifications to Indian environment for fine-tuning the credit risk management. The success of credit risk models impinges on time series data on historical loan loss rates and other model variables, spanning multiple credit cycles. Banks may, therefore, endeavour building adequate database for switching over to credit risk modeling after a specified period of time.

Loan Review Mechanism (LRM)

LRM is an effective tool for constantly evaluating the quality of loan book and to bring about qualitative improvements in credit administration. Banks should, therefore, put in place proper LRM for large value accounts with responsibilities assigned in various areas such as evaluating the effectiveness of loan administration, maintaining the integrity of credit grading process, assessing the loan loss provision, portfolio quality, etc. The complexity and scope of LRM normally vary based on banks' size, type of operations and management practices. It may be independent of the CRMD or even separate department in large banks.

The main objectives of LRM could be to:

1. identify promptly loans which develop credit weaknesses and initiate timely corrective action;
2. evaluate portfolio quality and isolate potential problem areas;
3. provide information for determining adequacy of loan loss provision;
4. assess the adequacy of and adherence to, loan policies and procedures, and to monitor compliance with relevant laws and regulations; and
5. provide top management with information on credit administration, including credit sanction process, risk evaluation and post-sanction follow-up.

Accurate and timely credit grading is one of the basic components of an effective LRM. Credit grading involves assessment of credit quality, identification of problem loans and assignment of risk ratings. A proper credit grading system should support evaluating the portfolio quality and establishing loan loss provisions. Given the importance and subjective nature of credit rating, the credit ratings awarded by credit administration department (CAD) should be subjected to review by loan review officers who are independent of loan administration.

Conclusion

Credit risk is a very essential component of risk management and in the world of burgeoning CAD and a falling growth rate especially in a country like India, it becomes all the more imperative for the banks and FIs to cater to the needs of the investor community and at the same time be prudent in the credit risk management. The paper provides some insights into the various credit risk models used in the market today and some issues of risk pricing, risk rating, etc. The recent financial crisis has shown all how important is the issue of lending and hence, the countries across the world have also accepted it. Therefore, now the need of the hour is to respond through appropriate credit risk models as per the credit culture and risk appetite of the countries and avoid occurrence of such crisis.

References

Bagchi, S.K. (2003). "Credit Risk Management: A Panacea or Conundrum?", *SBI Monthly Review* 42(10): 497-504.

Bandyopadhyay, Arindam (2006). "Predicting Probability of Default of Indian Corporate Bonds: Logistic and Z-Score Model Approaches", *The Journal of Risk Finance* 7(3): 255-72.

Deventer, D.V. and K. Imai (2003). *Credit Risk Models and the Basel Accords*. John Wiley & Sons (Asia) Pvt. Ltd.

Hu, J. (2007). "Assessing the Credit Risk of CDOs Backed by Structured Finance Securities", *Journal of Structured Finance* 13 (3): 43-59.

Mian, R.A. and A. Sufi (2009). "The Consequences of Mortgage Credit Expansion: Evidence from the U.S. Mortgage Default Crisis", *Quarterly Journal of Economics* 124(4): 1449-96.

Moody's Investors Service (2002). *Default & Recovery Rates of Corporate Bond Issuers 1970-2001*. February.

———. (2007). *U.S. Subprime: Overview of Recent Refinements to Moody's Methodology*. July 24.

Muninarayanappa and Nirmala (2004). "Credit Risk Management in Banks: Key Issues", *Journal of Accounting & Finance* 18(1): 94-98.

Reserve Bank of India (2002). *Guidance Note on Credit Risk Management*. Mumbai: Department of Banking Operations and Development. October 12.

Senior Supervisors Group Survey (2009). *Risk Management Lessons from the Global Banking Crisis of 2008*. October 21.

SECTION II

Risk Management in Banks

3 Project Finance and Risk Management in Infrastructure Financing by Indian Banks

Vikas Srivastava

Introduction

An economy cannot grow without heavy investment in infrastructure. Infrastructure is the physical framework of facilities through which goods and services are provided to the public. Investment in infrastructure has a multiplier effect on the economy. According to World Bank estimates, with 1.0 per cent increase in infrastructure spending, household access to safe water increases by 0.3 per cent, paved roads by 0.8 per cent, power 1.5 per cent and telecommunications 1.7 per cent. There is no doubt that in times of economic slowdown, pushing up investment in infrastructure as a percentage of gross domestic product (GDP) will prove countercyclical.

The *India Infrastructure Report, 1996*, defined infrastructure as: the physical framework of facilities through which goods and services are provided to the public. Infrastructure linkage to the economy is multiple and complex because it directly affects production and consumption, creates negative and positive spill-over effects (externalities) and involves large flow of expenditure. The Reserve Bank of India (RBI) in its circular dated November 30, 2007 (DBOD No. BP.BC.52/21.04.048/2007-08), defined infrastructure as: "Developing or developing and operating or developing, operating and maintaining an infrastructure facility in energy, logistics and transportation, telecom, urban and industrial infrastructure, agro-processing, construction for storage of agro-products, schools and hospitals, pipelines for oil, petroleum and gas, water and sanitation." This definition includes both physical and social infrastructure services. This research, however, focuses only on the issues of financing of the key physical infrastructure services by commercial banks.

However, there are signs that investment in infrastructure is slowing down. According to initial estimates of the Twelfth Plan, in order to sustain GDP growth rate of nine per cent, the planned investment was ₹ 41,00,000 crore in infrastructure sector. These estimates are likely to be revised as we see funding gaps in this sector and a slowing economy.

Government funding is not a solution to fill this gap. The government is already struggling to contain a huge fiscal deficit. Private sector is struggling to get finances for infrastructure projects and slowdown in infrastructure investments looks imminent. The present economic downturn as well as the increase in overall construction cost has pushed a majority of the private sector infrastructure companies to tight liquidity position.

Some of the companies are on the verge of collapse due to reasons such as aggressive bidding, absence of traffic revenue as projected, delays in land acquisition, hurdles encountered in obtaining environmental clearances and utility shifting and failure to hand over ROW (Right of Way) on time. Other concerns of companies include delays in honoring price variations, escalations, change of scope, etc.

There is consensus among government policy makers and a growing realisation by the public that there is a need of increased public-private partnership (PPP) in infrastructure projects and of the necessity of commercialisation of infrastructure services. During the last 10 years, infrastructure is being developed through increasing investments by the private sector on a commercial basis under the 'private ownership and operation' approach. Under this option, the private entity not only operates the infrastructure, but also owns the allied assets. The various approaches can assume any of the following arrangements, the most important among them being: build operate transfer (BOT); build own operate (BOO); build own operate transfer (BOOT); build operate lease transfer (BOLT), management contract (MC) and service contract (SC).

Because of budgetary and other constraints faced by fund providers to infrastructure both equity (Sources: domestic developers, infrastructure focused companies, equipment and operations/maintenance suppliers, export credit agencies, multilateral agencies, private equity and infrastructure funds, etc.) and debt (Sources: bank loans, capital market bonds, international banks, pension and insurance funds, external commercial borrowings, etc.), the financing gap is quite huge. It has been pointed out that the debt financing gap can be as high as ₹ 162,496 crore.

The banking sector has been showing a compound annual growth rate (CAGR) of almost 30 per cent year on year growth in lending to infrastructure and infrastructure has almost a 33 per cent share in industrial credit by banks. The deployment of gross bank credit to infrastructure stands at ₹ 3,52,360 crore (*Handbook of Statistics on Indian Economy,* RBI).

Due to the necessity of private sector participation, the need for incurring heavy institutional debt and in order to provide a conducive environment for infrastructure funding and sustaining the growth momentum, the RBI has put in place several mechanisms to steer the fund flow from banking sector towards infrastructure and accordingly issued specific guidelines from time to time. Most importantly, the RBI has relaxed individual and group exposure norms from 5 to 10 per cent of banks' capital funds in the case of lending to infrastructure sector for single and group borrowers respectively. It has also relaxed norms for classification of infrastructure assets as non-performing assets (NPAs). The RBI has allowed the banks to use the take out financing mechanism (also through an ECB route) and in a phased manner to bridge the asset liability mismatches, issue long-term bonds to fund infrastructure, invest in bonds issued by unrated special purpose vehicles (SPVs) of infrastructure companies, subject to a maximum ceiling of 10 per cent of non-SLR (statutory liquidity ratio) investments, keeping the promoters shares in infrastructure SPV's out of capital market exposure and allowing banks to fund promoters equity.

Identification of the Problem and the Scope of Research

It is clear from the above discussions that there is a substantial gap between the investments required for the infrastructure sector and the finances available. In the absence of sophisticated debt and equity instruments to fund long-term infrastructure, bank finance has been sharing a heavy percentage of debt flow to infrastructure.

This leads to an undesirable and unhealthy asset liability mismatch. In addition, the combination of high capital costs and low operating costs of infrastructure projects implies that initial financing costs constitute a very large proportion of the total cost. Infrastructure project financing entails a complex and varied mix of financial and contractual arrangements between multiple parties. Apart from this, regulatory uncertainty increases the risk profile of infrastructure projects.

The divergence in growth rate of credit and NPAs has widened in the recent period, which could put further pressure on asset quality in the near term. The slippage ratio increased to 2.1 per cent as at the end of March 2012 from 1.6 per cent at March 2011 and 1.9 per cent at September 2011. The ratio of slippages plus restructured standard advances to recoveries (excluding up-gradations) also exhibited an increasing trend underscoring the concerns with respect to asset quality, and the need for proactive management of NPAs by banks.

As per the *Financial Stability Report* when an empirical analysis of the asset quality of banks' advances portfolio was conducted by adding back the advances written off by banks during the last five years and (separately) assuming that 15 per cent of restructured accounts slip into impaired category, the resultant ratios exhibited an increasing trend that calls for a closer look at the underlying management of NPAs by banks. The proportion of restructured standard advances to gross total advances increased from 3.45 per cent in March 2011 to 4.68 per cent in March 2012.

Meanwhile, the losses of state electricity boards (SEBs) have also been mounting, adding to the concerns about asset quality in the sector. Asset quality of banks' credit to the airlines industry came under some stress in recent periods, driven largely by the performance of some specific airline companies. Sharp increase in restructured and impaired assets saw the share of Infrastructure lending sector increase in the aggregate banking sector NPAs. In fact, the growth in restructured and impaired assets in Infrastructure sector is higher than the growth in credit. There was significant concentration discernible in distribution of credit to the airline sector as 10 banks accounted for almost 86 per cent of total bank credit to this sector.

As at the end of March 2012, nearly three quarters of the advances of banks, which have an exposure of above ₹ 10 billion to the airline industry, were either impaired or restructured. Public sector banks (PSBs) accounted for the major share of these exposures. Going forward, the sectors are likely to continue facing funding constraints and could also be affected by prevalent policy uncertainties. These could pose challenges to the asset quality of credit to these sectors.

Against the above backdrop, a few questions arise:

1. Do Indian banks' credit officers have the adequate expertise to evaluate and finance infrastructure projects ensuring safety of funds?
2. Does the infrastructure appraisal process provide the mechanism to identify and measure the inherent risks with due diligence?

The absence of a straightforward answer to the above questions is itself quite disconcerting. Indian bankers are on a learning curve with regard to understanding the mechanics of infrastructure financing. For that matter, the project promoters, policy makers and regulators are not better off. The lack of lending expertise exhibits the poor confidence level of lenders, which in turn may be contributing to impeding the growth of infrastructure. This lacuna requires a fresh look at the way projects are being appraised by the bankers. It is apparent that the standard appraisal employed in traditional corporate financing—primarily based on the strength of the promoter, financial viability and the security safeguards—is not able to capture the entire complexities involved in financing infrastructure projects

Concepts and Review of Literature

The literature survey differentiates between the traditional corporate financing structure and the modern infrastructure projects financing.

To elaborate, in the traditional form of financing, as defined by Pandey (2005) and Chandra (2005) and commonly known as corporate financing or the balance sheet financing, although the financing is done for a project, the lender looks at the cash flows and assets of the whole company in order to gauge its ability to service the debt and provide security. However, in modern project financing, lenders base their credit appraisals on the projected revenues from the operation of the facility, and also on its assets including any revenue-producing contracts and other potential cash flows as collateral for the debt, rather than on the general assets or the credit (credibility) of the sponsor of the project. In this regard, studies by Adelson (1970), Quirin (1977), McConnell and Muscarella (1985) are important. They termed these (projects) as tactical decisions which demand different perspectives both from the investors and the lenders as they are driven by contractual structures and are able to encash future opportunities. Similar definitions have been given by Finnerty (1996), Nevitt and Fabozzi (2000), Hoffman (2001), and Esty and Sesia (2005). Infrastructure in India, as gleaned from the studies by Ghemawat (2000) and Mehta (2001), follows the project financing method. These definitions of project finance highlight some of the basic characteristics of the project financing method such as: (i) the creation of a separate entity, popularly known as special purpose entity or special purpose vehicle (SPE/SPV). The SPV has a defined objective and definite life; (ii) the equity holding pattern which may involve 3 or 4 equity sponsors; (iii) the non-recourse debt, which implies that the debt component provided by lenders is on non-recourse basis and the lenders have no claim on the equity of sponsors for the repayment of the debt but fully rely on the project's cash flows for the debt servicing, (iv) high leverage, and (v) the complex contractual structure.

However, apart from the comprehensive research carried out by Balu (2002), and a few research articles notably by Chandra (2005), Chen (2006) and Modi (2008) and some mention of these issues in various research reports, including those in the *India Infrastructure Report, 1996*, and Deepak Parekh Committee Report 2007, extensive and organised research has not been carried out on the structural issues and the impact that various project parties and contracts in this structure has on the appraisal done by Indian bankers. As far as risk measurement in project finance is concerned, study by Orgeldinger (2006) is important since it uses probability distribution models to measure credit risk in the infrastructure sector. This research, apart from focusing on stand-alone practices of assessing risk, like sensitivity analysis, scenario analysis, simulation and break-even analysis, also focuses on measuring risk through the credit scoring mechanism. Most of the credit risk models based on discriminant analysis focus on corporate loans rather than on project finance loans.

Therefore, a need is felt for a detailed research that takes into account the entire process of infrastructure project appraisal, which includes methods and techniques for scrutinising contractual and legal issues and structural aspects of the project, besides the managerial, technical, marketing, construction, financial and economic aspects of appraisal. As banks move from standardised approach to internal rating based (IRB) approach for Basel II compliance, the research into the rating models and the issues therein assumes importance. Literature review points out that research in this area is based on secondary data, and it is necessary to understand the bankers' perspective towards appraising and financing infrastructure through primary data.

The research will focus specifically on power and road sector as these two sectors command more than 80 per cent of disbursement done by scheduled commercial banks.

Research Methodology

Based on the identification of problems and the knowledge gaps that exist in the literature, the present research has the following objectives:

1. To examine the existing framework for appraisal and risk measurement by Indian banks in financing infrastructure projects.
2. To analyse and evaluate the credit rating mechanisms that banks use for measurement of risk and to statistically examine the attitude of credit officers towards relative importance of risk variables under each factor used in credit scoring in the power and road sector.
3. To draw conclusions from the study on project appraisal and risk measurement practices and survey results, identify gaps and offer suggestions for improving the methods.

Research Design

The following steps explain the research design.

Step 1: Study the project documents and the appraisal notes of participating banks. Qualitative research using depth interviews and structured observation method. Only those proposals which were sanctioned prior to 2004 (2002 onwards) were covered since the files already contained the follow-up and monitoring remarks.

Step 2: Prepare a detailed note on project appraisal and risk measurement practices (descriptive research).

Step 3: Examine the application of the process described above on chosen sectors: power and road, and identify the appropriate risk variables.

Step 5: Identify the above risk variables and test the perception of credit officers intra-sector on the credit rating mechanism used by banks by conducting a survey on the officers who have appraised projects in road and power sectors. Transition matrix of the data for five years is created for ratings given by the banks to seek rating migration and probability of default (PD) estimates in the above risk measurement system.

Step 6: Identify the gaps and suggest an alternate project appraisal and risk measurement technique which may be unique to a particular sector.

For the survey, a structured questionnaire was used for collecting data. Primary scales used in the questionnaire were nominal and interval scale and non-comparative scaling techniques and itemised rating scale in particular based on five point Likert scale was used. Coefficient alpha which is a measure of internal reliability of the scale items was 0.78. It tended to increase with the increase in number of scale items during the pre-test. Since the scales were pre-tested on a sample size of 30, an adequately positive opinion on the content validity of the scale was found.

The study included collection of data from public sector banks, other scheduled commercial banks including private banks and financial institutions and central banking institutions like the RBI and the National Bank for Agriculture and Rural Development (NABARD). The data are drawn largely from the PSBs. Further, a sample of 70 credit officers was picked for the attitude survey from the above sample using non-probability sampling technique, particularly quota sampling, was used. Forty-eight projects which had achieved financial closure and those banks in the sample that had rated projects using the CRISIL's risk assessment model (RAM) model for financing were selected for creating a transition matrix. The rating migration was captured for the years 2004-2008. Some of the selected projects had already achieved the commencement stage of operations during this period.

Hypothesis Testing

Two hypothesis were tested for drawing conclusions.

Hypothesis 1

For project appraisal and risk analysis, hypothesis testing is related to differences between the mean of two samples—credit officers who have appraised projects in the road sector and the power sector.

- H0 = Attitude of credit officers towards relative importance of credit scoring sub-variables on the overall credit score of each element of risk, as used in credit rating mechanism, is not different from sector to sector while appraising projects in the chosen sectors of road and power.
- H1 = Attitude of credit officers towards relative importance of credit scoring sub-variables on the overall credit score of each element of risk, as used in credit rating mechanism, depends on inherent risks unique to the sector and status of the promoter.

Hypothesis 2

For the structural differences between corporate and project finance, hypothesis testing is related to differences between mean of the two samples, that is credit officers who have appraised projects in infrastructure sector as well as in traditional projects started by corporate sponsor.

- H0 = Banks are using 'with recourse' structure to fund infrastructure projects, which is not different from financing corporate projects.
- H1 = Banks are using project finance structure to fund infrastructure projects with 'no or limited recourse,' which is different from financing corporate projects.

In the present research, since the alternate hypothesis lacks direction, two-tailed tests were used for testing the differences in the hypothesis.

Both parametric and non-parametric tests were used. As data for corporate and infrastructure projects as well as road and power sectors were drawn from the same group of respondents, it was considered as paired data, and therefore, the researcher adopted the paired sample t test. For data which are collected on the nominal scale, an important non-parametric test called the Wilcoxin matched-pairs single ranks test is conducted. The test statistic z is computed from positive and negative rank sums. The level of significance was fixed at 5 per cent or 0.05 because an intolerably high level of significance would have increased the Type II errors.

The risk sub-variables, selected under each factor of the credit scoring model which is used for attitude surveys, should be able to distinguish the critical risk drivers for the two sectors under focus—i.e., road and power. A statistical test for examining the difference among means for two or more populations is termed as analysis of variances (ANOVA). Since the researcher is doing the test for each risk sub-variable under each factor, the one-way ANOVA is done.

Results and Interpretation of Qualitative Research

Infrastructure project financing in India follows the project finance structure which means that lenders are advancing funds essentially on a 'non-recourse' or 'limited-recourse' basis as explained in the literature review. Therefore, bankers are required to ensure appropriate risk sharing, allocation and mitigation through a robust legal, contractual and structural framework as the promoters have legally and structurally separated their balance sheet from project vehicle.

The key project players include: sponsors, government, the SPV, lenders, engineering procurement and construction (EPC), contractor operations and management contractor, suppliers and customers (off-takers). Their inter-relationship with the SPVs for executing projects is explained through Figure 3.1.

Project appraisal includes: appraisal of management, technical, construction, market, legal and *force majeure* (regulatory/political) issues. The collateral support, equity pledge, corporate and personal guarantees

Figure 3.1

Project Structure

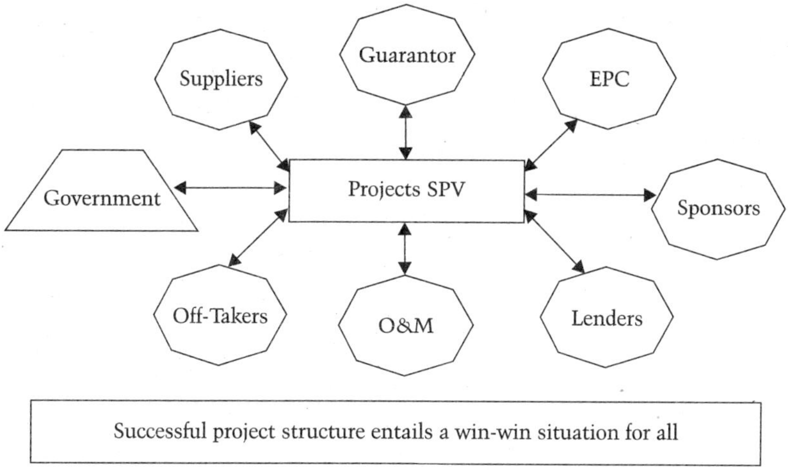

being minimal and the first charge limited to project assets, there is hardly any tangible security for mortgage and hypothecation. Therefore, lenders reinforce the security structure through mix of contracts and agreements, which try and allocate the risk to a counterparty which is best placed to mitigate that risk. The most important of these are: (i) the concession agreement which gives the private party the right to develop the infrastructure asset and also provides the terms and conditions which ensure compensation under political and non-political *force majeure* clauses; (ii) the shareholders' agreement, which binds the shareholders; (iii) the fuel supply and transport agreement which binds suppliers in the case of power project; (iv) the agreement with the government for ensuring state/centre support; (v) the EPC contract with construction contractor for a fixed time fixed price in order to prevent cost and time overruns; (vi) operations and management (O&M) contract with a reputed contractor; (vii) the substitution contract to mitigate distress; (viii) the power purchase agreement (PPA) with the off-takers (SEBs); (ix) the escrow charge on the off-takers account; and (x) the trust and retention account with appropriate waterfall mechanism which taps all cash flows of the borrower. All these agreements, contracts and charges are assigned to the banker as security with the prescribed *ad valorem* stamp duty. All the project documents and financing documents along with the key contract agreements listed above are called 'Transaction Documents.' The strength of the transaction documents forms the basis of the Project Appraisal by the bankers. The reports of the Lender's Independent Engineer (LIE) and Lender's Legal Counsel (LLC) therefore become important. If all the project parties are bound by iron-clad contracts at this stage and all the potential risks and loopholes are plugged, then there is little chance of the project not being successful.

Risk assessment is generally made with the help of stand-alone risk measurement ratios for the calculation and assessment of borrower's requirements. The most important being the debt service coverage ratio (DSCR) and the loan to value (LTV) calculations. Sensitivity and scenario analyses are performed on the cash flows and generally a pessimistic view is taken. Using a standardised rating model, risk scoring is done which leads to rating the 'class' of the borrower. This would reveal the probability of default through an appropriate balancing exercise. Various elements of risk such as sponsor risk, demand and price risk, cost and time overrun risk, legal and contractual risk, operational risk, funding risk, *force majeure* risk, which includes political risk, environmental and social risks are identified at all the stages of the project; in short the entire gamut of development, construction and operation comes under the lender's hawk-eye.

The researcher then evaluates the applicability of the above-discussed procedure for project appraisal and risk mitigation to the road and power sectors and traces out the sector-wise adaptations that bankers use when they move from general to sector-specific appraisals. It is observed that though the broader elements of appraisal remain the same as described above, there are subtle issues which are purely sectoral, which creep in when project appraisal takes place in individual sectors.

It becomes quite clear that management and financial appraisal is done on almost similar parameters in both the sectors. Risk measurement uses the same parameters and sensitivity analysis in both the sectors. However, the economic and structural drivers across the two sectors are different. While in the road sector, the technological appraisal focuses on the site and structures; in power, it assumes significance as better technology and better equipments will lead to higher efficiency and a better plant load factor. In terms of construction issues, the EPC contractor plays a critical role in the road sector as it is essentially a construction project and as observed from the case studies, the vetting of EPC costs takes a much serious role than in the power sector. Market risks are substantially mitigated in power sector on account of a strong power purchase agreement than in roads where traffic determines the success of the project. Hence, traffic assessment is given due weightage in the road sector, whereas in the power sector, the escrowable capacity of the SEB and the demand-supply gap in electricity are given due importance. The road sector has a well-defined concession agreement and therefore the legal and *force majeure* issues change dramatically on account of different regulations across sectors.

However, the dilemma is that when risk assessment is made by means of a credit scoring model, it is done on the same factors and sub-variables across both the sectors. Many a time, managers give scores based on their personal perceptions. Using the same factors and dividing them into sub-variables, based on descriptive research, an attitude survey was done on the appraising officers with the help of a structured questionnaire. The key results are discussed as below.

Testing of Hypothesis and Interpretation of Results

Results and Interpretation of Attitude Survey

The summary of results of the survey conducted on rating parameters for road and power sectors is given in Table 3.1.

The paired sample t test results clearly demonstrate that there is a statistically significant difference in the credit officers' attitude towards various sub-variables used for rating factors such as management quality, market potential, technology, construction, operation, legal, *force majeure* and funding issues regarding both road and power sectors. Similarly, in risk identification, which was done on nominal scales using checklists and the Wilcoxin matched pairs sign rank test, a significant difference was found in the attitude of credit officers across the sectors.

Table 3.1

Summary of Statistics: Project Appraisal and Risk Measurement

(Paired Sample t Test)

No.	Parameter	Comparative Statistics					
		Difference of mean Road-Power	Std. Deviation	Corr	Df	Paired t test	Sign (2-tailed) at 0.05
1.	Management Quality	- 1.77	2.04	0.220	69	-7.275	0.000
2.	Market Potential - Demand Issues	- 2.84	2.3445	0.113	69	-10.145	0.000
3.	Market Potential - Price Issues	-5.64	2.7454	-0.01	69	-17.19	0.000
4.	Technological Issues	- 5.51	2.43	0.161	69	-18.985	0.000
5.	Construction Issues	- 3.86	2.41	0.138	69	-13.39	0.000
6.	Operational Issues	- 2.62	2.03	0.055	69	-10.79	0.000
7.	Legal Issues	-3.10	2.23	0.270	69	-11.64	0.000
8.	Force Majeure Issues	-4.70	2.10	0.319	69	-18.71	0.000
9.	Funding Issues	-2.50	2.19	0.162	69	-9.543	0.000

Table 3.2

On-way Analysis of Variances

(Only Factors Not Statistically Significant are Listed)

Criteria	Mean Road	Mean Power	ANOVA Statistics	F Value	P Value at 0.05 Significance Level
Management Quality					
Sponsors' Track record	4.27	4.28	DF=1, MS =0.007	0.010	0.918
Sponsors Financial Prudence	4.63	4.65	DF=1, MS =0.028	0.070	0.791
Market Potential–Demand Issues					
Competition from New Entrants	3.19	3.10	DF =1, MS = 0.25	0.58	0.446
Technical Issues					
LIE Opinion on Aggressiveness	3.66	3.83	DF=1, MS = 1.02	1.82	0.178
Construction Issues					
Liquidated Damages	3.86	3.81	DF=1, MS = 0.064	0.11	0.735
Operational Issues					
Track Record of O&M Contractor	3.77	3.87	DF=1, MS= 0.35	0.96	0.328
Defining Events of Default	4.59	4.46	DF=1, MS=0.573	0.903	0.343
Legal Issues					
Enforceability of Rights/Remedies	4.53	4.59	DF=1, MS = 0.114	0.230	0.631
Funding Issues					
Stability of Cash Flows	4.63	4.50	DF=1, MS = 0.57	2.00	0.159
Reasonableness of Capital Costs	3.80	4.39	DF=1, MS=0.114	0.230	0.631
Viability and Bankability of Project	4.24	3.93	DF=1, MS=0.345	6.86	0.090

However, when the one-way ANOVA test was conducted across all sub-variables under each category of appraisal, it was found that the results are not statistically significant, indicating that the credit officers' attitude does not change for these sub-variables across the sectors with respect to the following factors—sponsors' track record, financial strength of borrowers, prudence in management appraisal, importance of lenders' independent engineer's report on technological issues, importance of liquidated damages in construction issues, track record of O&M contractor in operational issues, legal enforceability of contracts in legal and *force majeure* issues. In fact, credit officers place high importance on stability of cash flows, reasonableness of capital costs and viability and bankability of projects.

Thus, based on the above tests, the null hypothesis:

1. 'H0 = Attitude of credit officers towards relative importance of credit scoring sub-variables on the over-all credit score of each element of risk, as used in credit rating mechanism, is not different from sector to sector while appraising projects in the above chosen sectors,' can be rejected

and the alternate hypothesis:

2. 'H1 = Attitude of credit officers towards relative importance of credit scoring variables on the over-all credit score of each element of risk, as used in credit rating mechanism, depends on inherent risks unique to the sector and status of a promoter,' can be accepted.

Summary statistics of the survey conducted to find out the credit officers' attitude on structure of infrastructure projects as against corporate projects are summarised in Table 3.3.

There is no statistical difference in how the credit officers view the track record and financial strength of sponsors while appraising infrastructure or corporate projects. However, one of the elements that clearly differentiates corporate finance from project finance is in the practice of having recourse to the balance sheet or absolute dependence on sponsors' cash flows as in the case of the former rather than on project cash flows as in the case of the latter. Dependence on legal and contractual structure and preset range of appraising ratios is uniform across the sectors, there are significant statistical differences in the attitudes of appraising officers between corporate and infrastructure projects. This is further substantiated by data which was collected on nominal scale and tested by Wilcoxin matched pairs signed ranks test.

Table 3.3

Summary of Statistics: Project Structure

(Paired Sample t Test)

No.	Parameter	Comparative Statistics						
		Mean (Corp. Projects)	*Mean (Infra Projects)*	*Std. Deviation*	*Corr.*	*Df*	*Paired t test*	*Sign (2 tailed)* at 0.05
1.	Sponsors' track record/ Financial support to project	4.84	4.86	0.50	0.048	69	-0.241	0.810
2.	Repayment dependence only on project cash flows	3.81	4.81	0.98	0.234	69	-8.555	0.000
3.	Recourse to balance sheet of sponsor	4.43	2.79	0.72	0.023	69	19.01	0.000
4.	Legal/Contractual dependence	2.74	4.64	0.80	0.070	69	-19.83	0.000
5.	Ideal/Acceptable financial ratios	4.79	3.07	0.70	0.063	69	20.35	0.000

Therefore, the null hypothesis which says that:

1. 'Banks are using 'with recourse' structure to fund Infrastructure Projects which is not different from financing corporate projects' is rejected,

and, the alternate hypothesis which says that:

2. 'Banks are using Project Finance structure to fund Infrastructure Projects with 'no or limited recourse' which is different from financing corporate projects' was accepted.

In addition, the following key facts were revealed by the survey *vis-à-vis* banks' appraisal and risk identification methodology.

1. ***Management Appraisal/Quality***: Very high importance is given to the transparent shareholders' agreement, sponsors' track record and sponsors' financial prudence by the appraising officers. Though the t test (p value = 0.000 at 0.05 significance) shows that there is

a significant difference in the attitude of credit officers on relative importance of all factors contributing to the management appraisal in road and power sectors, the analysis of variance results shows that the difference is not significant in factors like sponsors' track record (p value = 0.918 at significance level of 0.05) and financial prudence (p value of 0.791 at significance level of 0.05).

2. **Market Potential/Risk, Demand and Price Issues:** In demand issues, high importance is given by the lender' appraising officers to the long-term demand gap (often given by the willingness to pay survey, origin destination surveys conducted by lenders' independent engineers) and alternate routes in the road sector. In pricing issues for the road sector, toll rates and their escalation clauses are given high importance by the appraising officers. In the power sector, contractual agreement with the buyer (power purchase agreement and its terms and conditions) is given the highest importance by the appraising officers. High importance is also given to factors like long-term demand-supply gap or presence of a contingent buyer. In pricing issues, a very high importance is given by the appraising officers to the bid amount given by the borrower and as to whether the same will be able to service the costs. Also the highest importance is given to factors like off-taker's (SEB) ability to service payments and whether any contractual agreement like take or pay is signed with them. However, the t test results show (p value =0.000 at a significance level of 0.05) that there is a significant difference in attitude towards both the demand and pricing issues across sectors. The ANOVA results also show a significant difference across all factors in demand and pricing issues except for competition from new entrants (p value 0.446 at significance level of 0.05) in case of demand issues.

3. **Technology Issues/Risk:** In technological issues, great importance is given to lenders' independent engineer's report with regard to the road sector (right of way) as also the design and land acquisition issues. In the power sector, the highest importance is given to technological and operational risks involved since plant's load factors depend on technologies and many a times bids are dependant on efficiencies of super-critical technologies. Also in

the power sector, testing and commissioning are given very high importance because power purchase agreement is often linked to it. Clearances from the government agencies like Pollution Control Board, Ministries of Environment and Finance are also given high importance, as many power projects depend on satisfactory resolution of these issues. However, the t test results show (p value=0.000 at a significance level of 0.05) that there is a significant difference in the attitude towards technological issues across sectors. The ANOVAs results also show a significant difference across all factors in technological issues except that of lender's independent engineer's report (p value 0.178 at significance level of 0.05).

4. **Construction Issues/Risk:** In the road sector, great importance is given to the 'Fixed time-Fixed price' EPC contract, and also to ensure that it is benchmarked against similar contracts with adequate liquidated damages. In the case of power sector, the highest importance is given to all these issues and also to the engineer's comments on aggressiveness of the EPC contract. The parent company's guarantees are also sought particularly against cost overrun. Regarding time overruns, it is often sought to be protected by liquidated damages, though it is capped at 20 per cent. However, the t test results show (p value = 0.000 at a significance level of 0.05) that there is a significant difference in the attitude towards construction issues across sectors. The ANOVA results also show a significant difference across all factors in construction issues except for liquidated damages (p value = 0.735 at significance level of 0.05), which is a part of all EPC contracts and is independent of the sector. Time and cost overruns and implementation issues are given the highest scores by bankers.
5. **Operations Issues/Risk:** In the road contract, the track record and pricing of O&M contract are given the highest importance. If the O&M contractor is good, the banker is assured of adequate flow of funds into the TRA account; consequently, the task of surveillance and monitoring also becomes easier. As far as power is concerned, the highest importance is given to supply/input linkages as many a power projects fail when these are not properly secured. Contracts

like fuel supply and transport agreements are also entered into. Rest of the factors described above in the case of road are also given high importance, and, in the case of power, clause for quick replacement, if suboptimal performance is noticed, is to be included. However, the t test results show (p value = 0.000 at a significance level of 0.05) that there is a significant difference in the attitude towards operational issues across sectors. The ANOVA results also show a significant difference across all factors regarding operational issues except for track record of O&M contractor (p value = 0.328 at significance level of 0.05) and for defining events of default and bonuses (p value = 0.343 at a significance level of 0.05), which are independent of the sectors and also part of the normal due diligence to be exercised by the lenders.

6. **Legal Issues/Risk:** In the case of road sector, the appraising officers give the highest importance to enforceability of rights and remedies as well as legal opinion on documentation and dispute redressal mechanism. In the case of power, apart from these factors, trustee and inter-creditor issues are also given sufficiently high importance. However, the t test results show (p value = 0.000 at a significance level of 0.05) that there is a significant difference in the attitude of bankers towards legal issues across sectors. The ANOVA results also shows a significant difference across all factors in legal issues except for enforceability of contracts (p value = 0.631 at significance level of 0.05).

7. ***Force Majeure* Issues/Risk:** *Force majeure* issues are of two kinds, political and non-political. In both the sectors, high importance is given to identification of issues and termination of benefits which help protect the banker in times of crisis. Insurance and coverage of supply default is given high importance in the case of the power sector. However, the t test results show (p value = 0.000 at a significance level of 0.05) that there is a significant difference in the attitude towards *force majeure* issues across sectors. The ANOVA results also show a significant difference across all factors in *force majeure* issues.

8. **Funding Issues/Risks**: Bankability and viability of projects and stability of cash flows have been considered as the most important factors by bankers for the road sector, whereas for power, in addition to these factors, equity commitment from sponsors and reasonableness of capital costs are also considered very important. As the projects are financed on non-recourse basis, stability of cash flows is important for both the sectors. Bankers generally apply diligence to project costs, means of finance and projected cash flows given by the borrower, and these are assessed for both the sectors. Tenor of loans and building a reasonable cushion between the tenor of loan and tenor of concession agreement are also crucial.

As both the null hypotheses are rejected, it can be inferred that for appraisal and risk identification, the issues involved in each of the sectors are significantly different, except for the evaluation of the promoter. Hence, each project and each sector is unique in itself. Each sub-sector of the infrastructure is also inherently unique in terms of its administrative and organisational structures, the regulatory framework governing their operations, the sophistication of technologies adopted and the degree of commercialisation. This being true, then, it can naturally be inferred that if banks are using the same credit scoring model across sectors, it will lead to deficiency in assessment of risk rating and also inappropriate pricing decision as the attitude of credit officers towards factors of appraisal is (statistically) significantly different across sectors. Therefore, in infrastructure projects, where it is inferred that each project in each sector is unique, bankers need a unique credit rating mechanism, with detailed sector-specific guidelines.

Results of Analysis of Credit Risk Model: Measurement of Risk

The survey results on risk measurement techniques points out that almost all banks use CRISIL Risk Assessment Model for measuring risk in infrastructure projects. Data were collected for all project special purpose vehicle ratings done by CRISIL for the period from 2004 to 2008. The total number of project vehicles rated were 1289. Out of these, 351 (27%) projects were BBB rated and 290 (23%) projects were BB rated. It means that 50 per cent of projects rated on CRISIL model were rated BBB and BB.

The calculation of counter party credit risk, according to Basel II capital accord, involves estimation of probability of default that could be derived from corresponding transition matrix.

The transition matrix represents rating migration from one rating level to another within the selected rating system and during the time period of one year. The last column of transition matrix represents probabilities of default. From the projects identified above, 48 projects of the companies were selected as sample. These projects were chosen as they had reached financial closure and had achieved commencement of operations. The result of the transition matrix is given in Table 3.4.

Table 3.4

Transition Matrix (N=248), 2005-2010

(Figures in percentage)

	AAA (Excellent safety and repayment)	*AA (Very good safety and repayment)*	*A (Good safety and repayment)*	*BBB (Ordinary safety and repayment)*	*BB (Less ordinary safety and repayment)*	*B (Low safety and repayment)*	*C (Unsafe)*	*D (Default)*
AAA	97.00	3.00	0.00	0.00	0.00	0.00	0.00	0.00
AA	8.00	92.00	0.00	0.00	0.00	0.00	0.00	0.00
A	0.00	4.50	90.00	5.50	0.00	0.00	0.00	0.00
BBB	0.00	0.00	8.00	89.00	3.00	0.00	0.00	0.00
BB	0.00	0.00	0.00	3.00	88.00	6.00	0.00	3.00
B	0.00	0.00	0.00	3.00	8.00	83.00	3.00	3.00
C	0.00	0.00	0.00	0.00	10.00	0.00	50.00	40.00
D	0.00	0.00	0.00	0.00	0.00	0.00	0.00	100

The transition matrix clearly shows certain aspects about the CRISIL Risk Assessment Model. The first is that it provides enough granuality among the rating classes. It is evident that the rating is quite stable in all grades, which may be termed as Investment Grade AAA (97.00) (indicating that 97.00 per cent of the rated projects continued with the same grade year after year, over a one-year horizon, during the five-year period); similarly AA (92.00%), A (90.00%) and BBB (89.00%). Thereafter for speculative rating like BB, B and C, the stability declines from 88 to 50 per cent, indicating that migration across each rating grade has increased. The migration to default is 3 per cent in BB, 3.00 per cent in B and 40 per cent in C grades.

That means, the lower rating is able to capture defaults quite well. This is remarkably true for C grade, though the rating grade looks quite unstable. As shown by the data in Table 3.4, the percentage of loans being rated BBB is quite high. However, it becomes clear that BBB loans show a zero probability of default and a remarkable upward migration, which may be due to projects reaching commencement of operation date in between the observation periods. Reaching commencement of operations drastically reduces project risks. In fact, the biggest risk that projects in India face is implementation risk because many projects do not commence operations on the scheduled date. This shows that both A and BBB grades which attract prime lending rate (PLR) + pricing may be reviewed along with the risk mitigants since a very significant percentage of projects shows an upward migration.

The high percentage of upward migration in BBB rating grades suggests that banks are conservative in rating infrastructure loans till the time the project starts earning revenues. However, if the sector-specific rating mechanism along with the effect of risk mitigants is used, it may have an effect on the rating of loans and subsequently on their pricing.

Recommendations and Suggestions

Depending on the credit risk that a particular project faces, the bank has to make adequate provision for capital against it. Expected credit risk loss (EL) is intended to provide reserve requirements for doubtful accounts, help calculate PLR (default premium), price the credit risky instruments (bonds and exotic options), and project the risk-adjusted profitability (e.g., risk-adjusted return on capital; RAROC). The bank may suffer greater loss than what was expected, say, during economic downturns. These losses are called unexpected losses (ULs) or uncertain losses. Strong capital base is required to absorb the unexpected losses as and when they occur. Credit ratings represent an objective opinion of a company's or a credit instrument's inherent financial strength which can project a summary of the diverse risk factors indicating either the financial health or the default probability of the borrower. Accordingly, capital provisioning has to be done in direct relation to the overall risk rating of the credit portfolio. With the advent of Basel II, the capital requirements have increased and are the maximum (22%) in the case of project loans. Besides, if the bankers, trained and accustomed to decades of security-backed lending, rate the project loans on the basis of non-recourse/limited recourse at a higher level, without regard to legal and contractual structure, the capital provisioning requirement for these loans is likely to shoot up, thus increasing the pricing. Consequently, this would make it costly for project developers and will directly impact on the viability of many of the projects. Similar results have been obtained by the transition matrix created for the loan ratings done by the CRISIL Risk Assessment Model.

As Indian commercial banks start appreciating the need for a structured credit risk management framework, it is imperative for them to incorporate some mechanism that will comprehensively and objectively capture and evaluate the credit worthiness of infrastructure project developers against the perspective of the changing scenario. Therefore, it is suggested that the credit rating officer at the branch/corporate credit department initiates the process of rating exercise. It is also imperative to obtain the industry rating from the economic cell, which should also specify critical contracts and regulations for a particular sector as well as set sector-specific benchmarks so as to avoid perceptual errors.

A conceptual framework is discussed in the research (Orgedlinger, 2006) which breaks down the process of risk measurement into four steps: (i) identification of sources of risk; (ii) modelling for uncertainty which includes the measuring uncertainties in their dimensions: (a) impact of risk drivers, (b) likelihood of risk driver happening and (c) risk concentration; (iii) aggregating risk concentration scores with their respective weights; and (iv) aggregating scores leading to credit risk rating. Each rating grade needs to be higher than the hurdle rate used by the banker for that particular rating class. If the appraising officer can give the likelihood and impact scores along with risk mitigant scores, a better rating exercise can be done for the project which will keep its dynamic nature intact. The raw scores can then be modelled by the credit risk department to arrive at the risk rating of the project.

Corresponding to the rating, the research report suggests an appraisal format which takes into account all the eight factors used in the survey and the most important sub-variables already identified by the statistical research. It is suggested, however, that the benchmarks need to be changed from sector to sector so as to retain the dynamic content of the model, and simultaneously the appraising officers also should be advised. It is expected that this model will automatically lead to the exact calculation or measurement of the inherent risk, because the credit officers will be able simultaneously to give scores on the likelihood impact and mitigants as suggested in the conceptual framework.

This appraisal format, as it takes the score of risk mitigants and appropriate hair-cuts into effect and the sub-variables selected are on the basis of primary data, is expected to improve the existing risk assessment model. However, quantitative validation on bank's data needs to be carried out.

Conclusion

The role of social sciences to study the future developments in banking and infrastructure finance in particular has been acknowledged by senior bankers. Infrastructure development will set India on its path to become a superpower. Especially post-financial meltdown, there is bound to be a tremendous thrust for infrastructure development because investment in infrastructure is seen to be counter-cyclical and recession-proof. Because the Indian banks have been mandated to boost the infrastructure growth, the research on project appraisal and risk measurement in infrastructure financing was undertaken, keeping in view the larger role they have to play in the nation's over-all development. Towards this end, the present study attempts to strengthen the efforts of banks to step up the credit flow to the various infrastructure sectors of the Indian economy.

References

Adelson, R.M. (1970). "Discounted Cash Flow: Can we Discount it?", *Journal of Business Finance* 2: 50-66.

Altman, E.I. (1968). "Financial Ratios, Discriminant Analysis and the Prediction of Corporate Bankruptcy", *The Journal of Finance*: 589-609. September.

Balu, K. (2002). *Infrastructure Financing by Indian Banks and Financial Institutions*. Mumbai: Indian Institute of Bankers.

Basel Committee on Banking Supervision (2001). *Internal Rating-Based Approach to Specialized Lending*.

Beenhakker, H.L. (1997). *Risk Management in Project Finance and Implementation*. Westport, CT: Quorum Books.

Chandra, P. (2002). *Projects: Planning, Analysis, Financing, Implementation and Review.* 5th edition. CTM -TMH Professional Series. New Delhi: Tata McGraw Hill.

———. (2005). *Projects: Planning, Analysis, Financing, Implementation and Review.* 5th edition. CTM-TMH Professional Series. New Delhi: Tata McGraw Hill.

Chen, A.H., J.W. Kensinger and J.D. Martin (1989). *Project Financing as a Means of Preserving Financial Flexibility.* University of Texas.

———. (2006). *Project Financing as a Means of Preserving Financial Flexibility.* University of Texas.

Dailami, Mansoor, Ilya Lipkovich and John Van Dyck (1999). *INFRISK: A Computer Simulated Approach to Risk Management.* Washington, DC: World Bank.

Esty, B. and A. Sesia Jr. (2005). *An Overview of Project Finance: 2004 Update*, Harvard Business School, Case #205-65

Fabozzi, F. and P. Nevitt (2000). *Project Financing (7th ed.).* London, UK: Euromoney Publications.

Finnerty, J.D. (1996). *Project Finance: Asset-Based Financial Engineering.* New York: John Wiley & Sons.

Flyvbjerg, B.N. Bruzelius and W. Rothengatter (2003). *Megaprojects and Risk: An Anatomy of Ambition.* Port Chester, New York: Cambridge University Press.

Ghemawat, P. (2005). *Commitment: The Dynamics of Strategy.* New York: Free Press.

Hoffman, S.L. (2001). *The Law and Business of International Project Finance.* 2nd ed. The Hague, The Netherlands: Transnational Publishers Inc. and New York: Kluwer Law International.

McConnell, J.J. and C.J. Muscarella (1985). "Corporate Capital Expenditure Decisions and the Market Value of the Firm", *Journal of Financial Economics* 14: 399-422, September.

Mehta, A. (2001). "Reflection on Enron", in *Globalization: A Symposium on the Challenges of Closer Global Integration.*

Modi, Chetan (2008). *India's Huge Infrastructural Needs: Will Foreign Lenders Respond?.* Moodys Investor Service.

Mohan, Rakesh (1996). *The India Infrastructure Report.*

Nevitt, P.K. and F.J. Fabozzi (2000). *Project Financing.* 7th ed. London, UK: Euromoney Books.

Orgeldinger, John (2006). "The Development of Basel II Confirming Model", *Journal of Structured Finance* 11(4): 84-95. (Winter).

Pandey, I. (2005). *Financial Management.* 9th ed. New Delhi: Vikas Publishing House Pvt. Ltd.

Project Finance Recovery Study (2002). *Standard & Poor's Risk Solution.* March. p.5.

Quirin, G.D. (1977). *The Capital Expenditure Decision.* Richard D. Irwin.

Standard and Poor's (1999). *Infrastructure Finance: Project Finance.*

4

Board Size, Composition and its Impact on the Performance of ICICI Bank

S. Sudalai Muthu and R. Hariharan

Corporate Governance in Banks in India

Governance issues were not an important consideration until the adoption of the economic reforms program in India in 1991. With gradual integration with global markets and increasing number of Indian corporates accessing global markets and getting listed on overseas exchanges, public concerns have become more focused on the effective protection of investors' interest, the need to move towards international standards in terms of disclosure by the corporate sector (Ghosh, 2007).

Recent scandals in the financial sector have brought corporate governance at the forefront of academic and supervisory attention. Banks' versatile role in the economic system has caught regulatory and supervisory interest around the world in an effort to inspire high-quality corporate governance standards. Board structure, in the sense of board size and composition, and its impact on corporate performance constitutes an indispensable and, at the same time, prevalent theme of the corporate governance discussion (Agoraki *et al.*, 2009).

Banks are different from other corporates in important respects, and that makes corporate governance of banks not only different but also more critical. Banks lubricate the wheels of the real economy, are the conduits of monetary policy transmission and constitute the economy's payment and settlement system. By the very nature of their business, banks are highly leveraged. Banks are interconnected in diverse, complex and oftentimes opaque ways underscoring their 'contagion' potential. If a bank fails, the impact can spread rapidly through to other banks with potentially serious consequences for the entire financial system and the macro economy.

A series of structural reforms raised the profile and importance of corporate governance in banks. The 'structural' reform measures included mandating a higher proportion of independent directors on the boards; inducting board members with diverse sets of skills and expertise; and setting up of board committees for key functions like risk management, compensation, investor grievances redressal and nomination of directors. Structural reforms were furthered by the implementation of the Ganguly Committee recommendations relating to the role and responsibilities of the boards of directors, training facilities for directors and, most importantly, application of 'fit and proper' norms for directors.

Overview of ICICI Bank

ICICI Bank is India's second-largest bank with total assets of ₹ 4,736.47 billion (US$ 93 billion) and profit after tax ₹ 64.65 billion (US$ 1,271 million) for the year ended March 31, 2012. It as a network of 2,777 branches and 10,021 automated teller machines (ATMs) in India, and has a presence in 19 countries, including India. It also offers a wide range of banking products and financial services to corporate and retail customers through a variety of delivery channels and through its specialised subsidiaries in the areas of investment banking, life and non-life insurance, venture capital and asset management. ICICI Bank's equity shares are listed in India on Bombay Stock Exchange (BSE) and the National Stock Exchange (NSE) of India Limited and its American Depositary Receipts (ADRs) are listed on the New York Stock Exchange (NYSE). Board of Directors in the ICICI Bank's including eminent individuals with a wealth of experience in international business, management consulting, banking and financial services.

The ICICI Bank website serves as a key investor awareness facility, allowing stakeholders to access information on ICICI Bank at their convenience. It also dedicated investor relations personnel who play a proactive role in disseminating information to both analysts and investors and respond to specific queries. For the third consecutive year, ICICI Bank ranked second in 'India's 50 Biggest Financial Companies' in the BW

Real 500 by *Business World*. ICICI Bank in the private sector bank (PSB) category won the Best Technology Bank of the year, Best Financial Inclusion Initiative and Best Use of Technology in Training and e-Learning by Indian Bank's Association (IBA) Technology Awards. The Bank also received the first runner up for Best Online Bank, Best Customer Relationship Initiative and Best Use of Mobility Technology in Banking by IBA Technology Awards.

Literature Review Board Size, Composition and Performance

The size and composition of the board of directors constitute of the most essential corporate governance themes and have caught the attention of academics and regulators alike (Agoraki *et al.*, 2009). The board composition plays an important role in corporate performance. The composition of board consists of both insider and outsider directors. Mostly insiders are members of the top management teams and employees of the company. Outside directors have no such association (Chatterjee, 2011). Klein (2002) and Andres and Vallelado (2008) who argue that a large board size should be preferred because of possibility of specialisation for more effective monitoring and advising functions. In the view of researchers such as Fama and Jensen (1983); Lipton and Lorsch (1992); and Yermack (1996), small board size should be preferred. Dhawan (2006) supported this finding by pointing out that the size of the board increases with turnover, but only up to a certain level, beyond which the increasing turnover does not have any influence. Hence, knowledge and skill of the board members are of paramount importance, rather than the size of the board.

Dwivedi and Jain (2005), in their study on board size and firm value, also suggested a positive relationship. On the other hand, there are studies which point to a negative relationship between board size and firm performance in the Indian context. Ghosh (2006) study on the relationship between financial performance and board parameters which include board size found that larger board size tends to have a negative influence on firm performance.

Most of the literature survey talks on the board composition and its firm performance or *vice versa* (Bhagat and Black, 2001). Board size also shows no consistent correlation with firm performance, some other studies found negative correlation. Some research studies reveal that large board size leads to improved firm performance, whereas there have also been evidence of larger boards being inefficient in nature.

Pearce and Zahra (1992) and Dalton *et al.* (1999) argue that as board size increases, the strategic decision making capabilities of the board increase, but Golden and Zajac (2001) argued that smaller boards are assumed to have inadequate confidence and unclear understanding in making strategic changes. If the board size increases, the cost associated with it, like coordination cost and communication costs, also increases (Raheja, 2005). Yermack (1996) empirically demonstrated that there is a negative relationship between board size and firm performance. Indicating operating efficiency and profitability are negatively related to the board size.

There is relationship between the inside directors and the firm performance in bank; prior research papers say it does not support a clear relation between board independence and firm performance. It can be said with the example of an early work by Vance (1964) that there exists a positive correlation between the inside directors and a firm performance. Conflicting with this, the results of Adams and Mehran (2005) show a significant positive relationship between board size and bank performance, as measured by Tobin's Q. Although the structure of the bank holding company was found to be related to board size, the positive effects of a larger board were still visible after taking it into account. In addition, while they find no significant relation between the proportion of outside directors and bank performance, they show that firms with boards dominated by outsiders do perform better.

Hermalin and Weisbach (1991) argued that there is no relationship between board composition and firm performance. They suggested that it is good to have inside directors' presence in the board of directors, as it helps CEOs to maximise value by providing both advice and knowledge about the day-to-day operations of the company. They also suggested that top management has control over board selection. In the view of Bhagat and Black (1999), there is no strong correlation between board independence and firm performance. They stated that different firms need different degrees of board independence, depending upon their growth rate.

The work of Staikouras *et al.* (2007) examined a sample of 58 out of the 100 largest, in terms of total assets, credit institutions operating in Europe for the period between 2002 and 2004. Their analysis inferred that bank profitability—measured in terms of return on assets (ROA), return on equity (ROE) and Tobin's Q—is negatively and significantly related to the size of the board of directors. Finally, Pathan *et al.* (2008), using a dataset of the Thai commercial banks over the period 1999-2003, also obtained a negative relation between board size and both ROE and ROA.

Objectives and Hypotheses

The paper mainly focused to on discussions on board size, composition and firm performance:

1. To identify any relationship between board size and board composition in the ICICI bank.
2. To assess any relationship between performance and the board composition in the ICICI bank.

To achieve these objectives, the following hypotheses are developed.

H_0^1: There is no relationship between board size and board composition in the ICICI bank.

H_1^2: There is relationship between performance and board composition in the ICICI bank.

H_0^3: There is no relationship among the performance and performance measure indicator (return on asset, deposits and net interest margin) in the ICICI bank.

Methodology

Sample

The sample includes only the ICICI Bank which is listed in both NSE and BSE in India and it's a leading private corporate bank with second largest market capitalisation in the private bank in India.

Data

The secondary data collected from the ICICI bank website like corporate governance report, management discussion and balance sheet and board composition of directors, profitability ratio, liabilities and executive summary are collected from Centre for Monitoring Indian Economy (CMIE) Pvt. Ltd. from the year 2007 to 2012.

Variables and Statistics

The variables taken for the study are board size, outside and inside directors (for board composition), meeting per year, sitting fee and director's salary for board characteristics. The Tobin's Q ratio, ROA, net interest margin (NIM), return on average equity (ROAE), loans, advances, non-performing asset (NPA) and deposits are used to measure the bank performance. The descriptive statistics tools is used to find out the mean, standard deviation, maximum and minimum value for all the variables. Correlation is used to find out the relationship between the board size and composition of the board, and regression is used for estimating the relationships among variables between board size and performance in the ICICI bank. The regression equation for the purpose of finding out the determinants of performance and board composition is as follows.

Tobin Q (performance) = $\alpha + \beta_1$ ROA + β_2 DEP + β_3 BOR + β_4 LA + β_5 INV + β_6 RONW + β_7 BOZ + β_8 NIM + β_9 ROE + β_{10} NPA + β_{11} SF + β_{12} DS + C.

Analysis and Findings

Table 4.1 shows the mean, median, standard deviation, maximum and minimum values of the following variables: board size, outside directors, inside directors, meeting per year, sitting fee, director's salary, Tobin's Q, ROA, ROE, NIM and return on net worth of ICICI bank.

Table 4.1

Descriptive Statistics

Variable	*N*	*Mean*	*Median*	*Std. Dev*	*Max*	*Min*
Board Size	6	18.33	18.5	2.42	21	14
Outside Directors	6	12.5	12.5	1.64	15	10
Inside Directors	6	5.83	6	.983	7	4
Meetings per year	6	7	7	1.54	9	5
Sitting fee	6	4.016	3.95	.318	4.60	3.70
Director's salary	6	40.16	38.80	3.76	46.80	36.90
Tobin's Q	6	3.24	3.34	.55	3.85	2.43
Return on Asset	6	1.11	1.040	.214	1.45	.86
Return on Average Equity	6	10.26	10.34	2.27	13.40	7.70
Net Interest Margin	6	2.94	2.52	1.27	5.50	2.20
Return on net worth	6	9.83	10.16	2.33	12.91	6.98

Source: Computed results are based on compiled data collected from CMIE Prowess Pvt. Ltd.

In Table 4.1, the mean and median size of the board are 18.33 and 18.5 directors, respectively, which is higher than the average board size (12) reported for non-financial firms (Yermack, 1996, Rosenstein and Wyatt, 1997; Klein, 1998; Vafeas, 1999; Andres *et al.*, 2005), but close to the 17 directors obtained by Adams and Mehran (2005) in the period 1995-1999 for banks. The board size of ICICI bank is larger. The mean of the outside directors is 12.5 which is higher than the mean of the inside directors of 5.83. This shows that the most of the directors are outside in the ICICI bank. The number of meetings per year mean is 7 which is less than the 8.48 meetings reported by Adams and Mehran (2005).

The mean and median of sitting fee of the director are 4.01 and 3.95 respectively and the director's salary of maximum and minimum value lies between 46.80 and 36.90 which depicts that the salary depends upon the number of directors in the board. The mean and median of the Tobin's q are 3.24 and 3.34 respectively which is greater than ratio of 1, which indicates that the market value of the ICICI bank is based solely on its assets. The mean of ROA is 1.11; it indicates that the return earned on asset is less in the ICICI bank on their total asset. The ROAE mean is 10.26 which indicates that ICICI bank board is good in deploying the shareholder's capital, net interest margin mean is 2.94 and return on net worth mean is 9.83.

Figure 4.1

Board Composition in the ICICI Bank

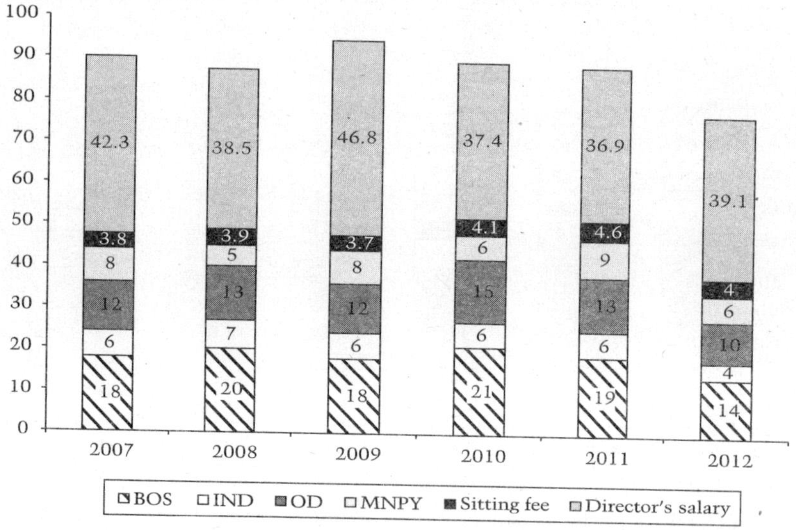

Source: Computed results are based on compiled data collected from CMIE Prowess Pvt. Ltd.

Figure 4.1 indicates the ICICI Bank board composition includes board size, inside, outside director, number of meeting per year, sitting fee and director's salary. It explains that the board composition from the year 2007 to 2012. The board size of ICICI Bank in the year 2010 was 21, which was larger than the board size in the year 2007 which was 18 only, but it was decreased to 14 in the year 2012. It shows the board size in the ICICI bank is larger. The inside directors in the ICICI bank were larger in the year 2008 (7) which reduced to 4 in the year 2012. The outside directors in the year 2010 were 15 which was highest in the ICICI bank which decreased to 10 in the year 2012. Larger number of meetings were conducted in the year 2011 and less meetings were conducted in 2012. The sitting fee of bank was high in the year 2011 because the number of meetings occurred was more in that year compared to other years. The director salary in the year 2009 was highest and it was fluctuating because of the composition of director in the board was increasing and decreasing in the bank.

Figure 4.2

Performance Indicator of the ICICI Bank

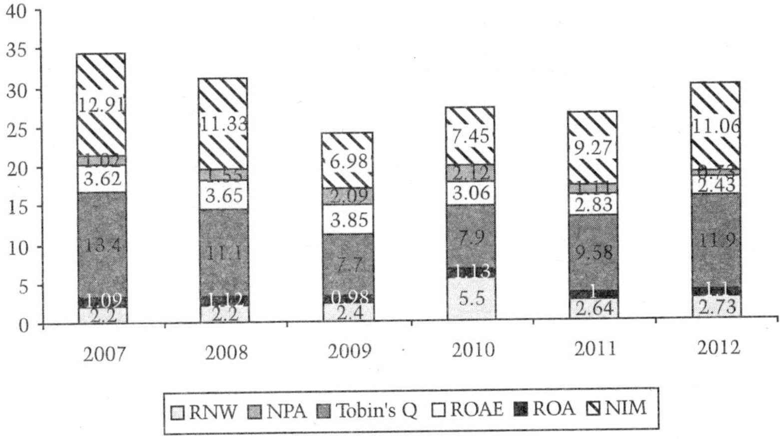

Source: Same as Figure 4.1.

Figure 4.2 shows about the ICICI bank performance in the terms of NIM, ROA, ROE, Tobin's Q ratio, NPA and return on net worth (RNW). From the chart, it's clearly indicated that NIM, ROA, ROE, Tobin's Q ratio, NPA and RNW were fluctuating between 2007 and 2012.

The Relationship between the Board Size and Board Composition in the ICICI Bank

H_0^1: There is no relationship between the board size and board composition in the ICICI bank.

Table 4.2 reveals the correlation between the board size and bank composition in the ICICI bank.

From the table, it is observed that correlation coefficient is significant for the board size and composition in the ICIC bank. So it rejects the null hypothesis (H_0^1). Hence, there is no relationship between the board size and composition in the ICICI bank.

Table 4.2

Board Composition and Bank Performance in the ICICI Bank

		Board size	*Inside directors*	*Outside directors*	*Meeting per year*	*Director's salary*	*Sitting fee*
		Pearson Correlation Coefficients (two-tailed significance levels in parentheses; sample size = 6)					
Correlation coefficient between board size and composition in the ICICI Bank	Board size	1	.025*	.003**	.920	.656	.744
	Inside directors		1	.137	1.000	.962	.920
	Outside directors			1	.882	.485	.582
	Meeting per year				1	.533	.531
	Director's salary					1	.087
	Sitting fee						1

Notes: *: Correlation is significant at the 0.05 level (two-tailed).

**: Correlation is significant at the 0.01 level (two-tailed).

Source: Computed results are based on compiled data collected from CMIE Prowess Pvt. Ltd.

Performance and Board Composition in the ICICI Bank

H_1^2: There is relationship between performance and board composition in the ICICI bank.

H_0^3: There is no relationship between the performance dependent variable and independent variables (ROA and NIM) in the ICICI bank.

The table depicts regression analysis of performance and board composition in the ICICI bank.

Regression analysis in Table 4.3 is used to find out whether there is any relationship between the performance and board composition in ICICI bank. The calculated coefficient of board size is found to be insignificant. So the null hypothesis is not rejected. So the null hypothesis is accepted (H_1^2). Hence there is relationship between performance and board composition in the ICICI bank. But the calculated coefficients of deposits, ROA and NIM are found to be significant. So the null hypothesis is rejected (H_0^3). Hence there is no relationship between the performance and performance measure indicator (ROA and NIM) in the ICICI bank. The R^2 value is nearly 97 per cent (.970), proving that the predictor variables of performance are 97 per cent, while there are other variables that determine performance. The F stat is also significant (0.14), indicating that the variance in the predictor variables is associated with the variation in performance.

Table 4.3

Regression Results of Performance and Board Composition in the ICICI Bank

Variables	*Unstandardised Coefficients*	*'t' value*	*Sig.*
(Constant)	6.450	19.610	.000
Return on asset	-.940**	-9.417	.003
Deposits	.500	3.370	.043
Borrowings	-.329	-.796	.484
Loan and advances	.366	1.506	.229
Investment	-.127	-.506	.648
Return on net worth	.307	1.543	.221
Board size	-.132	-.436	.692
Net interest margin	-.399*	-3.991	.028
Return on equity	.287	1.343	.272
Non-performing asset	-.417	-1.313	.281
Sitting fee	-.191	-.680	.546
Director salary	.173	.578	.604
R^2			.970
Adjusted R square			.951
F stat			0.14*

Note: *.Significant at 0.05 level; **Significant at 0.01 level.

Source: Computed results are based on compiled data collected from CMIE Prowess Pvt. Ltd.

Conclusion

The ICICI Bank is the second largest and market capitalisation private sector bank in India. The bank consists of larger board size, which has no significant relationship with the board composition. The result of the regression analysis reveals that the bank performance has significant relationship with the board compositions. These clearly implied that bank performances are based on the performance indicator measure in the bank like deposits, ROA and NIM. It shows that the bank accumulates large deposits and asset in their balance sheet.

References

Adams, R. and D. Ferreira (2007). "A Theory of Friendly Boards", *Journal of Finance* 62: 217-50.

Adams, R. and H. Mehran (2003). "Is Corporate Governance Different for Bank Holding Companies?", *Federal Reserve Bank of NY Economic Policy Review*: 123-42, April.

———. (2005). *Corporate Performance, Board Structure and its Determinants in the Banking Industry.* EFA 2005 Moscow Meetings. August 8. Available at SSRN: *http://ssrn.com/abstract=302593.*

Agoraki, Maria-Eleni, Manthos D. Delis and Panagiotis Staikouras (2009). "The Effect of Board Size and Composition on Bank Efficiency", Retrieved from *http://mpra.ub.uni-muenchen.de/18548/MRAP Paper No.18548.* Posted November 11, 2009/12:15.

Anderson, C.R. and M.D. Reeb (2003). "Founding-family Ownership and Firm Performance: Evidence from the S&P500", *The Journal of Finance* LVIII(3): 1301-28.

Andres, P., V. Azofra and F.J. Lopez (2005). "Corporate Boards in OECD Countries: Size, Composition, Compensation, Functioning and Effectiveness", *Corporate Governance: An International Review* 13: 197–210.

Andres, P.D. and E. Vallelado (2008). "Corporate Governance in Banking: The Role of the Board of Directors", *Journal of Banking & Finance* 32: 2570-80.

Bhagat, Sanjai and Bernard Black (1999), "The Uncertain Relationship between Board Composition and Firm Performance", *Business Lawyer* 54: 921-63.

———. (2001). "The Non-correlation between Board Independence and Long Term Firm Performance", *Journal of Corporation Law* 27: 231-74; Stanford Law School John M. Olin Program Law and Economics, *Working Paper* No.185.

Chatterjee, D. (2011). "Board Composition and Performance in Indian Firms: A Comparative Analysis Empirical", *The International Journal of Management Science and Information Technology (IJMSIT)* 1(2): 1-15, October-December.

Dalton D.R., C.M. Daily, J.L. Johnson and A.E. Ellstrand (1999). "Number of Directors and Financial Performance: A Meta-Analysis", *Academy of Management Journal* 42(6).

Dhawan, Jyothi (2006). "Board of Directors and Corporate Governance in Large Listed Firms in India", *The ICFAI Journal of Corporate Governance* 5(3): 39-61.

Donaldson, L. and J.H. Davis (1991). "Stewardship Theory or Agency Theory: CEO Governance and Shareholder Returns", *Australian Journal of Management* 16: 49-64.

Dwivedi, Neeraj and Arun Jain (2005). "Corporate Governance and Performance of Indian Firms: The Effect of Board Size and Ownership", *Employee Responsibilities and Rights Journal* 17(3): 161-72.

Fama, E.F. and M.C. Jensen (1983). "Agency Problems and Residual Claims", *Journal of Law and Economics* 26: 327-49.

Ghosh, Saibal (2006). "Do Board Characteristics Affect Corporate Performance? Firm-Level Evidence for India", *Applied Economics Letters* 13(7): 435-43.

———. (2007). "Bank Monitoring, Managerial Owership and Tobin's Q: An Empirical Analysis for India", *Managerial and Decision Economics* 28: 129-143. DOI: 10.1002/mde. 1315.

Golden, B.R. and E.J. Zajac (2001). "When Will Boards Influence Strategy? Inclination Power=Strategic Change", *Strategic Management Journal* 22: 1087-111.

Hermalin, Benjamin E. and Michael S. Weisbach (1991). "The Effects of Board Composition and Direct Incentives on Firm Performance", *The Journal of the Financial Management Association* 20(4): 101-12.

———. (2003). "Boards of Directors as an Endogenously Determined Institution: A Survey of the Economic Literature", *Economic Policy Review* 9(1): 7-26.

Jackling, B. and S. Johl (2009). "Board Structure and Firm Performance: Evidence from India's Top Companies", *Corporate Governance: An International Review* 17(4): 492-509.

Klein, A. (1998) "Firm Performance and Board Committee Structure," *Journal of Law and Economics* 41: 275-99.

———. (2002). "Audit Committee, Board of Director Characteristics, and Earnings Management", *Journal of Accounting and Economics* 33: 375–400.

Lipton, Martin and Jay W. Lorsch (1992). "A Modest Proposal for Improved Corporate Governance", *Business Lawyer* 48(l): 59-77.

Pathan, S., M. Skully and J. Wickramanyake (2008). "Reforms in Thai Bank Governance: An Aftermath of the Asian Financial Crisis", *International Review of Financial Analysis* 17(2): 345-65.

Pearce, John A. and Shaker A. Zahra (1992). "Board Composition from a Strategic Contingency Perspective", *Journal of Management Studies* 29: 411-38.

———. (2000). "Board Composition from a Strategic Contingency Perspective", *Journal of Management Studies* 29: 411-38.

Raheja, Charu (2005). "Determine of Board Size and Composition: A Theory of Corporate Boards", *Journal of Finance and Quantitative Analysis* 40: 283-306.

Rosenstein, S. and J.G. Wyatt (1997). "Inside Directors, Board Effectiveness and Shareholder Wealth", *Journal of Financial Economics* 44: 229-50.

Sharma, J.P. (2011). *Corporate Governance, Business Ethics and CSR*: New Delhi: Ane Books Pvt Ltd. p.79.

Simpson, W.G. and A.E. Gleason (1999). "Board Structure, Ownership, and Financial Distress in Banking Firms", *International Review of Economics & Finance* 8: 281-92.

Staikouras, P.K., C.K. Staikouras and M.E.K. Agoraki (2007). The Effect of Board Size and Composition on European Bank Performance", *European Journal of Law and Economics* 23: 1–27.

Vafeas, N. (1999). "Board Meeting Frequency and Firm Performance", *Journal of Financial Economics* 53: 113-42.

Vance, Stanley C. (1964). *Board of Directors: Structure and Performance*. Eugene, OR: University of Oregon Press.

Yermack, David (1996). "Higher Market Valuation of Companies with a Small Board of Directors", *Journal of Financial Economics* 40: 185-211.

5

Risk Management System in Banking

P.S. Subha Prada

Introduction

Risk is a fundamental element that drives financial behaviour. Future of banking will rest on the effectiveness and efficiency of risk management dynamics. Only those banks that have an effective enterprise risk management (ERM) will survive and flourish in the long run. As was evident in the 2008 financial crisis, with failure of one bank lies the systemic risk i.e., the risk of a single financial failure having a cascading effect and bringing down the entire financial system. To avoid this, banks need a proactive system of identifying and eliminating risk—i.e., over and above the regulatory requirements. That is, they need a robust risk management system in place. A good risk management system for a bank is shaped by two important variables. While one is the types of risks the bank is exposed to, the other is the measurement techniques available for the quantification of measurable risks. The following section describes the types of risks banks are exposed to and subsequently the techniques adopted for measuring and managing risks that a bank faces.

Risk: Risk is a situation involving exposure to danger, in simplest terms. The term was used to denote the danger at sea. The business dictionary defines it as the probability or threat of liability or loss or other negative occurrence that is caused by external or internal vulnerabilities and that may be neutralised through pre-emptive action. Therefore risk is an inherent part of any activity, business, industry or economy.

Risk management: The identification, analysis, assessment, control and minimisation or elimination of risk is called risk management. It may include the process of risk assumption, risk avoidance, risk retention, risk transfer, etc., to manage risk.

ERM is an integrated approach to risk management that includes practices and processes the board and management use to define their business model and strategy and prudently manage their risk exposure.

As with any other change, there has been some resistance to change to ERM in the beginning as it was considered as an expensive exercise that requires considerable time and effort with little value addition in return. But time and the recent global recession triggered with the collapse of Lehman Brothers, Fannie Mae and the like and the European financial crisis have re-emphasised the vulnerability of the banking system and the role of the banking system in ensuring financial stability of an economy. The recent financial meltdown of the USA and Europe has made importance of risk management paramount and made it an integral part of businesses worldwide in general and banking in particular. ERM in banking became a necessity as the financial turmoil could have been averted with a robust risk management mechanism.

Need for Risk Management in Banks

In the past, banking environment in India was regulated and was having a limited risk exposure. However, present day banking is exposed to numerous risks because of its increased level of operations and the diversified services the banks offer. ERM in banking allows a bank to identify and assess risks before they become a threat to the survival of the bank. It allows the banks to identify the credit risk, liquidity risk and other operational risks and take appropriate risk management measures to minimise the loss. ERM acts as an alert system that identifies risk indicators to identify the severity of risk and the urgency to attend to it.

Risk is defined broadly as the volatility of the value of the bank. Banks are constantly exposed to different kinds of risks like credit risk and market risk, operational risk in their business of offering financial services to customers. Though banks were initially acting as agents to lend money, the dynamic business environment and the intense competition owing to liberalisation has compelled banks to add a plethora of innovations in their portfolio of services thereby exposing the banks to additional risks.

In this backdrop, the paper intends to study the risks faced by banks, the sources of risks and the various risk assessment and management techniques followed by banks.

Types of Risks

Banks in the process of providing financial services are exposed to a variety of risks as credit risk, interest rate risk, foreign exchange risk, liquidity risk, operational risk, legal risk, regulatory and other risks that are highly capable of having a contagion effect by spreading the risks to other entities of the financial system.

Credit Risk

This is the most common risk that banks are exposed to. It refers to the risk of loss due to default or deterioration in credit quality of the obligor. It arises because of the borrower's unwillingness or inability to repay either the principal or the interest. Earlier the credit risk only included the risk of default. The deterioration in the credit quality was added later because of mark to market credit portfolios. Credit risk can be attributed to both external as well as internal factors. While the state of the economy, the interest rates, the variations in the foreign exchange rates, volatility of the equity prices and the regulatory environment make up the external factors, the internal factors could be inadequate loan administration policies, faulty appraisal of the borrower's financial position, improper risk pricing, absence of a post-sanction review transform as the internal factors leading to credit risk.

Market Risk

When the banking environment was highly regulated, the risk it was exposed to was limited and was mainly in the form of credit risk. Gradually as the banking environment was deregulated and liberalised, it was susceptible to many other kinds of risks caused by variations in the market variables as interest rates, foreign exchange rates, equity prices, commodity prices, etc. The risk to earnings arose from changes in interest rates or forex rates or from fluctuations in bond, equity or commodity prices. Banks are subject to market risk in both the management of their balance sheets and in their trading operations. Market risk comprises the following.

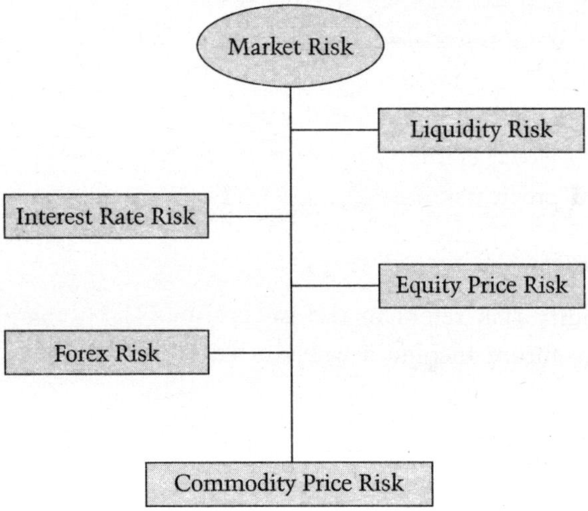

Interest Rate Risk

Interest rate risk refers to the potential loss an institution faces because of the movement in the rates of interest. It is capable of adversely affecting the net interest income, asset value and cash flows of the bank. Interest risk management aims at reducing the probable loss and ensures that there is a commensurate return for the risk accepted. It also assesses the risk stemming from maturity and re-pricing mismatches.

Foreign Exchange Risk

A bank is exposed to foreign exchange risk because of adverse exchange rate movement during a period in which it has an open position, either spot or forward or both in same foreign currency. Even in case where spot or forward positions in individual currencies are balanced, the maturity pattern of forward transactions may produce mismatches. There is also a settlement risk arising out of default of the counter party and out of time lag in settlement of one currency in one centre and the settlement of another currency in another time zone.

Currency risk is the possibility that exchange rate changes will alter the expected amount of principal and return of the lending or investment. At times, banks may try to cope with this specific risk on the lending side by shifting the risk associated with exchange rate fluctuations to the borrowers. However the risk does not get extinguished, but only gets converted in to credit risk.

Commodity Risk

Commodity risk refers to the uncertainties in the future market value and the future income because of the volatility in the process of commodities.

Equity Risk

Equity risk is due to volatility in equity prices.

Liquidity Risk

Banks generally have deposits that have shorter maturities compared to loans. Banks therefore need adequate liquidity to provide a cushion to withdrawals. Liquidity is the ability of banks to accommodate deposits as well as reduction in liabilities and to fund loan growth.

Operational Risk

Operational risk arises from implementation of business functions in an organisation. It arises because of frauds, errors and internal processes, legal risks, environmental risks, etc.

Risks Considered for Management

Banks are primarily payment agents for customers to borrow and lend money. Over the period of time, banks started diversifying into other activities. However these services do not have direct balance sheet implications, as the market participants utilising these services use their own balance sheet to facilitate the transactions and to absorb the risks associated with them. They rely on the generally accepted accounting procedures rather than an economic balance sheet. In spite of this, banks face many kinds of risks in on-balance-sheet businesses. Hence this forms the focus of risk management procedures.

The banking firms generally adopt the following steps to implement a risk management system which basically constitutes the following four elements:

1. Standards and reports,
2. Position limits and rules,
3. Investment guidelines and strategies,
4. Incentive contracts and compensation.

These tools are generally established to measure the exposure, define procedures to manage these exposures, limit individual positions to acceptable levels and encourage risk management in compliance with the organisational goals and objectives.

Comprehensive Risk Management Process

Risks faced by banks are not independent to each other. There is always a linkage found between various risks faced by banks. If a bank lends a client on a floating rate of interest, an increase in the market interest rate will increase the obligation of borrower which might lead to a default in case the client is not able to make the repayment. In this situation, interest rate risk leads to credit risk. Hence the risk management process should be multidimensional.

With reference to banks, the process of risk management comprises of managing various risk exposures that a bank is exposed to by constantly and actively revising the asset-liability portfolio with the aim of maximising profits. It involves ensuring that maturity profiles of assets match that of liabilities.

A risk management system should act as an advance warning system to the sensitivity of the bank adverse changes in the environment. It should focus on the profitability and long-term viability of the bank. All levels of management i.e., board of directors, middle management and lower management should have a role in the risk management process.

A comprehensive risk management process can comprise the following steps:

1. Define risk appetite of the organisation.

2. Have effective supervisory setup for risk management information system (MIS), monitoring and control.
3. Set standards, reports, rules, investment guidelines, incentives and compensation.
4. Strengthen the compliance system to take care of requirement.
5. Contingency mechanism to identify stress situations.
6. Select/develop risk measurement models and approaches for various risks.
7. Develop risk culture and communicate risk management objectives.
8. Define organisational structure, roles, responsibilities and accountability.
9. Identify the risks faced by the organisation.
10. Measure, assess and aggregate risks. Allocate resources.
11. Determine treatment for each risk identified.
12. Develop and implement risk-specific management strategies.
13. Evaluate the efficacy of the strategies implemented above.
14. Review frequently all components for improvement and feedback.
15. Update the process to keep up with internal and external changes.

The following section deals with the measurement and management of three most important risks that banks are exposed to, namely, the market risk, credit risk and operational risk.

Risk Management Techniques

Market Risk Management

Measurement of Market Risk

Changes in market parameters such as market volatility, liquidity, currency fluctuations, change in interest rates, slowdown in the economy, etc., lead to market risk that affects the earnings or asset-liability composition of the bank. The market risk emanates more because of the trading activities of the bank than because of the traditional activities. The market risk measurement is critical for the financial solvency of a bank or any financial institution as it gives vital information for managerial decision making in areas as risk exposure *vis-à-vis* capital resources. This helps the management in revising its risk allocation from risky activities to ones that are less risky and more profitable. The market risk is measured in terms of value-at-risk (VaR), earnings at risk (EaR) and daily EaR.

The VaR Measure

The term VaR was coined by Guldimann in late 1980's and has revolutionised market risk measurement for financial institutions. It attempts to summarise the total risk in a portfolio of financial assets and is extensively used by financial institutions. It is also used by central bank regulators in determining the capital a bank has to maintain to reflect the market risk it is exposed to. Traditionally market risk is being analysed by VaR models. The VaR model estimates the maximum amount that a bank can lose with a given certainty over a given period of time for a given trading portfolio. They summarise the risk exposure for a given portfolio. The model estimates the sensitivity of different components of a portfolio to small price changes like a one basis point change in interest rate or a one per cent change in exchange rates and assumes that the market prices follow a particular statistical distribution. The manager can make use of statistical theory to estimate potential losses with a degree of confidence.

The model can also be elaborated to measure the correlations between different components in a portfolio allowing to predict the extent to which prices in different markets tend to move together. This model can also be used to measure other aspects of risk such as the liquidity of the portfolio i.e., the ease with which an institution can liquidate or close risk propositions. Few of the international banks are incorporating the liquidity effects in greater detail in their VaR models. Parametric VaRs based on simulation of portfolio based on historical price data are extensively being used in place of statistical theory to predict price movements. This method revalues a portfolio directly at current and previous market prices measured over a period of time. It then uses the extreme simulated values as basis to predict losses on a portfolio.

The portfolio manger attempts to make a statement to the extent of certainty that the loss will not be more than ₹ V in the next N days. The variable V is the VaR of the portfolio. It is a function of the time horizon and the confidence level. It is the loss level over the time period (specified by the horizon) that the manager is X per cent certain (X specified by the confidence level) will not be exceeded.

A bank's capital for market risk is computed by regulators using N = 10 and X = 99. In other words, the emphasis is on loss level over a 10-day period that is expected to exceed only 1 per cent of the time. The market risk capital required for a bank to maintain is generally k times the 10-day 99 per cent VaR, in which the multiplier k is chosen by the regulators.

When N days is the time horizon and X per cent is the confidence level, VaR is the loss corresponding to the (100-X)th percentile of the distribution of the change in the value of the portfolio over the next N days. For instance, if the daily VaR of trading portfolio of a financial institution is ₹ 3 crore at 99 per cent confidence level, it means that there is only one chance in a hundred, under normal market conditions, that a loss greater than this amount will occur. This figure summarises the bank's exposure to market risk as the probability of an adverse move. The above figure shows VaR when the change in the value of a portfolio is approximately normally distributed. VaR will change if the time horizon or the holding period changes which will depend in turn on the liquidity of the instrument/market. With the help of VaR, it can be said with varying degrees of certainty that potential loss will not exceed a certain limit. VaR will change with different levels of certainty. It is a method of assessing risk using standard statistical techniques. It is the maximum loss over a target horizon such that there is a low, predetermined probability that the actual loss will be larger.

Approaches to Measure Market Risks

The Risk Metrics Model

A risk management model aims at estimating losses for a day as a single estimate that might be unfavourable for business activities. The RiskMetrics model was developed by J.P. Morgan in 1994. It involves a variance/covariance matrix of risk and correlation measures. It makes use of exponentially weighted moving average forecast to model variances. RiskMetrics forecasts risks for monthly horizons. The one-day exponential model is extrapolated to estimate volatility the next day and is extended so on. The market risk exposure of a financial institution can be measured on a daily basis through RiskMetrics. The main concern of a financial institution (FI) is how much loss it is likely to suffer on a day of adverse market conditions.

The daily Earnings at Risk of a financial institution = Rupee market value of the position * Price sensitivity of the position * Potential adverse move in yield.

As the product of price sensitivity and adverse yield move represents the price volatility of an asset,

Daily Earnings at Risk = (Rupee market value of the position) * (Price volatility)

Daily Price Volatility = (Price sensitivity to a small change in yield) * (Adverse Daily yield move)

N – day VaR = 1-day VaR * $\sqrt{N}$.

Historical Simulation

Historical simulation is one of the methods of estimating VaR. The method relies on the past data as an indicator of the direction in the future. The procedure for VaR calculation involves:

1. Identification of market variables like interest rates, exchange rates, equity prices, etc., affecting the portfolio.
2. Observations pertaining to the identified variables over the specified period of time are then collected. This gives as many alternative scenarios for what can take place between the present and the future.
3. A table is prepared that shows the values of the market variables the following day if their percentage changes between today and the following day are the same as they were between day i-1 and dayi.

Model Building Approach

Volatility in model-based approach is measured on a daily basis and the volatility of an asset is represented as volatility per day. It is calculated as volatility per year/√252 assuming 252 trading days in a year.

Volatility per day is calculated based on the volatility per year of the stock in the portfolio. A product of volatility per day and the value of the stock in the portfolio is obtained which is the standard deviation of the daily changes in the value of the position. In this approach, the change in the value of the stock is assumed to be normal and the mean is assumed to be zero. The method uses standard deviation and mean to arrive at the potential loss of a stock or an asset for a given time horizon and confidence level. VaR is estimated statistically with the help of these parameters.

Monte Carlo Simulation Approach

Model building approach can be implemented using this approach by adopting the following procedure.

1. The value of the portfolio today is determined using the current values of market variables.
2. A confidence level and holding period is chosen to calculate the potential loss.
3. A random generator of variables is run and the value of the asset/ portfolio is calculated using parameters appropriate for the selected holding period.
4. The profit and loss values of the asset are calculated as the difference between the simulated and the current values.
5. The profit and loss values are ranked and the value at the given confidence level is the VaR according to the Monte Carlo simulation.

Stress Testing

Stress testing of a portfolio involves estimating how the portfolio of a bank would have performed under some of the extreme market conditions observed in the past few years. It describes the techniques adopted by banks to gauge their susceptibility to exceptional but possible events. It involves identification of underlying variables and their movements and deciding on the extent of the stress these variables need to be subject. Once this is done, the portfolio is subject to shocks. The effect of particular market movements can be analysed by revaluing the portfolio. A summary of the effects of various shocks and their magnitudes is prepared in the form of a stress report. These tests summarise the bank's exposure to extreme but possible circumstances.

The objective of stress testing is different from that of VaR. It aims at examining the effects of extreme events on a portfolio.

Scenario Analysis

Scenario analysis is a leading stress testing technique. It specifies the shocks that might possibly affect several risk factors simultaneously in case an extreme event occurs. The scenarios are sometimes initiated by the senior management or by recent news.

Scenario analysis involves the following procedure:

1. Few scenarios that are capable of adversely affecting the market in which the bank operates are created.
2. The changes in each of the risk factors and their impact on the value of the portfolio for the given scenario are calculated.
3. The portfolio is then tested on a regular basis to estimate the probable loss under each scenario.
4. The scenarios are reviewed periodically.

Sensitivity Analysis

This tool, also called the 'what-if' analysis, is a very useful tool in determining the effect of change in market variables like interest rates, credit spreads, exchange rates, equity prices, etc., on the value of the portfolio. The simplest form of sensitivity analysis identifies the short-term impact of predefined moves in market variables on portfolio value; for instance a +/- 2 per cent, 4 per cent or a 6 per cent change in exchange rate. In certain instances, these parameters are also moved by a unit amount like a 5 per cent rise or a 10 basis point rise. These tests can also be historical in the sense that the analysis may examine the worst case movements in each or any of the risk factors

Market Risk Management Techniques

FIs manage market risk by: (i) either quantifying and controlling each risk separately, or (ii) by implementing scenario analysis.

Stop Loss Method of Hedging

Under the Stop Loss Method, the bank writes a call option at a certain strike price. The strategy is such that if the price of the underlying asset exceeds the strike price, the bank purchases the security at the strike price. If the price falls below, banks sell the security at the strike price. The strategy aims at holding a naked position when the price is below the strike price and hold a covered position when the price rises above strike price. This ensures that banks own the security when the option closes in the money and does not own it when the option closes out of the money.

However, this strategy might involve high hedging costs as it involves continuous selling and buying of stock.

Option Greeks

These are advanced strategies of hedging. Option Greeks are mathematical outputs of Option Valuation Model that is used in prediction of future movements in option values. Some of them are:

Delta (Δ): It refers to the change in the value of an option for a given change in the price of the underlying security.

$\Delta = \delta P/\delta S$ where P is the option price and S is the price of the underlying security.

Call option Deltas give positive relationship signifying that a price increase in the underlying asset will lead to an increase in the Call option value. Put option Deltas show a negative relationship indicating that an increase in price of the underlying security will lead to a fall in the Put option value.

Delta is determined by change in the prices of underlying security and the passage of time. This is to say that as time passes, value of Delta changes. Banks adopting the Delta hedging strategy should hedge the position on a continuous basis which is called re-balancing of Delta Hedging.

Theta (θ): As we are aware, the value of an option decreases over time. The time value element of an option will slowly move towards zero as it approaches the expiry date. The theta of a portfolio of derivatives can be defined as the rate of change in the value of the portfolio with reference time assuming that all other factors remain constant. It is the time decay of the portfolio. It is mostly negative as the value of an option decreases as the time to maturity decreases.

Gamma (γ): Gamma of a portfolio of derivatives can be defined as the rate of change of Delta of the portfolio against the price of the underlying asset. It predicts movements in Delta. A small gamma calls for lesser need of interventions to make portfolio delta neutral, as it indicates that delta changes only slowly. On the other hand, a high gamma requires a dynamic hedging strategy as the delta is highly sensitive to the change in the price of the underlying asset. It could prove disastrous if the portfolio is kept unhedged.

Vega (ν): Vega of a portfolio of derivatives can be defined as the rate of change in the value of a portfolio with respect to the volatility of the underlying asset. A high vega indicates the high sensitivity of the portfolio even to small changes in volatility, whereas a low vega indicates that a volatility of the asset has a very little impact on the value of the portfolio.

Rho (ρ): Rho specifies the relationship between the value of the portfolio of derivatives and the change in the interest rate. It is the rate of change in the value of a portfolio of derivatives with respect to change in interest rate.

Computation of VaR

The procedure for computation of VaR involves:

1. Calculating the market value of the portfolio.
2. Calculating the standard deviation of the portfolio.
3. Specifying the time horizon of the portfolio which is usually 10 days and dividing it by the number of trading days in a year, which is usually 252 days ($\sqrt{N/252}$).
4. Specifying a confidence level, assuming a normal distribution and retrieving corresponding value from the table.

5. Calculating VaR as a product of all the above i.e., (a) × (b) × (c) × (d).

As mentioned earlier, VaR gives the cxpected maximum loss over a given time horizon with a given confidence level.

Capital Charge for Market Risk

The Bank for International Settlement (BIS) allowed large banks to use internal model to calculate market risk. However it has specified the following things to be considered for calculating capital changes for market risk:

1. The bank must define an adverse change in rates at 99 per cent confidence level, that is use a product of σ x 2.33.
2. Banks are required to assume a minimum holding period of 10 days.

Banks are required to consider capital charger higher of the two:

1. previous day's VaR,
2. average daily VaR over a period of 60 days times a multiplication factor with minimum value of 3. That is capital charges = 10 days x 3.

Credit Risk Management

Measurement of Credit Risk

Since lending is the main business of a bank, it is exposed to credit risk in extending credit facilities to corporate, individuals and government. It takes this risk for better returns to its lenders and stakeholders. The banks price their loans to cover the cost of borrowings, the spread and the credit risk involved in lending. Credit quality and the type of loan play a crucial role in credit risk management.

Some of the popular credit risk measurement models used are default risk model, credit scoring model, mortality rate model, term structure model, J.P. Morgan's CreditMetricsTM, Credit Suisse Financial Products' (CSFP's) CreditRisk+TM, KMV's Credit MonitorTM , McKinsey's CreditPortfolio ViewTM , risk-adjusted return on capital (RAROC) Models, etc.

Default Risk Model

This is a qualitative model which uses information on borrower and market variables to make a credit decision. The borrower's reputation, borrower-lender relationship, borrower leverage or capital structure, volatility of earnings and the security provided are evaluated as borrower-specific factors. The market variables that are considered are business cycle, interest rates, etc.

Credit Scoring Model

This is a quantitative model in which the borrower's attributes are quantified to obtain a score indicating the probability of default. To implement this model, information on cash flows and financial ratios are essential. Data identification in this model is followed by default risk probability scoring using statistical techniques. Two methods are generally used for credit scoring—linear probability model and linear discriminant model.

Under linear probability model, historical data for financial ratios are input in the model to examine repayment experience on old loans. This is used as a basis to forecast repayment for new loans.

Altman's Z Score Model

The borrowers are categorised into—high and low default risk categories based on past observed experience, under the linear discriminant model. This model is also called as Altman's Z score model. The variable Z is an overall measure of default risk classification of a borrower. The variable takes its value from several financial ratios of the borrower and weighted importance of these ratios. The weights assigned are based on extensive research on the past loan repayment bahaviour of the borrower.

$$Z = 1.2\,X_1 + 1.4\,X_2 + 3.3\,X_3 + 0.6\,X_4 + 1.0\,X_5$$

where

X_1 = working capital/total asset ratio,

X_2 = retained earning/total asset ratio,

X_3 = earnings before interest and taxes (EBIT)/total asset ratio,

X_4 = market value of equity (MVE)/book value of long-term debt ratio,

X_5 = sales/total asset ratio.

The higher the Z value, the lower is the default risk of the borrower. A value of Z being less than 1.81 is considered a high default risk. In such cases, the bank may take a decision by either charging a risk premium or waiting till the score is improved.

RAROC Model

The RAROC model includes default risk in pricing of loan. Return on asset (ROA) is computed on the basis of loan at risk at the time of default, since if loan becomes non-performing asset (NPA), provision has to be made out of the bank's capital.

RAROC = Annual Income on Loan/Loan Risk or capital at Risk. A loan is approved if the RAROC is higher than the benchmark rate of bank for return on capital (ROC).

Measuring Credit Risk for a Portfolio of Credit Assets

While the above methods deal with measuring risk for a single loan, they cannot be applied for measuring credit risk for a portfolio of credit assets since correlations exist between loans in a portfolio. The degree to which the loans tend to default simultaneously is reflected by the correlation among them. As correlation effects are complex and difficult to observe, some models were developed for measuring credit risk of a portfolio based on certain financial assumptions. These models are Credit Risk + Model, Credit Metrics Model, KMV Portfolio Manager Model and the Modern Portfolio theory.

The Credit Risk + Model

This model developed by CSFP makes use of statistics of historical losses and is based on the actuarial model. It is generally used for analysing default risk on a large portfolio with small loans rather than portfolios that contain small number of big loans. However, the major limitation of this approach is linking the credit risk with market risk. These are overcome in the subsequent methods.

The CreditMetrics Model

The model correlates defaults in a portfolio of loans. It generates random values for each of the company's assets and if the value is very low, the model simulates a default. It is difficult to calculate a loan's market value and volatility of loan value over a period, as loans are not actively traded in the market. Hence, on the basis of credit rating, probability of change in rating in next one year, recovery rate on defaulted loans and yield spread in the bond market, a hypothetical market value and volatility is calculated. Then the portfolio VaR due to credit-VaR is estimated. A rating system with probabilities of migrating from one credit quality to another over a given time horizon is the main element of credit-VaR proposed by J.P. Morgan.

KMV Portfolio Manager Model

The banks are required to determine the expected return on loans R, the risk of a loan (σ) and correlation of default risks between loans (ρ). The return on loan is measured on the basis of fee paid on loan and spread on loan. The risk on loan refelcts the volatility of loan default rate which is used to calculate unexpected loss. The expected returns for loans and variances are calculated and then risk and return of the portfolio is calculated.

Modern Portfolio Theory

If the portfolio of banks has widely traded assets or loans and it is easy to calculate loan return, portfolio diversification model is used to measure credit risk exposure. According to this theory, banks can diversify credit risk as long as returns on different assets are not correlated positively. Banks can create a minimum variance portfolio.

Credit Risk Management Techniques

It is one of the oldest risks that banks are exposed to. It was the predominant risk that banks were focused on till Basel introduced market risk. Banks maintained capital adequacy based on credit risk. Credit risk is managed through internal monitoring system and credit derivatives.

Internal monitoring system manages credit risk through internal credit monitoring process, appraisal system, loan review mechanism, credit approving process, limits on large credit exposures, standards for loan collateral, portfolio management, risk concentration, risk monitoring and evaluation, pricing of loans, ratings of loans, rating review, provisioning, regulatory/legal compliance, etc.

Through the use of credit derivatives, several methods like credit default swaps, total return swaps, credit spread forwards and options, credit linked notes, securitisation, etc., have been evolved to manage credit risk.

Credit risk management of banks is reflected in profitability of bank, liquidity position of bank and level of NPAs. The primary concern for banks in credit risk management is to maximise RAROC while maintaining credit quality and quantity. Though the biggest source of credit risk is loans, few other sources like off balance sheet items as corporate guarantee, line of credit, etc., also expose the banks to further credit risk.

Credit risk management process in banks should take care of the following:

1. Identification and measurement of credit risk using credit scoring models and internal mechanisms.
2. Pricing of loans based on risk associated with each loan.
3. Assessment of adverse impact of assets' exposure on bank financials as NPA assessment.
4. Adopting the apt approach for risk mitigation.
5. Hedging the credit risk by using appropriate derivative product.
6. Continuous monitoring and review of hedging strategy in changing scenario of the market for loans.

Operational Risk Management

Measurement of Operational Risk

Operational risk is also an important risk for a bank. It evolves as a result of inadequacy of failure of people, processes, systems or external factors. Management of operational risk is different from other risks, as it is difficult to quantify variables in this. Even top most banks find it tedious to manage operational risk.

Sources of operational risk:

1. Employee: internal frauds and human errors,
2. Technology: failure and obsolescence,
3. Capital Assets: destruction,
4. Customer Relationship: customer services and legal disputes,
5. External: theft and external frauds,
6. Transaction: execution and booking.

The factors contributing to operational risk need to be identified carefully to minimise losses.

Approaches for Measuring Operational Risk

1. **Quantitative Approach**: It quantifies losses from different sources of risk. Judgment is based on information collected from databases and tries to pool information on historical events and current state of affairs. Historical events include financial losses and near misses which could have culminated into losses but did not happen or were controlled.

2. **Structural Approach:** This approach uses a causality model that defines set of linkages between various processes and the probability of loss events. This approach allows banks to channelise their efforts on the links that have a high probability of losses.

3. **Historical Approach:** The approach is based on historical events which are used to extrapolate future outcome. This approach is statistical and makes minimal assumptions about the causes and methods of loss.

4. **Modern Approach:** This approach combines all the methods mentioned above. It uses judgment, structure and loss experience to measure operational risk. Basel also recommends such an approach to measure operational risk.

Operational Risk Management

Operational risk management talks about the importance of non-quantifiable loss events to the businesses. Under extreme and adverse conditions, the magnitude of loss due to operational risk is huge compared to any other risk and threatens the survival of the business entity because the loss amount cannot be estimated and recovered.

Moody's Analytical Framework for Operational Risk Management in Banks

Operational risk management gives a competitive edge to banks as it improves the quality and stability of their earnings. The rapid growth of financial services sector has seen tremendous advances in the sphere of risk management with operational risk receiving greater importance. Operational risk management is primarily concerned with good governance, vigilance and continuous improvement. It has a significant contribution towards improving organisational performance. Operational risk is capable of affecting organisational reputation, credit ratings and stock prices. Moody's operational risk assessment is based on five thrust areas.

1. General Background: It includes definitions, boundaries, driving forces, management, impact of key risks, operation risk profile document, reports, etc.
2. Leadership: It covers areas of corporate governance, culture, ethics, strategy and management.
3. Organisational Efficiency and Effectiveness: It envisages operational risk framework, development stages, key risks and priorities.
4. External Factors: It includes contingency planning, outsourcing, insurance.
5. Reports and Results: It envisages reports, performance assessment, data, quantification and modelling, validation and verification.

This framework provides background information to support future risk assessment meetings and is not comprehensive.

Conclusion

Though there is so much of importance associated with the need for risk management in banks and the global economy is yet to recover from the aftershock of the recent global financial crises seen in the developed nations, there is a long way to go in implementing a robust and fool proof risk management system in Indian banking system. Several research studies have proved that there is a huge gap between the desired and the present risk management system. The initiatives taken are only baby steps and might prove inadequate in case of a financial catastrophe. Though each bank has its own risk management system depending on its risk tolerance, the overall objective should be to look at it holistically as an ERM system that can ultimately add value to the enterprise by increasing return on capital, efficient allocation of capital, stability of earnings through careful and meticulous risk measurement and management.

References

Asthana, P.N. (2009). *Financial Risk Management*. Himalaya Publishing House.

Dedman, Richard and Simon Robert-Tissot (2001). "Risk Management: Where Banks Fail", *Balance Sheet* 9(2): 16–19.

Hull, John C. (2003). *Options, Futures and Other Derivatives*. Pearson Education.

Raghavan, R.S. (2003). "Risk Management in Banks", *Chartered Accountant*, February.

Suresh, N., S. Anil Kumar and D.M. Gowda (2009). "Credit Risk Management in Commercial Banks", *Curie* 2(4). BITS Pilani.

Talwar, Shalini (2011). "Averting Bank Distress in Internationalized Financial System: Evolving a Comprehensive Risk Management Process", *The IUP Journal of Financial Risk Management* VIII(4).

Vyas, Madhuri and Sachin Singh (2010). "Risk Management in Banking Sector", *BVIMR Management Edge* 4(1).

6 Operational Risk in Dynamic Banking Industry

Aathira K. and R. Shanthi

Introduction

The choice of the appropriate definition is important as the industry starts to tackle operational risk. Definitional options for operational risk are strategically significant: as the definition becomes broader and encompasses more potential sources of loss, operational risk management moves beyond the ambit of any existing departmentally based risk manager, and potentially involves greater organisational change and 'lots of stepping on toes.' It is apparent that the nature of operational risk and the requirements on how to deal with this type of risk are very different from the classical risk categories of market and credit risk.

A survey by the Basel committee's Risk Management Group found that around 47,000 operational risks are reported on an average and banks had allocated approximately 15 per cent of their capital for operational risk. The trend towards greater dependence on technology, greater competition among banks and globalisation have left the banking industry more exposed to operational risk than ever before. Only the direct losses associated with internal and external events are captured within the scope of the Basel II definition. The Basel definition may be an attempt to provide a scope for non-financial risk, but the key problem is that the categories of non-financial risks are heterogeneous as well as inherently overlapping within itself and with credit and market risk. The definition for operational risk is kept on changing in accordance with global change. So merely giving definition for operational risk does not fetch any vibrant result.

Objectives of the Study

1. To assess the trend of operational risk definition over a period of time.
2. To examine the definitional issues of operational risk.

Literature Review

1. Kuritzkes (2002) investigated problem in Basel II operational risk definition and says that the Bank for International Settlement (BIS) II definition applies to only a subset of non-financial risks. This definition is under inclusive in two key respects: ignores business risk, strategic and reputation risks, as well as any opportunity costs associated with operational failures.
2. Savic (2008) defines operational risk in terms of information technology (IT) aspect at a present time: new products, product sophistication, new distribution channels, new markets, new technology, complexity of technology, e-commerce, business volume, new legislation, globalisation, regulatory pressure, mergers and acquisitions, reorganisations, staff turnover, cultural diversity of staff and clients.
3. Dima (2009) describes operational risk is a term with a variety of meanings within the banking industry, therefore for internal purposes, bank may choose to adopt their own definitions. This internal definition should respect the individual situation of every bank, such as its size, and sophistication, its nature and complexity of its activities in an economic manner, considering the full range of material operational risks facing the bank and captures the most significant causes of severe operational losses.
4. Izhar (2010) argued that in Islamic banking, operational risk definition may include *Shariah* non-compliance along with Basel II definition.

Table 6.1

Operational Risk Defined by Various Institutions

Year	*Institution/Author*	*Definition*
1994	Comptroller's Handbook	The risk of loss occurring as a result of inadequate system and control; human errors; or management failure.
1997	Schwartz and Smith	Operational risk is the risk of loss arising from human error, management failure and fraud; or from shortcomings in system or controls.
1998	Standard Bank annual report	Operational risk is defined as a potential loss arising from malfunctions in automated systems; failures in internal financial and administrative controls; and non-compliance with the bank's policies and procedures.
2000	Erasmus research report	Operational risk as risk of loss arising from breakdowns in internal controls established to ensure the proper functioning of people, system and functions.
January 2001	BCBS (Basel Committee for Banking Supervision)	Operational risk is the risk of 'direct and indirect loss' resulting from inadequate or failed internal processes, people or systems or from external events.
September 2001	BCBS Consultative document	Operational risk is the risk of loss resulting from inadequate or failed internal processes, people or systems or from external events*
2003	US Securities and Exchange Commission (SEC)	The risk of loss due to the breakdown of controls within the firm including, but not limited to unidentified limit excesses, unauthorised trading, fraud in trading or in bank office functions, inexperienced personnel, and unstable and easily accessed computer system.
2004	Buchelt and Untregger	Operational risk as "a highly varied and interrelated set of risks with different origins."
2011	Deutsche Bank	Operational risk is the potential for failure (incl. the legal component) in relation to employees, contractual specifications and documentations, technology, infrastructure failure and disasters, external influences and customer relationship.

Note: Earlier banks usually refer operational risk as "any risk not categorised as market or credit risk and some have defined it as the risk of loss arising from various types of human or technical error" (BCBS, 1998).

* The widely accepted definition was proposed by and adapted by Basel Committee in January 2001. After the collapse of major financial institutions in world, British Bankers' Association (BBA), International Swaps and Derivatives Association (ISDA), Robert Morris Associated with Pricewater House Coopers prepared a report about the best practices in operational risk management which defined operational risk as 'BCBS definition' and later it was adapted by the Basel committee.

Source: Author's concept compiled from selected sources.

Dimensions of Operational Risk

All the definitions mainly focused on four factors as People, process, system and external events. The widely accepted definition of Basel II was from the point of cause factors of operational risk. The logic behind it was the causing factors create some events that may be end with operational loss.

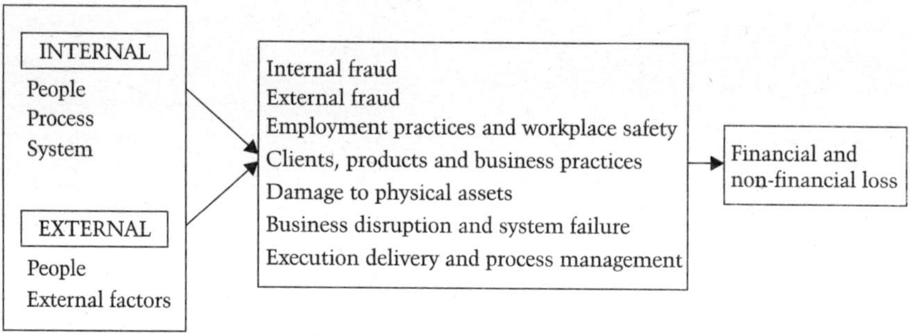

People: Employee fraud, employers liability, health and safety, lack of knowledge and skill, loss of key personnel etc. concentration problems, overtime, insufficient knowledge of products or procedures and fraud by employees (Cooper, 1999; O'Brien, Smith *et al.*, 1999; Brink, 2002; Harmantzis, 2003).

Process: Bank operates with large number of transaction to deliver services to customer. The risk stands at every process that banks have undertaken. The risk may include accounting error, capacity risk, product complexity, project risk, transaction error and valuation error.

System: All banks around the world are operated with the help of computer system. Hence small error in data entry will affect the operation and data quality; security breach, system failure, system suitability, system compatibility, etc., are the other factors to be considered.

External event: The environment under which the bank functions poses some threat and it cannot be controlled but can be mitigated through insurance or reserves. External events include fire, legal, terrorism, theft, earthquake, etc.

Measurement of Operational Risk

The operational risk can be quantified through measurement methods suggested by Basel II. Basically as a initiator, banks follow basic method known as basic indicator approach (BIA). The next stage is standard approach (SA) and those who well versed and well equipped with technology, skill and loss of data can apply advanced measurement approach (AMA) in banks.

Basic Indicator Approach

Under the BIA, banks have to hold capital for operational risk equal to a fixed percentage (alpha) of a single indicator which has currently been proposed to be 'gross income.' This approach is available for all banks irrespective of their level of sophistication. The charge may be expressed as follows:

KBIA = [(GI* ∝)]/n,

where

KBIA = the capital charge under the BIA.

GI = annual gross income over the previous three years

∝ = 15% set by the Committee

n = number of the previous three years for which gross income is positive.

The Standardised Approach (TSA)

Bank's activities are divided into eight business lines: corporate finance, trading and sales, retail banking, commercial banking, payment and settlement, agency services, asset management, and retail brokerage. The capital charge for each business line is calculated by multiplying gross income by a factor (denoted by beta) assigned to that business line.

KTSA = {S1-3 years max [] (GI1-8*β1-8)0]}/3

where

KTSA = the capital charge under TSA

GI1-8 = annual gross income in a given year, for each business lines

β1-8 = a fixed percentage, set by the Committee, relating the level of required capital to the level of the gross income for each of the eight business lines.

Advanced Measurement Approach (AMA)

Under AMA approach, the banks use individual methodology for calculation of operational risk exposure, losses and the minimum capital requirement. Banks are required to factor in four key elements in designing their advanced measurement approach framework: internal loss data, external loss data, scenario analysis, and bank-specific business environmental and internal control factors (Janakiraman, 2008).

Criticism on operational risk definition:

1. The difficulty related to operational risk is defined from a wide and narrow perspective.
2. The definition is 'casual-based' providing a breakdown of operational risk into four risk categories based on its source: people; process; system; and external factors.
3. In BCBS January 2001 definition, 'indirect loss' was not properly interpreted in terms of nature and the measure of indirect losses. So it was redefined in September 2001 BCBS consultative paper. Capturing indirect losses objectively is perceived to be more difficult but indirect losses may be far higher than direct losses and may therefore be the most significant source of non-financial risk (Brink, 2002)
4. Again the redefined definition includes legal risk but not reputational risk, business risk or strategic risk and cultural risk.
5. Ramadurai *et al.* (2004) state that the adoption of this definition for measurement proposes does not let institutions "off the hook" from managing reputational and business risk.
6. The Islamic bank cannot fully adopt operational risk definition as it entails legal risk, reputational risk, inclusion of *Shariah* non-compliance risk and fiduciary risk. *Shariah* non-compliance risk means risk arising from Islamic banks failure to comply with the

Shariah rules and principles. Fiduciary risk arises when a bank fails to perform in accordance with explicit and implicit standard applicable to their fiduciary.

Indian Bank's Approach towards Operational Risk

"Banks may adopt any one of the approaches, it is intended that they will benchmark their operational risk management systems with the various options and aim to move towards more sophisticated approaches" (RBI, 2005).

Almost all banks are in beginning stage in operation risk management and they adopt BIA for capital measurement. We can take this stage as a transformation period as many banks shifting their approaches from BIA to SA and AMA. Indian banks will be in golden age when entire banking industry will work with AMA approach. Because it demonstrates the soundness and sustainability of the banking system since banks having full loss data are self-sufficient to tackle and track any problem arising out of operations.

Indian banks lack in historical loss database. In order to make our banking system intact with global competitors, Indian Bankers Association in collaboration with 14 other banks set up the Credit and Operational Risk Data Exchange (CORDEx), with a view to collect, consolidate, and report the data on anonymity basis at an industry level relating to operational risk losses and credit risk losses to establish industry-wide benchmark which can facilitate adoption of advanced approaches for risk management under Basel II.

Table 6.2 provides the details of India's top 10 banks approach towards operational risk and capital charge on that date. Some banks seem to have huge regulatory capital to upgrade from BIA to AMA. The higher level of capital shows banks capacity to mitigate the risk to gain incentives of risk management.

Table 6.2

Top 10 Indian Banks and their Operational Risk (OR) Capital Charge

Rank	*Name of the Bank*	*OR Capital Charge*	*OR Capital Charge (Amt in cr)*
1.	State Bank of India (SBI)	BIA	7918.10
2.	Punjab National Bank (PNB)	BIA	1699.37
3.	Bank of Baroda (BoB)	BIA	1295.68
4.	IDBI Bank	BIA	686.37
5.	Syndicate Bank	BIA	542.36
6.	Bank of India (BoI)	BIA	1318.73
7.	Canara Bank	BIA	971.92
8.	Union Bank of India (UBI)	BIA	954.45
9.	Corporation Bank	BIA	473.18
10.	Bank of Maharashtra	BIA	356.03

Source: Rank is given by Indian ranker; *Annual Report (2011-12)* of concern banks.

International Level Operational Risk Database

The Operational Risk Data Exchange Association (ORX) was founded in 2002 with the primary objective of creating a platform for the secure and anonymised exchange of high-quality operational risk loss data. Today the ORX operates the world's leading operational risk loss data consortium for the financial services industry. The ORX Global Loss Database contains 269,430 operational risk loss events, each event over €20,000 in value, to a total value of €121 billion. The ORX is owned and controlled, on an equal basis, by its 62 member firms.

Table 6.3 gives examples of few experiences over the past few years and there are many more reported and unreported incidents that could be added to the list. However, what is important is that none of these examples represent straight market or credit risk, but all are examples of lack of procedures, systems or managerial control. It proves that supervisory bodies of financial institutions have to acknowledge operational risk as one of the most important types of risks within the banking sector. All these events brought into focus the issues of management and controls. The failure suggests that no single factor actually triggered the failure. As from example the direct losses of internal and external events may not be the most significant source of non-financial risk.

Table 6.3

Historic Events in Operational Risk

Year	*Bank*	*Operational Event*	*Loss Amount*
1994	Bankers trust	Lawsuits occurred due to inadequate explanation on derivative products	195 million dollar
	Orange County, USA	Bankruptcy due to lack of expert risk oversight and competence	1100 million dollar
1995	Barings Bank; United Kingdom	Rouge trade occurred in the transaction of Nikkei Future due to inadequate segregation of duties	826 million dollar
	Daiwa Bank: New York	Rogue trade involved in an employee in NY branch continued for 11 years.	1100 million dollar
1997	National Westminster Bank	A trader of swaption manipulated the volatility.	77 million pound
2001	Enron Corporation: USA	Poor information from accountant and management	750 million dollar
	September 11 terrorist attack: New York	Terrorist attack cause huge loss to financial institutions and settlement of New York Stock Exchange and NASDAQ for four days	140 million dollar
2002	Allied Irish Bank: Ireland	'Complex and very determined fraud' by misplaced proprietary trading strategy and repeated falsifying bank statement.	750 million dollar
	Mizuho Financial Group: Japan	System troubles related to mergers caused various problems such as delays in settlement of customer's payment on public utilities.	1.8 billion yen
	All first financial	Rouge Trading	700 million dollar
	Household Finance	Misleading sales practices	484 million dollar
2005	MasterCard International; USA	Security failure and internal fraud	Not yet estimated

Source: Adapted from Jorion (2003), Bonson *et al.* (2008) and de Fontnouvelle (2003).

Findings of the Study

1. The study reveals that operational risk is not static in nature. It emerges and changes in tone with operating environment. Operational risk definition should be tailored finely for dynamic environment.
2. The definition will be more meaningful and appropriate if it encompasses geographic variables (country specific) since developed

and developing countries follow the same framework for different operational settings.

3. The Basel II definition argued with some variables which are not included in its sub-categorisation. They are as follows.

Cultural risk: Risk culture which essentially is the way a company conceives risk and implements risk management in daily business. A key difference between a Western workplace and one set in South America, the Middle East or East Asia is what academics describe as cultural power distance. This is essentially the degree of hierarchy within an organisation or society. Low cultural power distance societies and organisations are more collegial, with value placed on social flow and less formality. The added operational risk arising from these cultural differences does not have to confound us. There are many contexts in which culturally driven operational risk can threaten the performance of business.

Strategic risk: Strategic risks are those that arise from the fundamental decisions that directors take concerning an organisation's objectives. Essentially, strategic risks are the risks of failing to achieve these business objectives.

Reputational risk: Generally reputational risk is considered as more valuable asset, but most of the institutions do not include reputational or brand exposure as a component for their operational risk assessment in order to quantify risk. Because reputational damage is a source of leverage for other risk sources rather than being a risk source itself.

Systemic risk: Systemic risk leads to collapse of entire banking industry which was observed in aftermath of 2007 credit crunch followed by global financial crisis.

Conclusion

Awareness of operational risk in banking sector is growing everywhere. A definition with unified and systemic perspective in operational risk will promote the financial stability. And if the history of the original Accord is any guide, it may take atleast a decade to revise even regulations that are widely viewed as dysfunctional. The definition of operational risk completes as a whole only when the current and future risk parameters are properly balanced.

References

Basel Committee on Banking Supervision (2001). *Working Paper on the Regulatory Treatment of Operational Risk.* September.

BCBS (1998). *Operational Risk Management.*

Bonson, E., T. Escobar F. and Flores (2008). "Operational Risk Measurement in Banking Institutions and Investment Firms: New European Evidences", *Financial Markets, Institutions and Instruments* 17(4): 287-307.

Brink, G.J. (2002). *Operational Risk: The New Challenge for Banks.* New York: Palgrave.

Buchelt, R. and S. Unteregger (2004). "Cultural Risk and Risk Culture: Operational Risk after Basel II", *Financial Stability Report* 6.

Chernaboi, Anna, S.T. Rachev and F.J. Fabozzi (2007). *Operational Risk: A Guide to Basel II Capital Requirements, Models, and Analysis.* Wiley Finance Inc.

Chorafas, D. (2005). "Operational Risk Control with Basel II: Basic Principles and Capital Requirements", Oxford; Elsevier Finance.

Cooper, L. (1999). "Operational Risk: Fear the Worst", *Risk Magazine*, July.

Credit Suisse Group (2001). *The New Basel Capital Accord.* Consultative Paper. January 16. Comments May 30.

de Fontnouvelle, Patrick (2003). *Capital and Risk: New Evidence on Implications of Large Operational Losses*, Federal Reserve Bank of Boston.

Dima, Alina (2009). "Operational Risk Assessment Tools for Quality Management in Banking Services", *Amfiteatru Economic* XI(26), June.

Graham, Judith (2008). *Cultural Aspects of Operational Risk: OpRisk & Compliance.* December.

Harmantzis, F. (2003). "Risky Business: Turbulent Times Focus Attention on Operational Risk Management in Financial Services", Available at *http://www.orms-today.org/orms-2-03/frrisk.html*

Herring, Richard J (2002). The Basel 2 Approach to Bank Operational Risk: Regulation on the Wrong Track, 38th Annual conference on *Bank Structure and Competition of the Federal Reserve Bank of Chicago,* May 9.

Hiwatashi, Junji and H. Ashida (2002). *Advancing Operational Risk Management Using Japanese Banking Experiences.* Federal Reserve Bank of Chicago.

Izhar, Hylmun (2010). "Identifying Operational Risk Exposures in Islamic Banking", *Kyoto Bulletin of Islamic Area Studies* 3-2: 17–53 (March).

Janakiraman, Usha (2008). "Operational Risk Management in Indian Banks in the Context of Basel II: A Survey of the State of Preparedness and Challenges in Developing the Framework", *Asia Pacific Journal of Finance and Banking Research* 2(2).

Jameson, R. (2001). "Between RAROC and a Hard Place", *erisk.com.* February.

Jorion, Philip (2003). Financial risk manager Hand book. New Jersey: John Wiley & Sons, Inc.

Kuritzkes, Andrew (2002). "Operational Risk Capital: A Problem of Definition", *The Journal* of Risk Finance 4(1): 47-56.

Loader, David (2007). *Operational Risk Managing: Key Component of Operations Risk.* Butterworth Heinemann.

O'Brien, N., B. Smith and M. Allen (1999). "The Case for Quantification: Operational Risk Special Report", *Risk Magazine*, July.

Power, Michael (2003). "The Invention of Operational Risk", ESRC centre for analysis of risk and regulation, *Discussion paper* No: 16.

Ramadurai, K., K. Olson, D. Andrews, G. Scott and T. Beck (2004). *The Oldest Tale but the Newest Story: Operational Risk and the Evolution of its Measurement under Basel II*. FITCH Ratings Special Report. January.

RBI (2005). Reserve Bank of India Guidance Note on Operational Risk Management dated October 15.

RMA (1999). *British Operational Risk the Next Frontier.* Bankers' Association, RMA, ISDA, supported by Pricewaterhouse Coopers.

Savic, Ana (2008). *Managing IT-related Operational Risks*. Belgrade: ICT College.

7 Risk Management in the Microfinance Sector

Veenapani

Introduction

Microfinance deals with provision of loans and other financial services to low income clients. Of late the microfinance industry has shown tremendous growth. Several studies have supported the fact that microfinance has proved to be a poverty alleviation tool. However in the recent past, several sporadic incidents have caught the attention of the government. Microfinance institutions (MFIs) are charging a very high rate of interest, the securitisation deal between ICICI and SHARE Microfin Ltd. was one of the largest deals in this sector. The number of suicides by microfinance lenders in Andhra Pradesh has raised several questions on regulation in this sector. Some studies (Chandrashekar, 2010) on one side have indicated that the microfinance bubble is to burst, and on the other hand some studies (Mosley, 2002) show that the microfinance programmes have a great impact on social and economic conditions of the poor. Under the microfinance regulation, MFIs cannot charge an interest rate greater than 24 per cent. Sustainability of MFIs will be threatened if these institutions do not manage their inherent risks. Microfinance institutions evaluate their performance on both financial and social objectives. Risk management strategies adopted by MFIs are different from the other sectors, where institutions are driven solely by profit. Many MFIs have grown rapidly, serving more customers and larger geographic areas, and offering a wider range of financial services and products.

MFIs need to design risk management tools and approaches that respond to their specific clients, lending methodologies, operating environments, and financial and social performance objectives.

Those MFIs that rely on depositors and other borrowed sources of funds are also vulnerable to changes in interest rates. These MFIs at times have to waive off loan installments on social grounds. The paper highlights the inherent risks faced by MFIs and suggests strategies to mitigate various risks faced by the microfinance sector. The paper being conceptual in nature does not adopt any methodology, but is based on risk and mitigation strategies that can be adopted by Indian MFIs to mitigate risks.

Objective of the Study

The main objective of the study is to identify various risks faced by the microfinance sector and suggest possible strategies to mitigate these risks.

Risks in the Microfinance Sector

Risk is the possibility of an adverse event occurring and its potential for negative implications to a MFI. Risk management is the process of managing the probability of the severity of the adverse event to an acceptable limit set by the MFI.

Many MFIs have grown rapidly and are serving more number of clients. The products offered by these MFIs have increased and some MFIs are now offering customised services to their clients. MFIs rely on market-driven sources of funds from outside investors or from local deposits or member savings. Preserving access to these funds calls for good financial performance and avoidance of unexpected losses. The operational environment of MFIs also provides a huge challenge. MFIs needs to design risk management tools and approaches that respond to their specific clients, lending methodologies, operating environments, and financial and social performance objectives. Figure 7.1 illustrates various risks faced by the microfinance sector.

Operational Risk

Operational risk arises due to the vulnerabilities confronted by MFIs in their daily operations, which may result in loss of their assets. Some of the operational risks faced by an MFI are unique, like an MFI may lose its money through bad loans, fraud or theft. Hence, emphasis is laid on credit risk and risk due to fraud.

Figure 7.1

Risks Faced by Microfinance Sector

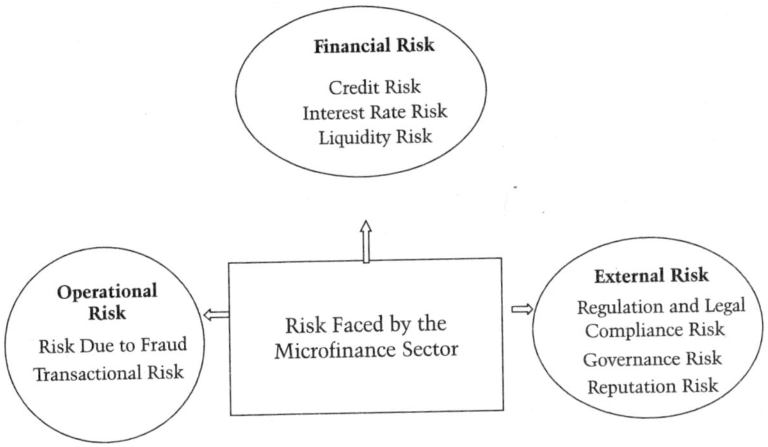

Risk Due to Fraud

MFIs are vulnerable to fraud as money changes hands. Weak management information system within MFIs fosters fraud. Risk due to fraud is high in this sector. Fraud should be detected on time as it involves volunteered savings of the members and reputation of the firm. Given the volume and number of transactions managed by an MFI on a daily basis, as well as the reality that cash travels or is wired constantly from the hands of borrowers to loan officers/branches and ultimately to the head office, MFIs require constant monitoring of cash management and procedures for the detection of fraud. Fraudulent cases include instances of phantom borrowers being created. Instances of group leaders being involved in fraud are quite common. The leader, who is the custodian of the pooled savings of the group, may utilise the fund for her personal use.

Transaction Risk

MFIs handle a high volume of small transactions daily, increasing the chances of transaction risk. In banks, the loans are disbursed by trained staff, usually for larger sum, with due verification. The same degree of verification is not possible, as this will increase the transaction cost.

Inconsistency in the data pertaining to loan repayment is seen. The data recorder by the group in some instances was found to be different from the records maintained at MFI office. This is evident when untrained field staff is appointed to collect the repayments.

Financial Risk

Under financial risk, MFIs are exposed to credit risk, interest rate risk and liquidity risk.

Credit Risk

This is the most commonly addressed risk in microfinance, arising due to non-payment of loans by the beneficiary. It encompasses a loss in income resulting from the MFI's inability to collect anticipated interest earnings as well as the loss of principle resulting from loan defaults.

Credit risk includes both transaction risk and portfolio risk. One microloan will not impact credit risk as these loans are very small, however delinquency can spread from a handful of loans to a significant portion of the portfolio. In order to manage their credit risks, some MFIs have refused further loans to all groups belonging to the hamlet, if one group fails to pay the loan. This practice is against the Reserve Bank of India (RBI) norms for group lending.

Interest Rate Risk

MFIs that use savings deposits as a source of loan funds must have sufficient cash to fund loans and withdrawals from savings. Those MFIs that rely on depositors and other borrowed sources of funds are also vulnerable to changes in interest rates.

When the terms and interest rates of MFI's assets and liabilities show a mismatch, interest rate risk arises. The spread between interest earnings and interest payments will narrow when interest rate on short-term liabilities arise before adjusting the lending rate.

Liquidity Risk

If an MFI borrows extensively to finance loan disbursements, bill payments, etc., their liquidity risk increases. In Bangladesh, MFIs faced the risk of floods, which increased their credit and liquidity risks, as borrower's businesses slowed down and their homes were destroyed or damaged. Under such cases loans are waived off under social considerations. MFIs have to maintain higher cash reserves during such situations to avoid liquidity risk.

External Risks

External risks are unique to this sector. Microfinance sector being unregulated, the risk of regulations is high. Several legal forms of MFIs exist, inviting legal compliance risks. Governance and reputation risks are also very significant to this sector.

Regulations and Legal Compliance Risk

Recently Indian Government has laid down norms for the otherwise unregulated microfinance sector. Ceiling on the interest rates has forced MFIs to cut down on their costs. These costs are high for an MFI as compared to other lending institutions, since it involves extension of loans without collateral and outreach of clients in remote areas.

MFIs operate under different legal structures. An non-governmental organisation (NGO)-MFIs operates without facing any taxation or much intervention, thus facilitating easy operation. A for-profit MFI has to fulfill regulatory norms, more reporting and is subject to scrutiny. Compliance risk arises out of violations or non-conformance with laws, rules, regulations, prescribed practices or ethical standards which vary from country to country.

Governance Risk

MFIs are particularly vulnerable to governance risks resulting from their institutional structure and ownership. MFIs that operate as credit unions face a different type of governance issue. Their boards comprise client members, most of whom are net borrowers whose focus is more on reducing lending rates, than on the institution's well-being.

Reputation Risk

Reputation risk refers to the risk to earnings or capital arising from negative public opinion, which may affect an MFI's ability to sell products and services or its access to capital or cash funds. Reputations are much easier to lose than to rebuild, and should be valued as an intangible asset for any organisation.

Steps to Mitigate Financial Risks in the Microfinance Sector

1. MFIs can mitigate credit risk and avoid defaults by proper screening of their clients. Since group lending without collateral is common mode of loan disbursement, a Group Recognition Test (GRT) can be conducted to assess the clients who are genuinely interested in the microfinance programme. Client screening helps to identify clients who are willing and have the ability to pay their loans.

2. Since loans are not based on any guarantee or collateral, peer pressure acts as collateral. If any member does not clear his dues, the other members are denied further loans. This puts pressure on the defaulter by the other members to clear his dues.

3. MFIs can mitigate a significant portion of default risk by designing loan products that meet client's needs. Loan product feature includes the loan size, interest rate, repayment schedule, collateral requirements and any other special terms. Loan products should be designed to address the specific purpose for which the loan is intended. For example, a loan to meet medical emergencies might have a different repayment schedule than a loan for a sewing machine.

4. MFIs should ensure that loan amounts are within the repaying capacity of the borrowers. Large amount of loans will lead to low credit absorption and credit will be diverted to non-productive use.

5. Loan monitoring and follow-up should be taken up by the MFI staff. Multiple loans should be discouraged.

6. MFIs can address the capacity issue by extending the loan term and making the installments smaller. The frequency of repayment (weekly or monthly) allows an MFI to control credit risk. However care has to be taken that the clients keep in mind that access to

next loan is a primary repayment incentive. This will reduce the interest rate risks.

7. Pricing of the loan is very important. The MFIs cannot charge a low interest rate as they have to cover the cost of delivery and other costs, and it could affect the sustainability of the MFI. A high interest rate on the other hand may lead to insufficient clients and it will be difficult for the MFI to maintain a healthy portfolio.
8. External borrowing for huge sum should be weighed beforehand, as this may lead to liquidity risk. Securitisation will help MFIs to mitigate liquidity risk.

Steps to Mitigate Transactional Risk

1. In order to reduce the transactional costs, MFI can adopt information technology (IT). Use of smart cards, where the client ID and loan information is fed, can be connected to the server at the MFI office.
2. Simple, correct and consistent procedures for cash transactions should be followed.
3. Internal auditing of funds should be taken up by MFI to check frauds.
4. Clients should be encouraged to speak out against corrupt staff.
5. Staff should be paid adequately and should be rotated. Staff, who tend to cater to the same group may become dominating and try to influence the members and siphon off their money.
6. Establishment of control units and random checking by higher official will check risk due to fraud.

Steps to Mitigate External Risk

1. MFIs have to be aware of the latest regulations in the sector and comply with them on time.
2. Ethical values have to be incorporated by the staff of the MFI.

3. Transparency in operation and adhering to MFI's mission should be followed by the governing body.
4. Regular auditing of clients statements and adhering to norms, without commercialising microfinance should be the strategy of the firm.
5. MFIs should balance their social and financial performance. Institutions working only for profits will have to pay a heavy price, if the savings of the clients are being misused.
6. MFI has to tackle desertion. Desertion refers to clients who choose not to take a new loan after paying off an existing loan. Clients may leave because a competing MFI offers loan products better suited to their needs. MFIs that do not make appropriate accommodations for these clients find that they lose the borrowers they most needed to keep. It is very important that an MFI should conduct 'exit interviews' with at least a portion of clients who do not apply for a new loan. The MFI needs to know if there is a growing trend of client desertion because of certain undesirable characteristics of MFI. This will help MFIs to keep up their reputation.

Conclusion

The paper has tried to identify major risks faced by the microfinance sector, which is different from other lending institutions. Some of these risks are inherent due to the clientele profile, the nature of loan disbursement and the social cause attached to the microfinance sector. An attempt has been made to suggest some strategies to mitigate risks in this sector, however with the massive growth of microfinance sector, new regulations coming into force, MFIs have to face more challenges and manage new risks, as demand for new products and services in this sector is rising.

References

Basu, Debabrata, Manas Mohan Adhikary and D. Biswas (2006). *Participatory Monitoring and Evaluation of Development Programs—Practioners Guide*. Udaipur, India: Agrotech Publishing Academy.

Capestake, James (2004). "Social Performance Assessment of Microfinance—Cost effective or Costly Indulgence?", *Small Enterprise Development* 15(3): 11-18.

Chandrashekar, Vaishnavi (2010). "In India, Warnings of a Microfinance Bubble" in the *Christian Science Monitor*, June 30.

Cheng and Wu (2005). *Better Corporate Governance Results in Higher Profit and Lower Risk*. New York: Institutional Shareholder Services.

Cracknell, David (2004). "Electronic Banking for the Poor-Panacea, Potential and Pitfalls", *Small Enterprise Development—An international Journal of Microfinance and Business Development* 15(4): 8-25.

Fukaya, Kurumi and Narayana Shadagopan (2001). *Microfinance Regulations in India*. New Delhi: Sa - Dhan.

Grootacrt, Christiann and Thierry Van Bastelarr (2002). *Understanding and Measuring Social Capital—A Multidisciplinary Tool for Practitioners*. Washington D.C.: World Bank.

Haper, Malcolm (2003). *Practical Microfinance: A Training Guide for South Asia*. New Delhi: Vistaar Publications.

Hexter, E. and S. Gates (2005). *From Risk Management to Risk Strategy*. Report No. R-1363-05-RR. New York: The Conference Board.

IMF (n.d.). *International Financial Statistics*, IMF Data.

Karmakar, K.G. (2008). *Microfinance in India*. New Delhi: Sage Publications.

Lam, J. (2003). *Enterprise Risk Management: From Incentives to Controls*. New Jersey: John Wiley and Sons.

Mosley, Paul (2002). "The Use of Control Groups in Impact Assessment for Microfinance", *Working Paper No*.19, International Labour Office, ILO, Geneva, Retrieved November, 2012, from *www.org/wcmsp5/groups/public/---ed- emp/documents/publication/wcms_118267.pdf*

Rath, Nilakantha (2007). "On the Microfinance Regulation Bill 2007", *EPW* XLII(37): 3692-3.

Yadav, Shalini and S.L. Kumbhare (2009). "Transaction Costs under SHG—Bank Linkage Program", *Bank Quest—Journal of Indian Institute of Banking and Finance* 79(1): 30-4.

8 Basel Risk Based Capital Requirements and Banks' Behaviour

A Simultaneous Equation Modelling from Mauritius

Polodoo Virendra and
Kesseven Padachi

Introduction

Following the failure of German Herstatt Bank in 1974, there was a need to enhance soundness and stability of the international banking system. The Basel Committee was set up and the first capital accord came into effect in 1988. Banks were required to meet a common solvency ratio of 8 per cent. Capital requirements act as a safeguard against insolvency, increase public credibility and prevent systemic crises.

Moreover, Mauritian banks are conservative and adopted ratios above 15 per cent on average. Yet, since the late 1990s, there is excess liquidity in the Mauritius banking system. An analysis of bank's response to the Basel risk-based capital requirement is pertinent to Mauritius because banks play a pertinent role in channelling financial resources.

Although there have been several studies conducted to analyse the effect of Basel requirements (both I and II) on bank behaviour, most studies are concentrated in Europe and USA. Studies in Mauritius are rather scant as the Basel Accord I came into effect in 1994 and there were subsequent amendments. There have also been various changes in the banking industry in terms of entry and exit which renders a problem of data availability. Also, Basel II was implemented in 2009 and hence the paper confines itself to Basel I due to data unavailability. This paper contributes to the literature by analysing the effect of capital requirements on bank behaviour using nine banks which existed for the period 1994-2011.

To achieve its aim, the rest of this paper is organised as follows: part 2 gives the literature review; part 3 explains Basel capital requirements in Mauritius; part 4 discusses the data sources and methodology, and specifies the model to be estimated; part 5 gives the results and analysis; and part 6 concludes the paper.

Review of Literature

Among the main reasons to substantiate capital regulation is the necessity to prevent incentive by banks to shift their risk behaviour by pricing deposit insurance inadequately. Although risk-sensitive deposit insurance brings in short run stability in the banking system, it discourages banks to hold sufficient capital and may in the long run lead to banking instability. Whether capital accords can fruitfully eradicate moral hazard problems of the foregoing type has been the centre of discussions for more than three decades.

The pioneering literature emanates from Pyle (1971) and Hart and Jaffe (1974). The authors assume banks to be utility-maximisers under a portfolio approach and in this regards, Koehn and Santomero (1980) postulate that by introducing higher capital requirements, banks will engage in more risky assets. Such reallocation will have greater impact on large banks which already hold a higher proportion of riskier assets to capital. Furlong and Keeley (1989) criticised this view by employing an option model and postulate that by introducing capital requirements, banks are not encouraged to hold more risky assets. According to Van Roy (2008), the mean variance framework in the case of Furlong and Keeley (1989) is incorrect as it does not sufficiently label the investment opportunity set of the bank and ignores the option value of deposit insurance as well as the likelihood of bank failure.

Kim and Santomero (1988) postulate that to discourage banks to shift their risk behaviour, banks should be forced to observe risk-related capital ratios. Yet, Rochet (1992) stipulates that if the aim of banks is to maximise the value of their future profits, risk-based capital requirements cannot pre-empt them from engaging in very risky activities.

Based on the foregoing, the theories regarding capital requirements and bank behaviour are equivocal such that a proper direction and nature of the link is rather hard to gauge. Yet according to the Jackson *et al.* (1999) of Bank for International Settlements (BIS), the extent to which capital requirements are made compulsory determines the extent to which it will influence credit risk. Also, the sensitiveness of capital and risk to capital requirements also depends on market discipline. Hence, the impact of capital requirements and bank behaviour and *vice versa* is an empirical issue which is addressed in the following section.

As far as empirical literature is concerned, following the pioneering work of Shrieves and Dahl (1992), there have been many researches carried out regarding the impact of capital requirements on bank behaviour. Note that recent studies in developed countries regarding the impact of Basel I on bank behaviour are scant given that researchers have started to investigate the impact of Basel II.

Using a simultaneous equation model (SEM) and three-stage least squares (3SLS), Shrieves and Dahl (1992) analysed the impact of Basel I on bank behaviour in the USA. The author found that the impact depends on whether capital requirements reflect the true exposure of the banks to risk. Other main studies carried out are by Aggarwal and Jacques (1998), Rime (2000), Hussain and Hassan (2005) and Ramessur and Polodoo (2011). Aggarwal and Jacques (1998) used the SEM for the USA by employing generalised method of moments (GMM) and found a positive impact of capital requirements on risk for the year 1991 while a negative impact is noted for the other years. Similarly, Rime (2000) employed the SEM but as methodology used IV approach and found a negative on risk but a positive impact on capital adjustment. Hussain and Hassan (2005) conducted the same study for 11 developing countries using SEM but employed a dual methodology of GMM and 3SLS and found that capital requirements do not increase the capital ratios but reduce portfolio risk of banks. Last, but not least, using the same methodology like Hussain and Hassan (2005), Ramessur and Polodoo (2011) found no effect on changes in capital and risk of Mauritian banks. Other studies are given in Annexure Table A-8.1.

Basel Capital Requirements in Mauritius

Pursuant to the Banking Act 1988 and the Basel Accord I, the Bank of Mauritius issued a guideline on capital adequacy and the capital to risk weighted assets ratio of 8 per cent was to be observed by all Mauritian banks as from 15 November 1993. However, it was found that the flat 8 per cent ratio did not adequately differentiates underlying risks and in January 1997, the ratio was raised to 9 per cent and eventually to 10 per cent in July 1997, a period when all banks in Mauritius were required to increase their paid-up capital.

Under Basel II which is structured on three pillars: minimum capital requirements (Pillar I), the supervisory review process (Pillar II) and market discipline (Pillar III), which was fully implemented in Mauritius in 2009, has the overall minimum capital requirements for the banking system staying generally unchanged. Regulators are required to keep on demanding capital cushions in addition to the minimum requirements.

The trend in the average risk-based capital requirements observed by the Mauritian banks is provided in Figure 8.1.

Figure 8.1

Average Ratio of Basel Capital Requirement Observed by Mauritian Banks (1994-2011)

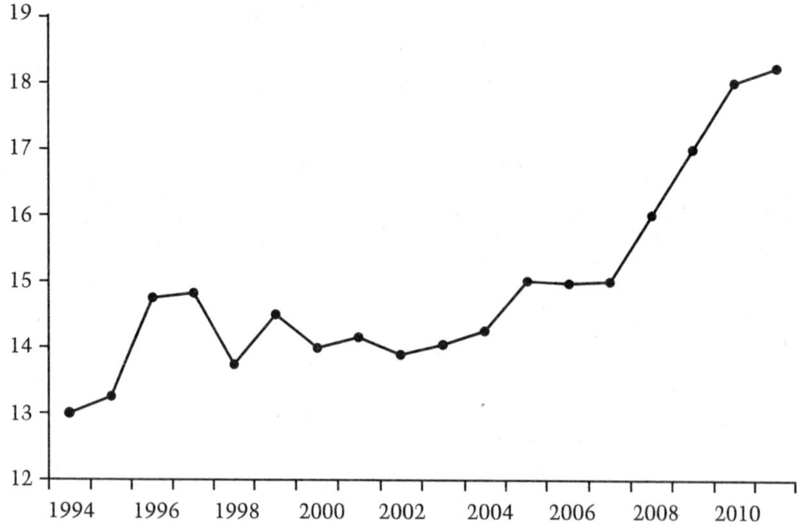

Source: Author's own illustration using data from Banks' Annual Reports, Various Issues.

From Figure 8.1, it is clear that the average ratio observed by the Mauritian banks is well above the ratio of 10 per cent prescribed the Bank of Mauritius, suggesting that banks in Mauritius are very conservative and risk averse. An individual analysis of the ratios among various banks shows that the ratios vary a lot because of differences in accounting policies and nature of operations.

Data Sources and Methodology

Data was obtained from the Registrar of Companies and from the Annual Reports of the banks taken in the sample. Since Basel I became effective in Mauritius in November 1993, sample data start in 1994 and end in 2011. Given that some banks started operations in the late 2000s, only nine banks are taken in the sample.

The study is a panel data analysis. According to Mouchart (2004), panel data analysis is more advantageous. Panel data analysis considers the fact that the banks differ in terms of accounting policies and standards. Panel data analysis removes all biases associated with the need to averaging or aggregation since in panel data, all banks' data are included.

Moreover, to achieve the aim of this paper, equations 7 and 8 are estimated using random coefficient (RC) estimates. According to Hondroyiannis *et al.* (2005), the RC model is a two-stage model which admits both individual-level and population-level effects. It is known to be robust against data that are not missing completely at random. However, the equations are first estimated using ordinary least squares (OLS) to check for heteroskedasticity (Breusch-Pagan/Cook-Weisberg Test), multicollinearity (variance inflating factor) and whether the model is well specified (Ramsey Reset Test). Heteroskedasticity occurs when the variance of the error terms differs across observations. Multicollinearity exists when the independent variables are found to be collinear. Also, Harris-Tzavalis' (1999) unit root test will be carried out to check for stationarity of the data set. Hondroyiannis *et al.* (2005) postulate that (RC) estimates give better estimates than the OLS, GMM and 3SLS. RC is also known as the time varying model, as it allows the intercepts and slopes to vary between the banks and through time and at a point in time. Further, there is no need to include dummy variables to take into account omitted variables and it controls for problems like endogeneity (good for simultaneous equations like our model) as well as measurement errors. There is also no need to look for instrumental variables as in GMM. Parameter constancy tests from the RC estimates give an insight as to whether the model is wrongly specified or not.

To follow Shrieves and Dahl (1992), a simultaneous equation model is developed. Yet, only variables deemed important for Mauritian banks are included. Assuming that capital and risk are simultaneously determined, the Shrieves and Dahl (1992) model is explained as follows:

$$\Delta Cap_{i,t} = \Delta^d Cap_{i,t} + X_{it} \qquad [1]$$

$$\Delta Risk_{i,t} = \Delta^d Risk_{i,t} + Y_{it} \qquad [2]$$

ΔCap and $\Delta Risk$ represent variations in capital and risk ratios respectively for bank i in period t. The first terms on the right-hand side of both equations are changes in capital and credit risk of the banks; X_{it} and Y_{it} show factors outside the bank controls which affects their capital and risk levels. Banks adjust their capital and risk using a partial adjustment procedure.

$$\Delta^d Cap_{i,t} = \omega(Cap^*_{i,t} - Cap_{i,t-1}) ; \qquad [3]$$

$$\Delta^d Risk_{i,t} = \Psi(Risk^*_{i,t} - Risk_{i,t-1}) . \qquad [4]$$

$Cap^*_{i,t}$ and $Risk^*_{i,t}$ denote capital and risk ratios, targeted for commercial bank i in year t. Replacing Equations 3 and 4 in equations 1 and 2, we have the following:

$$\Delta Cap_{i,t} = \omega(Cap^*_{i,t} - Cap_{i,t-1}) + X_{it} ; \qquad [5]$$

$$\Delta Risk_{i,t} = \Psi(Risk^*_{i,t} - Risk_{i,t-1}) + Y_{it} . \qquad [6]$$

Equation 5 says that changes in capital are dependent on the difference between target and actual capital and other factors outside the bank's control. Similarly, equation 6 says that changes in risks are dependent on the difference between target and actual risk. ω and Ψ show the swiftness of banks in adjusting their prevailing capital or risk to the targeted levels.

Based on the foregoing, the model for Mauritian banks is derived as follows:

$$\Delta Cap_{i,t} = \omega_0 - \omega_1 CG_{i,t} - \omega_2 ITA_{i,t} + \omega_3 ROA_{i,t} - \omega_4 GRGDP_{i,t} + \omega_5 \Delta RISK_{i,t} - \omega_6 Cap_{i,t-1} + X_{i,t} \quad [7]$$

$$\Delta RISK_{i,t} = \Psi_0 + \Psi_1 CG_{i,t} - \Psi_2 ITA_{i,t} - \Psi_3 ROA_{i,t} + \Psi_4 GRGDP_{i,t} + \Psi_5 \Delta Cap_{i,t} - \Psi_6 RISK_{i,t-1} + Y_{i,t} \quad [8]$$

- ROA—Return on Assets—is current profits of the banks and is expected to have a positive impact on capital as banks have a preference to increase their capital ratios through return earnings and not additional equities (Rime, 2000). However ROA has a negative impact on risk as a rise in credit risk (depicted by non-performing loans) diminishes bank profits.
- ITA—Ratio of Investment in Securities to Total Assets. ITA is expected to have a negative impact on both capital and risk. Hussain and Hassan (2005) stipulate that an increase in ITA reduces the capital ratios of banks when retained earnings are used to invest in treasury bills. ITA also reduces credit risk as less funds are available to advance as loans
- CG—Credit Growth. According to Rime (2000), CG is expected to negatively affect the capital ratio and positively affect risk of banks. As credit grows, bad debts increase (risk) and profits falls which leads to falling reserves and hence capital.
- GRGDP—Growth in real gross domestic products. As the economy grows, loans and advances of banks increase. As a result, a greater proportion goes to increasing bad debts (risk) which in turn reduces profitability, reserves and hence capital. Hence a positive impact is expected on risk and a negative impact is expected on capital.

Causality between Capital and Risk

It is expected that changes in risk positively affects changes in capital and *vice versa*. By having higher capital ratios, banks are encouraged to engage in risky activities by increasing their loans and advances.

Conversely, an increase in risk leads to an increase in profits, reserves and hence capital ratios of the banks.

We define the concepts of capital and risk. There are two definitions of capital employed in the empirical works: (i) the ratio of total capital (Tier 1+Tier 2 Capital) to risk-weighted assets and (ii) the ratio of capital to total assets. We employ the former definition, which is mostly used in the literature, especially by Jablecki (2009) and Awdeh *et al.* (2011) among others.

There are disagreements, however, regarding the measure of risk employed in the literature. Shrieves and Dahl (1992), Berger and Udell (1994), Rime (2000) and Van Roy (2003) among others employ the ratio of risk-weighted assets to total assets while Jablecki (2009) and Ramessur and Polodoo (2011) among others employ the ratio of non-performing loans. Given that credit risk is the main risk facing Mauritian banks, the ratio of non-performing loans is used in this paper

Based on the foregoing, the research questions to be investigated (the null hypothesis is denoted as H_0 and the alternative hypothesis is denoted as H_1) are as follows:

H_0: There is a simultaneous relationship between risk-based capital requirements and bank behaviour in Mauritius.

H_1: There is no simultaneous relationship between risk-based capital requirement and bank behaviour in Mauritius.

Results and Analysis

The diagnostic tests and regression results are given in the annexures. It is expected that Basel I does not impact on Mauritian banks behaviour. Thus, all the explanatory variables should be statistically insignificant except ROA (profitability) as higher profits significantly influence capital and risk of banks.

Turning to the diagnostic tests, it is clear from Annexure Table A-8.2 that the dataset does not suffer from unit root problems since the p-values from the Harris-Tzavalis tests are less than 0.05. Similarly, the Ramsey Reset tests from Annexure Table A-8.3 reveal no specification problems for both equations as depicted by the high F values relative to the p-values.

Similarly, variance inflating factors (VIFs) from Annexure Table A-8.4, reveals no multicollinearity problems. The Breusch-Pagan/Cook-Weisberg tests from Annexure C reveals large chi-squares as against the p-values, showing the presence of heteroskedasticity. Yet, given that the sample consists of both large and small banks, we accept heteroskedasticity.

The regression results are given in Annexure D in Annexure Tables A-8.4 (Δ Cap equation) and A-8.5 (Δ Risk equation). As expected, the RC estimates show that all the independent variables are insignificant for the Δ Cap equation. To be significant, the p-values need to be less than 0.05 at 95 per cent confidence interval.

Results for Δ Cap Equation

In contrast with Shrieves and Dahl (1992), the p-value of the lagged capital (0.451) in the Cap equation is insignificant, meaning that an increase in capital in the previous year leads to an increase of only 0.28 per cent in capital in the current year. This could mean that the increase in capital emanates from an increase in the portfolio of loans of banks, increasing their profits and hence increasing their reserves and profits, albeit such a situation is from a minority of banks in the sample as evidenced by a coefficient of 0.028.

The insignificance of ITA [as opposed Aggarwal and Jacques (1997)] and credit growth [as against Rime (2000)] suggests that owing to excess liquidity in the banking system, most of the excess are used to invest in treasury bills/loans and not retained earnings, thus insignificant in explaining changes in capital.

Further, the insignificance of real GDP growth (as against Rime, 2000) is explained by the fact that since the early 2000s, owing to closure of several textile firms, which lost their competitiveness on the world market, some banks incurred huge bad debts and losses resulting in erosion of their capital base. However, most banks in the sample hold well-diversified portfolio such that losses from textiles were compensated.

The insignificance of change in risk is due to the fact that Mauritian banks employ experts in debt recovery and are adopting much strict risk management policies.

Lastly, the insignificance of ROA is due to the fact that higher profits are used to invest in treasury bills to finance growing public deficit, thus do not add to reserves and capital of the company.

Results for Δ Risk Equation

For the Risk equation, only ROA is significant (similar to Rime, 2000) in explaining changes in risk, all other independent variables being insignificant. This shows that with increased profitability, the banks enjoy economies of scale by employing experienced and expert analysts to give good credit risk loans and advances and debt recovery. The same reason is advanced for the insignificance of credit growth (in line with Chiuri *et al.*, 2001). Change in capital is insignificant in explaining risk changes (in contrast with Hussain and Hassan, 2005). This clearly reflects the fact that Mauritian banks observe higher capital requirements than those prescribed by Accord I and engage in less risky loans and advances. In line with Aggarwal and Jacques (1998), ITA is also insignificant in explaining risk confirming that credit risk depends crucially on the ability of the banks to manage efficiently their credit risks through the employment of experts. The insignificance of lagged risk (in line with Ramessur and Polodoo, 2011) is explained by the fact that due to the employment of experts in debt recovery, bad credit risks were being recovered which explains the low rate of non-performing loans in the industry (below 5%).

In contrast with Rime (2000), real GDP growth rate is also insignificant in explaining changes in risk. Risks in Mauritian emanate from bad loans and despite the decline of traditional sectors like textiles and sugar, the risks were insignificantly affected as banks hold well-diversified portfolio of loans and advances.

Is there Simultaneity?

The results obtained from both equations suggest that there is no simultaneity between capital requirements and risk changes. Change in risk is insignificant in explaining change in capital and change in capital is insignificant in explaining change in risk. The results confirm that Mauritian banks' capital decisions are independent on credit risk decisions, that is, these decisions are separately being taken.

The result for parameter constancy test for both equations gives large χ^2 relative to Prob > χ^2 which means that the models are well specified and invalid inferences are avoided. Wald tests also indicate fine goodness of fit as indicated by high Wald χ^2 values.

Conclusion

This paper provides evidence regarding the impact of Basel risk-based requirements on bank capital and risk behaviour of Mauritian banks. The results so obtained are in contrast with existing empirical studies such that capital regulation does not impact on bank capital and risk behaviour in Mauritius.

From the Δ Cap equation, lagged capital is insignificant showing that an increase in capital emanates from an increase in the portfolio of loans of banks, increasing their profits and hence increasing their reserves and profits. Investment to total assets is also insignicant showing that instead of retained earnings, excess liquidity in the Mauritian banking system is used for investment purposes. The insignificance of change in risk is due to the fact that Mauritian banks employ experts in debt recovery and are adopting much strict risk management policies. ROA is also insignificant as higher profits are used to invest in treasury bills to finance growing public deficit, thus do not add to reserves and capital of the company.

As far as Δ Risk equation is concerned, only ROA is significant in explaining changes in risk, meaning that with increased profitability, the banks enjoy economies of scale by employing experienced and expert analysts to give good credit risk loans and advances and debt recovery. The latter reason also explains the insignificance of credit growth and lagged risk. Change in capital could not explain changes in risk as Mauritian banks observe higher capital requirements than those prescribed by Accord I and engage in less risky loans and advances.

In a nutshell, the results obtained from the change in both capital and risk equations suggest that there is no simultaneity between capital requirements and risk changes. Change in risk is insignificant in explaining change in capital and change in capital is insignificant in explaining change in risk. The results confirm that Mauritian banks' capital decisions are independent on credit risk decisions, that is, these decisions are separately being taken. The result for parameter constancy test for both equations gives large χ^2 relative to Prob > χ^2 which means that the models are well specified and invalid inferences are avoided. Wald tests also indicate fine goodness of fit as indicated by high Wald χ^2 values.

Nonetheless, the study takes into account only nine domestic banks. Data from offshore banks could also have been included. Yet, the problem is that the accounting policies of offshore banks differ a lot from domestic banks such that it would have been a tedious exercise to include them. Moreover, most of the data are taken from the banks' financial statements. Although financial statements give a true and fair view of the state of financial affairs, they are subject to window dressing such that the results so obtained might be misleading.

Given that this paper concentrates on the impact of Basel I, future research should be geared towards analysing the impact of Basel II on bank behaviour. Also, only nine banks are included in the sample. Future studies should include almost all onshore and offshore banks as well as following the Banking Act 2004, the difference between onshore and offshore banks seems to fade away.

References

Aggarwal, R. and K. Jacques (1998). "A Simultaneous Equations Estimation of the Impact of Prompt Corrective Action on Bank Capital and Risk," in *Financial Services at the Crossroads: Capital Regulation in the 21st Century*, Conference, 26-27 February 1998, Federal Reserve Bank of New York.

Ambrose, Brent, M. LaCour-Little and A.B. Sanders (2003). "Does Regulatory Capital Arbitrage or Asymmetric Information Drive Securitisation?", Unpublished paper, University of Kentucky and Ohio State University.

Awdeh, A., C. Moussawi and F. Machrouh (2011). "The Effect of Capital Requirements on Banking Risk", *International Research Journal of Finance and Economics* 66: 133-46.

Bank of Mauritius Annual Report, Various Issues.

Berger, A. and G. Udell (1994). "Did Risk-Based Capital Allocate Bank Credit and Cause a "Credit Crunch" in the United States?", *Journal of Money, Credit, and Banking* 26: 585-628.

Chiuri, Concetta Maria, Giovanni Ferri and Giovanni Majnoni (2001). "The Macroeconomic Impact of Bank Capital Requirements in Emerging Economies: Past Evidence to Assess the Future," *Policy Research Working Paper Series 2605*. The World Bank.

Ediz, S., I. Michael and W. Perraudin (1998). *Bank Capital Dynamics and Regulatory Policy*. Bank of England.

Furlong, F.T. and M.C. Keeley (1989). "Capital Regulation and Bank Risk-taking: A Note", *Journal of Banking and Finance* 13: 883-91.

Hart, O.D. and D.M. Jaffe (1974). "On the Application of Portfolio Theory to Depository Financial Intermediaries", *Review of Economic Studies* 41: 129-47.

Harris, R.O.F. and E. Tzavalis (1999). "Inference for Unit Roots in Dynamic Panels where the Time Dimension is Fixed," *Journal of Econometrics* 91: 201-26.

Hondroyiannis, G., P.A.V.B. Swamy, G. Tavlas and M. Ulan (2005). "Some Further Evidence on Exchange-Rate Volatility and Exports," Working Papers 28, Bank of Greece.

Hussain, M.E. and M.K. Hassan (2005). "Basel Capital Requirements and Bank Credit Risk Taking in Developing Countries", *Working Paper*, University of New Orleans/Drexel University, LeBow College of Business, Department of Finance.

Jackson, P., C. Furfine, H. Groeneveld, D. Hancock, D. Jones, W. Perraudin, L. Radecki and M. Yoneyama (1999). "Capital Requirements and Bank Behaviour: The Impact of the Basel Accord", *Basel Committee on Banking Supervision Working Papers*, no. 1, April.

Jacques, K. and P.J. Nigro (1997). "Risk-Based Capital, Portfolio Risk and Bank Capital: A Simultaneous Equations Approach", *Journal of Economics and Business* 49: 533-47.

Jablecki, J. (2009). The Impact of Basel I Capital Requirements on Bank Behavior and the Efficacy of Onetary Policy. *International Journal of Economic Sciences and Applied Research* 2(1): 16-35.

Kim, D. and A.M. Santomero (1988). "Risk in Banking and Capital Regulation", *Journal of Finance* 43: 1219-33.

Koehn, M. and A.M. Santomero (1980). "Regulation of Bank Capital and Portfolio Risk", *Journal of Finance* 35: 1235-44.

Mouchart, M. (2004). "The Econometrics of Panel Data" Institut de statistique Université catholique de Louvain, March.

Peek, J. and E. Rosengren (1995). "Bank Regulation and the Credit Crunch," *Journal of Banking and Finance* 19: 679-92.

Porter (2009). "The Impact of Bank Capital Requirements on Bank Risk: An Econometric Puzzle and a Proposed Solution", *Banks and Bank Systems* 4(1).

Pyle, D.H. (1971). "On the theory of Financial Intermediation", *Journal of Finance* 26: 737-47.

Ramessur, T.S. and V. Polodoo (2011). "The Impact of Basel Risk Based Capital Requirement (Accord 1) on Bank Performance in the Context of a Small Service-Based Island Economy", *International Journal of Small Economies* 2(1): 15-35.

Rime, B. (2000). *Capital Requirements and Bank Behaviour: Empirical Evidence for Switzerland*. Swiss National Bank.

Rochet, J. (1992). "Capital Requirements and the Behavior of Commercial Banks", *European Economic Review* 36: 1137-78.

Shrieves, R.E. and D. Dahl (1992). "The Relationship Between Risk and Capital in Commercial Banks", *Journal of Banking & Finance* 16(2): 439-57.

Van Roy, P. (2003). "Impact of the 1988 Basle Accord on Bank's Capital Ratios and Credit Risk Taking: An International Study", European Center for Advanced Research in Economics and Statistics, *Working Paper*. Universite Libre de Bruxelles.

———. (2008). "Capital Requirements and Bank Behavior in the Early 1990s: Cross-country Evidence", *International Journal of Central Banking* 4(3): 29-60.

Annexure A

Table A-8.1

Summary of Empirical Studies-Impact of Basel I on Bank Behaviour

Author and Year	*Model*	*Methodology*	*Result*
Berger and Udell (1994)-USA	SEM	3SLS	No effect on bank behaviour
Jacques and Nigro (1997)-USA	SEM	3SLS	Negative impact on credit risk
Aggarwal and Jacques (1998)-USA	SEM	Generalised Method of Moments (GMM)	Positive impact on risk in 1991 Negative impact for the other years.
Ediz *et al.* (1998)-UK	dynamic, multivariate panel regression model	Instrumental Variables Approach (IV)	Positive impact on bank behaviour. Banks adjust their capital rather than adjusting their portfolio of loans or other risky assets.
Rime (2000)- Switzerland	SEM	IV	Negative impact on risk but positive impact on capital adjustment
Van Roy (2003)- 7 OECD countries	dynamic, multivariate panel regression model	3SLS	Alterations in capital and risk were negatively linked. Regulations were ineffective in raising the capital ratio of undercapitalised banking Institutions in France and Italy.
Porter (2009)- USA	Unrestricted and Restricted econometric model-Stochastic Frontier Analysis	IV	Positive impact on Capital No impact on risk
Peek and Rosengren (1995)- 16 emerging economies.	dynamic, multivariate panel regression model	OLS	Capital requirements lead to a fall in supply of credit
Hussain and Hassan (2005)- 11 developing countries	SEM	GMM and 3SLS	Capital requirements did not increase the capital ratios but did reduce portfolio risk of banks
Van Roy (2008)- 6 G10 countries	SEM	3SLS	Only USA: weakly capitalised banks increase their capital ratios. Other countries: no indication of changes in capital and risk-weighted assets
Jablecki (2009)-G10 countries	dynamic, multivariate panel regression model	OLS	-Encouraged regulatory capital arbitrage - negative effect on bank lending
Ramessur and Polodoo (2011)-Mauritius	SEM	GMM and 3SLS	No effect on changes in capital and risk.

Source: Own Illustration.

Annexure B

Unit Root Tests, Ramsey Rest Test and Multicollinearity Tests

Table A-8.2

Harris-Tzavalis Unit Root Results

Rho value for	*statistic*	*z-value*	*p-value*
Lagged Capital	0.4556	-4.1271	0.0001
Lagged Risk	0.6413	-5.8731	0.0002
Change in risk	0.6935	-3.1047	0.0234
Change in Capital	0.5931	-3.5566	0.0041
Credit Growth	0.7940	-3.2311	0.0213
Investment to Total Assets	0.8293	-3.7238	0.0122
Return on Assets	0.4827	-4.2011	0.0011
Growth in Real GDP	0.6739	-4.7659	0.0000

Source: Stata 11 output.

Table A-8.3

Ramsey Reset Test Results

Variables	*Δ Cap equation*	*Δ Risk equation*
F(4,118)	10.92	11.08
Prob>F	0.1089	0.0004

Source: Stata 11 output.

Table A-8.4

Multicollinearity Tests: VIF (Variance Inflating Factor)

Regressands	*VIF-Δ Cap*	*1/VIF*	*VIF-Δ Risk*	*1/VIF*
Lagged Capital	2.17	1.89	-	-
Lagged Risk	-	-	2.34	1.92
Change in risk	2.32	1.94	-	-
Change in Capital	-	-	2.25	1.87
Credit Growth	1.67	1.84	1.77	1.08
Investment to total assets	1.09	1.07	1.04	1.33
Return on Assets	1.22	1.28	1.41	1.58
Growth in Real GDP	1.88	1.73	1.68	1.99

Source: Stata 11 Output.

The above results makes it clear that there is no multicollinearity since the VIFs are less than 10.

Annexure C

Test for Heteroskedasticity

Results Breusch-Pagan/Cook-Weisberg Test for Cap equation

Chi2(1) = 9.23

Prob>chi2 =0.0002

Results for Breusch-Pagan/Cook-Weisberg Test for Change in Risk equation

Chi2(1) = 10.84

Prob>chi2 =0.0006

Annexure D

Random Coefficient Estimates (@95 per cent Confidence Interval)

Table A-8.5

RC Estimates for Δ Cap Equation

Predictors	*Coefficient*	*P-value*	*Standard Error*
Constant	-11.49	0.315	-2.34
Lagged capital	0.283	0.451	0.67
Change in Capital	9.823	0.663	0.99
Change in risk	-0.067	0.838	-0.46
Credit Growth	-0.435	0.315	-2.38
Investment to Total Assets	-7.221	0.281	-2.48
Real GDP Growth	4.199	0.475	0.82
Return on Assets	8.648	0.697	0.65
Test for Parameter Constancy			
$\chi^2(28)$= 42.55			
Prob > χ^2= 0.0034	*Wald $\chi^2(7)$ = 17.62*		
Prob > χ^2= 0.0001			

Table A-8.6

RC Estimates for Δ Risk Equation

Predictors	*Coefficient*	*P-value*	*Standard Error*
Constant	-33.684	0.355	-2.27
Lagged Risk	-0.0047	0.763	-0.05
Change in Risk	7.624	0.457	0.46
Change in Capital	-0.048	0.715	-0.33
Credit Growth	-0.118	0.423	-2.14
Investment to Total assets	-3.842	0.151	-1.23
Growth in Real GDP	2.147	0.427	1.11
Return on Assets	-18.673	0.001	-4.30
Test for Parameter Constancy			
$\chi^2(28)$= 49.11			
Prob > χ^2= 0.0028	Wald $\chi^2(7)$ = 14.31		
Prob > χ^2= 0.001			

Source: Stata 11 Output.

SECTION III

Risk Management and Insurance Industry

9 A Conceptual Study on Insurers Changing Preference Towards Principle-Based Solvency Assessment Models

V. Jayalakshmi and
Pardhasaradhi Madasu

Introduction

Insurance is a highly regulated sector of the economy. It is so regulated because of 'risky' nature of its business. The regulator is always concerned with the protection of the policyholders. Maintaining good financial health of the insurer is the primary goal of the regulators. The financial health of an insurance company is measured by a metric named 'Solvency.' A solvency for any financial institution (including insurance companies) corresponds to its capacity to meet its liabilities without any hassle. We can say that a financial institution is insolvent in the following two situations: first, the financial institution's assets are not sufficient to meet its liabilities and second, even if the assets are sufficient to meet the liabilities but do not have liquidity so that the claims are met on time. In other words, 'solvency' is a part of 'prudential norms.' According to the International Association of Insurance Supervisors (IAIS) (2002), an insurance company is solvent "if it is able to fulfill its obligation under all contracts under all reasonably foreseeable circumstances." Hence, solvency norms form the most important supervisory aspect of insurance.

Generally, an insurer (equally applicable to any other financial institution like banks) has to maintain more assets than their existing liabilities. Excess of value of the assets over the value of the liabilities can be referred as 'solvency margins.' These margins are akin to 'capital adequacy' requirements of banks. This margin is required so that unanticipated claims can be taken care off. If the unanticipated claims are not taken care, than there is a possibility of the insurer becoming insolvent and this may lead to 'systemic risk.' The solvency ratio is a way investors can measure the company's ability to meet its long-term obligations The regulators will decide the amount of 'solvency margins' such that a crisis is avoided. The first uniformed solvency margin requirement was introduced in early 1970, in Europe. Until 1970, the only requirement to be satisfied by a life insurance company was that, after the distribution of surplus, if any, the value of its assets should not be less than the value of its liabilities. The early regulation primarily dealt with the 'paid-up-capital' of the insurer. Even in the present globalised and liberalised world of business, the regulators are emphasising on 'risk-based capital' (RBC) as the basis of capital adequacy for banks and solvency for insurers. RBC exists in various forms and degrees in all the countries. The regulators will prescribe the RBC by adopting different approaches ranging from the rudimentary fixed ratio approach to a more advanced level of stochastic modelling as in the UK and Canada.

Literature Review

In the recent past, the insurers are showing preference for the flexible principle-based solvency assessment model in place of rule-based solvency assessment model. Eling *et al.* (2007) have argued in favor of a flexible scheme, where RBC standards are used as guidelines—to assist insurers in managing their risk structures rather than as absolute requirements. They argued that flexibility is likely to yield a variety of risk strategies, limiting the possibility of systemic risk inherent in using a single standard model for all or even most insurers. One of the most important features of principle-based solvency assessment models is the possible use of internal, instead of standard-risk models to determine the required capital. As per the European Commission (2002a), the internal models are expected to result in more accurate analysis, control, and management of the insurer's financial situation than do the more generic standard models. A model will become eligible for internal model if it is certified by the supervisor. This process of certification requires lot of documentation with respect to the selected model. Apart from the approval from the supervisor, the model requires periodic examination. The movement towards the principle-based models also has inbuilt checks and balances. For example, European Commission (2005) prescribes that if an internal model is used to estimate the minimum capital required (MCR), than that amount of prescribed capital cannot be less than MCR given by Solvency-I rules.

Solvency-II is the principle-based solvency model for insurance. This is based on the Basel-II three-pillar structure, which is supposed to create a level playing field for the market participants. Studies by Eling *et al.* (2007) and Steffen (2008) dealt with development and main features of Solvency-II. Studies by Duverne and Le Douit (2009) discuss and compare recent developments in Solvency-II and the International Financial Reporting Standards (IFRS). Some impact studies were also conducted. For example, the impact of Solvency-II on regulation in countries like Bermuda is analysed by Elderfield (2009).

Some of the studies have compared different approaches that are adopted in insurance regulation for determining solvency. For example, Eling and Holzmüller (2008) compared four regulatory schemes for the insurance industry that represent different approaches to regulation, e.g., the use of static factor models or a dynamic rating-based approach. They concluded that there are major differences, especially in the applied risk measure, the potential use of internal models, and the quantification of operational and catastrophe risk. Apart from comparing the various approaches, Eling *et al.* (2009), Cummins and Phillips (2009), Vaughan (2009), as well as Von Bomhard (2010) have made studies to understand the similarities and differences between US RBC Standard and the Solvency-II regime

The comprehensive understanding of the above studies lead us to an understanding that the regulators (both in banking and insurance) are looking for the dynamic and risk sensitive approaches for framing prudential norms rather than rigid static models. In the present paper, the changing preference of the insurance regulators towards the principle-based solvency approach is discussed. The paper is divided into three major segments: (i) overview of solvency models, (ii) global scenario, and (iii) Indian scenario.

Overview of Solvency Models

Solvency assessment models are used to arrive at the MCR. Generally, the solvency assessment models can be categorised into static, accounting-based models and dynamic, cash-flow-based models. In the former, the capital requirements are arrived at by applying a certain calculation methodology on static (i.e., fixed at a given date), accounting basis like balance sheet position or profit and loss (P&L) position, whereas in the latter models, cash flow projections are taken as a basis rather than fixed positions.

Static, accounting-based models are further classified into simple factor-based models and risk factor-based models. Both these models apply well defined factors, therefore they are called as 'rules-based models'. Under the 'rules-based model,' clear rules are mentioned on what positions the factors are to be applied to and the factors are typically clearly defined as well. The Solvency-I is an example of simple factor-based model as the life insurance capital requirements are arrived at by multiplying a factor of 4 per cent to the mathematical reserves of participating business (for unit-linked business the factor is reduced to 1%) plus a factor of 0.3 per cent to the sum-at-risk. Risk factor-based models are the most prevalent in the industry. They apply fixed ratios to select accounting positions. The ratios are frequently calibrated to cover the underlying risk to a certain confidence level. It provides a series of risk factors that need to be applied to clearly define underlying accounting positions in order to arrive at the various risk capital numbers, which later are aggregated assuming correlations.

On the other hand, the dynamic/cash-flow-based assessment models are also classified into scenario-based model and purely principle-based models. In the former, the impact of clearly defined scenarios on the solvency of the firm is measured. To some extant, this is also a rule-based approach because the scenarios are well defined. Coming to purely principles-based models, no rules will be specified for the measurement of risk and associated capital. The insurance company is required to arrive at its own view of the capital requirement on the basis of internal models. An example of this is the UK-FSA's (Financial Services Authority) requirement for insurance companies to arrive at the individual capital assessment (ICA) using internal models that comply with the principles put forward in the UK-FSA Policy Statement 04/16.

In the recent past, the regulators are moving from a rule-based approach to a principle-based approach. The motivation to do so is that the standard-formulaic approach in arriving at the MCR is difficult to apply to all the players and flexibility is lacking. The principle-based model does not prescribe any specifics, but provides flexibility for individual interpretation. This approach will require judgment, which in turn requires reliable data.

Global Scenario

Globally the countries are moving from 'rule-based solvency standards' to 'principles-based solvency regulations.' It is now widely viewed that rule-based models are inadequate to prescribe the 'capital requirement' for the insurance companies. It is now argued that the rule-based solvency models are not able to properly relate the capital with the risks taken up by the insurance companies. The major difference between the rule-based solvency models and the principles-based solvency models is that the onus of estimating the capital required for the insurance company is shifted from the regulator to the management of the insurance company. The UK has taken the first step towards including the concept of the self-assessment by introducing FSA that introduced the ICAS (Individual Capital Adequacy Standard) regime in 2004. Switzerland followed suit in 2006 with the risk-based Swiss Solvency Test (SST). Initially, North America and Bermuda were hesitant to introduce risk-based solvency models for (re)insurers. However, in January 2008, the Bermuda Monetary Authority announced the phased introduction of RBC requirements to replace the current solvency margin regime, to be known as the Bermuda Solvency Capital Requirement (BSCR). In the same year, Brazil has also moved towards risk-based solvency models. In Asia-Pacific region, the Australian regulator Australian Prudential Regulation Authority (APRA) has taken the initiative to introduce risk-based solvency regulatory regime.

The European Union (EU) is all geared up to move from Solvency-I to Solvency-II. Solvency regulations have evolved over a period of time from simple ratio-based methods to complex risk-based approach. Life insurance directives [European Economic Community (EEC), 1979] and the non-life insurance directives (EEC 1973) can be considered the starting point of a formal set of solvency requirements that insurance companies were required to fulfil in a competitive and uncertain environment. The early day solvency regulations were significant to be understood. The significance emerges from the mere fact that they are the starting point of the journey. The early days of solvency regulation revolved around the 'minimum solvency margin' or 'required solvency margin.' During 2002, Solvency-I was introduced and it provided a simple, but robust mechanism to regulate the insurer's solvency. Some industry experts call the early regulations as 'Solvency-0.' Solvency-I has established more realistic minimum capital requirements, but still it does not reflect the true risk faced by insurance companies. Solvency-I was a simple factor-based model. One of the major differences from the early regulation of solvency (Solvency-0) and Solvency-I was that the insurers were required to meet the 'required solvency margin' norms on the date of the latest balance sheet whereas Solvency-I stipulated that solvency requirement should be met at all times and not just on the latest date of balance sheet. Apart from this, Solvency-I prescribed special guidelines for permanent health insurance contracts and unit-linked insurance contracts.

In the recent past, the financial markets have changed and perception about risk management also has undergone change. In these changed times, Solvency-II is gaining importance in the insurance sector. The Solvency-II directive is a new regulatory framework for the European insurance industry that adopts a more dynamic risk-based approach. On April 22, 2009, the European Parliament approved the 'Solvency-II' framework directive, due to become effective from January 1st, 2013. Industry experts are feeling that the implementation may be deferred to January 1st, 2014. Solvency-II is a fundamental review of the capital adequacy regime for the European insurance industry. Solvency-II (also referred as 'Basel for Insurers') will be adopted by all 27 EU member states plus three of the European Economic Area (EEA) countries. As a consistent European standard, it aims to establish a revised set of EU-wide capital requirements and risk management standards that will replace the current solvency requirements. Solvency-II aims to achieve consistency across Europe and includes the following key ideas:

1. Market consistent balance sheets.
2. RBC.
3. Own risk and solvency assessment (ORSA).

4. Senior management accountability; and
5. Supervisory assessment.

Solvency-II should help to protect policyholders' interests more effectively by making firm failure less likely, and by reducing the probability of consumer loss or market disruption. The new norms will reflect all types of risks faced by the insurance companies. The fundamental shift from Solvency-I to Solvency-II is the change in the approach *viz.*, shift to principles-based approach from rule-based approach.

Solvency-II framework follows the Basel Accord approach, with three-pillar structure which will bring the insurance and reinsurance regulation more in line with the banking regulation.

- **Pillar 1** consists of the quantitative requirements (e.g., the amount of capital an insurer should hold). The pillar 1 framework set out qualitative and quantitative requirements for calculation of technical provisions and solvency capital requirement (SCR) using either a standard formula given by the regulators or an internal model developed by the (re)insurance company.
- **Pillar 2** sets out requirements for the governance and risk management of insurers, as well as for the effective supervision of insurers. It defines governance requirements for risk management, internal controls, audit and outsourcing. This pillar allows the regulators to impose additional capital requirements, depending on the assessment of a company's risk management and corporate governance, and whether the Pillar 1 measure adequately reflects the risk profile.
- **Pillar 3** focuses on disclosure and transparency requirements. This pillar prescribes the information requirements for reporting to supervisors and public disclosure.

As per the report titled "Solvency-II's Long Reach: Beyond Europe" prepared by RGA International Reinsurance Company Limited (2010), the Solvency-II will have many and varied impacts outside EU. RGA summarises the extra-territorial impacts of Solvency-II into these four categories:

1. Non-EU subsidiaries of EU groups.
2. EU subsidiaries of non-EU groups.
3. Recognition by EU insurers of reinsurance purchased from non-EU reinsurers.
4. Non-EU countries that will eventually adopt a new capital and regulatory regime like Solvency-II.

EU adopting Solvency-II will certainly have influence on the solvency assessment model to be adopted by the non-EU insurance regulators. IRDA is not an exception.

Indian Scenario

In India, the insurance reforms are relatively new. The insurance space in India is being regulated by IRDA only from 2002. IRDA was established "to protect the interests of the policyholders, to regulate, promote and ensure orderly growth of the insurance industry...." IRDA is still gearing up to meet the new challenges. The major challenges before the Indian regulator (as well as other Insurance regulators in Asia-Pacific region) are:

- Capital adequacy.
- Risk management.
- Adoption to IFRS.
- Data control.
- Statutory reporting.
- Cost pressures.
- Shortage of skilled resources.

Over a period of time the insurance regulator in India is managing to cope with the challenges faced by the insurance sector. Initially, Union Ministry of Finance has constituted a committee in 1994 to recommend norms for the 'solvency margins' for the Indian insurance companies. The group studied the insurance regulations of many countries before framing the current regulations. The initial IRDA regulations of 2000 addressed issues related to valuation of assets and liabilities, solvency margin as well as the minimum capital requirement for setting up of insurance companies. As per the IRDA (assets, liabilities and solvency margin of insurers) Rules 2000, both life and general insurance companies need to maintain solvency margins. India's solvency regulation is a hybrid of the UK and Canadian norms. The regulator mandated all insurance companies to file their solvency position as at the end of each quarter. Basically, the IRDA is following updated version of Solvency-I. The IAIS has proposed the implementation of Solvency II guidelines in India.

At present, the Indian insurance industry follows a simple formulaic approach and is related to the total amount of business that an insurer transacts. Recently, IRDA has asked the companies to calculate the 'Economic Capital' and report them. IRDA has published a report on calculation of economic capital as a reference for Indian insurers. Insurers are required to conduct a calculation of economic capital and submit a report every year starting from 31st March, 2010. This move is in sync with Solvency-II norms.

Apart from the above, IRDA is planning to shift the insurance companies solvency assessment models and models to compute the economic capital to a risk-based solvency assessment models from the present factor-based solvency model. This step is one way moving forward towards the Solvency-II norms. The Indian insurance companies have to move towards the Solvency-II model because of the nature of the Indian insurance sector. If we observe the structure of the Indian insurance sector, we can find that out of 23 Indian private life insurers, 22 already have foreign partners and in the case of 21 general insurance companies, most of them have foreign tie-ups. Apart from the existing investment by the foreign partners, the FDI norm amendment may bring in more foreign partners. The recent approval by the Union Cabinet for hike in the FDI limit from 26 per cent to 49 per cent can also be seen as a move for allowing the insurance companies to raise more capital in tune with the risk-sensitive models. In these circumstances, Solvency-II norms will have impact far beyond EU. Any life, property and casualty or private health insurer that is headquartered in Europe, has subsidiaries that operate there or competes in non-EU markets where European insurers have a significant presence will need to conform to its provisions or adapt to them. Insurers that are not directly touched by Solvency-II may be able to seize competitive advantages from rivals subject to the new rules. To understand the impact of moving from a formula-based model of capital adequacy to risk-based model, we have to wait and watch the happening globally.

Conclusion

In the recent past, regulations (especially that are relating to 'economic capital') for the financial services sector is becoming more stringent and transparent. The recent financial market turmoil has highlighted the weaknesses in the system and has highlighted the need for more transparency and flexibility in setting the prudential standards (relating to capital, liquidity, valuations and reporting) for the financial service sector. The regulators are shifting their focus from an over-simplistic 'one-size-fits-all' rule-based approach to principle-based 'risk-sensitive internal model' approach. In one sense, the financial sector regulators are looking at dynamic models in place of static models. To assess the risk on a dynamic basis, the insurance companies are required to develop internal models to better measure the risks they take. Banking sector had a good experience with Basel Accord and this has influenced the insurance sector. EU legislative has initiated Solvency-II for insurance sector. Solvency-II is a fundamental review of the capital adequacy regime for the European insurance industry. It aims to establish a revised set of EU-wide capital requirements and risk management standards that will replace the current solvency requirements. This initiative has a lot of influence on other insurance regulators all over the world.

Indian insurance regulator IRDA is also closely watching the transition to the new norms. The new regulations regarding capital reserves and risk management are being aligned with the Solvency-II norms. As of now solvency norms of Indian insurers are based on Solvency-I norms (which are simple formulaic rule-based model). Not only this, IRDA is also taking initiatives to align the insurance financial reporting with IFRS. Further, IRDA has also come out with 'Corporate Governance' guidelines for insurers. All these initiatives are going to bring a change in the solvency assessment and reporting of insurance companies in India as well as other nations in Asia-Pacific region.

Scope for Further Study

This paper being a conceptual paper focused majorly on the theoretical framework of solvency models and the change in the preference of the financial sector regulators. Further studies can focus on the impact of the shift from static models to dynamic models. The impact can be seen in the amount of capital raised from the financial markets, usage of innovative financial instruments, development and implementation of new software technologies, human resources development and also on the regulations of other players in the financial markets.

References

Cummins, D. and R.D. Phillips (2009). "Capital Adequacy and Insurance Risk-based Capital Systems", *Journal of Insurance Regulation* 28(1): 25–72.

Duverne, D. and J. Le Douit (2009). "IFRS Phase II and Solvency II: Key Issues, Current Debates", *Geneva Papers on Risk and Insurance—Issues and Practice* 34(1): 47–55.

Elderfield, M. (2009). "Solvency II: Setting the Pace for Regulatory Change", *Geneva Paperson Risk and Insurance—Issues and Practice* 34(1): 35–41.

Eling, M. and T. Parnitzke (2007). "Dynamic Financial Analysis: Conception, Classification, and Implementation", *Risk Management and Insurance Review* 10(1): 33–50.

Eling, M., H. Schmeiser and J.T. Schmit (2007). "The Solvency II Process: Overview and Critical Analysis", *Risk Management and Insurance Review* 10(1): 69–85.

Eling, M., R.W. Klein and J.T. Schmit (2009). "Insurance Regulation in the United States and the European Union—A Comparison", *Independent Policy Report*. The Independent Institute.

European Commission (2002a). "Risk Models of Insurance Companies or Groups", Markt/2515/02, *Working Paper*, 2002-05-17, Brussels.

———. (2002b). "Considerations on the Design of a Future Prudential Supervisory System", Markt/2535/02, *Working Paper*, 2002-11-28, Brussels.

———. (2003a). "Design of a Future Prudential Supervisory System in the EU—Recommendations by the Commission Services", Markt/2509/03, *Working Paper*, 2003-03-03, Brussels.

———. (2003b). "Solvency II—Reflections on the General Outline of a Framework Directive and Mandates for Further Technical Work", Markt/2539/03, *Working Paper*, 2003-09-19, Brussels.

———. (2004a). "Solvency II—Organisation of Work, Discussion on Pillar I Work Areas and Suggestions of Further Work on Pillar II for CEIOPS", Markt/2543/03, *Working Paper*, 2004-02-11, Brussels.

———. (2004b). "The Draft Second Wave Calls for Advice from CEIOPS and Stakeholder Consultation on Solvency II", Markt/2515/04, *Working Paper*, 2004-10-11, Brussels.

IAIS Solvency & Actuarial Issues Sub-committe (2002). *Principles on Capital Adequacy and Solvency*. Basle, Switzerland: IAIS. January.

RGA International Reinsurance Company Limited (2010). "Solvency-II's Long Reach: Beyond Europe", Press Release by Reinsurance Group of America Inc. Available at: *http://www.rgare.com/media-center/Documents/10253_Solvency_ Brochure_EN-FINAL-LowRes.pdf*

Steffen, T. (2008). "Solvency II and the Work of CEIOPS", *Geneva Papers on Risk and Insurance—Issues and Practice* 33(1): 60–65.

Vaughan, T.M. (2009). "The Implications of Solvency II for U.S. Insurance Regulation", Policy Brief, Networks Financial Institute at Indiana State University.

Von Bomhard, N. (2010). "The Advantages of a Global Solvency Standard", *Geneva Papers on Risk and Insurance—Issues and Practice* 35(1): 79–91.

10 Risk Management and Enterprise Risk Management (ERM) Practices for Non-life Insurance Companies

Ruchi Agarwal and Jake Ansell

Risk Management Background

Risk concerns a future event with several potential outcomes. Some of the outcomes will lead to loss while others may be either neutral or beneficial. The potential losses are a concern for the businesses and individuals, and require management. In the 17th century, with the advent of the Industrial Revolution, with an increase in loss of goods, loss of ships and war raised concern with the growing merchant classes, especially among the sea-faring trade. This uncertainty about the loss and its management led to the development of marine insurance industry and hence the first insurance companies (Huybrechts and Van Hooydouk, 2000). Subsequently insurance principles developed by utilising the law of large numbers.

Five stages of risk management can be said to have evolved over the period since the 17th century. These are: classic risk management (CRM), traditional risk management (TRM), integrated risk management (IRM), enterprise risk management (ERM) and governance, risk and compliance (GRC). CRM can be characterised as the period in which the definition and terms related to risk management evolved and risk management was recognised as an important stream in insurance companies. TRM focused more on risk inside the companies. IRM superseded CRM and emphasised on the risk associated with the stakeholders like third party liability risk, public liability risk, etc. ERM took a holistic view of the external risks and integrated it with the company's objectives. The final stage is aligning the risk management with corporate governance under GRC practices (see Figure 10.1 for the development of risk management over time).

Figure 10.1

Development Stages of the Risk Management

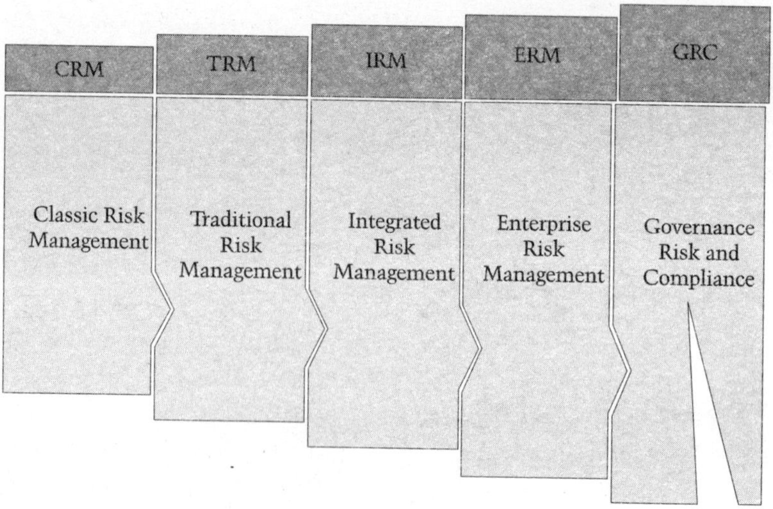

During the period of CRM, the definition of probability of loss, severity of loss, probable maximum loss (PML), estimated maximum loss (EML) and principles of insurance were the focus of insurance companies. Realisation by insurance companies of the need to manage their own risk by making risk pools and transfer the risk to reinsurance companies and retrocession companies added new dimension to the CRM. Very little research has been published on risk management within insurance companies until 1950 (Cummins, 1987; Weiss and Qiu, 2008).

The birth of risk communication internally within the companies, incorporation of formal risk prevention and mitigation methods helped in defining the accountability for risk among the line managers and supervisors. Furthermore, it increased the level of awareness and education among the managers and corporates towards risk management. The risk like market risk, credit risk, liquidity risk and operation risk related to each separate department like underwriting, claims, accounting, marketing in insurance companies were managed by their unit heads or the managers in silos (Cumming and Hirtle, 2001; Hoyt, 2003; Meulbroek, 2002; Miccolis *et al.*, 2000). During this period, the companies started giving formal training, workshop and education to its employees to manage the internal risk (Nielson *et al.*, 2005). Within the same period, the definition of risk management evolved. According to Bannister and Bawcutt (1981), risk management is "the identification, measurement and economic control of risks that threaten the assets and earnings of a business or other enterprise" (Crockford, 1982).

The Insurance industry faced financial turmoil with rising liability claims from third parties (Nielson *et al.*, 2005) and public liability claims e.g.: Asbestos claims in the US, high claims in particular region due to natural catastrophes, 9/11 terrorist attack, etc. Rapidly growing claims impacted on insurers' capital and solvency margins. This made insurance companies realise the need to think 'outside the box' and raised concerns for its stakeholders. Over the period of time, directors and officers liability claims became an important concern for many corporates. Burgeoning third party claims which led to higher premium, worker compensation pay outs and LMX spiral shorten the capacity and availability of reinsurance and retrocession. Repercussions of series of insolvency of insurance companies and reinsurance companies (Chen and Wong, 2004) led to increase in the role of credit rating agencies and strict regulatory regime. IRM is now often used by insurance companies for credit rating purpose which help the companies in setting new risk control language to compare with other companies (Mikes, 2005). IRM involves the identification, assessment of collective risk that affects firm value and implementation of firm-wide strategy to manage those risk (Meulbroek, 2002).

IRM helped organisation in bringing together various risks which were earlier managed by each department in separate silos. With the growth and geographical expansion of insurance companies in other countries, there is a clear need to align this integrated risk in holistic manner with organisational objective. The origin of the ERM framework was started with the Committee of Sponsoring Organisations of the Treadway Commission (COSO) along with Price Waterhouse Coopers (PWC) to evaluate and improve their organisations ERM which states that "ERM encompasses the way to align risk appetite and strategy, enhance risk response like risk avoidance, reduction, sharing and acceptance" (COSO, 2004).

ERM is a holistic approach, but sadly there are various definitions of ERM. Under the ERM framework, insurance risk, investments risk, credit risk, asset-liability management risk, liquidity risk, operational risk and environmental risks are covered. ERM is an on-going learning process where enterprise management should set clearly defined business model, well-articulated risk appetite and risk strategy, and risk exposure accumulation. It helps in developing well-integrated business processes for sales, marketing, underwriting, pricing, claims handling, reserving and investment functions and processes and developed and tested robust risk valuation and risk model that are operational for day-to-day business engagement of insurance companies. Towers Watson (2010) published a highly valuable report on ERM with six major findings regarding risk and capital management progress among insurers worldwide and ERM performance in crisis.

Good governance is a desirable state for all the companies where three terms GRC are closely related. Risk Governance is the ability to facilitate decision making about risk within modern society and is developed through gaining maturity in dealing with risks, having established the procedures, and ensuring everyone understands the approaches through training and effective implementation of the approaches aligned to the strategic objective of the organisation (Andreeva *et al.*, 2012). Through compliance it ensures the stated requirements are implemented. GRC implementation in companies encourages embedding rules, processes and control. It also provides better transparency, efficiency and accuracy in day to day working.

The Economic Intelligence Unit (EIU)[1] finds insurers have major problems in dealing with complex procedures which are difficult to model or automate, inconsistent methodologies, incompatible technologies, reconciling inconsistent or redundant data from multiple sources, boundaries issues between the departments with managers trying to hold authority in their own domain and too many manual processes, etc. (Economic Intelligence Unit, 2009).

1. EIU surveyed 446 senior executives in which 58 were from insurance industry.

Terms Used and Differentiation, Tensions between ERM and TRM and Silo Approach

It is unfortunate that ERM has not been clearly defined, but this reflects the dynamism within the environment of insurance companies which are subject to many different types of risk. Six terms have been used as synonyms for ERM; these are enterprise wide risk management (EWRM), holistic risk management (HRM), corporate risk management (CRRM), business risk management (BRM), integrated risk management (IRM) and strategic risk management (SRM).

While a few authors hold different view, most suggest that risk management can be divided into two categories: TRM and ERM. They support the view that the individual risk categories are separately managed in risk silos under TRM while ERM is synonymous with IRM, HRM, EWRM and SRM (Hoyt and Liebenberg, 2011; Casualty Actuarial Society, 2003). Some authors further elaborate the terms and have shown little differentiation from ERM (Mikes, 2005; D'Arcy, 2001).

Difference between TRM and ERM

TRM employed a silo approach; risk is managed by individual, not integrated with the other risk present in the organisation. ERM considers all risk in a holistic manner, integrating it with organisational objective (Hoyt, 2003; McShane *et al.*, 2011; Meulbroek, 2002; Miccolis *et al.*, 2000; Nielson *et al.*, 2005; Shenkir and Walker, 2011). Some authors argue that ERM helps in creating more value for the firm by increasing their capital efficiency and reducing the stock price volatility and supports overall better informed decision making (Hoyt and Liebenberg, 2008). More commonly, it could be understood that ERM supports interrelating the risk with each other to visualise the overall value to the organisation. For example a change in underwriting terms and condition might be able to reduce policy risk but can increase the risk of default by the policy holders in paying the premium, may impact reinsurance contracts and overall credit rating.

TRM empowers head of a department or unit managers to take decisions for their department or unit. This is contrary to this ERM which provides power to chief risk officer (CRO), chief executive officer (CEO) and board of directors to take the decision; sometimes the risk committee and audit committee along with the top management take the decision regarding risk matters (Adams *et al.*, 2011; Nocco *et al.*, 2006). The committee member and top management may have expertise and skills from diverse fields, are able to identify, analyse and correlate the risk from different perspectives which is not possible through risk managed in silos.

TRM is based on simple approach to follow compliance set by the regulator or the company internal risk management policy. In case of ERM, however, the compliance map becomes more complex and harder for the regulator to follow, especially when there are so many international regulations in place like COSO, Sarbanes-Oxley (SOX), Basel, Solvency, IRDA, etc., with too many guidelines that are costly to implement. The decision under ERM is influenced by too many people who can create chaos and confusion in implementation, sometimes there are delays as well in taking decisions.

Under TRM, risk needs to be prevented and controlled but under ERM, risk is viewed as an opportunity for profits and linked to organisational risk appetite. ERM uses the simulation and modelling techniques which help in offsetting some risk automatically by exploiting natural hedges which is not possible through traditional risk management VaR (value at risk) techniques of correlated risk (D'Arcy, 2001).

Need of ERM and Interest in Research

Deregulation, globalisation, cut throat competition, expansion and growth in emerging markets, consolidation and joint venture of the companies, fast moving technology changes in information technology (IT) and e-commerce, advance in technology, product innovation, recent financial crisis, increase in natural catastrophes shackle the regulators and raise concerns for the organisations. There is a need to think beyond the current practices and look for changes in their existing risk management policies and practices (Thomson, 2007).

Most of the research till now is related to Value of Firm and ERM and few of the paper explored its implementation of ERM while very few papers concern themselves with insurance industry implementation.

Definition of ERM Given by Regulatory Bodies and Standards

The Cadbury Report (1992) started with a significant contribution related to corporate governance which was further developed by Turnbull (2001) on internal controls and risk management. These reports helped in building an initial platform for risk management framework in UK companies. Its latest version published in 2008 elaborated more on the relationship between chairman and chief executive officer, role of non-executive directors, reporting on internal controls and financial reporting of all registered companies in the UK (Deighton and Dix, 2009). The consequence can be seen in the reflection of these regulations in listing rules of London Stock Exchange, Control and Transparency Act (KonTraG).

The direct impact of financial crisis and credit crunch especially the default of big companies like Enron lead US regulators to make rule-based stringent compliance to provide policy holder protection. Section 404 of (SOX) Act (2002) requires more transparency in the company's accounts, risk management, establishment and adherence of rule-based process, co-ordination and reporting of activities. This regulation emphasised some parts of ERM activities like co-ordination, adoption of risk-based approaches which affected the US market to a great extent (Thomson, 2007). In 2003, Section 303A of the New York Stock Exchange Listed Manual stated the requirement of chief executive officers, senior management and audit committee to work together to manage company's exposure to risk, however there is a need to emphasise ethical standard of risk by the audit committee (Votano *et al.*, 2004).

The need of ERM was recognised by the regulatory bodies as a part of good governance, co-ordination and reporting, however the definitions and guidelines for establishment of framework and scope of ERM remain as an open question. There is a clear requirement of set of ERM rules which are universally applicable, that can be followed by multinational companies (MNCs). As a consequence, this lead to emergence of involvement of four major interconnected parties to set guidelines for establishment of ERM; special commission formed by joint effort of various countries, financial service international regulatory bodies, actuarial bodies and credit rating bodies. A reflexion of this can be seen in most of the country's internal regulations of risk management and in stock exchanges' requirements (see Figure 10.2).

COSO (2004) published guidelines for Internal control integrated framework through ERM, which became one of the most cited pieces of regulation among the academic researchers (Boatright, 2011; COSO, 2004; Deighton and Dix, 2009; Manab *et al.*, 2012; O'Donnell, 2005; Shenkir and Walker, 2011; Thomson, 2007).

According to COSO (2004), ERM is a "process which is affected by an entity's board of directors, management and other personnel and applied in strategy setting across the enterprise. It also helps in identifying potential events that may affect the entity and manage risk to be within its risk appetite, to provide reasonable assurance regarding the achievement of entity objectives."

Solvency-II guidelines are based on set of principles which were tested in the market before execution in October 2012. It involves an integrated approach for insurance provision, capital requirement based on internal risk model of the company with the recognition of diversification and risk mitigation. It also establishes the link to International Accounting Standard Board work on insurance contracts. In ERM context, Pillar I focuses on identification and quantification of all risks given as per the balance sheet, Pillar II emphasises on good risk management practices and Pillar III works on disciplinary actions and its linkage with other stakeholders (Deighton and Dix, 2009). Pillar II focuses on ORSA (OwnRisk and Solvency Assessment) which seems to be a part of ERM. It could be interpreted that good risk management is a part of ERM practices followed by insurance organisation as per the Solvency-II regime.

According to the Casualty Actuarial Society (2003), ERM is defined as "The process by which organisations across all industries assess, control, exploit, finance and monitor risks from all sources. It supports increase in the organisation's short and long term value to its stakeholders."

According to Standard & Poor's (S&P) (2005), ERM is a "highly tailored analytic process which recognizes each insurer's unique structure, products, mix of business, potential earnings streams, cash flows, and investment strategy". It emphasised that ERM gains value by the benefits and risks of a diversified base of products, investments and geographic

Figure 10.2

The Bodies Creating the Need for ERM

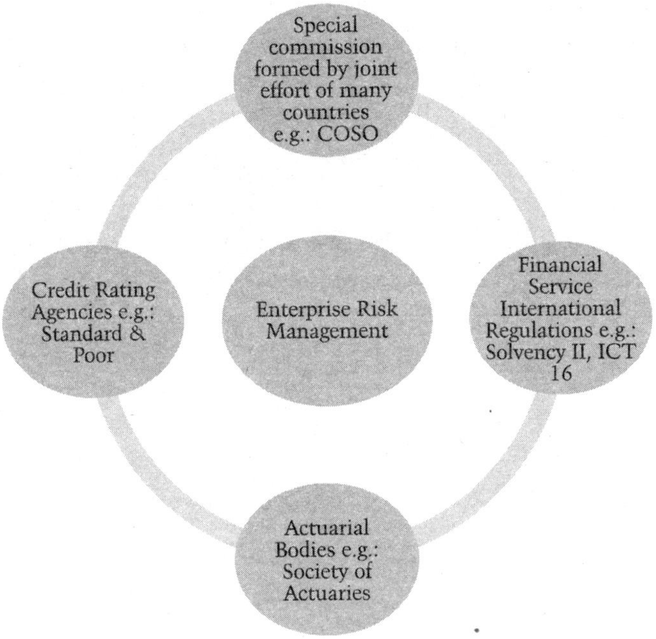

spread of risk (the benefits of uncorrelated or partially correlated risks). For evaluation, S&P looked at a company's processes in five areas: risk-management culture, risk control, extreme-event management, risk and capital models, and strategic risk management.

Interpretation of Enterprise Risk Management Definition

In this section, we observed that there are common elements in the above given definitions of ERM by Solvency-II (Sol II), COSO, Society of Actuaries (SoA) and Standard & Poor's (S&P) which are listed below:

1. ERM is affected by an entity's board of directors, management and other personnel (COSO).
2. ERM is applied in strategy setting (COSO); ERM is a part of SRM(S&P).

3. ERM must be applied across the enterprise (COSO).
4. ERM supports identifying potential events that may affect the entity (COSO), ERM helps in identification and quantification of risk (Sol II), ERM helps in assessing, controlling, exploiting and monitoring risk (SoA), risk control is a major element of ERM (S&P).
5. ERM helps in managing the risk to be within its risk appetite (COSO), ERM supports Good Risk Management practices (Solvency-II), ERM recognises each insurer's unique structure, products, mix of business, potential earnings streams, cash flows and investment strategy (S&P).
6. ERM process should provide reasonable assurance regarding the achievement of entity objectives (COSO).
7. ERM helps in developing internal risk model of the company with the recognition of diversification and risk mitigation (Sol II), It is a process that recognises the benefits and risks of a diversified base of products, investments and geographic spread of risk that can quantify the benefits of uncorrelated or partially correlated risks (S&P).
8. ERM has linkage with other stakeholders (e.g., following accounting standards) (Solvency-II).
9. ERM increase the organisation's short- and long-term value to its stakeholders (SoA).
10. Risk-management culture and extreme-event management are also the criteria to evaluate ERM practices in insurance companies (S&P).

ERM Definition: A Reflection from Regulations and Standards

On the basis of the essential element of ERM definition mentioned by COSO, Solvency II, Society of Actuaries and Standard & Poor's, we have developed a new definition of ERM

> ERM is an effective method of applying strategic risk management across the enterprise by a Chief Risk officer involving board of directors, top management, risk committee, audit committee and other personnel in decision making of identifying, quantification and control of the risk according to risk appetite of the enterprise. It supports in setting internal risk models to get benefit from uncorrelated or partially correlated risk and set up an ERM Framework involving risk communication, training and risk reporting.

Gaps in Implementation of Good Risk Management

There are very few papers, and regulation, which actually define good risk management and good ERM. There are few initial observations about barriers to implementation such as resistance to change, lack of education, lack of training and complex process which slow down the initiatives to implement ERM practices in insurance companies. Furthermore, with so many organisations (SOX, Solvency II, COSO, S&P and Society of Actuaries) with their distinct guidelines and regulations, and the involvement of too many parties/stakeholders (e.g., CEO, CRO, board of directors, Actuaries, Auditors, compliance officers, divisional heads, etc.) make ERM implementation even more time consuming and costly. Not only this, if insurance companies are able to develop it, there are no industry standard set criteria to compare or to know the level of effective implementation. All this makes it more complex, the misconception about good or bad ERM is during worst case scenarios such as deep recession and major natural catastrophe when good ERM could be said to have safeguarded the enterprise from foreseen and unforeseen losses. Equally, though, such outcome in worst case scenario may simply be to good fortune. Therefore good ERM practices cannot be just evaluated on the basis of single scenario rather should be tested against set of various combinations of different scenarios.

According to COSO (2004), the eight ERM components are the criteria to judge the effective implementation of ERM: internal environment (includes ethical values, risk appetite, risk attitude, risk culture), objective setting, identification of internal and external events, risk assessment, risk response, risk control, information and communication and risk evaluation. In other words, it can be interpreted that good ERM should ensure good internal environment, good risk management linked to organisational objective, good communication and regular monitoring of the process.

Few academician supports the argument that for good ERM implementation, practice of good risk management should be emphasised (Nielson *et al.*, 2005). While others argue that the tone of ERM should be set by the top management by setting example and it should not only link to organisational objective but also with each division's objective (Deighton and Dix, 2009). Sharing ERM implementation plan with entire stakeholders affects positively shareholders' value (Deighton and Dix, 2009), while in contrast, according to McShane *et al.* (2011, good risk management increases the value of the firm but surprisingly good ERM does not provide any additional value to the firm. It again questions the criteria to judge good ERM and actual definition of ERM considered.

Insurance companies are risk takers, therefore they are the most prone to the extreme risk events. It is obvious that they should have robust risk management system and set the example for other industries as well. If implementing ERM can create a robust financial system which will reduce the insolvency of the firms, create more value to not only shareholders but to all stakeholders in the companies, reduce cost, reduce unnecessary time spent on repetition of work, treating customer fairly, achieving enterprise objective, offsetting the risk by optimum diversification of portfolio of risk and provides risk as a profit opportunity, then it might be assessed as being good. Therefore, insurance companies should get benefit from ERM implementation, however the complex the set of issues they deal with may compromise achievement of this kind (Hoyt and Liebenberg, 2008; Santori, 2005).

Establishing Good Enterprise Risk Management Practice through Setting Benchmark

In this section, we express our beliefs in the way forward for ERM practice. It would be useful if all the regulatory bodies could combine to provide a common platform for setting the benchmark for ERM practices. It could start with identification of the best model of ERM across the countries which have been widely tested and tried, and that can be replicated in other countries. The process should be reviewed on a regular basis. The insurance companies can set ERM benchmark practices by following country level ERM practices after a group consensus with the local regulator and same can be done for the different department's level implementation. It will also help in defining the role of each stakeholder in ERM implementation process which will make this process less complex. Implementation of good ERM does not only involve its implementation in current scenario through best practices but also it needs to keep pace with the latest events and development in the field e.g., Basel III and Solvency-II.

It is possible to specify the requirements on management as follows. The board of directors, risk committee members and audit committee members should be given training for implementation of ERM. There should be written ERM policy that should be shared with all stakeholders. Obviously it will ensure better transparency in the financial system. CRO must be highly qualified in ERM and have sufficient experience with regular training updates. The insurance companies must share their experience and knowledge through common platform and should participate in international conferences.

ERM Issues and Implementation in the UK and Indian Insurance Companies

In this section, we will discuss how the Financial Services Authority (FSA) in the UK analysed the problems in implementation of ERM in insurance companies and how Indian insurance companies can bear in mind this model for their benefit. Obviously this can be replicated in other countries as well applying similar set of rules and take into account market conditions.

The FSA has performed a survey in 2003 and repeated it in 2006 to understand the implementation of ERM practices in insurance industry in the UK and has identified numerous issues. The major issues they found were: the problem of insufficient knowledge and experience within the committee structures (e.g., audit committee and risk committee) in handling risk, lack of clarity in understanding the risk appetite statements, also there is a gap between the definition of risk appetite and its application in operational risk, lack of consistency in risk management approach. Furthermore, it is also found that lack of information dissemination across the departments in insurance companies creates problems for management in setting priority. This issue could be addressed by analysing the risk trends and understanding the requirement for risk-based capital (FSA, 2006), but this may require an industry-based solution rather than an individual company approach.

FSA (2008) further explored how robust ERM in insurance companies could respond to changing scenarios and changes in internal or external factors and their potential impacts on existing system. It emphasises that management is required to take action to address such changes in the scenario because of external or internal factors. Thereafter analysing the scenarios, FSA suggested that there needed to be clarity in defining the triggers that would require a committee nominated person to act, and how these triggers might affect the financial calculations, any set of required actions brought about by change which ultimately define the overall response of the insurance company in respect of change of an internal or external factor, and considered a review of existing ERM practice.

Subsequently, Solvency-I and Solvency-II guidelines were issued in testing phase in part with the various deadlines and finally Solvency-II guidelines were implemented in the UK completely by October 2012.

IRDA, the regulatory body for insurance in India, had issued corporate governance guidelines (IRDA, 2009) which throw light on responsibilities and duties of director, CEO and compulsory formation of risk committee, preparing risk management policy and linking it to risk appetite. The implementation of ERM practices, however, is still in nascent stage in Indian market.[2] In year 2012, Indian insurance market is open to more foreign concerns and foreign equity stake has almost doubled from the last year, earlier a foreign multinational company could only have a 24 per cent stake of an insurance company in the Indian market, this has now increased to 49 per cent. It is interesting to observe that half of the foreign insurance companies that invested in Indian general insurance market are from 2 major countries of Europe (the UK and Germany). With the greater foreign direct investment (FDI), there will be a need for further research in the lucrative rapidly growing Indian market including on the state of ERM

2. There are 27 non-life insurance companies in India insurance market: 4 public sector general insurance companies, 17 private sector insurance companies, 4 health insurance companies and 2 specialised institutions.

implementation. They can bear in mind the UK model for the development following FSA.

Conclusion

This paper has explored the development of risk management and especially ERM. It has considered the difficulties that arise with the lack of a standard definition of ERM. In evaluating the value of ERM, the lack of standardisation of the term means it is difficult to assess good ERM or compare it with alternative forms such as TRM. We advocate the need for the development of standardisation to provide a benchmark to assess performance of companies and especially insurance companies which are inherently risk takers.

Clearly the UK has established procedures for reviewing the implementation of ERM which may help India to develop their own procedures. The need for robust evaluation is important as the introduction of foreign investment in the Indian insurance market needs to be managed to the benefit of not only shareholders but all other stakeholders.

References

Adams, M., C. Lin and H. Zou (2011). "Chief Executive Officer Incentives, Monitoring, and Corporate Risk Management: Evidence from Insurance Use", *Journal of Risk and Insurance* 78(3), doi:10.1111/j.1539-6975.2011.01409.x

Andreeva, G., J. Ansell and T. Harrison (2012). "Risk Governance and Accountability", *Working paper*, University of Edinburgh Business School

FSA (2008). *Insurance Sector Briefing: Risk and Capital Management Update*, September. Retrieved from *http://www.fsa.gov.uk/pubs/other/isb_risk_update.pdf*

Boatright, J.R. (2011). "Risk Management and the Responsible Corporation: How Sweeping the Invisible Hand?", *Business and Society Review* 116(1): 145–70. doi:10.1111/j.1467-8594.2011.00380.x

Casualty Actuarial Society (2003). "Overview of Enterprise Risk Management", Report, May.

Chen, R., and K.A. Wong (2004). The Determinants of Financial Health of Asian Insurance Companies. *Journal of Risk and Insurance* 71(3): 469–99. doi:10.1111/j.0022-4367.2004.00099.x

COSO (2004). *Enterprise Risk Management—Integrated Framework*, September. Retrieved from *http://www.mastercca.cnam.fr/PDF/SUPPORT DE COURS/CCG 206-207/CCG207-APPLYING-COSO.pdf*

Crockford, G. (1982). The Bibliography and History of Risk Management: Some Preliminary Observations. *The Geneva Papers on Risk and Insurance* 7(23): 169–79. Retrieved from *http://www.genevaassociation.org/PDF/Geneva_papers_on_Risk_and_Insurance/GA1982_GP7(23)_Crockford.pdf*

Cumming, C. and B. Hirtle (2001). "The Challenges of Risk Management in Diversified Financial Companies", *Economic Policy Review*. Retrieved from *http://papers.ssrn.com/sol3/papers.cfm?abstract_id=844215*

Cummins, J.D. (1987). "Presidential Address American Risk and Insurance Associaticn Revitalizing Risk and Insurance Educaticn and Research", *The Journal of Risk and Insurance* 54(1): 9-20.

D'Arcy, Stephen P. (2001). "Enterprise Risk Management", *Journal of Risk Management of Korea* 12(1): 207-28. Retrieved from *http://onlinelibrary.wiley.com/doi/10.1002/cbdv.200490137/abstract*

———. (2001). "Enterprise Risk Management," *Journal of Risk Management of Korea* 12(1): 207-28.

Deighton, S. and R. Dix (2009). Governance and Risk Management in United Kingdom Insurance Companies. *British Actuarial* ..., (March), 1–54. Retrieved from *https://www.actuaries.org.uk/sites/all/files/documents/pdf/sm20090323.pdf*

Economist Intelligence Unit (2009). "Strengthening Governance, Risk and Compliance in Insurance Industry". Retrieved from *http://viewswire.eiu.com/report_dl.asp?mode=fi&fi=1424467127.PDF*

FSA (2006). Briefing (November). Retrieved from *http://www.fsa.gov.uk/pubs/other/isb_risk.pdf*

Hoyt, R.E. (2003). The Determinant of Enterprise Risk Management: Evidence from the Appointment of Chief Risk Officers 6(1): 37–52.

Hoyt, R.E. and A.P. Liebenberg (2011). "The Value of Enterprise Risk Management", *Journal of Risk and Insurance* 78(4): 795–822. doi:10.1111/j.1539-6975.2011.01413.x.

Hoyt, R. and A. Liebenberg (2008). "The Value of Enterprise Risk Management: Evidence from the US Insurance Industry", unpublished paper, accessed at: *http://www.aria* ..., 1–22. Retrieved from *http://www.soa.org/library/monographs/other-monographs/2008/april/mono-2008-m-as08-1-hoyt.pdf*

Huybrechts, M., E. Van Hooydouk and C. Dieryck (2000). *Marine Insurance at the Turn of the Millennium, Volume 2* (Vol. 26, p. 260). Intersentia nv. Retrieved from *http://books.google.com/books?id=wrgfG1xLxeQC&pgis=1*

IRDA (2009). *Corporate Governance Guidelines*. Retrieved from *http://www.irdaindia.org/Investment/corpo_gov_anx_2_050809.pdf*

Manab, N.A., S.N. Othman and I. Kassim (2012). "Enterprise-wide Risk Management Best Practices: The Critical Success Factors", *OIDA International Journal of Sustainable Development* 04: 03. Retrieved from *http://www.ssrn.com/link/OIDA-Intl-Journal-Sustainable-Dev.html*

McShane, M.K., A. Nair and E. Rustambekov (2011). "Does Enterprise Risk Management Increase Firm Value?", *Journal of Accounting, Auditing & Finance* 26(4): 641–58. doi:10.1177/0148558X11409160.

Meulbroek, L.K. (2002). "A Senior Management Guide to Integrated Risk Management", *Journal of Applied Corporate Finance* 14(4): 56–70. doi:10.1111/j.1745-6622.2002.tb00449.x.

Miccolis, J., S. Shah and T. Tillinghast (2000). *Enterprise Risk Management: An Analytic Approach*. Retrieved from *http://scholar.google.co.uk/scholar?hl=en&q=miccolis+and+shah+2000&btnG=&as_sdt=1,5&as_sdtp=#0*

Mikes, A. (2005). Enterprise Risk Management in Action. ... Centre for Analysis of Risk and Regulation: Discussion ..., (August). Retrieved from *http://www2.lse.ac.uk/researchAndExpertise/units/CARR/pdf/DPs/Disspaper35.pdf*

Nielson, N.L., A.E. Kleffner and R.B. Lee (2005). "The Evolution of the Role of Risk Communication in Effective Risk Management", *Risk Management & Insurance Review* 8(2): 279–89.

Nocco, B.W., N. Insurance, D.A. Carter, D.A. Rogers, B.J. Simkins, R. Brealey, B. Cornell, *et al.* (2006). *Applied Corporate Finance.*

O'Donnell, E. (2005). "Enterprise Risk Management: A Systems-thinking Framework for the Event Identification Phase", *International Journal of Accounting Information Systems* 6(3): 177–95. doi:10.1016/j.accinf.2005.05.002

Santori, Laura, Mark Puccia, Grace Osborne, Rob Jones and Hans Wright (2005). "Evaluating the Enterprise Risk Management Practices of Insurance Companies", *Standard & Poor's Ratings Direct*, Available at: *http://www.aaa-riskfinance.nl/files/file/SP_ERM_Findings_July_07.pdf*

Shenkir, W.G. and P.L. Walker (2011). "Enterprise Risk Management: Frameworks, Elements, and Integration", *Institute of Management Accountants (IMA)*. Retrieved from *www.imanet.org*

Thomson, J.C. (2007). "S OX 404 and ERM : Perfect Partners . . . Or Not ?", *The Journal of Corporate Accounting & Finance* (March/April), 29–37. doi:10.1002/jcaf.

Votano, J., M. Parham and L. Hall (2004). "Final NYSE : Corporate Governance Rules", *Chemistry and Biodiversity* 1-18. Retrieved from *http://onlinelibrary.wiley.com/doi/10.1002/cbdv.200490137/abstract*

Watson, Towers (2010). Global Workforce Study: US. Report available at: *https://www.towerswatson.com/~/media/Pdf/Press/2010/03/TWGWS_2010_US_Media_Deck.ashx)*

Weiss, M.A. and J. Qiu (2008). "The Jouranl of Risk and Insurance : A 75-Year Historical Perspective", *Journal of Risk and Management* 75(2): 253–74.

11 Who Needs Life Insurance the Most?

Nitin Hande

Introduction

India's rapid rate of economic growth over the past decade has been one of the most significant developments in the global economy. This growth traces its origin in the introduction of economic liberalisation in the early 1990s, which has equipped India to exploit its economic potential and substantially raise the standard of living of its people. Together with other financial services, insurance services contributed 7 per cent of the country's gross domestic product (GDP) in 2011-12. A well-developed and evolved insurance sector is a boon for economic development, as it provides long-term funds for infrastructure development and concurrently strengthens the risk-taking ability of the country. Further, insurance has been a notable employment generator, not only for the insurance industry, but has also created significant demand for a range of associated professionals such as brokers, insurance advisors, agents, underwriters, claims managers and actuaries. By the nature of its business, insurance is closely linked to saving and investing. Life insurance, funded pension systems and non-life insurance have accumulated a significant amount of capital over time, which can be invested productively in the economy. The mutual dependence of insurance and capital markets plays an instrumental role in channeling funds and investment capabilities to augment the development potential of the Indian economy.

India's growing consumer class, rising insurance awareness, increasing domestic savings and investments are among the most critical factors that have positively driven the market penetration of the insurance products among its consumer segments. However, there are large untapped areas, which have yet not benefited from the upside of insurance. Imparting financial literacy, incentivising Indian households to transfer savings from physical assets to financial assets and taking the distribution network to rural areas are expected to help bring more and more individuals within the insurance circumference. The insurance industry in India has visibly progressed since the time when businesses were tightly regulated and concentrated in the hands of a few public sector insurers. Following the passage of the Insurance Regulatory and Development Authority (IRDA) Act in 1999, India abandoned public sector exclusivity in the insurance industry in favor of market-driven competition. This shift has brought about major changes to the industry. The new era of insurance development has seen the entry of international insurers, the proliferation of innovative products and distribution channels, and the raising of supervision standards. After liberalisation, insurance sector has witnessed a neverbefore hike in the sales of insurance products. Industry has witnessed strong growth in the insurance premiums, increased number of players, product innovation and its advanced regulatory framework. Due to impact of these factors, along with strong economic growth in the last few years, India has positioned as a regional insurance hub and a rapidly developing financial centre. The insurance industry is amid an exciting journey—there needs to be a persistent endeavour to sustain what has already been achieved as well as expand beyond the current level. Furthermore, several reforms and policy measures, especially during the last couple of years, have enabled a favourable environment for insurance companies to flourish in the country. The coming years are critical as the regulator stance and approach of market participants will govern the strength, stability and the sustained growth of the insurance sector.

The insurance sector has become a major contributor to economic development, especially to infrastructure development. This growth has been fueled by India's multiplying consumer class, rising insurance awareness, increasing domestic savings and investments. Moreover, it has been the joint effort of all stakeholders, including the government, regulator and insurance companies to enable the positive momentum of this industry. But scene is not ending here. In last few years, insurers were shifting weight from the philosophy of 'growth *versus* profitability' to the 'profitable growth.' As a result, the focus shifted from 'growth' to 'profitability,' with product pricing becoming more rational based on more conservative assumptions. Product innovation continued and traditional policies gained some foothold in an otherwise unit-linked incentive product (ULIP) driven market. But the story not ends here. Due to focus on profitability, a class of unorganised worker has remained to tap by Life Insurers. I think this is the class who needs Insurance service the most, but till out of the list. Most of unorganised workers find insurance as an investment tool rather than risk manager. To find out the reason behind these factors, we have to discuss about the concept of life insurance.

Concept of Life Insurance

Life insurance is generally considered a means of protecting one's family against the unforeseeable circumstance of the death of an earning member. However, there are a number of other benefits that are not apparent. Some benefits accrue to the individuals and their families, while others assist economic development. For instance, an insurance company takes the risk of large and uncertain losses in exchange for small premiums. This gives a sense of confidence and security to the insured individual through the protection of insurance in the event of an unfortunate incident. In large sized commercial and industrial organisations, it facilitates operations as many of the risks are transferred to the insurer. Insurance, particularly life insurance, is one of the ways of providing for the future. A life insurance policy which gives an annuity is a combination of protection and investment. It increases the creditworthiness of the assured person because it can provide funds for repayment in the event of death. It also reduces losses owing to theft, robbery, fire accidents, etc. In addition, it serves as a solution to social problems.

In India, the history of life insurance can be traced to 1818 when the Oriental Life Insurance Company started in Kolkata. This organisation was basically founded to serve European clients and hence Indians who opted for an insurance cover were charged a much higher premium. The reason given was that Indians had a lower life expectancy on account of their lifestyle, while in fact this was a planned effort to keep Indians out of any kind of progress. The company failed in 1834. Then, in 1870 the British Insurance Act was passed and the last three decades of 19th century saw the emergence of the Bombay Mutual Life Assurance Society (1871), which became the first organisation to charge the same premium from all residents of India irrespective of their origin or nationality. The Oriental (1874) and Empire of India (1897) insurance companies began their activities in the Bombay Residency in the late 19th century. This period, however, was dominated by foreign insurance offices such as Albert Life Assurance, Royal Insurance, and Liverpool and London Globe insurance, which did good business in India. Indian insurers played a massive part in competition before freedom. After 1956-1999, the life insurance industry in India consisted of only one state insurer, Life insurance Corporation of India (LIC). According to the IRDA, the life insurance industry in India at present consists of 23 life insurance companies.

Insurance is a form of risk management which is used primarily to hedge against the risk of a contingent, uncertain loss. Insurance is defined as the equitable transfer of the risk of loss, from one entity to another, in exchange for payment. Insurance is essentially an arrangement where the losses experienced by a few are extended among many who are exposed to similar risks. It is a protection against financial loss that may occur due to an unexpected event. The transaction involves the insured assuming a guaranteed and known, relatively small, loss in the form of payment to the insurer in exchange for the insurer's promise to compensate or indemnify the insured in the case of a large, possibly devastating, loss. The insured receives a contract called an insurance policy which details the conditions and circumstances under which the insured will be compensated. Life insurance or life assurance is a contract between the policy owner and the insurer, where the insurer agrees to pay the designated beneficiary a sum of money upon the occurrence of the insured individual's death or other event, such as terminal or critical illness. In return, the policy owner agrees to pay a stipulated amount at regular intervals or in lump sums. Life-based contracts tend to fall into two major categories:

1. Protection policies: designed to provide a benefit in case of a specified event, typically against lump sum payment. A common form of this policy is term insurance.

2. Investment policies: the main objective is to facilitate the growth of capital by single or regular premiums. The common forms in this category include whole life, universal life and variable life policies.

For instance, while compensation is available to victims of industrial injuries and road accidents, financial difficulties on account of old age, disability or death is minimised. Investment of accumulated resources by the insurer facilitates the overall development of the country. Capital is usually risk averse, but if insurers provide protection against risks, then several investors would come forward to invest their funds. In many developed countries, citizens are to a certain extent protected by social security schemes provided by the government. These schemes offer financial aid to citizens who are eligible on grounds of unemployment, old age, sickness, disability, etc. The social security scenario in India is quite different, having traditionally been the responsibility of the family or community. However, with industrialisation, urbanisation, breakup of the joint family system and weakening of family bondage, it has become necessary to provide social security arrangements that are institutionalised and regulated by the state rather than the society. Issues relating to social security are listed in the directive principles of state policy. While social security and insurance, employment and unemployment form Item 23 of the concurrent list, the welfare of labour including conditions of work, provident fund, employee's liability, workmen's compensation, invalidity and old age pension and maternity benefits form Item 24, also of the concurrent list. During the initial years of development planning, it was believed that with the process of development, a greater number of workers would join the organised sector and eventually get covered by formal social security arrangements. However, the actual experience has proved otherwise. There is now almost a stagnation of employment in the organised sector with increase in the inflow of workers into the informal sector.

Term Insurance: The Purest Form of Insurance

The unorganised workforce is characterised by scattered and fragmented areas of employment, seasonality, lack of job security and low legislative protection. Currently, out of an estimated workforce of nearly 400 million, only less than 10 per cent have the benefits of formal social security protection. Although the government has a few centrally funded social assistance programmes like National Old Age Schemes and National Family Benefit Schemes, the number of people covered as well as the benefits is very meager. Furthermore, in a country like India, where there is no provision for unemployment benefits, the concept of insurance becomes extremely important. An individual is exposed to various risks in daily life and it will surprise one to note how many of these can actually be insured. Life insurance and general insurance companies offer a variety of products covering different types of risks. Not only is there a dearth of knowledge about these, but also most individuals are not aware of the value that insurance, as an option, could add to their lives. While affordability and the place of insurance in the list of an individual's priority in this context are important questions, quite a few are uninsured purely due to lack of awareness about insurance as a protection tool and details about the types of insurances that are possible. All stakeholders have the responsibility of creating this awareness. Representatives of insurance companies are doing ground work but most of their efforts are for pulling customer to whole life plan. With a small earning Indian unorganised labour force has, it is a serious issue to prevent them from purest form of insurance. When making financial decisions, we like to stress that circumstances matter. Your wants and needs make one decision good for you and another decision good for me. This is less true, though, in deciding whether to purchase term or whole life insurance. Term life insurance is almost always the better option. First, let's get an understanding of each type of insurance, and then we'll look at why term life insurance is usually a smarter choice.

What is Whole Life Insurance?

As the name implies, whole life insurance is a life insurance policy that covers you for your entire life, assuming you are paying the premiums. The idea that the policy has no end date is appealing to some customers. Whole life insurance differs from term life insurance because it provides both a death benefit and a savings account. Insurance agents like to refer to these 'forced savings' as a form of retirement savings. You can withdraw or borrow against this cash value savings account portion of the policy. In addition, insurers sell this policy by emphasising that the cash value grows over time. If you outlive the life of the policy, you can receive cash back. Since a portion of your premiums are going towards this savings account, whole life premiums typically cost 5-10 times more than term life premiums.

What is Term Life Insurance?

Term life insurance is life insurance that covers you during the life, or term, of the policy. Terms range in length from 1 to 20 years. There is no forced savings associated with term life insurance. For this reason, term life policies tend to be less confusing and more convenient for policy holders than whole life policies. Term life premiums are also significantly cheaper than whole life premiums, particularly if you are under age 50. You usually pay an annual renewable premium that increases in cost every year. This differs from whole life policies' constant cost premiums.

Why is Term Life Insurance Better?

Whole life insurance is usually significantly more expensive than term life insurance. You would assume this means your whole life policy provides a noticeable extra benefit. One purported benefit is that you can receive life insurance beyond age 65. Term life policies typically won't cover you beyond age 65. On the surface, this might seem attractive, but it doesn't really matter. The idea of life insurance is it provides for the people who depend on you and won't be able to care for themselves in the case of your death. For example, life insurance is designed to help provide for young children if their parents pass away. By the time your term policy expires—likely around age 65—your kids will be old enough to care for themselves. In addition, most liabilities, like loans, will be repaid by that age.

So how else do insurers justify the much higher premiums for whole life policies? They say a portion of your premiums goes towards an investment—it might be bonds, money-market instruments, stocks, etc. You can borrow against this savings account, or you can use it as a retirement account. This might seem like a good idea, except these policies typically come with large commissions and high fees. In addition, there are much better ways to invest for retirement. So with whole life insurance you are essentially paying a higher premium in order to put money into a bad retirement investment. You would do better to take the difference in premiums between the term life and whole life policies and invest it in something like a mutual fund. Buying whole life insurance is not always a bad idea as the high premiums are suited for wealthier people. Whole life policy holders might benefit from using the whole life policy in their estate planning or by setting up an insurance trust to pay estate taxes. Borrowing or withdrawing from the cash value could be a useful investment strategy as well. However, in the vast majority of cases, choosing term life instead of whole life insurance is the smart decision, especially those who have very few earnings.

Let us compare both plans simultaneously, Mr A wants life coverage of 10 lakh, he will call his insurance advisor, his advisor can suggest him a plan that will give guaranteed return policy that is Endowment policy which cost Mr A annually ₹ 28500. After 30 years, A will get 10 lakh plus bonus appox. 25 lakh. Mr A may satisfy with these calculations and may purchase his policy. But chance of another two stories is also possible. Case 1. Mr A is smarter one and he may compare this policy with term insurance policy.

Term Plan	*Endowment Plan*
Premium: ₹ 4000/year	Premium: ₹ 28,500/year
Tenure of policy: 30 years	Tenure of policy: 30 years
Total Premium Paid = 4000 x 30 =120,000	Total Premium Paid = 28,500 x 30 =855,000

If Mr A is business-minded person, he can calculate rate of returns in endowment plan. He found that 6.75 per cent returns which he thinks in comparison of inflation rate 6.75 is very less. He will also go through the term insurance plan and after checking the difference between the two plans, he will invest in equity schemes of mutual fund and in stock market for that matter where he can earn 12–15 per cent. He will get around 66 lakh after 30 years. Even if he invests it in Public Provident Fund (PPF) which gives him 8 per cent returns, he will get 30 lakh. Case 2: Mr A doesn't afford premium of ₹ 28,500. So he downgrades himself to a plan of 5 lakh coverage. This case is very serious because Mr A has affordability to get good protection for his family through term insurance, but he is not aware of it. Term insurance is a way for them who want to protect their family with sound amount after their death. One should have to consider insurance as a tool of risk management not as an investment tool.

Retirement Solutions

Risk of cconomic death is worse than natural death. Self-earned pension in a new practice in India. Government is not carrying the burden of a pension furthermore. Pension has been transferred to private sector. Risk of economic death is big than natural death. As old age income determines your retirement life, everybody should be aware about these terms. When a person reaches the age of retirement, it means that he is no longer considered fit to give the same amount of hard work he could when he was younger. Since retirement comes at a time when people enter their old age, it is also a very tricky situation for them because they lose out on the regular income they were generating. Moreover, due to age-related factors, they come to encounter a lot of issues pertaining to their health and their quality of life can suffer a major setback. This is why a lot of people make the wise decision to invest their pension amount in different investment opportunities. Pension annuity is also one of those investment opportunities where pensioners can easily deposit the retirement fund they received. With the help of a pension annuity calculator, they can also find out the most profitable way to maximise the income generated from their invested retirement funds. Through the pension annuity calculator, you can put in your financial details and work out the payment you will be requiring after retirement. These details could include your current age, the retirement age, the income you earned at the time and the amount of money you want to put in the pension annuity. These annuities are provided by the insurance providers with whom you enter into an agreement. A large number of people still in service plan for the amount they receive after retirement by investing money in annuities through payouts they make every month. Consulting an expert on annuities, you can easily work out with the help of a pension annuity calculator what you are up for when you retire. The expert will take you over the kind of returns you will need at that stage, helping you understand the course of action that best suits your requirements. Even with the latent tax application on your annuities, the pension annuity calculator helps you calculate the taxes that will be levied when you withdraw the money. Moreover, it also helps you in deciding which type of annuity among the fixed type and variable type you should go for. Through pension annuity calculator, you can work out which of these options will be more viable for you considering your own situation and preferences.

If you make the decision to invest your retirement funds in annuity, it is highly recommended and advisable for you to calculate both benefits and risks with the pension annuity calculator. This may also help you to understand the different conditions that apply on the agreement you entered into with the insurance provider. Moreover, with the pension annuity calculator, you can easily assess the total amount that would be payable on your part and the amount that you will be receiving. In this way, it helps you to create a deeper understanding of the pros and cons of the agreement you are planning to get into. To provide self-earned pension in affordable price, New Pension System (NPS) was introduced. The government has, through an executive order dated 10th October, 2003, mandated Pension Fund Regulatory and Development Authority (PFRDA) to act as a regulator for the pension sector. The mandate of PFRDA is development and regulation of pension sector in India.

The NPS reflects the government's effort to find sustainable solutions to the problem of providing adequate retirement income. As a first step towards instituting pensionary reforms, the Government of India moved from a defined benefit pension to a defined contribution-based pension system by making it mandatory for its new recruits with effect from 1st January, 2004. Since 1st April, 2008, the pension contributions of Central Government employees covered by the NPS are being invested by professional pension fund managers (PFMs) in line with investment guidelines of government applicable to non-government provident funds.

The NPS architecture is transparent and will be web-enabled. It would allow a subscriber to monitor his/her investments and returns under NPS, the choice of PFM and the investment option would also rest with the subscriber. The design allows the subscriber to switch his/her investment options as well as pension funds. The facility for seamless portability and switch between PFMs is designed to enable subscribers to maintain a single pension account throughout their saving period. The NPS has been designed to enable the subscriber to make optimum decisions regarding his/her future and provide for his/her old age through systemic savings from the day he/she starts his/her employment. It seeks to inculcate the habit of saving for retirement among the citizens. PFRDA also intends to intensify its effort towards financial education and awareness as a part of its strategy to protect the interest of the subscribers. PFRDA's efforts are an important milestone in the development of a sustainable and efficient voluntary defined contribution based pension system in India.

NPS and Term Insurance both are useful for the class who do not have resources for savings especially the unorganised labour force, agriculture workers, craftsmen, industrial workers, etc. To measure awareness of these terms in different classes of society, a questionnaire of 15 questions was set and given to 50 insurance customers. Thirty industrial workers whose monthly salary is below 12,000 and 20 corporate workers whose monthly salary was above 12,000 were respondents. All answers given by them were filled in the chart. To find the trends of observations, all answers were converted into bar chart diagrams. Analysis of answers of all the questions is given below one by one.

Question no. 1: In your point of view insurance is the tool of.....

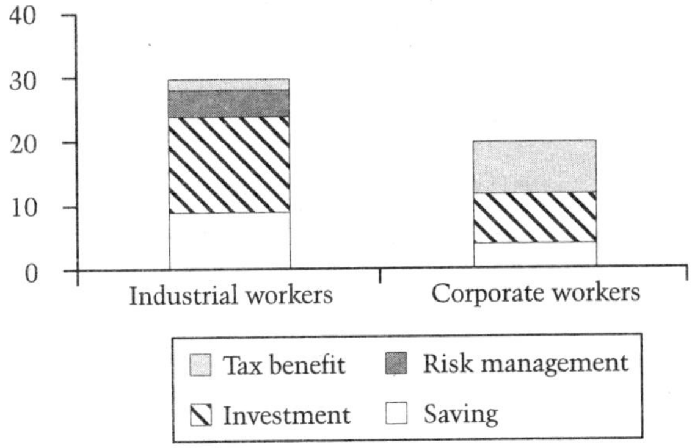

Question no. 2: Percentage of insurance premium against salary?

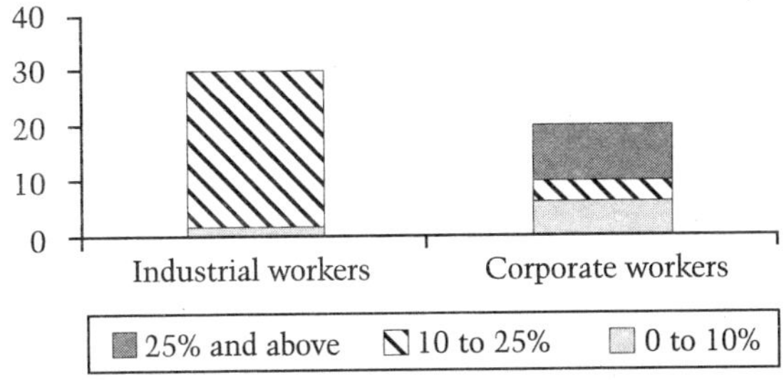

Question no. 3: Which type of policy you think is best for your needs?

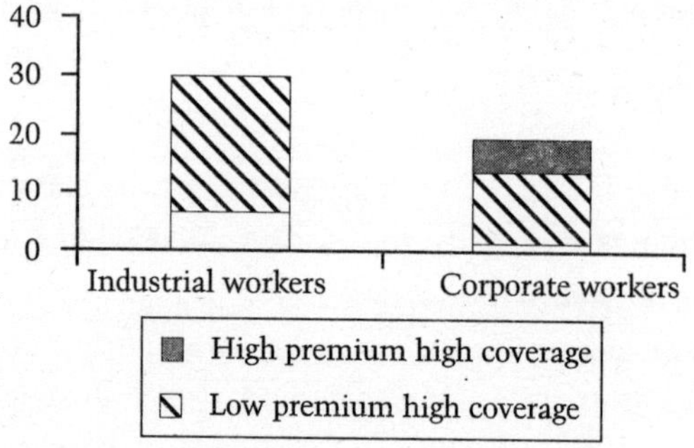

Question no. 4: Current insurance service provider?

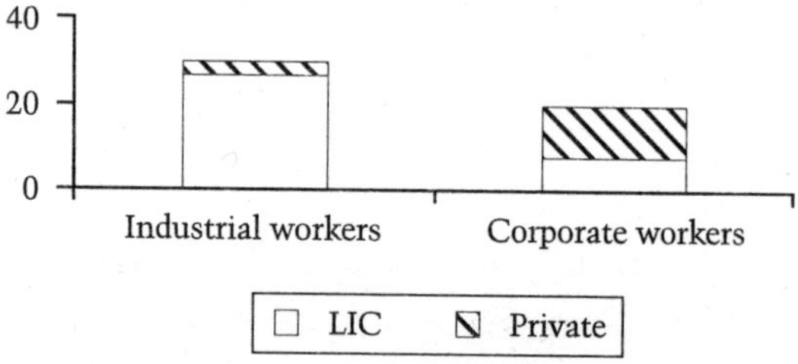

Question no. 5: Does LIC is more trustable than private companies?

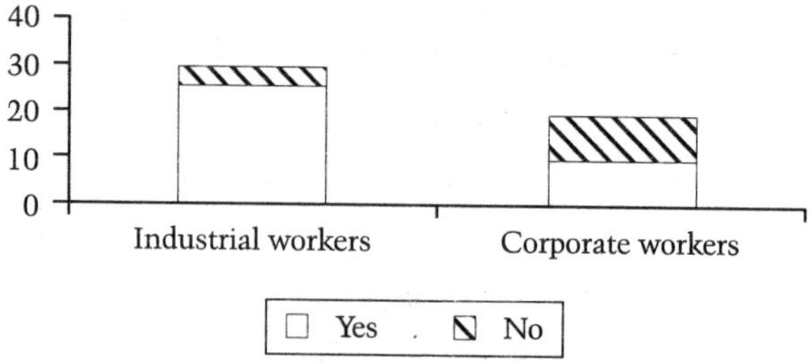

Question no. 6: Does LIC provides cheaper plans than private companies?

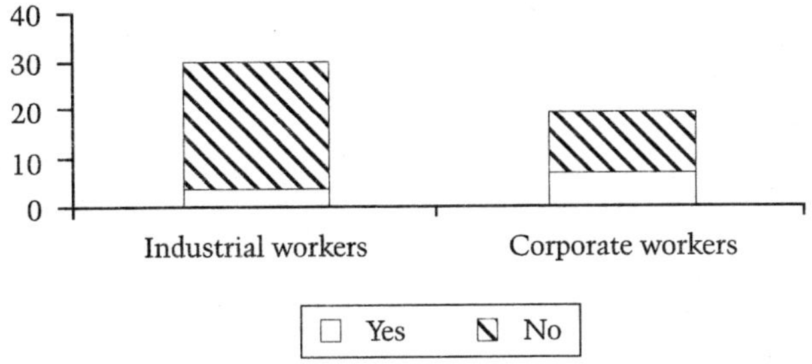

Question no. 7: Had you compared same category plans of different companies.?

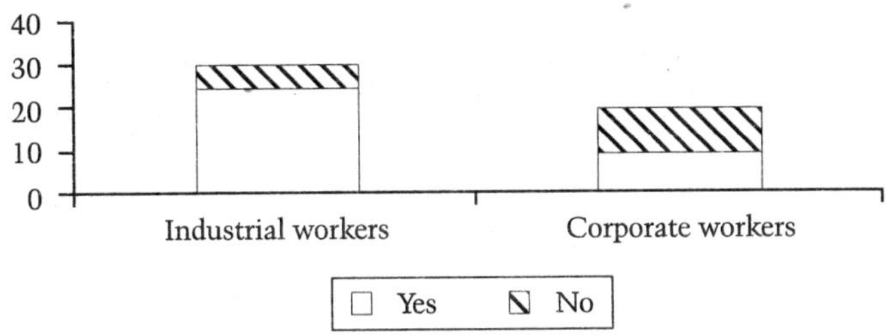

Question no. 8: Do you know term insurance?

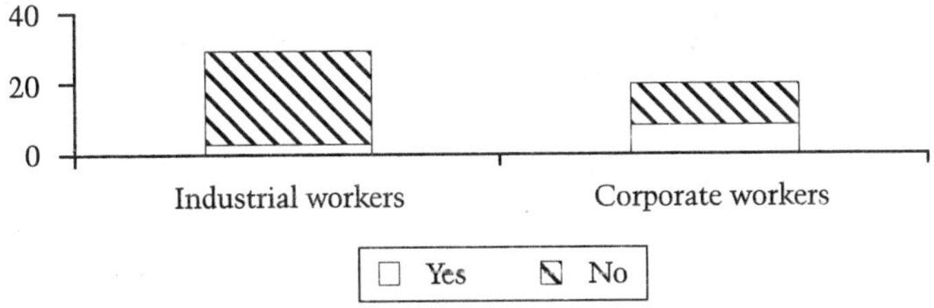

Question no.9: Did your insurance advisor advice you to purchase term insurance?

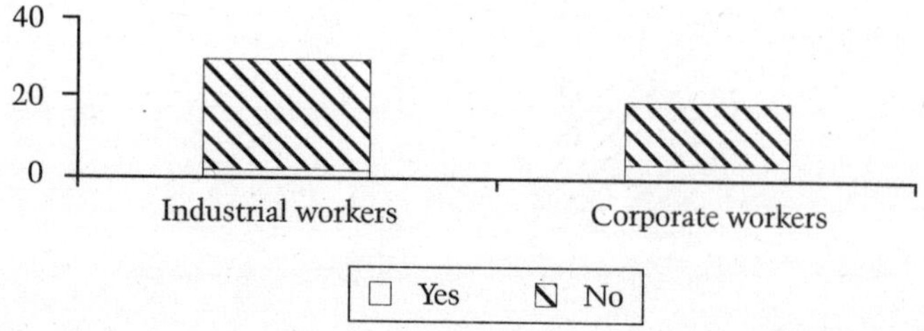

Question no. 10: Are you sure that you had taken enough coverage?

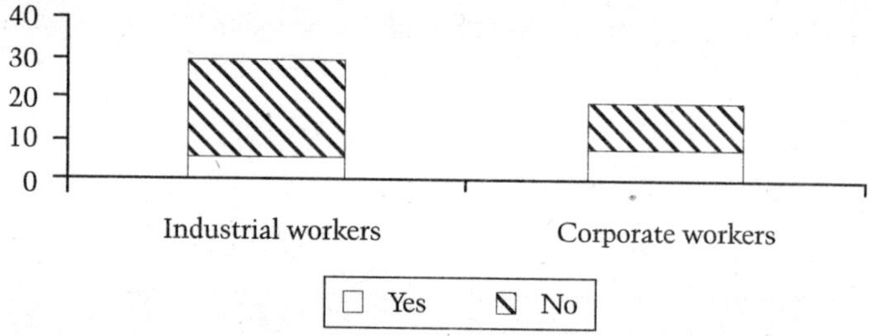

Question no. 11: Do you have any pension plan?

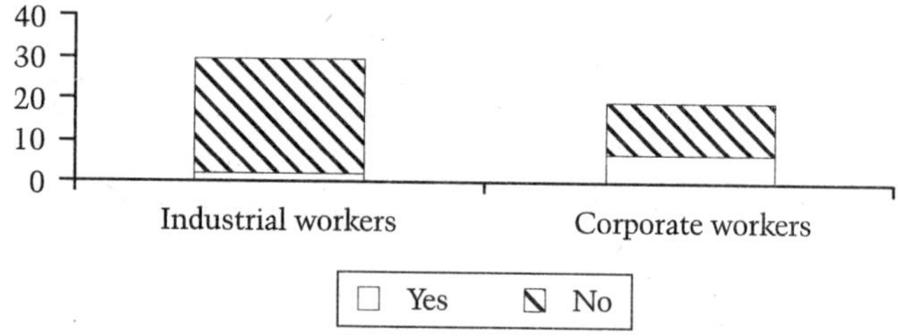

Question no. 12: Do you have any health plan?

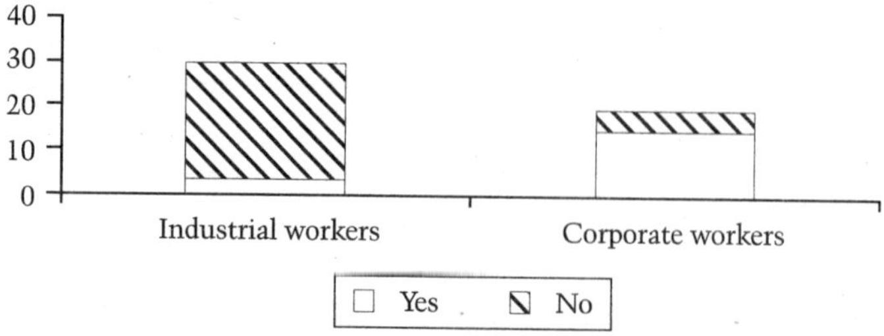

Question no. 13: Are you aware about NPS?

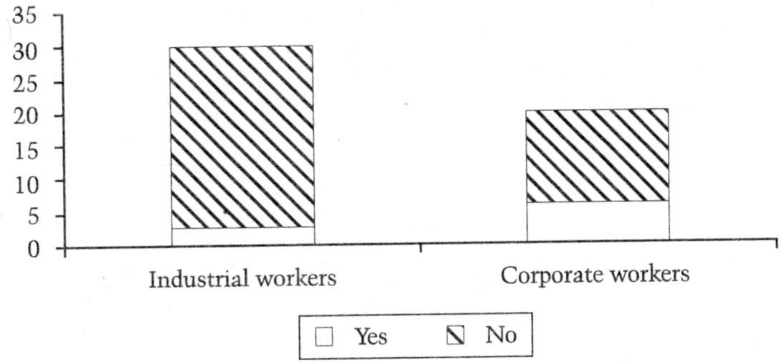

Question no. 14: Your experience with your insurer company?

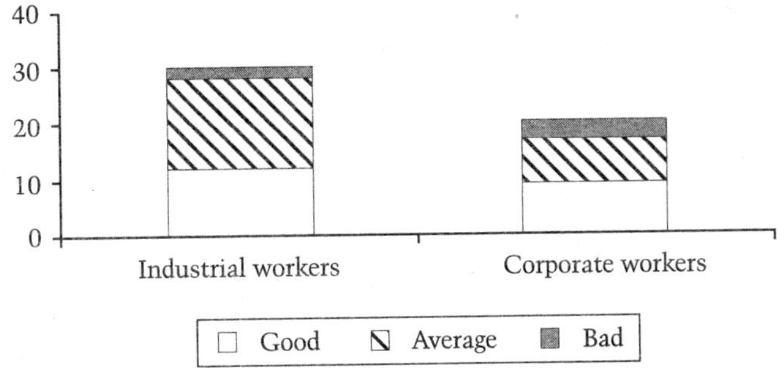

Question no. 15: Your experience with insurance advisor?

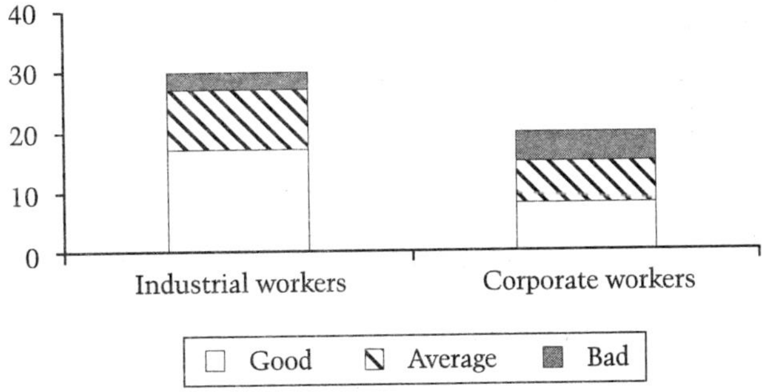

Table 11.1

Summary of Observations

Sr. no.	*Question Asked*	*Options*	*Industrial Workers (Total 30)*	*Corporate Workers (Total 20)*	*Overall (Total 50)*
1	In your point of view Insurance is the tool of.....	Saving	30%	20%	26%
		Investment	50%	0%	30%
		Risk management	13.33%	40%	24%
		Way to tax benefit	6.67%	40%	20%
2	Percentage of Insurance premium against salary?	Upto 10%	53.33%	30%	44%
		10% to 25%	20%	20%	20%
		Above 25%	26.67%	50%	36%
3	Which type of policy you think is best for your needs?	Low premium Low coverage	23.33%	10%	18%
		Low premium High coverage	76.67%	60%	70%
		High premium High coverage	0%	30%	12%
4	Current insurance service provider?	LIC	90%	40%	70%
		Private companies	10%	60%	30%
5	Does LIC is more trustable than private companies?	Yes	86.67%	50%	72%
		No	13.33%	50%	28%
6	Does LIC provide cheaper plans than private companies?	Yes	83.33%	45%	68%
		No	16.66%	55%	32%
7	Had you compare same category plans of different companies.	Yes	13.33%	35%	22%
		No	86.67%	65%	78%
8	Do you know Term Insurance?	Yes	10%	40%	22%
		No	90%	60%	78%
9	Did your insurance advisor advice you to purchase Term Insurance?	Yes	6.67%	20%	12%
		No	93.33%	80%	88%
10	Are you sure that you had taken enough coverage?	Yes	20%	40%	28%
		No	80%	60%	72%
11	Do you have any pension plan?	Yes	6.67%	35%	30%
		No	93.33%	65%	70%
12	Do you have any Health plan?	Yes	13.33%	75%	38%
		No	86.67%	25%	62%
13	Are you aware about NPS?	Yes	10%	30%	18%
		No	90%	70%	82%
14	Your experience with your insurer company?	Good	40%	45%	42%
		Average	53.33%	40%	48%
		Bad	6.67%	15%	10%
15	Your experience with Insurance Advisor?	Good	56.67%	40%	50%
		Average	33.33%	35%	34%
		Bad	10	25%	16%

Findings

As we are saying that insurance literacy is increasing but 78 per cent of respondent did not know tern insurance concept among which major part is from a low-income profile group. This was the group that should have be gone with term insurance because their earning is very small. So rather going with endowment plan, they can get good coverage in affordable price with term insurance. Members of this group should not consider insurance policy for tool of savings, as we know returns in the life insurance are always less than inflation rates. But 60 per cent of this group purchase policy for savings. . This group is not aware of various investment options as compare to corporate workers who are keener about various insurance products, various insurance companies and various investment tools. Many insurance advisors are forcing customer to purchase such insurance product that gives advisors good amount of commission. So they are hiding option of term insurance from customers. Numbers from Table 11.1 show that only 12 per cent respondents were intimated for term insurance by their advisors. In industrial workers, the rate was only 6.67 per cent. These numbers have their own voice. In my point of view, 78 per cent respondents miss the chance to get purest form of insurance just because their advisors want to make more money. This is malpractice of the business. Every human has tendency to get maximum benefit in minimum sacrifice. Here also 70 per cent of respondents want maximum coverage in minimum premium; 76.67 per cent of industrial workers want such protection but very few of them are aware about term insurance.

The purpose of launching NPS in India was to cover that sector which does not come under any form of socioeconomic security scheme. This is a way where unorganised labour force, farmers, craftsmen and industrial workers can be benefited with regular amount in their old age. But here awareness about NPS in industrial workers is very rare. In my point of view, efforts put in publicity and advertisement by governments are not upto their marks. Information regarding NPS should reach to the last person in the nation. In market, there are various pension plans of almost each and every insurer company but only corporate workers and middle class is showing interest in them. Here I think industrial workers are playing in blind. Because all that they are getting is spend on their daily needs. The little money what they can save or invest they used it for getting endowment policy. So after unfortunate death of breadwinner, their family will get very little amount which can't long last. In case of survival of him, he will get sum assured plus bonus which they think is a big amount at a time purchase policy. But inflection trends make that amount just to buy groundnuts, as trends show prices multiplies 10 times in 20 years. Most of customers from industrial workers know that interesting fact is these workers are satisfied with their insurance company and insurance agent and most of them are customer of LIC. Customer is not blaming that his advisor doesn't gave him proper information about most suitable policy. Most of customers think LIC is more trustable brand and LIC has cheaper plan than private companies.

Corporate workers are showing interest in health plan and pension plan but industrial workers are far behind in this factor. As life and health of industrial workers are more risky, risk factor is not forcing them to get suitable healthcare plan. Corporate workers can get earnings even after their retirement through consulting, but industrial workers don't have such options. They should manage a fund in their working age which can be used after retirement. But here in pension plans of insurance companies or NPS, they are not taking part. This is a serious issue. Most of corporate workers are also failing to compare plans of same category but of various companies.

Conclusion and Recommendations

Death or economical death of breadwinners disturbs entire life of dependents. As this is a socioeconomic problem, government has to do some regulations for unorganised workers. There should be mandatory health care policy, term insurance and participation in NPS to everybody. Insurance companies have to focus on term insurance which costs less and gives more coverage. There should be some provision for workers who work under non-organised sector. Publicity of NPS should have done more effectively. Healthcare insurance should also campaign in industrial sectors. Ministry of social welfare has to lead campaign for spreading insurance in every part of the nation and to every citizen of India. Unique identification (UID) Adhaar card can be use for enrolling low income group in social security schemes by giving direct subsidies to people below poverty line because this is a class of society who needs the life insurance most.

References

Ahuja, R. (2003). "Old Age Income Security for the Poor", *Economic & Political Weekly* 38(37).

Asher, M. (2010). "Pension Plans, Provident Fund Scheme and Retirement Policies: India's Social Security Reform Imperative", *ASCI Journal of Management* 39(1): 1-18.

Indian Statistic Institute. *Statistic Abstract*.

Maclean, F.J. (1931). *The Human Side of Insurance*. London: Sampson Low, Marston & Co.

Ray, R.M. (1941). *Life Insurance in India: Its History, Law, Practice and Problems*. Bombay: Allied Publishers.

Visaria, P. (2001). "Demographics of Aging in India", *Economic & Political Weekly* 36(22).

12 Dynamic, Evolving Reinsurance

A Relook at Risk Management Measures in the Indian Reinsurance Sector

Sudha Rajagopal and
Padma Srinivasan

Introduction

Reinsurance is defined by M. Grossmann as "the transfer of a part of the hazards or risk that a direct insurer assumes by way of insurance contract or legal provision on behalf of an insured, to a second insurer carrier, the Reinsurer, who has no direct contractual relationship with the insured."

Insurance or the risk taking and risk managing process is a three-tier function, with participation from individuals at the first and then specialised organisations at the two subsequent levels. The primary level of mitigation of risk is done by the individual himself, like protecting for very low level and easily discernable, estimatable downturns or uncertainty with instinctive safeguards and generally accepted and practised prudent actions.

At the next stage, the risks are managed in more financial terms by an equitable transfer to an insurer. The risk is defined, assessed and accordingly priced, with the insurer quoting an appropriate price as the premium for taking-on of the risks offered on transfer. If the risk in financial terms is sufficiently large, then the insured goes in for multiple insurers or coinsurance.

The insurers, once having underwritten the risks (quoting a premium) after due estimation of the loss probability, and taking on the business then wishes to safeguard themselves and their finances by further insuring their risks with a reinsurer. Thus, reinsurance is the third level of diversification and managing of risks occurring in the economy.

The major heads of business in insurance or lines of insurance businesses broadly are life and non-life segments. Non-life or general insurance business has couched in itself many lines of businesses: health, property and fire, motor, marine hull, and marine cargo, aviation and engineering to specify just the major heads. All of these risks collectively called the commercial risks lead to losses but which also have some databases to fall back on for loss probability calculation and estimations. So insurers i.e., insurance companies, hedge their exposures to these risks through the mechanism of reinsurance. There are the facultative or treaty reinsurance contracts, on a proportional or non-proportional basis as per the risk assessment done by the Risk Management Department.

Then there are catastrophe losses: huge losses which are a challenge to predict as to the number, intensity, timing and quantum of loss, arising due to both natural and man-made causes. Natural or Acts of God perils like earthquakes and seaquakes, hurricanes, storms and tsunamis all destroy life, property and cause huge economic loss at the time of occurrence and also give rise to a string of losses over a long time period. These losses, because of their characteristics of total uncertainty and huge magnitude, need to be necessarily hedged by the insurers. The latest updates on reinsurance business impact[1] in USA are:

Table 12.1

Reinsurance Business Impact Details

1.	Reinsurers experienced an historic level of catastrophe losses in 2011.
2.	Macroeconomic conditions, including the Eurozone debt crisis, continued to challenge the industry, making underwriting an even more critical component to profitability.
3.	There was a 9.5 per cent average increase in global property catastrophe rates on January 1, 2012, with wide-ranging rate movements at national, regional and even local levels depending on loss experience and exposure perceptions.
4.	Overall, 2011 catastrophe losses did not have much impact on hardening US casualty and workers' compensation reinsurance market pricing.
5.	The casualty reinsurance markets continue to be concerned about the level (and sustainability) of primary market pricing, with the impact being felt most strongly in selected lines of business and proportional treaties.

Similarly catastrophe losses arising due to man-made perils, primary among them being terrorist attacks, then sabotage, accidents involving peoples' lives and huge economic value, exposures to attacks with biological

1. *http://imr.marsh.com/Reports/UnitedStates.aspx?ID=71*

warfare, hazardous chemicals/materials, alternatively termed as *hazmat* in short; and all other such risks arising need to be insured against.

Figure 12.1

Global Property Catastrophe Reinsurance Rate on Line (ROL), Index

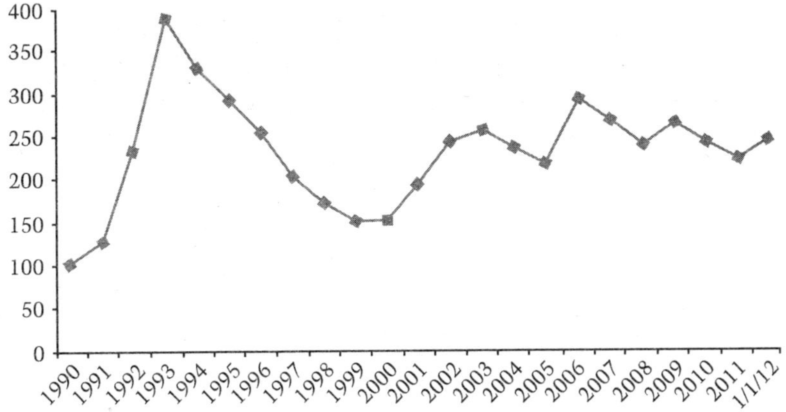

Source: Guy Carpenter & Company and LLC.

Global Reinsurance Market and Indian Contribution

The Indian insurance market has experienced little direct impact from the global financial downturn. Despite the troubles in the more developed insurance markets, total insurance premiums climbed almost 19 per cent to approximately INR 3 trillion (USD 65.86 billion) in the financial year leading up to 31 March, 2010.

Table 12.2

Insurance Market Conditions

Business Segment	*Price Change*
Global Property Catastrophe Reinsurance	Up 5% to 15%
Global Marine and Energy	Up 5% to 15%
Global Aviation and Aerospace	Flat to down 5%
Global Credit, Bond and Political Risk	Flat to down 20%*
Global Life/Accident Catastrophe Reinsurance	Flat
U.S. Property Catastrophe Reinsurance	Up 5% to 15%
U.S. Casualty Clash	Flat to up 5%
U.S. Workers' Compensation Catastrophe	Flat to down 5%
U.S. Directors and Officers	Up 5% to down 5%
U.S. Errors and Omissions	Up 5% to down 5%
U.S. Medical Professional Liability	Flat
U.S. Surety	Down 5% to 10%

Note: Based on individual performance.
Source: Guy Carpenter & Company, LIC.

As the insurance market has experienced an increase in total premiums, this has required the support of the reinsurance community. There are a number of drivers behind increased insurance—and subsequently reinsurance—demand. India is the second most populous nation in the world with 1.2 billion inhabitants and economic prospects are deemed better in India than for many developing markets.[2]

In India, Reinsurance Advisory Committee and Insurance Regulatory and Development Authority (IRDA) monitor the policy of reinsurance and IRDA requires that reinsurance be placed with the reinsures with a rating of BBB with Standard and Poor (Tripathy and Pal, 2005: 98).

Insurance Business and Reinsurance Market

It can be seen that there are two major lines of insurance business which need another tier of insurance covering them for the full benefit of economic value to flow through to the assets. These are risks which cover both the regular commercial and catastrophe (of both natural and man-made perils) lines of the insurance companies, businesses already underwritten by the insurers, economic values held in these assets are to be protected or insured, which are the major lines of reinsurance business.

The different phases of the sector can be seen distinctly under three periods. The different phases of the sector can be seen distinctly under three periods. These were: (a) the period prior to nationalisation of the non-life insurance business; (b) post-nationalisation till liberalisation; and then (c) liberalisation and entry of private and foreign players into general insurance business in India from the year 2000 onwards.

Insurance Act 1938 formed the foundation on which the then 100 odd companies engaged in non-life or general insurance business and operated in India till 1972. In 1972, the General Insurance Corporation of India (GIC) Act was enacted and in 1973, the sector was nationalised. All the 100 odd players were consolidated to form four public sector insurance companies namely United India Insurance Company, New India Insurance, Oriental Insurance and New India Assurance Company under the Holding Company GIC.

---

2. *http://reinsuranceasiaonline.com/articles/india-still-major-attraction*

There was only one GIC Re which was responsible for the entire reinsurance business and to oversee the reinsurance business among the four public sector undertakings (PSUs). The Tariff Advisory Committee or the TAC set out the products, pricing and terms of contract. It was entirely government operated complete with limits and coverage. GIC Re held the reinsurance business and the retroinsurance business. Since liberalisation in the year 2000 and functioning within IRDA's guidelines and monitoring, there are in total 25 PSU and private insurance companies doing business in India currently. But yet GIC Re remains to date the only reinsurer in India.

While reviewing the literature available on reinsurance, it can be noted that Cummins (2005) has pointed out the response of the worlds' reinsurance industry to recent mega catastrophes and provided recommendations for regulatory reforms that would improve the efficiency of reinsurance markets. Venkant Ramana (2008) analysed that insurance and reinsurance are the most booming industries, maintaining upward surge and an all-round growth, on both the domestic and global fronts, particularly in growing economies like India and China. Singh and Kumar (2009) have observed that the rapid expansion of public sector insurance companies since nationalisation has given rise to a number of problems related to the image, operational efficiency, productivity and the quality of portfolio of the system as a whole.

Reinsurance and Risk Management in India

The liberalisation process saw enabling provisions put out for the reinsurance business as well, inviting foreign reinsurers and capital but it was not met with enthusiastic and encouraging responses.

There were enough in-built gaps in the regulatory sections that enabled foreign reinsurance firms to do business, even without a formal branch or an established organisational office, in accordance with their objectives, scale and style. Thus the sole Indian reinsurer was at a comparative disadvantage in terms of establishment costs and regulatory aspects that governed its business operations. The inherent issues impacting the reinsurance apart from regulatory mandates are tightening insurer reserves, rating agency actions and cyber risks.

Within Indian boundaries, GIC Re would seem to be enjoying monopoly but in the real sense, it is practically dealing with the routine, low margin, high volume and inland business. The non-life insurers have to mandatorily cede 20 per cent to GIC Re and GIC Re in turn has to manage this risk. This risk management (domestic inland) *per se*, as per recorded, past business data, has not been an operational challenge. The revenues and reserves being built up have been growing at a nominal level.

The Asia Insurance Review, 2010, reports on 'Reinsurance market in India: The current state and the challenges ahead' which claims that life insurance companies are already looking for capital infusion to further grow the business in the market.

Reinsurance can be done on facultative basis, which is on a case-to-case basis, or covers entire lines of risks under the treaty reinsurance. Underwriting businesses on proportional basis will earn premium and also give rise to claims on proportional basis.

Reinsurance could very well be written on non-proportional basis, or on stop loss or excess of loss formats. Risk definition and assessment are the prime considerations while underwriting reinsurance. Subsequently the management of those risks and simultaneously investing with high returns will optimise reinsurance business finances.

The preparedness is to be in the scale of 1 in 200 claim possibilities which will need huge infusion of capital and more utilisation of opportunities arising, but with the present limited reserves and surplus, GIC Re faces a challenging business environment.

As per the Charter, GIC Re, functioning out of any of its single unitary branches abroad, potentially could underwrite/take on the entire quantum of risk capacity as of the entire company. While this will be highly profitable during non-claim years, even one catastrophe loss could bring on the near ruin probability. This probability has played out recently with the Australia/New Zealand floods situation.

Regulatory Norms on Reinsurers in India

The Indian reinsurance market, which is primarily regulated by the IRDA,[3] previously permitted Indian cedants to reinsure their risks with

1. An Indian reinsurance company registered with the IRDA and approved by the central government (currently, GIC Re, the national re-insurer of India, is the only registered Indian reinsurance company), and
2. Unregistered foreign reinsurers, provided they comply with the requirements stated in the IRDA (general insurance–reinsurance) Regulations 2000 and the IRDA (life insurance–reinsurance) Regulations 2000 (collectively referred to as 'the Regulations')

It is interesting to note that the reinsurance market in India has not been subject to much regulatory intervention, which is clear from the fact that the Regulations, which were notified in 2000, have remained substantially in the same form as they were when they were originally notified. Reinsurance in India has therefore remained largely market driven, though the guiding principle of the Regulations has always been to retain and maximise the retention of risk within India. The IRDA also required that insurers placing reinsurance with overseas reinsurers can only cede to companies that satisfy necessary requirements as stipulated in the Regulations. As per the Regulations, each insurer in India is free to structure its annual reinsurance programme in compliance with the Regulations, although the same must be submitted to the IRDA.[4]

IRDA Guidelines on Communication by Reinsurance Brokers

IRDA Reinsurance guidelines[5] provide that where the insurer needs to develop terms from the reinsurance markets before quoting its terms to the client, the insurer shall be free to use the services of any reinsurance broker of its choice.

---

3. *www.irda.gov.in*
4. *http://www.inhouselawyer.co.uk/index.php/india/9834-indias-insurance-regulatory-and-development-authority-takes-a-giant-leap-to-rein-in-cross-border-reinsurers*
5. *http://www.irda.gov.in/ADMINCMS/cms/frmGuidelines_Layout.aspx?page=PageNo1178&flag=1*

A composite broker shall not go to the reinsurance markets to develop terms in respect of cases referred to in (k) above, without the written prior authorisation of the insurer invited to quote terms for the insurance. Paras 2(i) and 2(j) of the Code of Conduct are relevant in this connection. It is important to emphasise that placement of reinsurance is entirely within the purview of the insurer, and neither the direct broker nor the client can direct the insurer where to place reinsurance and how much to reinsure. This does not prevent the client or the broker from enquiring about the insurer's own retention on the risk and the reinsurances that it will place and the security rating of reinsurers to be used, as a part of its examination whether to accept the insurer for its insurance requirements.

Further where reinsurance terms are developed as part of the process of quoting terms for direct insurance, the broker who is instructed to develop terms shall truthfully communicate to the insurer on whose behalf the reinsurance terms are developed, the basis of the quotation, the rates and terms and the list of reinsurers with written lines and the extent of likely support at those terms.

Findings and Conclusions

Viewed from the perspective of the primary level insurers, the present model of operations of the GIC Re, on the national or domestic operations front, fulfils all of the three major objectives Reinsurers are expected to achieve. The reinsurers existence is for increasing underwriting capacity of the insurers, cutting down the volatility and stabilising of their profits, and to afford an exit option for the insurers if so desired. This form of reinsurance ensures a protection layer and nominal growth path and level for the reinsurer himself while the business of reinsurance on the international domain has got the potential of growing exponentially, provided the risk management is on sound principles.

In conclusion, thus we see that risk is managed in the best possible manner with dynamic financial analysis, advanced hedging techniques including the concept of dynamic hedging and prudent business practices will enable GIC Re to rank among the best in the world in that class and category. The twin aspects of sound hedging and maximising returns on the back-end financial investments will establish reinsurance business on a firm and profitable platform.

The global reinsurance market has continued to show robustness in the face of persistent adverse conditions in the real economy in general and in financial markets in particular. This is the main conclusion reached by the International Association of Insurance Supervisors (IAIS) Global Reinsurance Market Report 2010. But the key macroeconomic challenges for this reinsurance industry in the days to come are: deleveraging cycle, changes in growth expectations, changes in inflationary/deflationary expectations, low investment returns and high investment volatility.

References

Chennappa, D. (2006). "Result of Liberalized India's Insurance Sector: Challenges and Opportunities", *The ICFAI Journal of Risk and Insurance* III(3): 65-75. July.

Culp, C.L. (2002). *The Art of Risk Management*, New York: John Wiley and Sons.

Cummins, David J. (2005). "Reinsurance for Natural and Man-made Catastrophes in the US: Current State of the Market and Regulatory Reforms of the Market and Regulatory Reforms".

Easwaran, P.S. (2007). "Growth of Indian Insurance Industry after Opening up to Private Sector", The Insurance Times, November, pp.19-21.

Rejda, George E. (2005). *Principles of Risk Management and Insurance*, 9th Edition. Boston: Addison-Wesley.

Gulati, Neelam C. (2009). *Principles of Insurance Management*. New Delhi: Excel Books.

Insurance Regulatory and Development Authority, *Annual Report 2009-10*.

Nema and Parul Jain (2012). *Growth of Insurance in India*.

Ruth, Gastel (2004). *Reinsurance: Fundamentals and New Challenges*. New York: Insurance Information Institute.

Singh, Manjit and Rohit Kumar (2009). *Indian Management Studies Journal*.

Tripathy, Nalini Prava and Prabir Pal (2005). *Insurance Theory and Practice*. New Delhi: Prentice Hall.

Venkant Ramana, B. (2008). "Insurance and Reinsurance: The Industry on the Growth Trajectory".

13 Insurance Industry in India

Shardul Admane

Introduction

Insurance is a form of risk management tool wherein the insured transfers his risk to the insurer on payment of a consideration called as premium. It is the most preferred form of risk transfer and is practised since centuries. The concept of insurance envisages the spreading of risk over large number of premium paying individuals or entities so that the collective corpus generated would be utilised to compensate the unfortunate few who are faced with the events or circumstances insured against.

Brief History

In India, insurance has a deep-rooted history. It finds mention in the writings of Manu (*Manusmrithi*), Yagnavalkya (*Dharmasastra*) and Kautilya (*Arthasastra*). The writings talk in terms of pooling of resources that could be re-distributed in times of calamities such as fire, floods, epidemics and famine. This was probably a pre-cursor to modern day insurance. Ancient Indian history has preserved the earliest traces of insurance in the form of marine trade loans and carriers' contracts. Insurance in India has evolved over time heavily drawing from other countries, England in particular.

The year 1818 saw the advent of modern life insurance business in India with the establishment of the Oriental Life Insurance Company in Calcutta. This company however failed in 1834. In 1829, the Madras Equitable had begun transacting life insurance business in the Madras Presidency. The year 1870 saw the enactment of the British Insurance Act and in the last three decades of the 19th century, the Bombay Mutual (1871), Oriental (1874) and Empire of India (1897) were started in the Bombay Residency.

In 1914, the Government of India started publishing returns of insurance companies in India. The Indian Life Assurance Companies Act of 1912 was the first statutory measure to regulate life business. In 1928, the Indian Insurance Companies Act was enacted to enable the government to collect statistical information about both life and non-life business transacted in India by Indian and foreign insurers including provident insurance societies. In order to protect the interest of the insurance public, the earlier legislation was consolidated and amended by the Insurance Act of 1938 with comprehensive provisions for effective control over the activities of insurers. It continues to be the principal legislation governing insurance business in India even today, though emended from time to time.

The Insurance Amendment Act of 1950 abolished principal agencies. However, there were a large number of insurance companies and the level of competition was high. There were also allegations of unfair trade practices. The Government of India, therefore, decided to nationalise insurance business. An ordinance was issued on 19th January, 1956, nationalising the life insurance sector, and Life Insurance Corporation (LIC) came into existence in the same year. The LIC absorbed 154 Indian, 16 non-Indian insurers and also 75 provident societies—245 Indian and foreign insurers in all. The LIC had monopoly till the late 1990s when the insurance sector was reopened to the private sector.

The history of general insurance dates back to the Industrial Revolution in the west and the consequent growth of sea-faring trade and commerce in the 17th century. It came to India as a legacy of British occupation. General insurance in India has its roots in the establishment of Triton Insurance Company Ltd., in the year 1850 in Calcutta by the British. In 1907, the Indian Mercantile Insurance Ltd. was set up. This was the first company to transact all classes of general insurance business. The year 1957 saw the formation of the General Insurance Council (GIC), a wing of the Insurance Associaton of India. The GIC framed a code of conduct for ensuring fair conduct and sound business practices.

In 1968, the Insurance Act was amended to regulate investments and set minimum solvency margins. The Tariff Advisory Committee was also set up then. In 1972 with the passing of the General Insurance Business (Nationalisation) Act, general insurance business was nationalised with effect from 1st January, 1973. One hundred seven insurers were amalgamated and grouped into four companies, namely National Insurance Company Ltd., the New India Assurance Company Ltd., the Oriental Insurance Company Ltd. and the United India Insurance Company Ltd. The GIC was incorporated as a company in 1971 and it commenced business on 1st January, 1973.

This millennium has seen insurance come a full circle in a journey extending to nearly 200 years. The process of re-opening of the sector had begun in the early 1990s and the last two decades have seen it been opened up substantially. In 1993, the government set up a committee under the chairmanship of R.N. Malhotra, former Governor of the Reserve Bank of India (RBI), to propose recommendations for reforms in the insurance sector. The objective was to complement the reforms initiated in the financial sector. The committee submitted its report in 1994 wherein, among other things, it was recommended that the private sector be permitted to enter the insurance industry. They stated that foreign companies be allowed to enter by floating Indian companies, preferably a joint venture with Indian partners.

Following the recommendations of the Malhotra Committee report, in 1999, the Insurance Regulatory and Development Authority (IRDA) was constituted as an autonomous body to regulate and develop the insurance industry. The IRDA was incorporated as a statutory body in April 2000. The key objectives of the IRDA include promotion of competition so as to enhance customer satisfaction through increased consumer choice and lower premiums, while ensuring the financial security of the insurance market.

The IRDA opened up the market in August 2000 with the invitation for application for registrations. Foreign companies were allowed ownership of up to 26 per cent in the capital of an insurance company in India. In December 2000, the subsidiaries of the GIC were restructured as independent companies and at the same time GIC was converted into a national re-insurer. Parliament passed a bill delinking the four subsidiaries from GIC in July 2002. The status of the insurance companies as on September 2012 is given in Table 13.1.

Table 13.1

Status of Insurance Companies, September 2012

Category	*No. of Companies*
Life Insurance Companies (including LIC)	24
Non-Life (General) Insurance Companies (including health insurers)	25
Reinsurers—General Insurance Corporation of India	01
Export Credit Guarantee Corporation	01
Agriculture Insurance Company Limited	01

Source: IRDA Annual Report 2012-13.

The insurance sector has been growing at a steady rate of 10-12 per cent, although growth has slowed during the last year. Together with banking services, insurance services add significantly to the country's gross domestic product (GDP). A well-developed and evolved insurance sector is a boon for economic development, as it provides long-term funds for infrastructure development at the same time strengthening the risk taking ability of the country.

The measure of insurance penetration and density reflects the level of development of the insurance sector in the country. The penetration and density of insurance in India as of 2011 was as follows:

	Penetration (%)	*Density (in USD)*
Life Insurance	3.40	49.0
General Insurance	0.70	10.0

Source: IRDA Annual Report 2011-12.

Insurance penetration is defined as the ratio of premium underwritten in a given year to the GDP. Insurance density is defined as the ratio of premium underwritten in a given year to the total population (measured in USD for convenience of comparison). Comparative position of penetration and density of insurance in selected countries is given in Figures 13.1A and 13.1B.

Unique Mission of IRDA

Apart from the usual function of regulation and supervision of the insurance sector in the country, the IRDA has also been mandated to

Figure 13.1

Insurance Penetration in Selected Countries in 2011

A

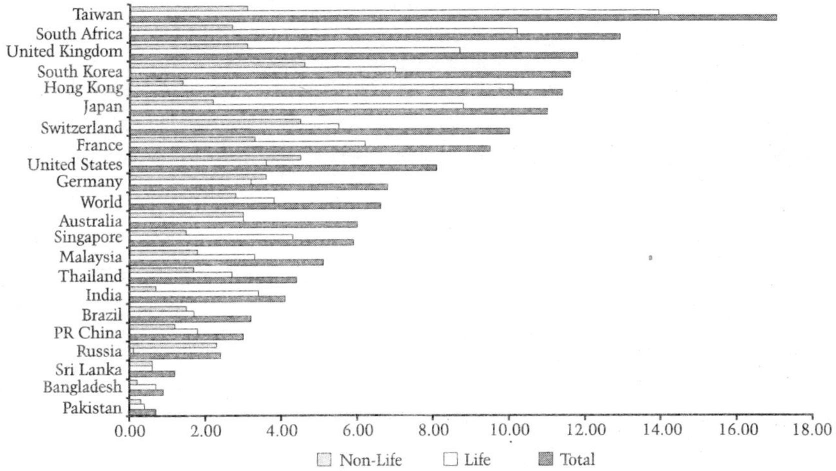

Source: *IRDA Annual Report 2011-12*.

B

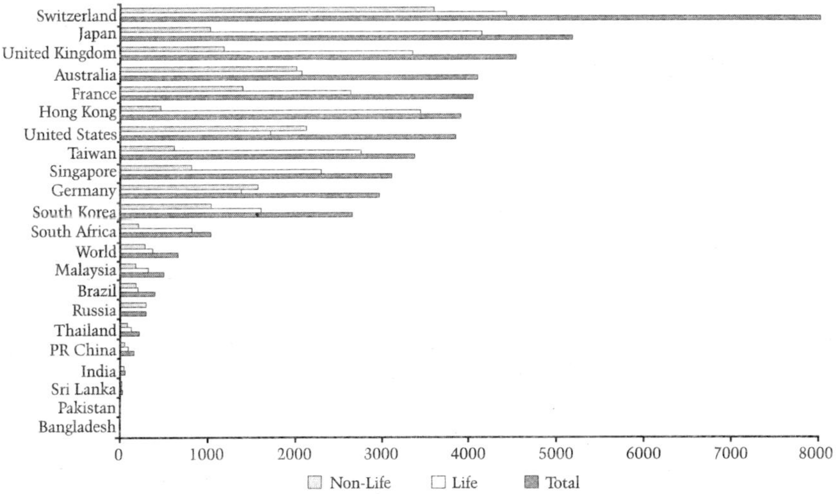

Source: Same as Figure 13.1.

ensure a balanced development of the insurance sector in the country. An important part of the mission statement of the Authority is:

> To bring about speedy and orderly growth of the insurance industry (including annuity and superannuation payments), for the benefit of the common man, and to provide long term funds for accelerating growth of the economy.

The penetration of insurance in India is very low as compared to the developed countries (as seen above) and also with respect to its peers, the developing nations. Insurance offers a potent tool to secure the financial interests of a population which does not have a formal system of social security provided by the state, especially for the large and varied unorganised section of the economy. With a huge population, the country offers both an opportunity as well as challenges to expand and grow the business while providing financial security to its population. At the same time-insurance also makes available a large pool of long-term funds that are required for the development of critical infrastructure in the country.

Regulatory Mechanism

The IRDA is the primary regulator for the insurance sector in India. It is under the purview of the Ministry of Finance, Department of Financial Services, Insurance Division. Insurance is a part of the financial sector, the others being banking and securities/capital market, regulated by the RBI and the Securities Exchange Board of India (SEBI). In 2010, an apex body, the Financial Stability and Development Council (FSDC), was formed under the aegis of the Ministry of Finance, with representation from all the financial sector regualtors, to achieve co-ordination and faster decision making on critical matters relating to the financial sector in the country.

The IRDA Act of 1999 provides for an Insurance Advisory Committee, a body consisting of experts drawn from various fields, that may be established by the Authority in order to assist and advise the Authority in making or revising the regualtions. In addition, there are the LIC and the GIC which represent the life insurance and general insurance companies in India respectively, that are involved in the consultative process for the development of Regulation. A separate body has also been recently established for helath insurance. Health insurance has gained significance in the past few years and presents its own peculiarities which need to be addressed differently. The new body, Health Insurance Forum, is expected to bridge the gap between the various stakeholders and bring in more transparency and efficiency in the health insurance space.

The tools for regulation are provided by various legislations, the prime legislation being: Insurance Act, 1938, and the Insurance Rules, 1939. It is supported by various other statutes such as the Life Insurance Corporation Act, 1956, the General Insurance Business (Nationalisation) Act, 1972, etc. The Authority has framed a set of regulations under the powers vested in it by virtue of section 26 of the IRDA Act, 1999. The regulations encompass various aspects of the insurance business like registration of various participants (such as insurers, brokers, agents, third party administrators (TPAs), etc.), format of financial statements and reports to be maintained and furnished to the Authority, investment of funds, etc. Apart from the above, various circulars, notifications and guidelines have been issued by the Authority from time to time on matters relating to the insurance sector.

The Authority has also instituted the Insurance Ombudsman in terms of the Redressal of Public greivances Rules, 1998, to provide relief to customers of insurance who resolve the complaints relating to settlement of claims under insurance policies. The Authority has also framed the Protection of Policyholder's Interests Regulations, 2002, in order to ensure timely settlement of claims in respect of life and non-life insurance policies.

The rationale for regulation stems from the fact that the insurance companies deal with funds collected as premiums from various contributors (policyholders) that should be made availabe to them in the event the insured event occurs. The broader objectives of regulations are as follows:

1. To ensure the financial health and stability of insurance companies
2. To safeguard public interest against fraudulent business practices by market participants
3. To even out any imperfections in the market
4. To follow socially desirable goals
5. To adhere to the global practices and standards of both business and regulation.

Insurance is the Business of Risk

Insurance companies that issue policies essentially undertake the risks of the policyholders in consideration of the premium paid by them. Insurance is thus, a business of risk wherein the risk of one party (insured) is transferred to another (insurer) at a price. The price or premium is scientifically determined based on various factors. Insurance offers a risk management tool whereby the insured generates fianncial capacity to face a large financial shock on payment of a relatively small consideration or premium. It is thus, one of the most convenient, cost-effective and preferred ways of delaing with risks over which one cannot exercise effective control or avoid totally.

Uncertainty is inherent in any risk and so it is with insurance acivity. The time of occurrence of any insured event (frequency) as well as the damage it could cause in the event of occurrence (severity) are highly uncertain. The insurers use various statistical and mathematical tools and models to guage the frequency and severity of risks in order to arrive at the premium rates and to determine the provisions to be made for unexpired risks. Insurance companies are organisations that deal in risk and therefore need to have systems in place to deal with them. The activity of underwriting or risk evaluation itself is fraught with the risk of adverse selection by the insurer. Insurers must achieve diversification of risks by spreading them over a large population covering wide geographical areas and across various categories of customers. This ensures that the damaging effects of adverse selection, if any, are minimised.

Supervision

The Regulator has to continuously supervise and monitor the operations and working of the various participants in the industry. For this purpose, the Authority seeks periodical returns and reports from various entities. The returns provide information about the level of business, distribution channels, operating expenses, corporate governance compliance status, solvency position, grievances of policyholders, etc. The frequency or periodicity of the returns is determined based on the critical nature of the reporting parameters. Apart from this, the Authority has a mechanism for on-site inspection of the regulated entities, by a team of its officers and external professionals, if necessary. The inspection is aimed at ensuring compliance with the applicable acts, rules, regulations and circulars and guidelines issued by the Authority. The inspection brings out valuable inputs which provide insight about the state of operations of various aspects of the insurance business and help in improving and strengthening the regulatory function.

The supervisory function also encompasses the examination of market conduct of insurers and intermediaries. The test of good conduct of business by insurers is whether policyholders are treated fairly both before the contract is entered into and throughout the lifecycle of the insurance policy, until all obligations under the contract have been satisfied. From the regulatory perspective, the pre-requisite is a proper framework including relevant laws, rules, regulations, guidelines, etc., within which the insurers and intermediaries operate. A good framework for conduct of business lays down benchmarks for various aspects of policyholder servicing. When it comes to monitoring and supervision, the Regulator should be able to identify concerns from a macro and systemic level and bring about required changes in the framework.

The two most critical aspects or functions of the insurance business are underwriting and investments. The insurers encounter risks while building and managing the underwriting portfolio as well as the investment portfolio. Underwriting is nothing but undertaking risks on behalf of the policyholders and there is a high degree of uncertainty about whether the risks would materialise. It is always a challenge for insurers to generate surplus out of underwriting activity and in such a scenario, there is an overwhelming dependence on the ability of the investment portfolio to generate adequate returns to keep the insure solvent and capable of meeting its commitments. The underwriting policy and the investment policy of the insurers thus become the key objects for the supervisors attention. Given the critical significance of investment function of insurers, they are required to adhere to a stringent set of regulations regarding investments. Lack of adequate attention to the investment function by an insurer could severely impair its ability to meet its commitments and put its very existence in jeopardy. The funds of policyholders are held by the insurers in fiduciary capacity and they need to be invested and managed strictly as per the regulatory stipulations in order to meet the needs of the policyholders, if necessary. The accumulated total investments held by the insurance sector as on 31st March 2012, was Rs. 16,80,527 crores.

An interesting aspect of the regulation and supervision function is that the Authority, while discharging its responsibilities, itself faces a huge reputation risk. Any slackness in supervisory activity might lead to an incident which could trigger a serious lack of confidence in the industry. Financial markets, both within an economy and globally, are becoming increasingly inter-linked and even a small event could result in catastrophic losses due to cascading effects, thereby putting not only an organisation or industry, but the system itself at risk.

Micro Insurance: Rural and Social Sector Obligations

In order to ensure a balanced and speedy expansion of insurance coverage in the country, the Authority has put in place the regulatory framework laying down the obligations of insurers to the rural and social sectors. These regulations impose obligations on insurers towards the rural population—to sell a specified percentage of policies and underwrite specified percentage of gross premium underwritten for life and non-life insurance companies respectively, and cover a specified number of lives/ assets belonging to people below poverty line or those pursuing certain traditional occupations. These obligations have been linked to the number of years of having been in operations of the respective insurer. The Government of India had set up a consulting group in 2003 to examine the existing insurance schemes for the rural poor, and on the basis of the group's recommendations, the Authority issued IRDA (Micro insurance) Regulations, 2005.

Initiatives

Some of the key initiatives the Authority has undertaken in the past few years to improve the market place are the following:

Insurance Information Bureau (IIB): IIB was formed in October 2009 with the objective of facilitating in the efficient functioning of the insurance sector as well as for the protection of the interests of the policyholders by providing reliable, timely and accurate information on the industry. The IIB aims to act as a single point of official reference for the entire insurance industry data and also to ensure that the data are available to various market players, researchers, policyholders and the public at large for real-time decision making. Some of the recently published *ad-hoc* reports include the following:

1. Claim Development Analysis of Motor Third Party Claims,
2. Motor Third Party Claims Analysis of claim severity by time lag bands and nature of loss,
3. Health Data Claim analysis by types of payment, and
4. Health Data Claims analysis on medical inflation.

Integrated Grievance Management System (IGMS): The implementation of IGMS has enabled the Authority to monitor the grievance mechanism of the industry more closely. IGMS acts as a whistle-blower for the industry and the regulator for undesirable market conduct, and it has resulted in speedy disposal of complaints by the insurers.

Insurance Repositories: The Authority has issued guidelines on insurance repositories and electronic issuances of insurance policies with a view to create insurance repositories in the insurance space. The main objective of creating an insurance repository is to provide policyholders a facility to keep insurance policies in electronic form and to undertake changes, modifications and revisions in the insurance policy with speed and accuracy in order to bring about efficiency, transparency and cost reduction in the issuance and maintenance of insurance policies.

Consumer awareness and education initiative: The IRDA along with other stakeholders of the industry has a responsibility of improving financial literacy in the country as well as to impart consumer education in insurance. Towards this end, the IRDA has been working on and has implemented various initiatives. In the area of financial literacy, the IRDA is also working with the other financial regulators, namely, the RBI, SEBI and Pension Fund Regulatory and Development Authority (PFRDA) through the FSDC platform on a common approach for the nation as a whole.

One of the major activities undertaken during the year was IRDA's Consumer Education website which was launched during the annual seminar held in June 2012 in Kolkata. The website (*www.policyholder.gov.in*) is comprehensive covering various areas of insurance and hosts the e-copies of IRDA's publications relating to consumer education as well. The Authority has also published policyholder handbooks for general public in all major Indian languages, which are available on the website. The IRDA also conducts and sponsors seminars/workshops, competitions, which have themes or focus on consumer education and empowerment.

The insurance industry in India today is poised to take a giant leap of growth. With the growing financial aspirations of a population that is witnessing rapid urbanisation, the demand for financial products for a secure future life is bound to rise. There is vast untapped market to be explored and the changing lifestyles and perspectives will fuel demand for better and innovative insurance products for the next few decades. The regulator has a vital role to play in the development and expansion of the market while maintaining appropriate balance and discipline.

References

Swiss Re: sigma reports.

IRDA Annual Reports.

SECTION IV
Risk Management and Hedging

14 Dynamic Relationships between Stock Market, Crude Oil and Gold Futures Markets

An Empirical Analysis of India

Pratap Kumar Jena, Phanindra Goyari and Debashis Acharya

Introduction

The study on the relationships between stock market, crude oil and gold market became more vibrant right after the collapsing of stock market during 2002 across the United States, Canada, Asia and European nations. But still there are huge gaps in the literature on this issue particularly for underdeveloped economies like India. The recent global financial crisis world-wide gave a lesson to researchers and policy makers to study on the possible relationships between these markets for an efficient portfolio diversification. Though these three markets are different from each other, prices of these three markets were not completely driven by their fundamental factors of demand-supply rather than the prices of each other and some other factors due to interaction between these markets. For example, the crisis in 2002 caused a boom in both the crude oil and gold prices and it continued till the first half of 2008. But in the second half of 2008, due to global financial crisis, there has been a decline in the price of crude oil from $147 per barrel to nearly 30 at the end of 2008 and also decreased by nearly 64 per cent in 2009, with an annual average price of $35 per barrel. But at the same time, the gold price also sharply declined from over $1000 per ounce to 700 or so (Zhang and Wei, 2010). But, after the economic recovery in 2009, there has been rises in the stock market, crude oil and gold prices. Therefore, it is very important for investors/traders to know what relationship exists between these three markets for their profitable investment and also for asset allocation.

The asset allocation can be achieved through two main channels: (i) diverting investment to different classes of assets and (ii) investing in similar classes of assets in multiple markets through international diversification (Cappiello *et al.*, 2003). Therefore, the collapse of financial market in 2008 brought into the notice of policy makers and investors to look into the correlationship between stock returns and commodity returns (like crude oil and gold). These three markets are different in their structures and nature, but they affect each other by a common shock. Though it is believed that there has been a negative correlation between the financial market and commodity markets, during the financial turmoil, commodity markets attract more attention to the investors to hedge against the financial risk as it is believed that commodities are more secured than the stock market. Thus, the major effect of global financial turbulence has shown in the commodity markets especially on two commodities, *viz.*, crude oil and gold futures markets. Therefore, this paper attempts to find out the relationship between stock prices, crude oil and gold futures prices in India.

Over the last two decades of research on stock market volatility, various studies examined the dynamics of the covariance of different assets. The existing studies mainly focused on the univariate volatilities, not correlations or covariances. Thus, in the above backdrop, it is an important issue from the research point of view to understand and to examine the linkages between stock market, crude oil and gold futures markets. The specific objectives of the present study are: first, to examine the long-run relationship between stock prices, crude oil and gold futures prices in India. Second, to examine both price and volatility spillovers using the dynamic conditional correlation (DCC) model between these three markets.

The rest of the paper is organised as follows. Section 2 provides the brief literature survey. While Section 3 outlines the estimation methods, Section 4 discusses the data and empirical results. Finally, the last section provides the concluding remarks.

Literature Review

There is a vast literature on exchange rate and stock market volatility, crude oil and stock market volatility, etc., studied comprehensively particularly by financial economists and practitioners. But there is still a huge gap in literature on the relationship between stock market, gold and crude oil futures markets. Studies examining the dynamic relationship between stock prices, crude oil and gold prices for India are relatively few in number. The financial crisis of 2002 and also recent crisis of 2008 have increased the importance to examine the interlinkages between these three markets. The available literatures on these three markets are theoretical as well empirical. The relationships between stock prices, crude oil and gold prices have three-fold features: (i) there is negative relationship between stocks and gold price. Gold price rises when stocks price falls, as gold is considered a safe or risk-free asset. (ii) Historically, there is positive relationship between gold and oil prices (Amritha, 2009). (iii) There are negative relationships between stock prices and crude oil prices, as higher crude oil prices translate into higher transport cost, production, heating oil cost, inflation, etc., which reduce corporate earnings (Pescatori and Beth, 2008). The relationship between price and volume is important to understand the theories of dissemination of information flow into the market. The market information affects financial prices in a random manner (Brailsford, 1994). Thus the asymmetric information between different traders ensures that markets are the most volatile as traders suck out and discover relevant information from one another. The dynamic relationship between volatility, futures trading and investor sentiment under different market conditions seems to differ depending on the market under investigation for different information and trader types (Hsueh *et al.*, 2008).

There are a large number of empirical studies on the relationship between stock prices, crude oil and gold prices both for developed and emerging nations. The empirical study on the relationship between the crude oil and gold market on price cointegration, causality and price discovery shows that the volatility of crude oil price is two times greater than the gold price. There are both short-term and long-term equilibrium relationships between these two markets and it is also interesting to know that both markets were affected by the common factors such as the US dollars exchange rate, economic fundamentals and geopolitical events. Similarly, there was significant unilateral linear causality between crude oil and gold market, and the crude oil market outweighs the gold in terms of price information (Zhang and Wei, 2010). The study on the reaction of international stock markets to oil shocks shows that the reaction of Canadian and US stock prices to oil shocks can be completely due to shocks on real cash flows but this result is not supported to in case of Japan and the UK (Jones and Kaul, 1996). Another study shows that the oil futures returns do lead some individual oil company stock returns but oil futures returns do not have much impact on broad-based market indices like the S&P 500 (Huang *et al.*, 1996). But, the relationship between these two markets is different when they use quarterly data from 1947 to 1991. Oil prices do have an effect on aggregate stock return (Jones and Kaul, 1996), but the analysis of daily data from 1979 to 1991 shows that there was no relationship between oil futures prices and aggregate stock returns (Huang *et al.*, 1996).

The linear and non-linear relationship between the daily futures prices and volumes of West Texas Intermediate (WTI) crude oil is examined by Moosa and Silvapulle (2000) using the unrestricted vector autoregression (VAR) model in the first differences or the error correction models. The study found that Hsio procedure showed the unidirectional causality from volume to price but the Back-Brock non-linear model indicated the bi-directional causality from price to volume

The investigation by Twite (2002) on the exposure of the stock prices of Australian gold-mining firms to changes in gold prices shows various possible explanations for the gold premium that reflects the difference between the discounted cash flow valuation of a gold-mining firm and the actual market value of the company. These explanations include the misuse of the discounted cash flow techniques and those drawn from the existence of real options like: resources/reserve ratio, number of operational mines, hedging levels, level and volatility of gold prices and firm size. The study also found that there is evidence of strong association between the gold premium, firm size and the volatility of gold prices as predicted by the option market but no relationship exists between the gold premium and other identified option characteristics.

Narayan *et al.* (2010) examined empirically whether the gold and crude oil futures markets are efficient or not using the Gregory and Hansen cointegration test for the period from 2 January, 1995, to 12 September,

2009. The study found that the gold and oil spot and futures markets up to the maturity of 10 months were cointegrated. This study also found that the oil market can be used to predict gold market prices and vice versa.

In the financial economics literature a large number of studies used the Autoregressive conditional hetroscedasticity (ARCH) and generalised ARCH (GARCH) models to model the volatilities in prices, either of financial assets or commodities. Engle (1982) proposed the ARCH model to model the volatilities in the financial market but later this model was developed by Bollersleve (1986) to the GARCH model by including the conditional variance of white noise error term itself. The common finding of such studies shows that the ARCH and GARCH models usually lead to a very high degree of conditional volatility to a shock. But, Diebold (1986) examined the persistence of conditional variances using the ARCH and GARCH models. He found that the persistence of high degree of volatility may be spurious if there are structural changes in the conditional volatility during the period of financial crisis or any outstanding shock, because switches in stock market regimes may be caused by low probability events. Similarly, Schwert (1990) and Nelson (1991) show that the standard ARCH and GARCH models are no longer flexible to describe any unforeseen events like financial crisis.

Therefore, there was introduction of multivariate conditional variance model was introduced to avoid the assumption like constant correlation coefficients in ARCH and GARCH models. Asymmetry in variances as well as covariances has been introduced by Kroner and Ng. There are very rare studies available which capture asymmetric effects in correlation in a multivariate GARCH model. Presently there are only two models developed to capture this; first, the asymmetric effects model by Kroner and Ng, they allow for asymmetric effects in both the variances and covariances. Another model alternative to the Kroner and Ng is the DCC GARCH model to capture asymmetries in variances but not in correlation. According to Engle and Sheppard (2001), any univariate GARCH model which is covariance stationary and assumes normally distributed errors (irrespective of the true error distribution) can be used to model the variances, as the model is estimated in two steps; first, variances are estimated using a univariate GARCH specification, and second, the parameters of the dynamic correlation are considered.

The asymmetries in conditional variances, covariances and correlations in international equity and bond returns were examined by Cappiello *et al.* (2003) using the DCC model of Engle and Sheppard (2001) using 15 years of weekly price for the period from 2 January, 1987 to 15 February, 2001. The study found that national equity index return series show strong asymmetries in conditional volatility but little evidence is seen in bond index returns. However, both bonds and equities exhibit asymmetry in conditional correlation, although in asymmetrically different manners.

Chang *et al.* (2011) examined the performance of four multivariate models such as constant conditional correlation (CCC), VARMA-GARCH, DCC, BEKK and diagonal BEKK, for the crude oil spot and futures returns of two major benchmark international crude oil markets. They found that the optimal portfolio weights of all multivariate volatility models for Brent suggested holding futures in large proportion than spot. But for WTI, DCC, BEKK and diagonal BEKK suggested holding crude oil futures to spot, but CCC and VARMA-GARCH suggested holding crude oil spot to futures. The hedging effectiveness indicates that the diagonal BEKK is the best (worst) model for optinal hedge ratio (OHR) calculation in terms of reducing the variance of the portfolio.

Similarly, the study by Kuper and Lestano (2007) on the dynamic linkages among financial markets in Thailand and Indonesia shows that while monetary policy pursued by Thailand authorities helped to defend the exchange rate at the outbreak of the financial crisis, there is little evidence for Indonesia at the end of 1998. The correlations between countries within each of the financial market reveal a certain degree of interdependence among countries, which is lower during crisis.

Thus, the above survey of literatures shows that most of the existing studies on the present topic used different time series techniques. Particularly, vast numbers of literatures are available which examined the financial/commodity market volatility using the ARCH and GARCH models but these models, in many cases, could not capture the dynamic relationship between variances or covariances. Therefore, to examine the dynamic relationship between variables, the present study has used the DCC GARCH model.

Methodology

The long-run relationship between stock prices, crude oil and gold futures price returns and trading volume is estimated using the univariate VAR model and Johansen cointegration techniques.

First, we consider the Johansen cointegration technique to examine the dynamic *long-run* relationship between stock market, gold and crude oil futures market in India. Thus, to test the cointegration model, following three steps are followed.

Step 1: The data series should be stationary and these are evaluated by the below unit root technique. After checking the order of the stationarity, we conducted the Johansen's cointegration test.

Step 2: A VAR model with p^{th} lags containing the study variables at time t can be written as:

1. $$y_t = \mu + A_1 y_{t-1} + \ldots + A_p y_{t-p} + \varepsilon_t , \quad (1)$$

where y_t is a $n \times 1$ vector of variables that are integrated of order one and ε_t is an $n \times 1$ vector of innovations. The second step involves to rewrite the VAR(p) model as:

$$\Delta y_t = \mu + \Pi y_{t-1} + \sum_{i=1}^{p-1} \Gamma \Delta y_{t-i} + \varepsilon_t \quad (2)$$

2. where $\Pi = \sum_{i=1}^{p} A_i - I$ and $\Gamma_i = -\sum_{J=i+i}^{p} A_j$,

where y_t is the vector of stock index, gold and crude oil futures price series, Δ denotes the first difference operator, ε_t is the vector of white noise error terms, Γ and Π are 2×2 coefficient matrices. Π matrix has two rank values, i.e., 1 (one) and 0 (zero). If the variables are not cointegrated, then the rank of Π = 0. But if these are cointegrated then rank of Π = 1.

Step 3: According to Johansen approach, there are two likelihood ratio tests, i.e., λ_{trace} and λ_{max}, to identify the cointegration. The test statistic λ_{trace} carries whether the number of cointegrating vector is 0 or 1. But λ_{max} test shows whether there is/are one or two cointegrating vectors for cointegration. In general, if r cointegrating vector is accepted, the two test statistics are:

1. $\lambda_{\text{trace}}(r) = -T \sum_{i=r+1}^{g} \ln(1-\hat{\lambda}_i$ (3)

2. $\lambda_{\max}(r, r+1) = -\text{Tn}(1-\hat{\lambda}_{r+1}$ (4)

where r is the number of cointegrated vectors and $\hat{\lambda}_i$ is the estimated value for the ith order eigenvalue from the Π matrix, T is the total sample period and g is the number of separate series to be examined.

The null hypothesis is tested for r = 0 or 1. If $r = 0$ is rejected, then there is cointegration between the variables. Thus, the value of r is continually increased until the null is no longer rejected. Johansen and Juselius (1990) provide the critical values of these statistics. The rank of Π matrix may be tested using the λ_{trace} and $\lambda_{\max}$.

Therefore, the error correction coefficients, α_i, serve two purposes (Pradhan and Bhat, 2009). These purposes are (i) 'to identify the direction of causality between spot and futures prices' and (ii) 'to measure the speed with which deviations from the long-run relationship are corrected by changes in the spot and futures prices.' Thus, the vector error correction model (VECM) allows the short run dynamic adjustment of the variables to the long-run behaviour of the endogenous variables in the Johansen model. The deviation from long-run equilibrium is corrected gradually through a series of partial short-run adjustments. The Akaike's information criteria (AIC) and Schwartz information criterion (SIC) are employed to determine the appropriate lag length.

To study the conditional correlationship between variables, the present study also uses the DCC model of Engle (2002). Now, the DCC model can be explained in the following way:

Asset (financial or commodity) price volatility is measured by using the ARCH or GARCH models of Bollersleve (1986). Now we can write the GARCH (1,1) model in the following way;

1. $x_{i,t} = \mu + \varepsilon_{i,t}, \qquad \varepsilon_{i,t} \sim N(0, h_{ii,t})$ (5)

2. $h_{ii,t} = \gamma_i + \alpha_i \varepsilon_{i,t-1}^2 + \beta_i h_{ii,t-1} \qquad i = 1, 2, \ldots\ldots N$. (6)

Subject to $\gamma_i > 0,\ \alpha_i,\ \beta_i \geq 0,\ \alpha_i + \beta_i < 1$. The coefficients α and β in the model determine the short-run dynamics of the resulting volatility time series. If the coefficient β is large, it shows that volatility is persistent. Similarly, if α is large, it indicates that volatility reacts intensely to recent market movements.

The covariance matrix of DCC (1,1) model can be expressed as

$H_t = D_t R_t D_t$, where $D_t = diag(h_{11,t}^{1/2} \ldots\ldots h_{NN,t}^{1/2})$ is a diagonal matrix of univariate GARCH volatility model.

$Rt = Q_t^{*-1} Q_t Q_t^{*-1}$ is the time varying correlation matrix, with $Q_t = (q_{ij,t})$ as described by

$$Q_t = (1 - a - b)\bar{Q} + a(\Xi_{t-1}\Xi'_{t-1}) + bQ_{t-1} \quad (7)$$

where $\bar{Q}$ is the N×N unconditional covariance matrix of standardised residuals, $\Xi = x_t / \sqrt{h_t}$ resulting from the first estimation,

$Q_t^* = (q_{ii,t}^*) = (\sqrt{q_{ii,t}})$ is a diagonal matrix composed of the square root of the ith diagonal elements of Q_t, and a and b are non-negative coefficients satisfying $a + b < 1$.

Now rewriting $R_t = Q_t^{*-1} Q_t Q_t^{*-1}$, the conditional correlation between assets i and j at time t can expressed as

$$\rho_{ij,t} = \frac{q_{ij,t}}{\sqrt{q_{ij,t}\, q_{jj,t}}}.$$

As with the GARCH (1,1) model, coefficients of the DCC (1,1) model are estimated by the maximum likelihood procedure using the algorithm of BFGS (Broyden-Fletcher-Goldfarb-Shanno). The log likelihood function, under the assumption of conditional multivariate normality, is

$$L(\vartheta) = -\frac{1}{2}[TN\ln(2\pi) + \sum_{t=1}^{T}(\ln|H_t| + \Xi_t H_t{}^{1}\Xi'_t)] \quad (8)$$

with $H_t = E_{t-1}(\Xi_t \Xi'_t)$ being the $N \times N$ conditional variance/covariance matrix.

By using the above framework, we can analyse the conditional correlations between commodity futures returns and returns of the traditional asset classes. Before estimating the DCC model, at first we have to check how they changed over time by simply regressing them on a constant and a time trend. Second, we have to study the relationship between conditional correlations and conditional volatilities by regressing the former on the latter as follows:

$$\rho_{TC,t} = \alpha + \beta_T \sqrt{h_{T,t}} + \beta_c \sqrt{h_{ct}} + \varepsilon_t \quad (9)$$

where the subscripts T and C refer to traditional asset and commodity futures respectively. If β_T is positive, it suggests that conditional return correlations between traditional asset and commodity futures rise with the volatility of traditional market. Similarly, if β_T is negative, it indicates that correlations between commodity futures and traditional asset fall in periods of high volatility in traditional asset market. Ultimately, this result would imply that the usefulness of commodity futures as a diversification tool increases in periods of above average market volatility.

Data and Estimation Results

The empirical analysis of the present study is based on daily futures price data of gold and crude oil and the Bombay Stock Exchange (BSE) stock index data. Gold and crude oil futures price data were collected from the website of the Multi Commodity Exchange (i.e., *www.mcxindia.com*) in India for the period from 01 June, 2005 to 31 December, 2010. Gold futures trading has six contracts in a year, one for every six months. Likewise, crude oil has 12 contracts in a year. This study includes both June and December contracts for gold futures. Due to differences in the contract maturity period, the study uses four futures contracts, namely, March, June, September and December contracts for crude oil. The daily stock index (Sensex) data were collected from the BSE from 1 June, 2005 to 31 December, 2010. The total sample after adjusting daily closing prices consists of 1340 daily prices for gold and crude oil, and 1340 days for BSE stock index. This study uses the returns of stock index price and two commodities futures price. It is estimated by :

$$R_t = \left(\frac{P_t - P_{t-1}}{P_{t-1}} \right) \times 100 \quad (10)$$

where, R_t is the daily percentage of stock index return and two commodities futures price return, P_t and P_{t-1} are the daily stock index and futures prices of commodities at time t and t-1.

Table 14.1

Summary Statistics of Stock, Crude Oil and Gold Futures Price Returns

	Sensex	*Crude Oil*	*Gold*
Mean	0.101	0.065	0.102
Std. Dev.	1.904	2.109	1.197
Skewness	0.329	0.619	0.097
Kurtosis	10.208	9.359	8.094
Jarque-Bera	2924.743	2343.365	1450.822
Probability	0.000	0.000	0.000
Sample size	1340	1340	1340

The summary statistics of BSE Sensex, crude oil and gold futures price returns are reported in Table 14.1. It is observed that the gold has the highest average returns 10.16 per cent, followed by sensex which provides 10.12 per cent average daily futures return. Crude oil futures provides the least average daily returns 6.51 per cent. In the sample period from 1 June, 2005 to 31 December, 2010, it is observed that the crude oil has the highest daily volatility 2.109 compared to the sensex and gold, whereas gold returns have the least volatility 1.197. The value of skewness and kurtosis indicates that all three variables are positively skewed and highly leptokurtic with respect to the normal distribution. Jarque-Bera statistics reject normality for each of the series at the 1 per cent level of significance.

In Table 14.2, we have reported the unconditional return correlations between sensex, crude oil and gold. As existing studies (Jensen *et al.*, 2000, Erb and Harvey, 2006) reported that stock returns have a very low correlation with commodity return, we also found that there are very low correlations between BSE sensex return with crude oil and gold futures return. The unconditional return correlation coefficient between sensex and crude oil future return is 0.17, which indicates that both sensex return and crude oil futures return are positively correlated in the study period. The positive correlationship between sensex return and gold future return is very low but negative i.e., -0.01, which implies that both markets are moving in opposite direction. Therefore, to choose which market provides better investment opportunities and an efficient asset allocation can be known from their risk and return relations. The standard deviation and the mean return of these three variables show that gold futures has the highest mean return with lowest standard deviation, whereas crude oil future has the lowest mean return with highest standard deviation, which implies that gold futures is more efficient in terms of more return with less risk than the sensex and crude oil future return. We have examined the long-run relationship between these three variables using the Johansen cointegration techniques to know how these three variables are behaving in the long run.

Table 14.2

Unconditional Return Correlation between Stock, Crude Oil and Gold

	SENSEX	*Crude Oil*	*Gold*
SENSEX	1.00	0.17*	-0.01
Crude Oil	0.17*	1.00	0.24*
Gold	-0.01	0.24*	1.00

Analysis of Johansen Cointegration Results

The long-run relationships between sensex, crude oil and gold futures returns are measured by the Johansen cointegration test. The results of the Johansen cointegration test for three variables are reported in Table 14.3 in two parts: Trace statistics and maximum statistics. Both test statistics are significant at 1 per cent level. Therefore, both the tests rejected the null hypothesis of no cointegration ($r=0$) at the 1 per cent level. This result shows that there exist three cointegrating vectors in the case of three variables. Hence, there is a long-term co-movement among these three variables.

Table 14.3

Results of Johansen Cointegration Test between Gold, Crude Oil and Stock Prices in India

Return		*Null Hypothesis*	*Alternative Hypothesis*	*Eigen Value*	*Statistics*	*Critical Values* 5%	1%
Sensex, Crude Oil and Gold	λ_{trace}	$r=0$	$r>0$	0.188	717.50*	29.80	35.46
		$r\leq 1$	$r>1$	0.153	439.28*	15.49	19.94
		$r\leq 2$	$r>2$	0.150	217.13*	3.84	6.63
	λ_{trace}	$r=0$	$r=1$	0.188	278.22*	21.13	25.86
		$r=1$	$r=2$	0.153	222.15*	14.26	18.52
		$r=2$	$r=3$	0.150	217.13*	3.84	6.63

Notes: r denotes the cointegration vector, *denotes significance at 11 per cent level.

Table 14.4

Results of the Vector Error Correction Model for Gold, Crude Oil and Stock

Explanatory Variables ↓	Δ *Stock*	Δ *Crude Oil*	Δ *Gold*
Intercept	-0.0002 [-0.0036]	-0.0015 [-0.0238]	-0.0009 [-0.0244]
Δ Stock Prices *t*-1	-0.1835* [-5.6493]	0.3494* [9.1398]	-0.0754* [-3.3734]
Δ Stock Prices *t*-2	-0.1161 [-4.4125]	0.2160* [6.9706]	-0.0448** [-2.4740]
Δ Crude Oil Prices *t*-1	0.2092 [8.0396]	-0.5252* [-17.1469]	-0.0671* [-3.7452]
Δ Crude Oil Prices *t*-2	0.1012 [4.3889]	-0.3109* [-11.4605]	-0.0376** [-2.3703]
Δ Gold Prices *t*-1	-0.3911* [-8.7548]	-0.2902* [-5.5199]	-0.5616* [-18.2580]
Δ Gold Prices *t*-2	-0.2918 [-7.3480]	-0.1290 [-2.7605]	-0.3032* [-11.091]
Z_{t-1}	-0.6130 [-17.5786]	-0.3755 [-9.1493]	0.1438* [5.9909]

Notes: Δ=first difference, and
*, **, ***, denote significance at 1 per cent, 5 per cent and 10 per cent levels respectively.

To justify the long-run relationship between sensex, crude oil and gold futures return, we have estimated the VECM for short-run dynamic adjustment of the variables. The optimum lag length for the VECM is selected by the AIC and SIC and these two models give 2 is the optimum lag-length for VECM. The estimated results of VECM for three variables at 2 lags are reported in Table 14.4. The results of the VECMs support the presence of cointegration tested above by the Johansen approach. The error correction coefficients Z_s, Z_c and Z_g for stock prices, crude oil and gold future returns are -0.613, -0.376 and 0.144 respectively and are significant at 1 per cent level. It reveals that the there is dynamic adjustment between these three variables for long-run equilibrium. The estimated coefficients show that each variables return is influenced by its own recent past returns as well as other two variables past returns.

Table 14.5

Summary Statistics of Conditional Correlations between Stock, Crude Oil and Gold Futures Returns

	Stock with Crude Oil	*Stock with Gold*	*Crude Oil with Gold*
Mean	0.068	0.032	0.279
Std. Dev.	0.040	0.163	0.156
Skewness	-0.205	0.338	-0.756
Kurtosis	3.174	3.335	3.903
Jarque-Bera	11.062	31.826	173.183
Probability	0.004	0.000	0.000
Observations	1340	1340	1340

Conditional Return Correlations and Conditional Volatilities between Stock, Crude Oil and Gold

Traditionally, many researchers have used the VAR model to examine the dynamic relationship between their study variables but this model could not capture the cross correlations between variances and covariances among the variables. Therefore, to examine the dynamic relationship between the study variables, we have used the Engle (2002) proposed DCC model. The summary statistics of conditional correlations estimated from the DCC model between three variables are reported in Table 14.5. It can be seen that the average conditional correlations (0.0677, 0.0318 and 0.2794 in Table 14.3) are same in magnitude with the unconditional correlations which are reported in Table 14.2. Similarly, the conditional correlations standard deviations between variables are divergent in volatilities to each other. The conditional correlations of sensex with crude oil standard deviations is 0.0402, whereas the conditional correlations standard deviations between sensex and gold is 0.1631. Similarly, the conditional correlations standard deviation of crude oil with gold is 0.1563. The result suggests that segmentation between sensex, crude oil and gold futures markets has increased over time. Therefore, to know how the conditional correlations between these three variables are affected with market shocks or volatility, we have estimated the conditional correlations against the market volatility of each variable.

The conditional correlations and conditional market volatility between sensex, crude oil and gold futures returns are reported in Table 14.6-14.8. In Table 14.6, we have reported the conditional correlation and conditional volatility between sensex and crude oil. The estimated result shows that β_S and β_C coefficient on $\sqrt{h_{s,i}}$ and $\sqrt{h_{c,i}}$ of Equation (1) are negative (-0.0034 and -0.003) and significant at 1 per cent level, indicating that conditional correlations between sensex and crude oil futures returns fall in periods when market risk rises. This means when there is increased crude oil return volatility, the correlations between sensex and crude oil fall. This is good news to institutional investors to diversify investment when market volatility is high that benefits of diversification are most needed (Engle, 2004). Similarly, in Table 14.7, we have reported the conditional correlation and conditional volatility between sensex and gold futures returns. It can be seen from Table 14.7 that the estimated β_S is native (-0.0089) and significant at 1 per cent level, whereas the coefficient β_G is negative (-0.0019) but not significant. This result indicates that there is fall in the conditional correlationship between sensex and gold, when there is increased market risk of two variables. The coefficient value of β_G in Table 16.8 is positive (0.0298) and significant at 1 per cent level. It indicates that if there is increased conditional volatility of gold return, it affects positively the conditional correlation between crude oil and gold.

Table 14.6

The Relation between Conditional Correlation and Conditional Volatility between Stock and Crude Oil

Variable	*Coefficient*	*Std. Error*	*t-Statistic*	*Prob.*
C	0.094	0.002	61.271	0.000
Z1	-0.003	0.000	-15.275	0.000
Z2	-0.003	0.000	-9.985	0.000
Adjusted R-squared	0.293			
Durbin-Watson stat	2.091			

Notes: Z1 and Z2 are conditional volatility of stock and crude oil, the results are derived by estimating the regression $\rho_{rci} = \alpha + \beta_Y \sqrt{h_{Y,i}} + \beta_C \sqrt{h_{C,i}} + \varepsilon_i$

where *T* and *C* stand for the stock and crude oil futures respectively,

ρ_{rci} is the conditional return correlation between stock and crude oil future return,

$\sqrt{h_i}$ is a conditional volatility and ε_i is an error term.

Table 14.7

The Relation between Conditional Correlation and Conditional Volatility between Stock and Gold Futures Return

Variable	*Coefficient*	*Std. Error*	*t-Statistic*	*Prob.*
C	0.068	0.007	9.631	0.000
Z1	-0.009	0.001	-7.636	0.000
Z2	-0.002	0.005	-0.406	0.685
Adjusted R-squared	0.063			
Durbin-Watson stat	0.021			

Notes: Same as Table 14.6.

Table 14.8

The Relation between Conditional Correlation and Conditional Volatility between Crude Oil and Gold Futures Return

Variable	*Coefficient*	*Std. Error*	*t-Statistic*	*Prob.*
C	0.331	0.007	47.381	0.000
Z2	-0.022	0.001	-17.111	0.000
Z3	0.030	0.004	7.649	0.000
Adjusted R-squared	0.178			
Durbin-Watson stat	0.077			

Notes: Same as Table 14.6.

Figure 14.1

The Relationship between Conditional Correlation and Conditional Volatility between Stock and Crude Oil Futures Returns

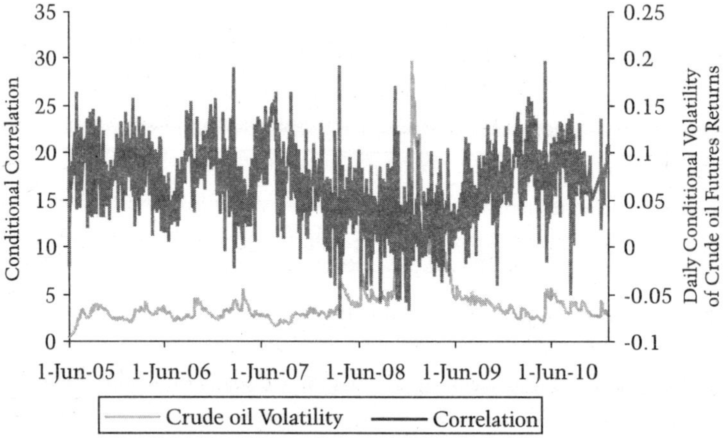

Figure 14.2

The Relationship between Conditional Correlation and Conditional Volatility between Stock and Gold Futures Returns

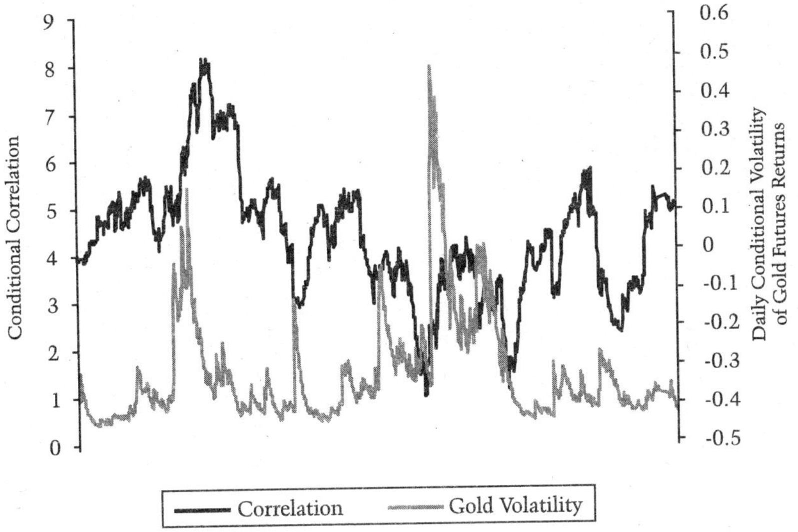

We have plotted the conditional correlations between these three variables in Figures 14.1-14.3. In Figure 14.1, we have plotted the conditional correlation between sensex and crude oil against the conditional volatility of crude oil future return. The figure shows that there has been negative relationship between conditional correlation and conditional volatility of crude oil. When there is an increase in the conditional volatility of crude oil futures returns (19 March 2007, 4 March 2008, 17 December 2008 and 10 May 2010), there has been a decline in conditional correlation between sensex and crude oil futures return. Alternatively, when there is a decline in conditional volatility of crude oil future returns, there is a spike in the conditional correlations between sensex and crude oil (22 November 2006, 27 July 2007 and 6 March 2010). Figure 14.1 clearly indicates the inverse relationship between conditional correlations between sensex and crude oil futures return with the conditional volatility of crude oil future return. It can be said from Table 14.6 that the average β_C coefficient is -0.003, which means 1 per cent rise in crude oil futures market risk leads, on average, to a 0.3 per cent fall in correlation and vice versa.

Figure 14.3

The Relationship between Conditional Correlation and Conditional Volatility between Gold and Crude Oil Futures Returns

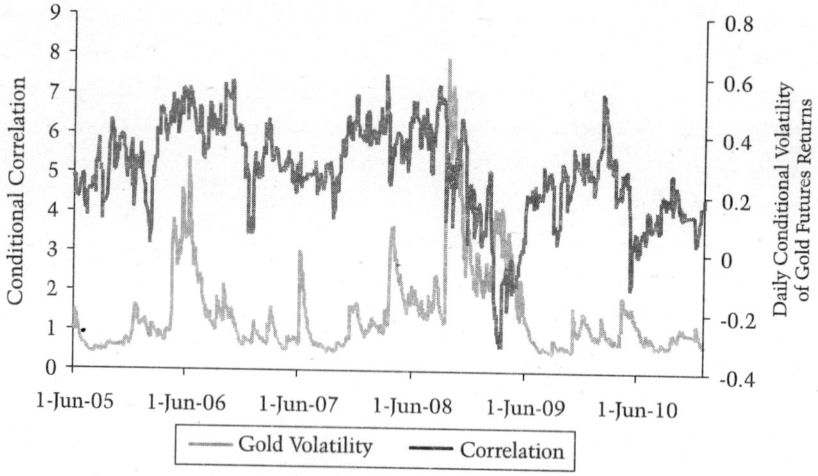

Similarly, if we look at Figure 14.2, it indicates the negative relationship between conditional correlations of sensex and gold futures returns with conditional volatility of gold futures returns. It shows that when there is an increase in conditional volatility of gold futures returns (14 June 2006, 7 June 2007, 25 March 2008 and 23 September 2008), there has been a fall in the conditional correlation between sensex and gold futures return. Likewise, when there is a fall in conditional volatility of gold futures return, there are spikes in conditional correlations between sensex and gold futures returns (7 August 2006, 17 August 2007, 2 January 2008 and 25 February 2010). This implies that both sensex and gold futures market are negatively related. This means when gold futures market poses diversification benefits in times of increased stock market (sensex), market stresses and vice versa. Now it can be said that from Table 14.7, the average β_G coefficient is -0.0019 that means a 1 per cent rise in gold futures market risk leads, on average, to a 0.19 per cent fall in correlation and vice versa. It indicates that investors/traders by allocating assets to gold futures during turbulence periods can benefit more from the decrease in correlation and the enhanced risk reduction that ensues.

Figure 14.3 shows the positive relationship between the conditional correlations between crude oil and gold futures returns with the conditional volatility of gold futures returns. The figure shows two types behaviour, first, the figure shows the positive relationship between the conditional correlations of crude oil and gold with conditional volatility of gold futures returns that means both are moving in a same direction up to 23 September, 2008. After that it can be seen that from 24 September to 30 December, 2010, both are in opposite direction. The most significant reason for this is during this period worldwide global financial crisis was realised; therefore, there has been largely fall in crude oil prices. On the other hand, though it is believed that gold is the most secure and risk-free asset, gold market attracts investors/traders, as a result there has been a rise in gold futures prices in India. Therefore, there has been positive relationship between the conditional correlation of crude oil and gold futures return with the conditional volatility of gold futures markets.

Summary and Conclusion

This paper examined the dynamic relationships between India's stock market, crude oil and gold futures market using daily data from 1 June, 2005 to 31 December, 2010. The cointegration result shows that there are both long- and short-term relationships between these three markets. The error correction model results show that the change of each variable returns is influenced not only by their own lag returns but also by other two variables' lag returns. The DCC model was used to examine the dynamic relationship between these three variables' returns and their volatility spillovers. This model showed the cross volatility relationships between these three markets. We found that there has been a negative relationship between the conditional correlations of stock market and crude oil futures market with the conditional volatility of crude oil futures return. Likewise, there is also a negative relationship between the conditional correlations of stock market and gold futures market with the conditional volatility of gold futures market. The DCC model provides a positive conditional correlation between crude oil and gold futures market with the conditional volatility of gold futures returns. But during the financial turmoil, both crude oil and gold futures market are negatively correlated.

References

Amritha, A.H. (2009). "Gold, Oil and Sensex: Has the Relationship Gone Awry?", *The Hindu Business Line*, January 12.

Bollersleve, T. (1986). "Generalised Autoregressive Conditional Heteroscedasticity", *Journal of Econometrics* 31: 307-27.

Brailsford, T.J. (1994). "The Empirical Relationship between Trading Volume, Returns and Volatility", *Working Paper 94-01*. University of Melborne.

Cappiello, L., R.F. Engle and K. Sheppard (2003). "Asymmetric Dynamics in the Correlations of Global Equity and Bond Returns", *WP Series*, European Central Bank.

Chang, C., M. McAleer and R. Tansuchat (2011). "Crude Oil Hedging Strategies using Dynamic Multivariate GARCH", *Energy Economics* 33: 912-23.

Diebold, F.X. (1986). "Modelling the Persistence of Conditional Variance: A Comment", *Econometric Reviews* 5: 51-56.

Engle, F.R. (2002). "Dynamic Conditional Heteroscedasticity Models", *Journal of Business and Economic Statistics* 20: 339-50.

Engle, R.F. (1982). "Autoregressive Conditional Heteroscedasticity with Estimates of the Variance of United Kingdom Inflation", *Econometrica* 50: 987-1007.

Engle, R.F. and K. Sheppard (2001). "Theoretical and Empirical Properties of Dynamic Conditional Correlation Multivariate GARCH", *NBER Working Paper*-8554.

Engle, R.F. and S. Manganelli (2004). "CAViaR: Conditional Autoregressive Value at Risk by Regression Quantiles", *Journal of Business & Economic Statistics* 22: 367-81. American Statistical Association.

Erb, C.B. and C.R. Harvey (2006). "The Tactical and Strategic Value of Commodity Futures", *Financial Analysts Journal* 62(2): 69-97.

Hsueh, P.L., Y.A. Liu and N.R. Lee (2008). "Dynamics of Volatility, Futures Trading, and Investor Sentiments Under Different Market Conditions", *International Research Journal of Finance and Economics* 20: 151-63.

Huang, R.D., R.W. Masulis and H.R. Stoll (1996). "Energy Shocks and Financial Markets", *Journal of Futures Market* 16(1): 1-27.

Jensen, G., R.R. Johnson and J. Mercer (2000). "Efficient use of Commodity Futures in Diversified Portfolios", *Journal of Futures Markets* 20: 489-506.

Johansen, S. and K. Juselius (1990). "Maximum Likelihood Estimation and Inference on Cointegration: With Application to the Demand for Money", *Journal of Oxford Bulletin of Economics and Statistics* 52(2):169-210.

Jones, C.M. and G. Kaul (1996). "Oil and the Stock Markets", *Journal of Finance* 51(2): 463-91.

Kuper, G. and L. Lestano (2007). "Dynamic Conditional Correlation Analysis of Financial Market Interdependence: An Application to Thailand and Indonesia", *Journal of Asian Economics* 18: 670-84.

Moosa, I.A. and P. Silvapulle (2000). "The Price-Volume Relationship in the Crude Oil Futures Market: Some Results based on Linear and Non-Linear Causality Testing", *International Review of Economics and Finance* 9: 11-30.

Narayan, P.K., S.N. Narayan and X. Zheng (2010). "Gold and Oil Futures Markets: Are Markets Efficient?", *Economics Working Paper-13*. Deakin University.

Nelson, D.B. (1991). "Conditional Heteroskedasticity in Asset Pricing: A New Approach", *Econometrica* 59: 347–70.

Pescatori, A. and M. Beth (2008). "Do Oil Prices Directly Affect the Stock Market?", *Research Paper*. Federal Reserve Bank of Cleveland.

Pradhan, K.C. and K. Sham Bhat (2009). "An Empirical Analysis of Price Discovery, Causality and Forecasting in the Nifty Futures Markets", *International Research Journal of Finance and Economics* 26: 83-92.

Schwert, G.W. (1990). "Why does Stock Market Volatility Change over time?" NBER-WP2798.

Twite, G. (2002). "Gold Prices, Exchange Rates, Gold Stocks and the Gold Premium", *Australian Journal of Management* 27(2): 123-40.

Zhang, Y. and M. Wei (2010). "The Crude Oil Market and the Gold Market: Evidence for Cointegration, Causality and Price Discovery", *Resources Policy* 35: 168-77.

15 An Analysis of the Dynamic Conditional Return Correlations between Commodity Futures Indices and Traditional Asset Markets in India

M.A. Lagesh and
Mohammed Kasim C.

Introduction

Portfolio diversification has been generally accepted as an important device to maximise the return from a group of assets of a single market or of different kinds of markets. The potential for portfolio diversification depends on the number of markets available for investment and the correlation between these markets (Rouwenhort, 2002). Interestingly, in India, the number of markets available for investment has recently increased, especially with the introduction of derivative trading in different kinds of assets such as equities, commodities and currencies, as well as with the introduction of corporate bond market.[1] It is now common that an investor with wide spectrum of investment opportunities invests not only in single type of assets, but also in different type of assets of different type of markets to obtain a well diversified portfolio. The benefits of such a diversification depend also on the correlation between the returns of assets of different markets. It was commonly agreed that an asset can provide

1. In India, Trading in Index Futures were introduced in June 2000 based on Sensex of Bombay Stock Exchange (BSE) and Nifty of National Stock Exchange (NSE). In June 2001, options on index were introduced for trading on these exchanges. Stock options on individual stocks were introduced in July 2001. Further, trading in stock futures was introduced in November 2001. Several national multi-commodity exchanges and regional commodity exchanges were set up since 2002.

superior returns to investor with well diversified portfolio only when it has little correlation with assets of other markets in the portfolio mix.

This argument is primarily based on the view that the risk arising from high price volatility in one market cannot be easily disseminated into another, if the markets are less correlated. Hence, less integration of asset markets always provides opportunity to an investor to compensate the loss in one market by trading in another market. However, in case of traditional asset markets like equity markets, the price fluctuations in one market can easily be disseminated into another, due to high degree of integration among markets across globe. Further, the contagion effect, i.e., the panic spread among markets soon after a financial a crisis, makes equity markets more vulnerable to foreign price fluctuations. The reverberations of any financial crisis, like recent subprime crisis, are now a days transmitted to various domestic equity markets across globe, through its effect on short-term capital flows that are highly speculative in nature. When financial crises occur, foreign institutional investors withdraw their funds from domestic markets. Such a sudden withdrawal leads to liquidity crunch in domestic equity market, ultimately resulting in huge stock market fall. India also experienced a stock market plunge as a result of recent financial crisis, with a drastic fall in Bombay Stock Exchange (BSE) and National Stock Exchange (NSE) indices. For instance, net flow of foreign institutional investments (FIIs) accounted for ₹ 7784.26 crore in February 2008, while it registered a negative figure as ₹ -13461 crore in October 2008 when massive gross sales, resulted out of global financial crisis, crossed the gross purchases. Consequently, NSE CNX Nifty plunged from 5223.5 to 2885.6 and so did BSE Sensex from 17578.72 to 9788.06 over the same period. In periods of such an equity market fall, an investor could reduce losses if he prudently invests some portion of his portfolio in a market which is least related with traditional asset markets.

Virtually, commodity future markets have little return correlation with traditional asset classes like stocks and bonds and thus are useful tools for portfolio diversification (Jensen *et al.*, 2000, Erb and Harvey, 2006, Daskalaki and Skiadopoulos, 2011). Further, correlations between commodity futures and equity returns tend to fall in turbulent periods, namely, when market risk increases (Chong and Miffre, 2008). Because the factors that drive commodity prices (e.g., weather and geopolitical conditions, supply constraints in the physical production and event risk) are distinct from those that determine the value of stocks and bonds (Daskalaki and Skiadopoulos, 2011, Geman, 2005). Hence, during periods of high volatility in equity markets, the investor could reallocate some of his portfolio to commodity futures to compensate the loss. Similarly, in periods of high volatility in short-term interest rates, the return correlation between the commodity futures and short-term interest rate securities tend to fall (Chong and Miffre, 2008). This suggests that during periods of interest rate fluctuations, the commodity futures could also be used together with short-term interest rate securities as fine portfolio diversifiers.

Several earlier studies have already established the diversification benefits of commodity futures without any ambiguity.[2] Earlier studies, comparing risk-return trade-off of portfolio of stocks alone and portfolio of stocks and commodities, showed that adding commodity futures reduces risk without sacrificing return (see Bodie and Rosansky, 1980; Fortenbery and Hauser, 1990; Conover *et al.*, 2010). Similarly, inclusion of commodity futures to traditional asset portfolio shifts the efficient frontier upwards (see Satyanarayan and Varangis, 1996; Abanomey and Mathur, 1999). Moreover, evidences put forth by some other earlier studies (Ankrim and Hensel, 1993, Jensen *et al.*, 2000; Idzorek, 2007) also suggest that incorporating commodity futures to traditional asset portfolio improves the risk-return trade-off of optimal portfolios.

Apart from the function of portfolio diversification, the commodity futures themselves have been growing as a separate asset class. They have started giving better returns to investors. They present positive skewness in their return distribution (Gorton and Rouwenhorst, 2006). Moreover, they serve as good hedge against inflation (Bodie and Rosansky, 1980; Bodie 1983; Daskalaki and Skiadopoulos, 2011). In India, volume and value of commodities future trading have been increasing at a significant rate since the first National Multi-Commodity Exchange (NMCE) was set up

2. Since our focus is on dynamic conditional correlation between commodity futures and traditional asset markets, we do not include a comprehensive review of literature on diversification benefits of commodity futures. However, for review of literature, see Jensen *et al.* (2000), Cheung and Miu (2010) and Daskalaki and Skiadopoulos (2011).

in November 2002 at Ahmedabad.[3] The total value of commodity futures trade increased from 0.66 lakh crore in 2002-03 to 21.34 lakh crore in 2005-06 and further increased to 77. 65 lakh crore in 2009-10.

However, among the various traded commodities, gold and silver account for half of turnover and by 2006 India had become home to the world's third largest derivative market for gold (Wells and Zibell, 2008). Further, during 2009-10, trading in Bullion, that includes precious metals like gold, silver and platinum, accounted for 40.75 per cent of total value of commodity trading. Such an outstanding growth of future trading in precious metals is mainly due to the fact that during periods of chaos in equity markets, investors treat commodity futures as refugee assets by reallocating a part of their traditional asset portfolio to commodity futures, especially gold futures.[4] All these facts imply that commodity futures in India have evolved as additional instruments for portfolio diversification and optimisation of risk-return trade-off. Hence, to investigate the potential for portfolio diversification benefits of commodity futures in Indian context, the present study focuses on the dynamic conditional correlation of commodity futures returns with that of traditional asset classes like stocks and bonds.

The literature on dynamic conditional correlation between traditional asset markets in general and equity markets in particular has been getting improved ever since advanced econometric techniques were developed, especially the class of multivariate generalised autoregressive conditional heteroscedasticity (GARCH) models which accounts for time varying conditional correlations. However, most studies analysed the dynamic conditional correlation between national and international equity markets to study the extent and nature of integration among the markets.[5] Some other studies analysed the conditional correlation between equity markets

3. Now there are 5 NMCEs and 16 recognised Commodity Specific Regional Exchanges. However, significant share of commodity trading takes place in NMCEs. For instance, during 2009-10, four NMCEs namely Multi Commodity Exchange (MCX), Mumbai, National Commodity and Derivatives Exchange (NCDEX), Mumbai, NMCE, Ahmedabad, and Indian Commodity Exchange, Ltd., New Delhi, contributed 98.86 per cent of the total value of the commodities traded.
4. Santhosh Kumar and Lagesh (2011) offer empirical validity to the 'safe heaven property' of gold futures in Indian context.
5. See Durai and Bhaduri (2011) for detailed review of national and international studies on dynamic conditional correlation between equity markets.

and bond markets.[6] On the other hand, studies analysing dynamic conditional correlation between stocks, bonds and commodity futures markets are scanty. Further, these studies are either in the context of developed countries or focused on important global equity and bond indices. For instance, Chong and Miffre (2008) examined the temporal changes in the conditional correlations between commodity futures returns and traditional asset returns using the major global equity and bond indices and commodity prices. Employing dynamic conditional correlation (DCC) GARCH model, they find that conditional correlation of commodity returns with stock index and Treasury bill returns fell over time, especially during periods of high volatility in equity prices and interest rates, suggesting that when market risk is high, the benefits of diversification is most appreciated. On the other hand, in case of long-term fixed income securities, conditional correlations tend to rise when volatility is high. On the contrary, Silvennoinen and Thorp (2010), by employing double smooth transition conditional correlation (DSTCC)-GARCH, showed that the correlation between returns to commodities and traditional stock and bond returns do not decline and further the integration of commodity and equity markets exhibited increases over the period 1990-2009 in case of selected developed countries like the USA and the UK.

However, to our knowledge, there is still paucity of study investigating the dynamic conditional correlation between stock, bond and commodity futures markets exclusively in the context of a developing country or an emerging economy, and more importantly, no such study is yet attempted in Indian context. Therefore, the present study seeks to analyse the dynamic conditional correlation between the returns of commodity futures, stocks, bond and Treasury bill indices markets in India, a major emerging economy.

The main distinction of the present study in this context is twofold. First, the study employs DCC-GARCH model to estimate the dynamic conditional correlation between returns of commodity futures indices and that of traditional asset markets such as stock, bond and Treasury bill indices markets in the context of a developing country. Second, we divide the study period into two, tranquil period and period of high volatility, i.e.,

6. Padhi and Lagesh (2010) present review of literature related to the dynamic conditional correlation between equity markets and bond markets.

crisis period, to study the differences in conditional correlations during these two periods. This is aimed at evaluating the diversification benefits of commodity futures when market volatility is high.

The remaining sections of the study is organised as follows. In the second section two, we discuss the data and methodology, while the third section presents the empirical results and discussions. The fourth section offers summary and conclusions.

Data and Methodology

Variables and Data Sources

The present study attempts to analyse the dynamic conditional correlation between the returns of commodity futures, stocks, bond and Treasury bill markets in India. For this purpose, we make use of the national commodity futures indices constructed by MCX India. These are COMDEX (an index represent all commodities), MCXMETAL, MCXENERGY and MCXAGRI which are representing the relevant sectors like metal, energy and agriculture. These indices are constructed from real time prices of exchange traded commodities/futures; each index is an indication of the price movements in the spot/futures market as a whole. Further, we introduced long-term bond index (LRLBND) as well as Treasury bill index (LRSBND) constructed by Clearing Corporation of India Limited (CCIL) as a proxy of Indian fixed income securities markets. CCIL constructed long-term bond indices in such a way that the securities included in the Broad index for a month would consist of top traded bonds of the previous month,[7] while Treasury bill index is based on 5 distinct sub-segments in terms of maturity buckets—(i) less than or equal to 60 days; (ii) between 61 and 120 days; (iii) between 121 and 240 days; (iv) between 241 and 360 days; and (v) 361 to 364 days. This includes all T-bills reported to the Negotiated Dealing System (NDS) of the Reserve Bank of India (RBI). As a proxy of Indian stock market, we selected S&P CNX Nifty

7. This index excludes bonds with maturities of less than 1.5 years, such as special bonds like oil bonds, Unit Trust of India (UTI) capitalisation bonds, floating rate bonds, bonds with call and put options, etc.

build up by NSE of India. S&P CNX Nifty is a well diversified 50 stock index accounting for 24 sectors of the economy.[8]

After adjusting for dates and missing observations, due to holidays, a total of 1612 daily observations over the period 7 June, 2005, to 30 September, 2011, were selected for the estimation. The total data set has been divided into two subsets to represent both tranquil period (pre-crisis period) and period of high volatility, i.e., recent global financial crisis periods. This is aimed at making a comparison between the temporal changes in the conditional correlations during normal period and volatility period. The reverberations of the global financial crisis, which started in the first half of 2008, reflected in Indian stock market by the mid of 2008, when net flow of FIIs became negative, due to huge withdrawal of investments by foreign investors. Starting from May 2008, FII monthly net flows registered negative figures consecutively until November 2008. As a result, the Indian stock markets experienced turbulent movements in their indices since mid of 2008.

Based on these observations, we have conducted a structural break test developed by Bai and Perron (1998) on stock market index to pick an exact date for the division purpose. Bai and Perron's test is considered as most sensitive index, which would identify potential breakpoints in the series that are formed due to recent global financial crisis. The Bai-Perron test determines endogenously the number of breakpoints and their corresponding dates when they are initially unknown. The number of breaks selected minimises the Bayesian information criterion (BIC). Result is reported in the appendix. According to this measure, there exist an optimal number of structural breaks in a given time series. According to the statistical criterion, selecting 9 July, 2008, break seems more appropriate. This date is common in all breaks considered in the test.

Therefore, we have selected 9 July, 2008 to divide the whole period. The tranquil period consists of 791 observations over the period 7 June, 2005, to 9 July, 2008. The second set represents the recent global financial crisis period that consists of 820 observations covering a period from 10

8. Visit *www.mcxindia.com*, *www.nseindia.com* and *www.ccilindia.com* for detailed explanation regarding the variables used in this study.

July, 2008, to 30 September, 2011. The return series for all indices are calculated with the following logarithmic formula:

$$R_t = \ln(\frac{P_t}{P_{t-1}})$$

Where 'ln' is a natural logarithmic operator, R_t is the return for period t, P_t is the level index price for period t.

Methodology

Simple (or rolling) correlation analysis is among the simplest method for examining the co-movement of financial variables. However, this method has been criticised for its limitations, especially to incorporate the time-varying variance which is the most common characteristics of a financial series.

We apply the bivariate DCC model proposed by Engle (2002) to examine the time-varying co-movement between commodity index futures and other traditional assets returns in India. DCC is a simplified multivariate generalised GARCH model. DCC has the flexibility of univariate GARCH models, but it still provides parsimonious correlation specifications without the computational difficulties of multivariate GARCH models.

The mean equation can be written as follows:

$$\begin{bmatrix} R_{i,t} \\ R_{j,t} \end{bmatrix} = \begin{bmatrix} \mu_{i,0} \\ \mu_{j,0} \end{bmatrix} + \begin{bmatrix} \varepsilon_{i,t} \\ \varepsilon_{i,t} \end{bmatrix} \quad (1)$$

where $\mu_{i,0}$ and $\mu_{j,0}$ are the unconditional means of commodity index and traditional asset returns to be estimated respectively and $\varepsilon_{i,t}$ and $\varepsilon_{j,t}$ are the residuals. The residuals of Equation (1) are assumed to be conditionally multivariate normal and the conditional covariance is specified using DCC analysis:

$$\varepsilon_{i,t} / I_{t-1} \sim N(0, H_t),\ H_t = \begin{bmatrix} \sigma^2_{i,t} & \sigma^2_{ij,t} \\ \sigma^2_{ji,t} & \sigma^2_{j,t} \end{bmatrix}$$

for i = commodity index and j= traditional asset

$$H_t = D_t R_t D_t \quad (2)$$

where I_{t-1} is the information set at time period *t-1*, *Ht* is the 2×2 conditional variance-covariance matrix at time t, R_t is the 2×2 time-varying correlation matrix at time *t* and *Dt* is a 2×2 diagonal matrix of time-varying standard deviations obtained from univariate GARCH (1,1) specifications:

$$h_{ii,t} = \omega_i + \alpha_{i,1}\,\varepsilon^2_{i,t-1} + \beta_{i,1} h_{ii,t-1} \tag{3}$$

for i = commodity index and j= traditional asset.

The conditional covariance terms are then assumed to follow the DCC (1, 1) specification:

$$h_{ij,t} = \rho_{ij,t}\sqrt{h_{ii,t}}\sqrt{h_{jj,t}}$$

$$\rho_{ij,t} = \frac{q_{ij,t}}{\sqrt{q_{ii,t}}\sqrt{q_{jj,t}}} \quad \textit{and}$$

$$q_{ij,t} = \bar{\rho}_{ij}(1-a-b) + aq_{ij,t-1} + b\eta_{i,t-1}\eta_{j,t-1} \tag{4}$$

for i = commodity index and j= traditional asset

where $q_{ij,t}$ is the conditional covariance between standardised residuals $(\eta_{i,t-1} = \varepsilon_{i,t}/\sqrt{h_{ii,t}})$ from Equation (1) and $\bar{\rho}_{ij}$ is the unconditional correlation between model residuals $(\varepsilon_{i,t})$. The average of $q_{ij,t}$ will be $\bar{\rho}_{ij}$ and the average variance will be 1. The $q_{ij,t}$ expression will be mean-reverting when a+b<1. The specification reduces the number of parameters to be estimated and makes the estimation and time-varying correlation more tractable.

As per Engle and Sheppard (2001) and Engle (2002), the DCC model can be estimated by using a two-stage approach to maximising the log-likelihood function. Let θ denote the parameters in D_t and Φ the parameters in R_t, then the log likelihood function is:

$$I_t(\Theta,\Phi)$$

$$= [-\frac{1}{2}\sum_{t=1}^{T}(n\log(2\pi) + \log|D_t|^2 + \varepsilon_t' D^{-2}\varepsilon_t)] +$$

$$[-\frac{1}{2}\sum_{t=1}^{T}(\log(2\pi) + \log|R_t| + \mu_t' R_t^{-1}\mu_t - \mu_t'\mu_t)]\,; \tag{5}$$

The first part of the likelihood function in Equation (5) is volatility, which is the sum of individual GARCH likelihoods. The log-likelihood function can be maximised in the first stage over the parameter in D_t. Given the estimated parameters in the first stage, the correlation component of the likelihood function in the second stage [the second part of the Equation (5)] can be maximised to estimate correlation coefficients. Quasi-maximum likelihood estimation (QMLE) of Bollerslev and Wooldridge (1992) is adopted in parameter estimation, which allows inference in the presence of departure from conditional normality.

Results and Discussions

Table 15.1 reports descriptive statistics on the return series of commodity, bond and stock market indices for whole, pre-crisis and crisis periods. Average returns reported in the first raw of each period indicate that commodity future indices provide higher return over whole, pre-crisis and crisis periods. Except Treasury bill index (LRSBND), which shows positive skewness in all periods, all other indices display mild negative skewness over whole and pre-crisis periods, while agricultural index (LRAGR) and stock market (LRNSE) return show mild positive skewness during crisis period. All the return series display significant leptokurtic behaviour as evidenced by large kurtosis with respect to the Gaussian distribution over whole, pre-crisis and crisis periods. Table 15.1 also displays Jarque-Bera test statistics for each period. The Jarque-Bera test statistics show that all the return series depart from the null hypothesis of normality distribution. Stationarity in the series is also checked by applying the augmented Dickey-Fuller (ADF) test. The results allow us to reject the null hypothesis that returns have unit root in favor of alternate hypothesis of stationarity at 1 per cent MacKinnon critical value in all periods under study.

Table 15.2 demonstrates the unconditional correlation between the returns of the commodity futures indices and other traditional assets in India for all three periods. It can be noted from panel 'A' that for over the whole period, the correlations of different commodity indices returns with stock index returns are very low. More importantly, the return of COMDEX (henceforth LRCDX), the index that represents all commodities, and the return of Nifty (henceforth LRNSE) show extremely low correlation

Table 15.1

Descriptive Statistics

Panel A: Whole Period							
	LRCDX	LRAGR	LRENR	LRMTL	LRSBND	LRLBND	LRNSE
Mean	0.0005	0.0005	0.0002	0.0007	0.0002	0.0003	0.0005
Median	0.0010	0.0004	0.0005	0.0014	0.0001	0.0002	0.0010
Maximum	0.2937	0.2051	0.4864	0.1356	0.0034	0.0229	0.1633
Minimum	-0.3082	-0.1928	-0.5194	-0.1377	-0.0029	-0.0479	-0.1301
Std. Dev.	0.0159	0.0131	0.0296	0.0145	0.0004	0.0031	0.0178
Skewness	-0.8399	-0.5600	-0.8160	-1.2590	0.2291	-1.8136	-0.0366
Kurtosis	163.5849	106.8413	157.2021	22.0550	14.2050	45.9348	10.7984
Jarque-Bera	1731177	723894.4	1596296	24798.18	8441.829	124621	4082.601
	(0.0000)	(0.0000)	(0.0000)	(0.0000)	(0.0000)	(0.0000)	(0.0000)
ADF	-50.100*	-23.402*	-34.4418*	-44.449*	-16.414*	-34.247*	-38.313*
	(0.0000)	(0.0000)	(0.0000)	(0.0000)	(0.0000)	(0.0000)	(0.0000)
Panel B: Pre-Crisis							
	LRCDX	LRAGR	LRENR	LRMTL	LRSBND	LRLBND	LRNSE
Mean	0.0009	0.0001	0.0011	0.0009	0.0002	0.0001	0.0009
Median	0.0012	0.0006	0.0009	0.0015	0.0002	0.0002	0.0014
Maximum	0.2937	0.0265	0.4864	0.1356	0.0034	0.0074	0.0672
Minimum	-0.3082	-0.1825	-0.5194	-0.1377	-0.0029	-0.0114	-0.0910
Std. Dev.	0.0186	0.0101	0.0370	0.0162	0.0004	0.0020	0.0170
Skewness	-0.9213	-7.6743	-0.8586	-1.4024	0.2193	-0.9709	-0.5727
Kurtosis	173.7127	136.8696	130.2872	25.8116	15.6340	8.8133	6.1626
Jarque-Bera	959396.7	597656.7	533413.8	17387.7	5260.434	1236.527	372.4133
	(0.0000)	(0.0000)	(0.0000)	(0.0000)	(0.0000)	(0.0000)	(0.0000)
ADF	-26.028*	-27.104*	-22.0221*	-34.000*	-36.076*	-25.356*	-27.499*
	(0.0000)	(0.0000)	(0.0000)	(0.0000)	(0.0000)	(0.0000)	(0.0000)
Panel C: Crisis							
	LRCDX	LRAGR	LRENR	LRMTL	LRSBND	LRLBND	LRNSE
Mean	0.0001	0.0009	-0.0005	0.0004	0.0002	0.0004	0.0003
Median	0.0007	0.0001	0.0001	0.0013	0.0001	0.0002	0.0005
Maximum	0.0559	0.2051	0.0789	0.0510	0.0015	0.0229	0.1633
Minimum	-0.0692	-0.1928	-0.0845	-0.0854	-0.0009	-0.0479	-0.1301
Std. Dev.	0.0126	0.0154	0.0199	0.0126	0.0003	0.0038	0.0185
Skewness	-0.5358	1.3760	-0.2358	-0.9216	0.1994	-1.7793	0.3727
Kurtosis	6.4984	84.4160	5.0710	7.8716	3.9986	37.1062	13.7742
Jarque-Bera	458.5223	227287.9	154.5201	929.1961	39.60135	40274.42	3994.877
	(0.0000)	(0.0000)	(0.0000)	(0.0000)	(0.0000)	(0.0000)	(0.0000)
ADF	-26.849*	-18.391*	-25.488*	-27.631*	-10.429*	-24.137*	-26.786*
	(0.0000)	(0.0000)	(0.0000)	(0.0000)	(0.0000)	(0.0000)	(0.0000)

(0.0054). Similarly, for the whole period Treasury bill index return (henceforth LRSBND) shows low negative correlations with LRCDX and energy index (henceforth LRENR) and low positive correlation with returns of index of agricultural commodities (henceforth LRAGR) and metals (henceforth LRMTL). Long-term bond index return (henceforth LRLBND) also shows a negative correlation with LRCDX and a very low positive correlation with returns of agricultural, energy and metal commodity indices. All this imply that commodity future returns move independently from equity and bond returns.

Table 15.2

Unconditional Correlation

	Panel A: Whole Period			
	LRCDX	*LRAGR*	*LRENR*	*LRMTL*
LRSBND	-0.0175	0.0251	-0.0214	0.0226
LRLBND	-0.0362	0.052	0.0184	0.0078
LRNSE	0.0054	0.0455	0.1032	0.0561
	Panel B: Pre-Crisis			
	LRCDX	*LRAGR*	*LRENR*	*LRMTL*
LRSBND	-0.0005	-0.0003	-0.0077	0.0492
LRLBND	-0.0016	0.0636	0.0089	-0.0082
LRNSE	0.0050	0.0296	0.0581	0.0313
	Panel C: Crisis			
	LRCDX	*LRAGR*	*LRENR*	*LRMTL*
LRSBND	-0.0538	0.0503	-0.0570	-0.0237
LRLBND	-0.0683	0.0469	0.0374	0.0205
LRNSE	0.0108	0.0574	0.1923	0.0873

As expected, during the pre-crisis period, commodity indices showed low and in some cases negative correlation with other traditional assets. As can be noted from panel 'C' of Table 15.2, there is an increase in the degree of correlation between the commodity indices and other traditional assets during the crisis period. However, when we compare this with the correlation between commodity indices and other traditional assets during whole period, the increase in the correlation is insignificant. This implies that commodity futures are good candidates for portfolio diversification.

To understand the dynamic conditional correlation between commodity futures indices and other traditional assets in India, we have employed DCC-GARCH model proposed by Engle (2002). This model accounts for the changes in volatility, and thereby be free from the potential upward bias during periods of financial turmoil. Figures 15.1 and 15.2 demonstrate the DCCs derived from DCC-GARCH (1,1) model for pre-crisis and crisis period respectively. Table 15.3 illustrates the descriptive statistics on DCC series.

Panel A of Table 15.3 reports descriptive statistics of the DCC during the pre-crisis period. During the pre-crisis period, in most cases, the average DCCs between commodity indices returns and other assets returns are very low, ranging from -0.00770 to 0.07064. In some cases, average DCCs between commodity indices and other assets are negative, especially between LRCDX and LRSBND, LRAGR and LRNSE, LRENR and LRLBND, and LRMTL and LRLBND. On the other hand, remaining cases show very low positive correlations. The highest range of the dynamic correlation in the pre-crisis period is between LRAGR and LRSBND i.e., 0.26303 to a minimum of -0.17498.

Panel B of Table 15.3 depicts descriptive statistics of the DCC during the crisis period. During this period, average conditional correlation showed low negative correlation in most cases. There is a clear evidence for negative correlation between LRCDX and LRLBND, LRCDX and LRSBND, LRENR and LRLBND, LRENR and LRSBND, LRMTL and LRLBND, and LRMTL and LRSBND. The low conditional correlations during pre-crisis and crisis period indicate that the commodity futures market and traditional asset markets in India become more separated and their returns are totally independent. These evidences reveal the portfolio diversification benefits of commodity and investors can maximise their risk-return trade-off by adding commodity futures to their portfolio.

Further, we have fitted trend line for every conditional correlation during crisis period to verify whether conditional correlations declined during crisis periods. The results given in Table 15.4 showed mixed trends, including negative and positive trends. The conditional correlation between LRAGR and LRLBND, LRAGR and LRSBND, and LRMTL and LRLBND showed negative trend, indicating that the conditional correlation of

Table 15.3

Descriptive Statistics on Dynamic Conditional Correlation

	Panel A: Pre-Crisis Period				*Panel B: Crisis Period*			
	Mean	*Median*	*Maximum*	*Minimum*	*Mean*	*Median*	*Maximum*	*Minimum*
LRCDX/LRLBND	0.02595	0.02595	0.02595	0.02595	-0.01562	-0.01687	0.54535	-0.5412
LRCDX/LRNSE	0.02230	0.02230	0.02230	0.02230	0.04812	0.04780	0.32620	-0.09998
LRCDX/LRSBND	-0.01296	-0.01310	0.15700	-0.18600	-0.03056	-0.03057	-0.02957	-0.03164
LRAGR/LRLBND	0.07084	0.07084	0.07109	0.07077	0.01756	0.01572	0.09436	-0.00496
LRAGR/LRNSE	-0.02946	-0.03285	0.12615	-0.14434	0.06497	0.06344	0.36193	-0.14658
LRAGR/LRSBND	0.03686	0.03718	0.26303	-0.17498	0.07606	0.06753	0.49065	-0.10994
LRENR/LRLBND	-0.00770	-0.00770	-0.00770	-0.00700	-0.02832	-0.02746	0.30692	-0.41043
LRENR/LRNSE	0.06574	0.06499	0.20800	-0.05294	0.18542	0.18542	0.18542	0.18542
LRENR/LRSBND	0.00541	0.00541	0.00541	0.00541	-0.10040	-0.10040	-0.10040	-0.10040
LRMTL/LRLBND	-0.01244	-0.01244	-0.01244	-0.01244	-0.01751	-0.01751	-0.01751	-0.01751
LRMTL/LRNSE	0.04671	0.04671	0.04671	0.04671	0.08746	0.08698	0.25233	-0.20850
LRMTL/LRSBND	0.06915	0.06915	0.06916	0.06914	-0.02640	-0.02640	-0.02637	-0.02644

agriculture commodity future returns with long-run bond returns and short run bond returns declined during the crisis period, so did the conditional correlation between the metal futures index returns and long-run bond returns. This suggests that the returns of these commodity futures and long-run and short-run bonds become more segmented during crisis periods. There is significant positive trend only in case of correlation between LRCDX and LRLBND. In all other cases, trend line is found to be insignificant.

Table 15.4

Time Trend of Conditional Correlations for Crisis Period

Dependent Variable(Corr.)	*Intercept*	*Trend*
LRCDX/LRLBND	-0.02694* (0.0000)	2.76E-05** (0.0430)
LRCDX/LRNSE	0.045892* (0.0000)	5.43E-06 (0.2178)
LRCDX/LRSBND	-0.03056* (0.0000)	1.25E-08 (0.7216)
LRAGR/LRLBND	0.023665* (0.0000)	-1.49E-05* (0.0000)
LRAGR/LRNSE	0.060782* (0.0000)	1.02E-05 (0.2491)
LRAGR/LRSBND	0.094743* (0.0000)	-4.56E-05* (0.0005)
LRENR/LRLBND	-0.022125* (0.0000)	-1.51E-05 (0.1146)
LRENR/LRNSE	0.185417* (0.0000)	1.86E-12 (0.6470)
LRENR/LRSBND	-0.100398* (0.0000)	-7.44E-18 (0.5477)
LRMTL/LRLBND	-0.017507* (0.0000)	-1.22E-17* (0.0001)
LRMTL/LRNSE	0.085252* (0.0000)	5.38E-06 (0.1448)
LRMTL/LRSBND	-0.026401* (0.0000)	1.61E-09 (0.1253)

Note: *, ** indicate significance at 1 per cent and 5 per cent level respectively.
Values in parenthesis are probability values.

Further, to understand the nature of relationship between conditional correlations and conditional market volatility in traditional asset markets during crisis period, we have regressed the conditional correlations on conditional market volatility. Such an analysis would be helpful to understand whether the conditional correlations between commodity future returns and returns of traditional assets declined during high volatility in traditional markets. The results given in Table 15.5 reveal mixed picture.

The relations between conditional market volatility of stock index and the conditional correlations of NSE stock index returns with agriculture commodity futures returns, Energy commodity futures returns and Metal commodity futures returns are inverse during crisis period. It reveals that the conditional correlations of these commodity indices returns with stock index declined in periods when market risk rises. This further indicates that the diversification benefits of commodity futures increases in periods of high risk in equity markets. The negative relation between stock market volatility and correlation of LRMTL (metals) and LRNSE warrants two things. When there is high volatility in equity market, investors could reallocate a portion of their stock portfolio to precious metals, and benefit more from decline in correlations. The benefits of such a diversification most realised when market risk is high. By and large, institutional investors treat the precious metals as refugee assets in periods of high market volatility.

Chong and Miffre (2008) identified the possible factors responsible for inverse relation between equity market volatility and conditional correlations of agricultural futures returns with equity index returns. First, any national or international instability negatively affects equity returns and positively affects commodity prices. Similarly, hike in inflation negatively affects equity markets and increases returns from commodities. Further, higher commodity prices increase the returns from long positions in commodity futures, however, on the other hand create high stock market volatility. Because commodities are inputs for most of the firms, an increase in commodity prices tends to increase costs and increase uncertainty in returns of a firm.

However, in case of CDX index returns, the relation between conditional market volatility of stock index and conditional correlations of NSE stock index returns and COMDEX returns is not significant.

However, the nature of relation is different for fixed income securities. The relationships between volatility in LRLBND and correlations of LRAGR, LRENR and LRMTL with LRLBND are found to be positive. It

Table 15.5

The Relation between Conditional Correlation and Conditional Market Volatility

Dependent Variable (Corr.)	*LRLBNDVOL*	*LRNSEVOL*	*LRSBNDVOL*	*LRCDXVOL*	*LRAGRVOL*	*LRENRVOL*	*LRMTLVOL*	*C*	*Adj. R Square*
LRCDX/LRLBND	-173.712500 (0.3332)			-14.047820 (0.7041)				-0.0108*** (0.0507) 0.049699	0.000977
LRCDX/LRNSE		0.481195 (0.8846)		-11.202870 (0.3952)				0.01407* (0.0000)	-0.000947
LRCDX/LRSBND			790.9343** (0.0190)	-0.54471* (0.0000)				-0.03055* (0.0000)	0.045802
LRAGR/LRLBND	245.4139* (0.0000)				-0.209103 (0.4292)			0.01407* (0.0000)	0.248467
LRAGR/LRNSE		-17.0905 (0.0002)			-4.07232* (0.0079)			0.07280* (0.0000)	0.021734
LRAGR/LRSBND			82737.050000 (0.4149)		-2.335958 (0.3079)			0.06828* (0.0000)	-0.000394
LRENR/LRLBND	982.055* (0.0000)					-58.200* (0.0000)		-0.02012* (0.0000)	0.033806
LRENR/LRNSE		-0.00007* (0.0071)				0.00001* (0.0000)		0.18541 (0.0000)	0.020400
LRENR/LRSBND			1.71E-07 (0.1047)			6.50E-1* (0.0000)		-0.10039* (0.0000)	0.064979
LRMTL/LRLBND	1.59E-1* (0.0000)						-3.53E-13 (0.9534)	-0.01750* (0.0000)	0.030306
LRMTL/LRNSE		-10.52480* (0.0000)					32.95333* (0.0001)	0.08599* (0.0000)	0.024447
LRMTL/LRSBND			19.14453** (0.0321)				-0.00831* (0.0001)	-0.02640* (0.0000)	0.016817

Notes: *, **, *** indicate significant at 1 %, 5 % and 10 % level respectively

Values in parenthesis are probability values.

reveals that the conditional correlation tends to move directly with the volatility of long-term fixed income securities. Similarly, there is only one significant relation between market volatility and conditional correlations when we consider the case of Treasury bill index returns. There is positive relation between market Treasury bill volatility and conditional correlation between LRMTL and LRSBND. This also shows that the conditional correlation tends to rise when Treasury bill volatility increases. In all other cases, the relations are found to be insignificant.

Summary and Conclusion

The study examined the dynamic conditional correlation of commodity futures returns with that of traditional asset classes like stocks and bonds to empirically analyse the potential for portfolio diversification benefits of commodity futures in Indian context. Using the daily data of notional commodity futures indices constructed by MCX India, long-term bond index (LRLBND) as well as Treasury bill index (LRSBND) constructed by CCIL and S&P CNX Nifty index of NSE for a period of six years, we have employed DCC-GARCH model proposed by Engle (2002) to study the dynamic conditional correlations. We have divided the study period into two pre-crisis and crisis period to study whether the movement of dynamic conditional correlations during periods of high market volatility in traditional asset markets varies.

Empirical results suggest that there exist very low dynamic conditional correlations between commodity futures indices returns and traditional asset indices returns, a clear evidence indicating the portfolio diversification benefits of commodity futures. Commodity futures become more segmented from traditional asset market, thus they can be effectively used for strategic asset allocation. The price movements in traditional asset markets do not affect the commodity futures returns. Therefore, one could maximise the risk-return trade-off by taking long-term position in commodity futures along with an equity portfolio, thereby any reduction in returns resulted out of high volatility traditional asset markets can be compensated.

Further, the conditional correlation between agriculture commodity future returns with long-run bond returns and short-run bond returns declined during the crisis period, so did the conditional correlation between the metal futures index returns and long-run bond returns. This suggests that the conditional correlations of returns of these commodity futures and long-run and short-run bonds declined during turbulent periods.

Moreover, study reveals that the conditional correlations of these commodity indices returns (agriculture, energy and metal) with stock index declined in periods when equity market risk rises. This further indicates that the diversification benefits of commodity futures increase in periods of high risk in equity markets. However, the conditional correlations commodity futures returns tend to move directly with the volatility of long-term and short-term fixed income securities. This could be due to the illiquidity and highly restrictive policies in Indian bond market.

References

Abanomey, W.S. and I. Mathur (1999). "The Hedging Benefits of Commodity Futures in International Portfolio Construction", *Journal of Alternative Investments* 2: 51–62.

Ankrim, E.M and C.R. Hensel (1993). "Commodities in Asset Allocation: A Real Asset Alternative to Real Estate?", *Financial Analysts Journal* 49: 20–29.

Bai, Jushan and Pierre Perron (1998). "Estimating and Testing Linear Models with Multiple Structural Changes", *Econometrica* 66(1): 47-78.

Bodie, Z. (1983). "Commodity Futures as a Hedge Against Inflation", *Journal of Portfolio Management* 12-17, Spring.

Bodie, Z. and V. Rosansky (1980). "Risk and Returns in Commodity Futures", *Financial Analysts Journal*: 27-39, May/June.

Bollerslev, T. and J.M. Wooldridge (1992). "Quasi-maximum Likelihood Estimation and Inference in Dynamics Models with Time-varying Covariances", *Econometric Reviews* 11(2).

Cheung, C.S. and Peter Miu (2010). "Diversification Benefits of Commodity Futures", *Journal of International Financial Markets, Institutions and Money* 20: 451-74.

Chong, J. and J. Miffre (2008). "Conditional Return Correlation between Commodity Futures and Traditional Assets", *Working Paper*, EDHEC Risk and Asset Management Research Cetntre, Lille Nice.

Conover, C.M., G.R. Jensen, R.R. Johnson and J.M. Mercer (2010). "Is Now the Time to Add Commodities to Your Portfolio?", *Journal of Investing* 19: 10–19.

Daskalaki, C. and G. Skiadopoulos (2011). "Should Investors Include Commodity in their Portfolios After all ? New Evidence", *Journal of Banking and Finance* 35: 2606-26.

Erb, C. and C. Harvey (2006). "The Strategic and Tactical Value of Commodity Futures", *Financial Analysts Journal* 62(2): 69-97.

Engle, R.F. (2002). "Dynamic Conditional Correlation: A Simple Class of Multivariate Generalised Autoregressive Conditional Heteroscedasticity Models", *Journal of Business and Economic Statistics* 20: 339-50.

Engle, R.F. and K.K. Sheppard (2001). "Theoretical and Empirical Properties of Dynamic Conditional Correlation Multivariate GARCH", *NBER Working Papers-8554*, National Bureau of Economic Research, Camridge.

Fortenbery, T.R. and R.J. Hauser (1990). "Investment Potential of Agricultural Futures Contracts", *American Journal of Agricultural Economics* 72: 721–26.

Forward Market Commission (2011). *Annual Report 2009-10*. Ministry of Consumer Affairs, Food and Public Distribution, Department of Consumer Affairs, Government of India, Mumbai.

Galvani, V. and A. Plourde (2010). "Portfolio Diversification in Energy Markets", *Energy Economics* 32: 257–68.

Geman, H. (2005). *Commodities and Commodity Derivatives: Modeling and Pricing for Agriculturals, Metals and Energy*. Chichester: John Wiley & Sons Ltd.

Gorton, G. and K. Rouwenhorst (2006). "Facts and Fantasies about Commodity Futures", *Financial Analysts Journal* 62(4): 86-93.

Idzorek, T.M. (2007). "Commodities and Strategic Asset Allocation", in, H. Till and J. Eagleeye (eds.). *Intelligent Commodity Investing*. London: Risk Books.

Jensen, G., R. Johnson and J. Mercer (2000). "Efficient Use of Commodity Futures in Diversified Portfolios", *Journal of Futures Markets* 20: 489-506.

Padhi, Puja and M.A. Lagesh (2010). "Correlation Dynamics between Stock and Bond Return: Evidence from India", *Arthavigyan* LII(4): 331-331.

Raja, S. Durai and Sumitra N. Bhaduri (2011). "Correlation Dynamics in Equity Markets: Evidence from Indian", *Research in International Buisness and Finance* 25: 69-75.

Rouwenhorst, K.G. (2002). "Long-term Global Market Volatility and Correlation", *Canadian Investment Review*, Summer, pp.31.

Santhosh Kumar, P.K. and M.A. Lagesh (2011). "A DCC Analysis of the 'Safe Haven' Property of Gold Against Stock Market: Some Recent Evidence from India", *Arthavigyan* LIII(2): 125-35.

Satyanarayan, S. and P. Varangis (1996). "Diversification Benefits of Commodity Assets in Global Portfolios", *Journal of Investing* 5: 69-78.

Silvennoinen, A. and S.J. Thorp (2010). "Financialization, Crisis and Commodity Correlation Dynamics", *Research Paper Series*. Sydney: Quantitative Finance Research Centre, University of Technology.

Teravista, T., D. Tjostheim and W.J.C. Granger (2010). *Modeling Nonlinear Economic Time Serie*. Oxford University Press.

Thorp, Susan and H. Silvennoinen (2010). "Financialisation, Crisis and Commodity Correlation Dynamics", *Research Paper* 267, Quantitative Finance Research Centre, University of Technology, Sydney.

Wells, Stephen and L. Schou-Zibell (2008). "India's Bond Market-developments and Challenges Ahead", *Working Paper Series on Regional Economic Integration*, No. 22, Asian Development Bank, Mandaluyong City, Philippines.

16 Risk in Black Scholes Option Pricing Model

Tuhin Mukherjee and
Biswajit Chakraborty

Introduction

In the early 1970s, Myron Scholes, Robert C. Merton and Fisher Black made an important breakthrough in the pricing of complex financial derivatives and it has become known as the Black-Scholes (BS) model. It was published in the *Journal of Political Economy* 81(3) (May-June 1973). Rubinstein (1994) states that the BS model is the most widely used formula, with embedded probabilities, in human history. In 1997, the importance of their model was recognised worldwide, when Myron Scholes and Robert C. Merton received the Nobel Prize for Economics. Unfortunately, Fisher Black died in 1995; otherwise he would have also received the award. The BS model proposed a partial differential equation for option pricing and its closed form solution. This model has had huge influence on the way that traders price and hedge options (Hull, 2006). McDonald (2006) argues that the BS model fails to consider all of the factors that enter into the pricing of an option. This model only accounts for the stock price, the exercise price, time to expiration, the dividends and the risk-free rate. Still its biggest strength is the possibility of estimating market volatility of an underlying asset, as a function of price and time without direct reference to specific investors characteristics like expected yield, risk aversion measure or utility function (Teneng, 2011).

The BS model constitutes the cornerstone of contemporary valuation theory in both discrete and continuous time finance. Despite their popularity and widespread use, the model is built on some non-real life assumptions about the market. These unrealistic and rigid assumptions are stated, explained, challenged and extended in several research papers in the last four decades (1973-2012). This paper attempts to give an outline of the BS model with its own discussion about its assumption and opinion of its implication.

Assumptions behind BS Model

Invariance Nature of Volatility

The BS model assumes that stock price is independent of all the previous trading. In this case, each trade contributes to the overall volatility in the same way. This is the constant volatility assumption.

In reality volatility can be relatively constant in a very short term, but it is never constant in longer term. Large price changes tend to be followed by another large price changes and vice versa leading to a property called volatility clustering. In fact, empirical evidence by Black (1976) himself shows that measures of volatilities are negatively correlated with asset price returns (leverage effect), while trading volumes or the number of trades are positively correlated. Hence volatility cannot be a constant over time (Carr, 2002). Some advanced option valuation models substitute BS's constant volatility with stochastic process-generated estimates. Followings are the other studies which we reviewed about such constancy of volatility assumption.

Rosenberg (1973) suggests that it follows an autoregressive scheme. Blattberg and Gonedes (1974) suggest that volatility of the underlying stock is stochastic and random. Their empirical results are also consistent with the results of Geske (1979). MacBeth and Merville (1980) found that the volatility of the underlying stock decreases as the stock price rises. Schoenmakers and Kloeden (1998) proposed an extension of the BS model by adding a term to the original Weiner term involving a smoother process, which was a challenge of constant volatility assumption. Yang (2006) found implied volatilities on the ASX 200 Index are unbiased and superior to historical instantaneous volatility in forecasting future realised volatility.

In summary, above review shows that statistical analysis on various stocks reveals long range dependence behaviour of the stock prices that is not consistent with classical BS model. This memory or non-deterministic trend behaviour is often seen as a reflection of market sentiments that oppose the assumption of volatility invariance.

Impossibility of Consistent Predictability

The BS model assumes that the underlying stock prices follow the geometric Brownian motion i.e., the price of a stock in time $t+1$ is independent from the price in time t (martingale property of Brownian motion). Hence stock moves in a manner referred to as a random walk. Random walk means that at any given moment, the price of the underlying stock can go up or down with the same probability. This is usually not true as stock prices are determined by many economic factors that cannot be assigned the same probability in the way they will affect the movement of stock prices. In other words, there may not be a single source of uncertainty driving say two assets even if one is a derivative of the other (in contrast to martingale representation theorem as mathematicians often assume).

Log Normally Distributed Price and Normally Distributed Return

This assumption is reasonable in the real world, though not fitting into observed financial data accurately. Asset returns have a finite variance and semi-heavy tails contrary to stable distributions like log normal with infinite variance and heavy tails (Clark, 1973). Duan (1999) suggested the tail properties of the underlying log-normal distribution are too small. In other words, the BS model assumes that the percentage changes in asset prices are log-normally distributed, ignoring the possibility of future losses and thus underestimating the financial risk. But it has been found empirically that when attempting to price options, traders do take into account the possibility of suffering loss.

As the time scale over which return of assets is calculated increases, the distribution of asset prices looks more like the normal distribution with heavy tails despite the fact that autocorrelation of asset prices is often insignificant (Rama, 2003).

Known Interest Rates with Zero Variance

It uses the risk-free rate to represent this constant and known interest rate. In the real world, there is no such thing as a risk-free rate, but it is possible to use a rate (like interest of nationalised banks) which is deemed to be stable enough. However, these rates can change in times of increased volatility.

In fact, the BS theory implies that fluctuation of the derivative and the underlying stock exactly and immediately cancels each other when combined in a certain proportion i.e., one unit of derivative with a short sale of $\partial c/\partial s$ units of the underlying, so that the 'hedge' portfolio is devoid of any impact of such fluctuation. This is obviously strongly unrealistic and there may exist a very brief period when no arbitrage condition may cease to hold and hence, returns on the 'hedge' portfolio may be different from risk-free rate.

One way to remove this anomaly is to obtain the parameters of the pricing model from empirics of the financial markets, what exactly J.P.Singh and S. Prabakaran did in 2006. They proposed a generalisation of the BS model by removing constancy of return assumption. They introduced a stochastic return for the 'hedge' portfolio. Their work is based on the Vasicek model for short term.

Thus the BS model immunised against price fluctuations of the underlying and its derivative through mutual interaction; other market factors that would impact the portfolio as a whole are not accounted for (e.g., factors affecting bond yields and interest rates, etc). Consequently, to assume that 'hedge' portfolio is completely risk free is an aberration; it is risk free only to the extent of risk that emanates from factors that impact the underlying and the derivatives in like manner and is still subject to risk and uncertainties that originate from factors that either do not affect the underlying and the derivative to equivalent extent or impact the portfolio as a unit entity.

Absence of Dividends

This assumption relates to the basic BS formula. In the real world, most companies pay dividends to their shareholders. The basic BS model was later adjusted for dividends, so there is a work around for this. A common way of adjusting the BS model for dividends is to subtract the discounted value of a future dividend from the stock price.

Absence of Transaction Costs

The model assumes that there are no fees for buying and selling options and stocks and no barriers to trading. Usually it is not true as stock brokers charge rates based on spreads and other criteria.

The BS formula is considered by some economist to be a 'self-fulfilling' prophecy (Cherian and Jarrow, 1994) in the following sense. Due to absence of transaction cost, investors can buy or sell stocks to maintain the hedge position within this self-financing strategy (i.e., without bringing or consuming wealth). This assumption is completely unrealistic in real life situations.

European Options Only

The BS model only proposed a pricing model for European option. The same partial differential equation (PDE) holds for European options with different boundary conditions of call and put options and their solutions satisfy put-call parity.

In contrast, American-style options can be exercised at any time during the life of the option. It makes American options more valuable due to their greater flexibility. The BS model did not address the issue of such American options. There are a lot of extended study of the BS model by other researchers who have taken care of such American options.

Possibility of Purchase or Sell of Fractions of Assets

This again is not plausible as purchasing/selling by investors are limited by the amount of money they can invest, policies of their companies and by the wish of sellers to sell or buyers to buy. It may not be possible to buy/sell fractions of options (say $\partial c/\partial s$ amount, for perfect hedging) as well. There are many recent studies by new researchers who have adjusted this factor in the extension of the BS model.

Risk-Neutral World

Another assumption of the BS model is risk-neutral valuation. In such risk neutral world, all individuals are indifferent to risk and require no compensation for risk. The BS model does not involve any variable that is affected by investors' risk preference (Derman and Kani, 1994). Therefore, the option can be valued as though the expected rate of return on all securities is the risk-free interest rate (Gray *et al.*, 2006).

No Arbitrage Opportunity

The BS model assumes that the market is efficient and thus there are no arbitrage activities in the market. The option value should reflect all available information regarding the option and its underlying assets. Therefore, market participants in the efficient market are not able to trade options to earn riskless profits (Wilson and Fung, 1991). This unrealistic assumption is challenged by so many researchers in recent days with their empirical findings.

In fact, it is extremely difficult to derive the correct mathematical model because the arbitrage opportunities do exist in the real world and are very hard to be incorporated into the option pricing model (Das and Sundaram, 1999; Ederington and Guan, 2002). So the ideal assumption concerning no arbitrage activities in the markets threatens the reliability of the BS model.

Absence of Discontinuous Jump

The continuous time finance framework of BS model does not allow jump, which is another limitation of BS model. There have been also other various attempts to extend the BS theory to incorporate stochastic volatility factor and discontinuous jumps in the stock price in order to take into account the volatility smile. These extended BS models always decompose the total change in stock price into 'normal' and 'abnormal' components. These models yield excess kurtosis and negative skew in the stock return distribution, which is consistent with the empirical evidence (Cox and Ross, 1976; Merton, 1976; Oldfield *et al.*, 1977). These normal components are modelled by the lognormal diffusion process (Ball and Torous, 1983). The 'abnormal' changes may be due to the receipt of any information which causes jumps in the price of the stock and is usually modelled by the Poisson process (Ball and Torous, 1983).

Other Issues behind BS Model

Since most of the limitations of BS model relate to fundamental aspects of the market, it is necessary to come up with models that will take into consideration some of the modified assumptions not addressed by BS model. Many models have been proposed over time, all attempting to mimic the characteristics of the market fully. Every aspect of the market cannot be considered in any given model, as every factor affecting the price of a financial security cannot be captured mathematically. We can only attempt to capture most of the aspects, which is proposed by Levy models (Dumenil and Levy, 2011) and other advanced models as follows.

Amin and Na (1993) finds ARCH models mitigate moneyness and time to maturity bias but not completely. Trautmann and Beinert (1994) estimate parameters of a jump-diffusion process on German capital markets, against the BS model. Similarly Das and Sundaram (1999) indicate jump-diffusion and stochastic volatility mitigate but do not eliminate volatility bias completely.

Ghaziri and Osman (2003) introduced AI approach to price the options using Neural Network and Fuzzy Logic. Since BS option pricing formula is only approximate, which leads to considerable errors, Trenev (2010) obtained a refined formula for pricing an option. Due to the fluctuation of financial markets from time to time, some of the input parameters in the BS model cannot always be expected in the precise sense. As a result Wu *et al.* (2011) applied fuzzy approach to the BS formula. Zmeskal (2012) used the input data in a form of fuzzy numbers in his approach to option pricing using BS model.

Conclusion

In 1973, Fisher Black and Myron Scholes ushered in the modern era of derivative securities with a seminal paper. In this paper, famous BS formula made its debut, and Ito calculus was unleashed upon the world of mathematical finance. (In fact the use of Weiner process in financial models dates back to the early years of the 20th century, in Bachelier's thesis. However, the success of the BS model assured that the Ito calculus would have a permanent place in the world of mathematical finance.)

Derman and Kani (1994) assert that the main appeals of the BS model are its simplicity and ease of implementation.

The BS formula, the most commonly used option pricing model today, follows some ideal assumptions like asset prices follow geometric Brownian motion with constant volatility σ and the asset returns are log-normally distributed, possibility on risk-neutral valuation, assuming that all the traders are indifferent to the risk, the arbitrage opportunities do not exist in the real world, etc. This paper challenges few such assumptions and attempted to sketch a brief idea of recent advancement on BS model by recent researchers after four decades (i.e., from 1973 to 2012) of the introduction of BS model.

References

Amin, K.I., and V.K. Na (1993). "Inferring Future Volatility from the Information in Implied Volatility Eurodollar Options: A New Approach", *Review of Financial Studies* 10(2): 333-67.

Ball, C.A. and W.N. Torous (1983). "A Simplified Jump Process for Common Stock Returns", *Journal of Financial and Quantitative Analysis* 18: 53–65.

Black, F. (1976). "Studies of Stock Price Volatility Changes", in *Proceedings of the 1976 Meetings of the American Statistical Association*. pp.171–81.

Blattberg, R.C. and N.J. Gonedes (1974). "A Comparison of the Stable and Student Distributions as Statistical Models for Stock Prices", *Journal of Business* 47: 244-80.

Carr, Peter and W. Liuren (2002), "Static Hedging of Standard Options", *CRIF Working Paper series* 22, Available at: *http://fordham.bepress.com/crif_working_papers/22*

Clark, P.K. (1973). "A Subordinated Stochastic Process Model with Finite Variance for Speculative Prices", *Econometrica* 41: 135-55.

Cox, John C. and Stephen A. Ross (1976). "The Valuation of Options for Alternative Stochastic Processes", *Journal of Financial Economics* 3: 145-66.

Cox, J.C., S.A. Ross and M. Rubinstein (1979). "Option Pricing: A Simplified Approach", *Journal of Financial Economics* 7: 229–63.

Das, S. and R. Sundaram (1999) "Of Smiles and Smirks: A Term Structure Perspective", *Journal of Financial and Quantitative Analysis* 34: 211-39.

Derman E. and I. Kani (1994). "Riding on a Smile", *RISK* 7(2): 32–39.

Duan, J.C. and J.G. Simonato (1999). "American Option Pricing under GARCH by a Markov Chain Approximation", *Working paper*. Hong Kong University of Science and Technology.

Dumenil, G. and D. Levy (2011). "Modeling Monetary Macroeconomics: Kalecki Reconsidered", *Metroeconomica* 63(1): 170–99.

Ederington, Louis H. and Wei Guan (2002). "Measuring Implied Volatility: Is an Average Better? Which Average?", *Journal of Futures Markets* 22(9): 811–37.

Geske, R. (1979). "The Valuation of Compound Options", *The Journal of Financial Economics* 7: 63-81.

Ghaziri, Hassan and Ibrahim H. Osman (2003). "A Neural Network Algorithm for the Traveling Salesman Problem with Backhauls", *Computers and Industrial Engineering* 44: 267-81.

Gray, Dale F., Robert C. Merton and Zvi Bodie (2006). "A New Framework for Analyzing and Managing Macro Financial Risks of an Economy", *NBER Working Papers* 12637. National Bureau of Economic Research Inc.

Hull, J.C. (2006). *Options, futures and Other Derivative Securities*. Upper Saddle River: Prentice Hall.

Jarrow, R.A. and C. Joseph (1994). "Options Markets, Self-Fulfilling Prophecies, and Implied Volatilities". Available at *http://ssrn.com/abstract=5703*

John, G.M. Schoenmakers and Peter E. Kloeden (1998). "Robust Option Replication for a Black-Scholes Model Extended with Nondeterministic Trends", *Journal of Applied Mathematics and Stochastic Analysis* 12(2): 113-20.

Kallianpur, G. and R.L Karandikar (1999). *Introduction to Option Pricing Theory*. Birkhauser.

Macbeth, J.D. and L.J. Merville (1980). "Tests of the Black-Scholes and Cox Call Option Valuation Models", *The Journal of Finance Volume* 35(2): 285–301.

Martin, R. (2003). "Globalization and Workers in Developing Countries", *Policy Research Working Paper Series* 2958. The World Bank.

Merton, Robert C. (1976). "Option Pricing when Underlying Stock Returns are Discontinuous", *Journal of Financial Economics* 3(1-2): 125-44. Elsevier.

McDonald, R. (2006). "The Role of Real Options in Capital Budgeting: Theory and Practice", *Journal of Applied Corporate Finance* 18(2): 28-39.

Oldfield, George Jr., Richard J. Rogalski and Robert A. Jarrow (1977). "An Autoregressive Jump Process for Common Stock Returns", *Journal of Financial Economics* 5(3): 389-418. Elsevier.

Omberg, E. (1987). "A Note on the Convergence of Binomial-Pricing and Compound-Option Models", *Journal of Finance* 42(2): 463–69.

Rosenberg, B. (1973). "Random Coefficient Models: The Analysis of a Cross Section of Time Series by Stochastically Convergent Parameter Regression", *Annals of Economic and Social Measurement* 2: 399-428.

Rubinstein, M. (1994). "Implied Binomial Trees", *Journal of Finance* 49(3): 771-818.

Shreve, S.E. (2004). *Stochastic Calculus for Finance I, II*. Springer.

Teneng, D. (2011). "Limitations of the Black-Scholes Model", *International Research Journal of Finance and Economics* 68: 99-102.

Trautmann, S. and M. Beinert (1994). "Stock Price Jumps and their Impact on Option Valutation", *Working paper*. Mainz, Germany: Johannes Gutenberg Universitat.

Trenev, D.V. (2010). "Spatial Scaling for the Numerical Approximation of Problems on Unbounded Domains", Texas Digital Library, Available at *http://repositories.tdl.org/tdl-ir/handle/1969.1/ETD-TAMU-2009-12-7280)*

Wilmott, P., S. Howison and J. Dewynne (1995). *The Mathematics of Financial Derivatives*. Cambridge Univ. Press.

Wilson, Ww and Hg Fung (1991). "Put-call Parity and Arbitrage Bounds for Options on Grain Futures", *American Journal of Agricultural Economics* 73(1): 55-65.

Wu, Ligang, Xiaojie Su, Peng Shi and Jianbin Qiu (2011). "Model Approximation for Discrete-Time-State-Delay Systems in the T–S Fuzzy Framework", *IEEE Transactions* 19(2): 366-78.

Zmeskal, Zdenek (2012). "Modelling the Sequential Real Options under Uncertainty and Vagueness (Fuzzy-Stochastic Approach)", *Proceedings of 30th International Conference Mathematical Methods in Economics*.

17 A Study of Various Hedging Instruments

An Overview of Corporate Hedging in India

Amit B. Mirji

Introduction

In 1971, the Bretton Woods system of administering fixed foreign exchange rates was abolished in favour of market-determination of foreign exchange rates; a regime of fluctuating exchange rates was introduced. Besides market-determined fluctuations, there was a lot of volatility in other markets around the world owing to increased inflation and the oil shock. Corporates struggled to cope with the uncertainty in profits, cash flows and future costs. It was then that financial derivatives—foreign currency, interest rate, and commodity derivatives—emerged as means of managing risks facing corporations.

In India, exchange rates were deregulated and were allowed to be determined by markets in 1993. The economic liberalisation of the early 1990s facilitated the introduction of derivatives based on interest rates and foreign exchange. However derivative use is still a highly regulated area due to the partial convertibility of the rupee. Currently forwards, swaps and options are available in India and the use of foreign currency derivatives is permitted for hedging purposes only.

This study aims to provide a perspective on managing the risk that firms face due to fluctuating exchange rates. It investigates the prudence in investing resources towards the purpose of hedging and then introduces the tools for risk management. These are then applied in the Indian context. The motivation of this study came from the recent rise in volatility in the money markets of the world and particularly in the US dollar, due to which

Indian exports are fast gaining a cost disadvantage. Hedging with derivative instruments is a feasible solution to this situation.

This report is organised in six sections. The next section presents the necessity of foreign exchange risk management and outlines the process of managing this risk. The third section discusses the various determinants of hedging decisions by firms, followed by an overview of corporate hedging in India in the fourth section. Evidence from major Indian firms from different sectors is summarised here and the fifth section concludes.

Foreign Exchange Risk Management: Process and Necessity

Firms dealing in multiple currencies face a risk (an unanticipated gain/loss) on account of sudden/unanticipated changes in exchange rates, quantified in terms of exposures. Exposure is defined as a contracted, projected or contingent cash flow whose magnitude is not certain at the moment and depends on the value of the foreign exchange rates. The process of identifying risks faced by the firm and implementing the process of protection from these risks by financial or operational hedging is defined as foreign exchange risk management. This paper limits its scope to hedging only the foreign exchange risks faced by firms.

Kinds of Foreign Exchange Exposure

Risk management techniques vary with the type of exposure (accounting or economic) and term of exposure. Accounting exposure, also called translation exposure, results from the need to restate foreign subsidiaries' financial statements into the parent's reporting currency and is the sensitivity of net income to the variation in the exchange rate between a foreign subsidiary and its parent.

Economic exposure is the extent to which a firm's market value, in any particular currency, is sensitive to unexpected changes in foreign currency. Currency fluctuations affect the value of the firm's operating cash flows, income statement and competitive position, hence market share and stock price. Currency fluctuations also affect a firm's balance sheet by changing the value of the firm's assets and liabilities, accounts payable, accounts receivables, inventory, loans in foreign currency, investments certificates of deposit (CDs) in foreign banks; this type of economic exposure is called balance sheet exposure. Transaction Exposure is a form of short-term economic exposure due to fixed price contracting in an atmosphere of exchange-rate volatility.

The most common definition of the measure of exchange-rate exposure is the sensitivity of the value of the firm, proxied by the firm's stock return, to an unanticipated change in an exchange rate. This is calculated by using the partial derivative function where the dependant variable is the firm's value and the independent variable is the exchange rate (Adler and Dumas, 1984).

Necessity of Managing Foreign Exchange Risk

A key assumption in the concept of foreign exchange risk is that exchange rate changes are not predictable and that this is determined by how efficient the markets for foreign exchange are. Research in the area of efficiency of foreign exchange markets has thus far been able to establish only a weak form of the efficient market hypothesis conclusively which implies that successive changes in exchange rates cannot be predicted by analysing the historical sequence of exchange rates (Soenen, 1979). However, when the efficient markets theory is applied to the foreign exchange market under floating exchange rates, there is some evidence to suggest that the present prices properly reflect all available information (Giddy and Dufey, 1992). This implies that exchange rates react to new information in an immediate and unbiased fashion, so that no one party can make a profit by this information and in any case, information on direction of the rates arrives randomly so exchange rates also fluctuate randomly. It implies that foreign exchange risk management cannot be done away with by employing resources to predict exchange rate changes.

Hedging as a Tool to Manage Foreign Exchange Risk

There is a spectrum of opinions regarding foreign exchange hedging. Some firms feel hedging techniques are speculative or do not fall in their area of expertise and hence do not venture into hedging practices. Other firms are unaware of being exposed to foreign exchange risks. There are a set of firms who only hedge some of their risks, while others are aware of the various risks they face, but are unaware of the methods to guard the firm against the risk. There is yet another set of companies who believe shareholder value cannot be increased by hedging the firm's foreign exchange risks, as shareholders can themselves individually hedge themselves against the same using instruments like forward contracts available in the market or diversify such risks out by manipulating their portfolio (Giddy and Dufey, 1992).

There are some explanations backed by theory about the irrelevance of managing the risk of change in exchange rates. For example, the International Fisher effect states that exchange rate changes are balanced out by interest rate changes and the Purchasing Power Parity theory suggests that exchange rate changes will be offset by changes in relative price indices/inflation since the Law of One Price should hold. Both these theories suggest that exchange rate changes are evened out in some form or the other. Also, the Unbiased Forward Rate theory suggests that locking in the forward exchange rate offers the same expected return and is an unbiased indicator of the future spot rate. But these theories are perfectly played out in perfect markets under homogeneous tax regimes. Also, exchange rate-linked changes in factors like inflation and interest rates take time to adjust and in the meanwhile, firms stand to lose out on adverse movements in the exchange rates.

The existence of different kinds of market imperfections, such as incomplete financial markets, positive transaction and information costs, probability of financial distress, and agency costs and restrictions on free trade, makes foreign exchange management an appropriate concern for corporate management (Giddy and Dufey, 1992). It has also been argued that a hedged firm, being less risky can secure debt more easily and enjoy a tax advantage (interest is excluded from tax while dividends are taxed). This would negate the Modigliani-Miller (MM) proposition as shareholders cannot duplicate such tax advantages. The MM argument that shareholders can hedge on their own is also not valid on account of high transaction costs and lack of knowledge about financial manipulations on the part of shareholders.

There is also a vast pool of research that proves the efficacy of managing foreign exchange risks and a significant amount of evidence showing the reduction of exposure with the use of tools for managing these exposures. In one of the more recent studies, Allayanis and Ofek (2001) use a multivariate analysis on a sample of S&P 500 non-financial firms and calculate a firm's exchange-rate exposure using the ratio of foreign sales to total sales as a proxy and isolate the impact of use of foreign currency derivatives (part of foreign exchange risk management) on a firm's foreign exchange exposures. They find a statistically significant association between the absolute value of the exposures and the 'absolute value' of the percentage use of foreign currency derivatives and prove that the use of derivatives in fact reduces exposure.

Foreign Exchange Risk Management Framework

Once a firm recognises its exposure, it then has to deploy resources in managing it. A heuristic for firms to manage this risk effectively is presented below which can be modified to suit firm-specific needs i.e., some or all the following tools could be used.

1. *Forecasts:* After determining its exposure, the first step for a firm is to develop a forecast on the market trends and what the main direction/trend is going to be on the foreign exchange rates. The period for forecasts is typically 6 months. It is important to base the forecasts on valid assumptions. Along with identifying trends, a probability should be estimated for the forecast coming true as well as how much the change would be.

2. *Risk Estimation:* Based on the forecast, a measure of the *Value at Risk* (VaR) (the actual profit or loss for a move in rates according to the forecast) and the *probability* of this risk should be ascertained. The risk that a transaction would fail due to *market-specific problems* should be taken into account. Finally, the Systems Risk that can arise due to inadequacies such as reporting gaps and implementation gaps in the firms' exposure management system should be estimated.

3. *Benchmarking:* Given the exposures and the risk estimates, the firm has to set its limits for handling foreign exchange exposure. The firm also has to decide whether to manage its exposures on a cost centre or profit centre basis. A cost centre approach is a defensive one and the main aim is to ensure that cash flows of a firm are not adversely affected beyond a point. A profit centre

approach on the other hand is a more aggressive approach where the firm decides to generate a net profit on its exposure over time.

4. *Hedging:* Based on the limits a firm set for itself to manage exposure, the firms then decide an appropriate hedging strategy. There are various financial instruments available for the firm to choose from: futures, forwards, options and swaps and issue of foreign debt. Hedging strategies and instruments are explored in a section.

5. *Stop Loss:* The firm's risk management decisions are based on forecasts which are but estimates of reasonably unpredictable trends. It is imperative to have stop loss arrangements in order to rescue the firm if the forecasts turn out wrong. For this, there should be certain monitoring systems in place to detect critical levels in the foreign exchange rates for appropriate measure to be taken.

Figure 17.1

Framework for Risk Management

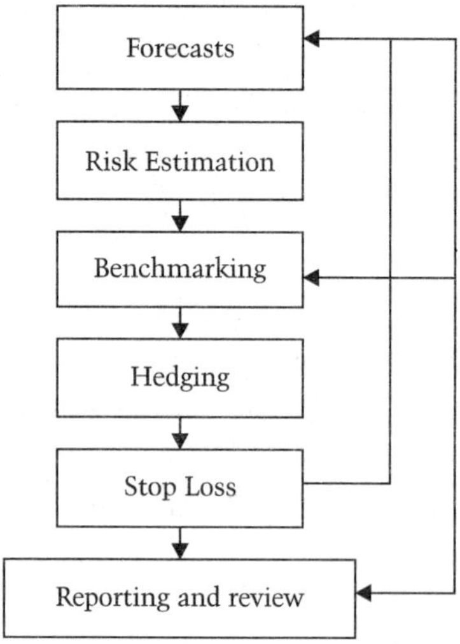

6. *Reporting and Review:* Risk management policies are typically subjected to review based on periodic reporting. The reports mainly include profit/loss status on open contracts after marking

to market, the actual exchange/interest rate achieved on each exposure, and profitability *vis-à-vis* the benchmark and the expected changes in overall exposure due to forecasted exchange/ interest rate movements. The review analyses whether the benchmarks set are valid and effective in controlling the exposures, what the market trends are and finally whether the overall strategy is working or needs change.

Hedging Strategies/Instruments

A derivative is a financial contract whose value is derived from the value of some other financial asset, such as a stock price, a commodity price, an exchange rate, an interest rate or even an index of prices. The main role of derivatives is that they reallocate risk among financial market participants and help to make financial markets more complete. This section outlines the hedging strategies using derivatives with foreign exchange being the only risk assumed.

1. *Forwards:* A forward is a made-to-measure agreement between two parties to buy/sell a specified amount of a currency at a specified rate on a particular date in the future. The depreciation of the receivable currency is hedged against by selling a currency forward. If the risk is that of a currency appreciation (if the firm has to buy that currency in future say for import), it can hedge by buying the currency forward. For example, if Reliance Industries Ltd. (RIL) wants to buy crude oil in US dollars for six months, it can enter into a forward contract to pay Indian rupee (INR) and buy USD and lock in a fixed exchange rate for INR-USD to be paid after six months regardless of the actual INR-dollar rate at the time. In this example the downside is an appreciation of dollar which is protected by a fixed forward contract. The main advantage of a forward is that it can be tailored to the specific needs of the firm and an exact hedge can be obtained. On the downside, these contracts are not marketable, they can't be sold to another party when they are no longer required and are binding.
2. *Futures:* A futures contract is similar to the forward contract but is more liquid because it is traded in an organised exchange i.e., the futures market. Depreciation of a currency can be hedged by

selling futures and appreciation can be hedged by buying futures. Advantages of futures are that there is a central market for futures which eliminates the problem of double coincidence. Futures require a small initial outlay (a proportion of the value of the future) with which significant amounts of money can be gained or lost with the actual forwards price fluctuations. This provides a sort of leverage. The previous example for a forward contract for RIL applies here also just that RIL will have to go to a USD futures exchange to purchase standardised dollar futures equal to the amount to be hedged as the risk is that of appreciation of the dollar. As mentioned earlier, the tailorability of the futures contract is limited i.e., only standard denominations of money can be bought instead of the exact amounts that are bought in forward contracts.

3. *Options:* A currency option is a contract giving the right, not the obligation, to buy or sell a specific quantity of one foreign currency in exchange for another at a fixed price, called the Exercise Price or Strike Price. The fixed nature of the exercise price reduces the uncertainty of exchange rate changes and limits the losses of open currency positions. Options are particularly suited as a hedging tool for contingent cash flows, as is the case in bidding processes. Call options are used if the risk is an upward trend in price (of the currency), while put options are used if the risk is a downward trend. Again taking the example of RIL which needs to purchase crude oil in USD in 6 months, if RIL buys a call option (as the risk is an upward trend in dollar rate), i.e., the right to buy a specified amount of dollars at a fixed rate on a specified date, there are two scenarios. If the exchange rate movement is favourable i.e., the dollar depreciates, then RIL can buy them at the spot rate as they have become cheaper. In the other case, if the dollar appreciates compared to today's spot rate, RIL can exercise the option to purchase it at the agreed strike price. In either case, RIL benefits by paying the lower price to purchase the dollar

4. *Swaps:* A swap is a foreign currency contract whereby the buyer and seller exchange equal initial principal amounts of two different currencies at the spot rate. The buyer and seller exchange fixed

or floating rate interest payments in their respective swapped currencies over the term of the contract. At maturity, the principal amount is effectively re-swapped at a predetermined exchange rate so that the parties end up with their original currencies. The advantage of swaps is that firms with limited appetite for exchange rate risk may move to a partially or completely hedged position through the mechanism of foreign currency swaps, while leaving the underlying borrowing intact. Apart from covering the exchange rate risk, swaps also allow firms to hedge the floating interest rate risk. Consider an export-oriented company that has entered into a swap for a notional principal of USD 1 mn at an exchange rate of 42/dollar. The company pays USD six-month London Interbank Offered Rate (LIBOR) to the bank and receives 11.00 per cent p.a. every six-month on 1st January and 1st July, till five years. Such a company would have earnings in Dollars and can use the same to pay interest for this kind of borrowing (in dollars rather than in rupee) thus hedging its exposures.

5. *Foreign Debt:* Foreign debt can be used to hedge foreign exchange exposure by taking advantage of the international Fischer effect relationship. This is demonstrated with the example of an exporter who has to receive a fixed amount of dollars in a few months from present. The exporter stands to lose if the domestic currency appreciates against that currency in the meanwhile so, to hedge this, he could take a loan in the foreign currency for the same time period and convert the same into domestic currency at the current exchange rate. The theory assures that the gain realised by investing the proceeds from the loan would match the interest rate payment (in the foreign currency) for the loan.

Choice of Hedging Instruments

The literature on the choice of hedging instruments is very scant. Among the available studies, Géczy *et al.* (1997) argue that currency swaps are more cost-effective for hedging foreign debt risk, while forward contracts are more cost-effective for hedging foreign operations risk. This is because foreign currency debt payments are long-term and predictable, which fit the long-term nature of currency swap contracts. Foreign currency revenues, on the other hand, are short-term and unpredictable, in line with the short-term nature of forward contracts. A survey done by Marshall (2000) also points out that currency swaps are better for hedging against translation risk, while forwards are better for hedging against transaction risk. This study also provides anecdotal evidence that pricing policy is the most popular means of hedging economic exposures.

These results however can differ for different currencies depending on the sensitivity of that currency to various market factors. Regulation in the foreign exchange markets of various countries may also skew such results.

Determinants of Hedging Decisions

The management of foreign exchange risk, as has been established so far, is a fairly complicated process. A firm, exposed to foreign exchange risk, needs to formulate a strategy to manage it, choosing from multiple alternatives. This section explores which factors firms take into consideration when formulating these strategies.

Production and Trade vs. Hedging Decisions

An important issue for multinational firms is the allocation of capital among different countries production and sales and at the same time hedging their exposure to the varying exchange rates. Research in this area suggests that the elements of exchange rate uncertainty and the attitude toward risk are irrelevant to the multinational firm's sales and production decisions (Broll,1993). Only the revenue function and cost of production are to be assessed, and the production and trade decisions in multiple countries are independent of the hedging decision.

The implication of this independence is that the presence of markets for hedging instruments greatly reduces the complexity involved in a firm's decision making as it can separate production and sales functions from the finance function. The firm avoids the need to form expectations about future exchange rates and formulation of risk preferences which entails high information costs.

Cost of Hedging

Hedging can be done through the derivatives market or through money markets (foreign debt). In either case, the cost of hedging should be the difference between value received from a hedged position and the value received if the firm did not hedge. In the presence of efficient markets, the cost of hedging in the forward market is the difference between the future spot rate and current forward rate plus any transactions cost associated with the forward contract. Similarly, the expected costs of hedging in the money market are the transactions cost plus the difference between the interest rate differential and the expected value of the difference between the current and future spot rates. In efficient markets, both types of hedging should produce similar results at the same costs, because interest rates and forward and spot exchange rates are determined simultaneously. The costs of hedging, assuming efficiency in foreign exchange markets result in pure transaction costs. The three main elements of these transaction costs are brokerage or service fees charged by dealers, information costs such as subscription to Reuter reports and news channels and administrative costs of exposure management.

Factors Affecting the Decision to Hedge Foreign Currency Risk

Research in the area of determinants of hedging separates the decision of a firm to hedge from that of how much to hedge. There is conclusive evidence to suggest that firms with larger size, research and development (R&D) expenditure and exposure to exchange rates through foreign sales and foreign trade are more likely to use derivatives (Allayanis and Ofek, 2001). First, the following points describes the factors that affect the decision to hedge and then the factors affecting the degree of hedging are considered.

1. *Firm size:* Firm size acts as a proxy for the cost of hedging or economies of scale. Risk management involves fixed costs of setting up of computer systems and training/hiring of personnel in foreign exchange management. Moreover, large firms might be considered as more creditworthy counterparties for forward or swap transactions, thus further reducing their cost of hedging. *The book value of assets is used as a measure of firm size.*

2. *Leverage:* According to the risk management literature, firms with high leverage have greater incentive to engage in hedging because doing so reduces the probability, and thus the expected cost of financial distress. Highly levered firms avoid foreign debt as a means to hedge and use derivatives.
3. *Liquidity and profitability:* Firms with highly liquid assets or high profitability have less incentive to engage in hedging because they are exposed to a lower probability of financial distress. *Liquidity is measured by the quick ratio, i.e., quick assets divided by current liabilities. Profitability is measured as earnings before interest and taxes (EBIT) divided by book assets.*
4. *Sales growth:* Sales growth is a factor determining decision to hedge as opportunities are more likely to be affected by the underinvestment problem. For these firms, hedging will reduce the probability of having to rely on external financing, which is costly for information asymmetry reasons, and thus enable them to enjoy uninterrupted high growth. *The measure of sales growth is obtained using the 3-year geometric average of yearly sales growth rates.*

As regards the degree of hedging, Allayanis and Ofek (2001) conclude that the sole determinants of the degree of hedging are exposure factors (foreign sales and trade). In other words, given that a firm decides to hedge, the decision of how much to hedge is affected solely by its exposure to foreign currency movements.

This discussion highlights how risk management systems have to be altered according to characteristics of the firm, hedging costs, nature of operations, tax considerations, regulatory requirements, etc. The next section discusses these issues in the Indian context and regulatory environment.

An Overview of Corporate Hedging in India

The move from a fixed exchange rate system to a market determined one as well as the development of derivatives markets in India has followed with the liberalisation of the economy since 1992. In this context, the market for hedging instruments is still in its developing stages. In order to understand the alternative hedging strategies that Indian firms can adopt, it is important to understand the regulatory framework for the use of derivatives here.

Development of Derivative Markets in India

The economic liberalisation of the early 1990s facilitated the introduction of derivatives based on interest rates and foreign exchange. Exchange rates were deregulated and market determined in 1993. By 1994, the rupee was made fully convertible on current account. The ban on futures trading of many commodities was lifted starting in the early 2000s. As of October 2007, even corporates have been allowed to write options in the atmosphere of high volatility.

Derivatives on stock indexes and individual stocks have grown rapidly since inception. In particular, single stock futures have become hugely popular. Institutional investors prefer to trade in the over-the-counter (OTC) markets to interest rate futures, where instruments such as interest rate swaps and forward rate agreements are thriving. Foreign exchange derivatives are less active than interest rate derivatives in India, even though they have been around for longer. OTC instruments in currency forwards and swaps are the most popular. Importers, exporters and banks use the rupee forward market to hedge their foreign currency exposure. Turnover and liquidity in this market has been increasing, although trading is mainly in shorter maturity contracts of one year or less. The typical forward contract is for one month, three months or six months with three months being the most common.

The Indian rupee, which is being traded on the Dubai Gold and Commodities Exchange (DGCX), crossed a turnover of $23.24 million in June 2007.

Regulatory Guidelines for the Use of Foreign Exchange Derivatives

With respect to foreign exchange derivatives involving rupee, residents have access to foreign exchange forward contracts, foreign currency-rupee swap instruments and currency options—both cross currency as well as foreign currency-rupee. In the case of derivatives involving only foreign currency, a range of products such as Interest Rate Swaps, Forward

Contracts and Options are allowed. While these products can be used for a variety of purposes, the fundamental requirement is the existence of an underlying exposure to foreign exchange risk i.e., derivatives can be used for hedging purposes only.

The Reserve Bank of India (RBI) has also formulated guidelines to simplify procedural/documentation requirements for small and medium enterprises (SME) sector. In order to ensure that SMEs understand the risks of these products, only banks with which they have credit relationship are allowed to offer such facilities. These facilities should also have some relationship with the turnover of the entity. Similarly, individuals have been permitted to hedge upto USD 100,000 on self-declaration basis.

Authorised dealer (AD) banks may also enter into forward contracts with residents in respect of transactions denominated in foreign currency but settled in Indian rupees including hedging the currency indexed exposure of importers in respect of customs duty payable on imports and price risks on commodities with a few exceptions. Domestic producers/users are allowed to hedge their price risk on aluminium, copper, lead, nickel and zinc as well as aviation turbine fuel in international commodity exchanges based on their underlying economic exposures. ADs are permitted to use innovative products like cross-currency options, interest rate swaps (IRS) and currency swaps, caps/collars and forward rate agreements (FRAs) in the international foreign exchange market. Foreign institutional investors (FIIs), persons resident outside India having foreign direct fnvestment (FDI) in India and non-resident Indians (NRIs) are allowed access to the forwards market to the extent of their exposure in the cash market.

Hedging Instruments for Indian Firms

The recent period has witnessed amplified volatility in the INR-USD exchange rates in the backdrop of the sub-prime crisis in the USA and increased dollar inflows into the Indian stock markets. In this context, the paper has attempted to study the choice of instruments adopted by prominent firms to stem their foreign exchange exposures. All the data for this have been compiled from the 2006-07 annual reports of the respective companies. A summary of the foreign exchange risk-hedging behaviour of select Indian firms is given in Table 17.1.

Table 17.1

Evidence of Derivative Use for Hedging FX Risk in Indian Firms

Instruments	*Currency (mn)*	*₹ (Cr.)*	*Nature of Exposure*
Reliance Industries		1064.49	Earnings in all businesses are linked to USD. The key input, crude oil, is purchased in USD. All export revenues are in foreign currency and local prices are based on import parity prices as well.
Currency Swaps		2939.76	
Forward Contracts		5764.10	
Maruti Udyog			
Forward Contracts	6411 (INR-JPY) 70 ($-INR)		Import/royalty payable in yen and exports receivables in dollars.
Currency swaps	124.70 (USD-INR)		Interest rate and forex risk.
Mahindra and Mahindra			
Forward Contracts	350 (INR-JPY) 2 (INR-EUR) 27.3($-INR)		Trade payables in yen and euro and export receivables in dollars
Currency Swaps	5390 (JPY-INR)		Interest rate and foreign exchange risk.
Arind Mills			
Forward Contracts	152.98 ($-INR) 2.25 (GBP-INR) 5 (INR-$)	703.67 21.88	Most of the revenue is either in dollars or linked to dollars due to export.
Option Contracts	122.5 ($-INR)	547.16	
Infosys			
Forward Contracts	119 ($-INR)	529	Revenues denominated in these currencies.
Options Contracts	4 ($-INR) 8 (INR-$)	18 36	
Range barrier options	2 ($-INR) 3 (EUR-INR)	971	
Tata Consultancy Services (TCS)			
Forward Contracts	15 (EUR-INR) 21 (GBR-INR)	265.75	Revenues largely denominted in foreign currency, predominantly USD, GBP and euro. Other currencies include Australian $, Canadian $, South African Rand, and Swiss Franc
Option Contracts	830 ($-INR) 47.5 (EUR-INR) 76.5 (GBP-INR)	4057	
Ranbaxy			
Forward Contracts		2894.589	Exposed on accounts receivable and loans payable. Exposure in USD and JPY
Dr. Reddy's Labs			
Forward Contracts	398 ($-INR) 11 (EUR-$)		Foreign currency earnings through export, currency requirements for settlement of liability for import of goods.
Options Contracts	30 (EUR-$)		

Notes: 1. $-INR forward contracts denote selling of USD forwards to convert revenues to INR. INR-$ forward contracts denote buying of USD forwards to meet USD payment obligations.

2. $-INR Option contracts are put options to sell USD. INR-$ are call options to buy USD.

Source: Compiled from 2006-07 Annual Reports of the respective companies.

Discussion on Hedging by Indian Firms

From Table 17.1, it can be seen that earnings of all the firms are linked to either USD, euro or pound as firms transact primarily in these foreign currencies globally. Forward contracts are commonly used and among these firms, Ranbaxy and RIL depend heavily on these contracts for their hedging requirements. As discussed earlier, forwards contracts can be tailored to the exact needs of the firm and this could be the reason for their popularity. The tailorability is a consideration as it enables the firms to match their exposures in an exact manner compared to exchange traded derivatives like futures that are standardised where exact matching is difficult.

RIL, Maruti Udyog and Mahindra and Mahindra are the only firms using currency swaps. Swap usage is a long-term strategy for hedging and suggests that the planning horizons for these companies are longer than those of other firms. These businesses, by nature, involve longer gestation periods and higher initial capital outlays and this could explain their long planning horizons.

Another observation is that TCS prefers to hedge its exposure to the USD through options rather than forwards. This strategy has been observed among many firms recently in India. This has been adopted due to the marked high volatility of the USD against the rupee. Options are more profitable instruments in volatile conditions as they offer unlimited upside profitability while hedging the downside risk, whereas there is a risk with forwards if the expectation of the exchange rate (the guess) is wrong as firms lose out on some profit. The use of range barrier options by Infosys also suggests a strategy to tackle the high volatility of the dollar exchange rates. Software firms have a limited domestic market and rely on exports for the major part of their revenues and hence require additional flexibility in hedging when the volatility is high. Another implication of this is that their planning horizons are shorter compared to capital-intensive firms.

It is evident that most Indian firms use forwards and options to hedge their foreign currency exposure. This implies that these firms choose short-term measures to hedge as opposed to foreign debt. This preference is possibly a consequence of their costs being in rupees, the absence of a rupee futures exchange in India and curbs on foreign debt. It also follows that most of these firms behave like Net Exporters and are adversely affected by appreciation of the local currency. There are a few firms which have import liabilities which would be adversely affected by rupee depreciation. However it must be pointed out that the data set considered for this study does not indicate how the use of foreign debt by these firms hedges their exposures to foreign exchange risk and whether such a strategy is used as a substitute or complement to hedging with derivatives.

Conclusion

Derivative being used for hedging are going to increase due to increased global linkages and volatile exchange rates. Firms need to look at instituting a sound risk management system and also need to formulate their hedging strategy that suits their specific firm characteristics and exposures.

In India, regulation has been steadily eased, and turnover and liquidity in the foreign currency derivative markets has increased, although the use is mainly in shorter maturity contracts of one year or less. Forward and option contracts are the more popular instruments. Regulators had initially only allowed certain banks to deal in this market, however now corporates can also write option contracts. There are many variants of these derivatives which investment banks across the world specialise in, and as the awareness and demand for these variants increase, the RBI would have to revise regulations.

For now, Indian companies are actively hedging their foreign exchanges risks with forwards, currency and interest rate swaps and different types of options such as call, put, cross-currency and range-barrier options. The high use of forward contracts by Indian firms also highlights the absence of a rupee futures exchange in India. However, the DGCX in June 2007 introduced rupee-dollar futures that could be traded on its exchanges and had provided another route for firms to hedge on a transparent basis. There are fears that the RBI's ability to control the partially convertible currency will be subdued by this introduction, but this issue is beyond the scope of this study. The partial convertibility of the rupee will be difficult to control if many exchanges offer such instruments and that will be a factor to consider for the RBI.

The Committee on Fuller Capital Account Convertibility had recommended that currency futures may be introduced subject to risks being contained through proper trading mechanism, structure of contracts and regulatory environment. Accordingly, the RBI in the Annual Policy Statement for the year 2007-08 proposed to set up a Working Group on Currency Futures to study the international experience and suggest a suitable framework to implement the proposal, in line with the current legal and regulatory framework.

The limitation of this study is that only one type of risk is assumed i.e., the foreign exchange risk. Also applicability of conclusion is limited as only very few firms were reviewed over just one time period. However the results from this exploratory study are encouraging and interesting, leading us to conclude that there is scope for more rigorous study along these lines.

References

Adler, M. and B. Dumas (1984). "Exposure to Currency Risk: Definition and Measurement", *Financial Management* 13: 41-50 (Summer).

Allayannis, George and Eli Ofek (2001). "Exchange Rate Exposure, Hedging, and the Use of Foreign Currency Derivatives", *Journal of International Money and Finance* 20(2): 273-96.

Broll, Udo (1993). "Foreign Production and International Hedging in a Multinational Firm", *Open Economies Review* 4: 425-32.

Gambhir, Neeraj and Manoj Goel (n.d.). *Foreign Exchange Derivatives Market in India—Status and Prospects*. Available at: *http://www.iief.com/Research/CHAP10.PDF*

Geczy, C., B.A. Minton and C. Schrand (1997). "Why Firms Use Currency Derivatives", *Journal of Finance* 52: 1323-54.

Giddy, Ian H. and Gunter Dufey (1992). *The Management of Foreign Exchange Risk*. Available at: *http://pages.stern.nyu.edu/~igiddy/fxrisk.htm*. (last accessed: March 2008).

Judge, Amrit (2003). *How Firms Hedge Foreign Currency Exposure: Foreign Currency Derivatives versus Foreign Currency Debt*. August.

Marshall, A.P. (2000). "Foreign Exchange Risk Management in UK, USA and Asia Pacific Multinational Companies", *Journal of Multinational Financial Management* 10: 185-211.

Muller and Verschoor (2005). *The Impact of Corporate Derivative Usage on Foreign Exchange Risk Exposure*. March. Available at *http://ssrn.com/abstract=676012*

Soenen, L.A. (1979). Efficient Market Implications for Foreign Exchange Exposure Management, DE ECONOMIST 127, NR. 2.

Soenen L.A. and Jeff Madura (1991). "Foreign Exchange Management: A Strategic Approach", *Long Range Planning* 24(5): 119-24.

Websites

http://www.newyorkfed.org/research/economists/sarkar/derivatives_in_india.pdf

http://www.ril.com/rportal/jsp/eportal/ListDownloadLibrary.jsp?DLID=866

http://www.infosys.com/investor/reports/annual/Infosys_AR06.pdf

http://www.arvindmills.com/finance/docs/qtr/0405/Arvind%20Mills%20Annual%20Report%20for%202006-07.pdf

http://www.rbi.org.in/Scripts/BS_FemaNotifications.aspx

18 The Hedging Scenario in Micro, Small and Medium Enterprises (MSMEs)[1]

Laila Memdani and Karthik Athelli

Introduction

In the world of globalisation where more and more firms are entering the international markets, they are being continuously exposed to foreign exchange rate volatility. Consequently, they are getting more inclined towards financial derivatives for effective foreign exchange risk management. This study aims to analyse the management of the foreign exchange risk by the small and medium enterprises (SMEs) by availing the currency hedging strategies. As the currency derivatives market is still at a nascent stage in India, the use of hedging strategies is a new concept for the firms. Information has been obtained by conducting primary research on the SMEs to determine the usage of the currency hedging strategies and the impact of the latest RBI guidelines (as on 11 December, 2011).

The RBI guidelines w.r.t. notification as on 15 December, 2011, titled 'Risk Management and Inter-bank dealings' on the foreign exchange transactions of SMEs, focuses on the following points:

1. Forward contracts booked by residents irrespective of the type and tenor of the underlying exposure, once cancelled, cannot be rebooked.

2. For Importers, 25 per cent of the average of the previous three financial years' (April to March) actual import/export turnover or the previous year's actual import/export turnover, whichever is higher.

1. With respect to the change in the RBI guidelines as on 15 December 2011.

a. In case of importers who have already utilised in excess of the revised/reduced limit, no further bookings may be allowed under this facility.

b. All forward contracts booked will be on fully deliverable basis. In case of cancellations, exchange gain, if any, should not be passed on to the customer.

3. All cash/tom/spot transactions by the authorised dealers (ADs) on behalf of clients will be undertaken for actual remittances/delivery only and cannot be cancelled/cash settled.

4. Forward contracts booked by the foreign institutional investors (FIIs), once cancelled, cannot be rebooked. However, be rolled over on or before maturity.

Literature Review

According to Jorion (1990), exchange rates are a major source of uncertainty for companies around the world, which is characteristically 4 times the interest rates and 10 times the inflation in terms of volatility. No single firm can avert the impact of international economic changes and foreign exchange rate fluctuations; foreign exchange risk management is of utmost importance for companies dealing in international trade.

Managers have to deal with currency rate exposures efficiently and effectively, to mitigate the losses, to prove their executive abilities and flexibilities. Thus, exchange risk management with the use of hedging strategies such as investing in derivative instruments is being used by firms all over the world, to "reduce the volatility in return earnings" (Froot *et al.*, 1993).

Currency exposure has come under the spotlight, in India, as companies were exposed to global competition. "The gradual liberalisation of Indian economy has resulted in substantial inflow of foreign capital into India" (Gambhir and Goel, n.d.). The demolishment of trade barriers and adoption of Open Door Policy has integrated the Indian economy with the world economy. Indian companies are entering the international markets; an active and rapidly expanding liquid foreign exchange (FX) derivative market has evolved providing a large range of hedging instruments for effective management of foreign exchange risks.

V.D.M.V Lakshmi (2008, cited in Devandra Singh, 2011) cited the decision taken by the RBI to allow exchange traded currency future in India as a gift to traders and investors as it is a standardised and transparent instrument to hedge their currency risk. The author provided an insight on how the currency future can be used by market participants to cover the exchange rate risk in currency market along with the legal framework and sanction approval procedure from the authorised agencies.

Nirvikar Singh (2008, cited in Devandra Singh, 2011) stated that off-shore non-deliverable forward markets have existed in India while the exchange traded currency futures were banned. However, in June 2007, trading of rupee future started on the Dubai Gold and Commodities Exchange (DGCX) prompting the RBI to set up a committee to look into this possibility for India. During 2007, rupee future trading on DGEX was not controlled by the RBI, showcasing that the new market was being used for short-term hedging, probably by parties engaged in international trade. He concluded with statement that the RBI policies need to be from the macroeconomic perspective for the growth of the financial sector in India.

Krishnan Sitaraman and Satish Prabhu (2010, cited in Devandra Singh, 2011) showed the procedure to mitigate exchange rate risk through illustrations. They showed the progress and development in the currency futures in India. The introduction of the currency options in the market was suggested by the authors.

Padmalatha Suresh (2008, cited in Devandra Singh, 2011) stated that the currency future has helped the undernourished Indian financial markets by explaining how the exchange traded futures are the answer to prevent systematic risks in the future. The RBI decision to extend the currency futures market to include three more currency pairs and the introduction of currency options in the future, as natural extension at the currency future market, was lauded by the author. The author analysed the performance of currency futures and provided insights on over-the-counter (OTC) markets and currency futures (INR/USD) traded on the National Stock Exchange (NSE) and Multi Commodity Exchange (MCX) showed a remarkable increase in the turnover of derivatives as a percentage of OTC forward turnover. The paper also cited some reasons for inefficient and illiquid market in India such as inadequacy of financial firms, regulators and structured barriers, frictions caused by taxes and suggested that currency futures are not an end in themselves but more positive actions from the regulators and government are expected to nourish the market.

Objectives

1. To find the Hedging opportunities to minimise the foreign exchange risk of the MSMEs.
2. To study the impact of the change in the RBI guidelines on the MSME sector

Methodology

A sample survey of 25 exporters and 25 importers (total of 50 SMEs) from Andhra Pradesh will be done with the help of a structured questionnaire to find out whether SMEs are availing the opportunities of hedging or not and the impact of the RBI guidelines on them.

Results and Findings

Twenty-five responses for each (importers and exporters) were collected through personal interviews with the SMEs. The industries and the products the SMEs interviewed deal in are shown in Table 18.1.

Table 18.1

List of Industries to which the SMEs Belong to and the Products Dealt in the FX

Industry	*Products*	*No. of Importers*	*No. of Exporters*
Agriculture and food products	Sugar, Sugarcane. Vermicelli, Masalas, Namkeens, Sweets	5	4
Engineering	Tramway and railway locomotives, rolling stock, Engineering Parts, Castings spares,	5	4
Software technology	Software developments	3	4
Textiles	Saris and cloth material	1	2
Power	Silicon rubber	1	1
Explosives	Explosives and Explosive Accessories	1	1
Pharmaceuticals	Medical Equipments, Reagents, Accessories, Spares and Re-Usuable	3	1
Glass	Reading Glasses		1
Chemicals	Sulphur, Ammonia, Urea, Rock	1	2
Tyers and Tubes	Tyres and Tubes, Spares	1	1
Sanitary	Sanitary ware	1	1
Electronic	Electronic Products	1	1
Paint	Paints and chemicals		1
Crops and Seeds	Seed and Crop technology	1	
Telecom	Telecom servicea	1	1

The profile of the SMEs dealing in the FX market is shown in Figures 18.1 and 18.2.

Figure 18.1

The Experience of the Export Firms Dealing in the Foreign Exchange Market

	Response Per cent	Response Count
Less than 1 year	0.0%	0
1-5 years	12.0%	3
5-10 years	40.0%	10
More than 10 years	48.0%	12
	Answered Question	25

Figure 18.2

The Experience of the Import Firms Dealing in the Foreign Exchange Market

	Response Per cent	Response Count
Less than 1 year	0.0%	0
1-5 years	25.0%	6
5-10 years	33.3%	8
More than 10 years	41.7%	10
	Answered Question	24

The Findings of the Research

Eighty-one per cent of the firms have been dealing in the FX market for more than 5 years. Forty per cent of the total firms have less than 25 per cent of their business outside India. The value of the exports and imports ranges from ₹ 40 lakhs to ₹ 13.56 crores and 63 per cent of the firms have more than 10 FX transactions per year, out of which 24 per cent

Figure 18.3

Percentage of Exports Out of the Total Sales of the Company

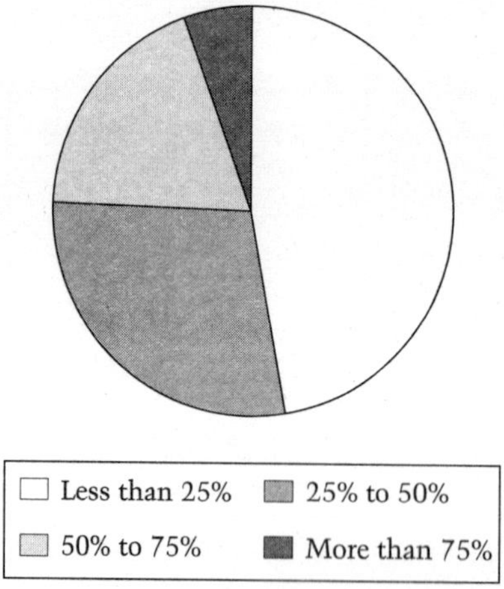

Figure 18.4

Percentage of Imports Out of the Total Purchases of the Company

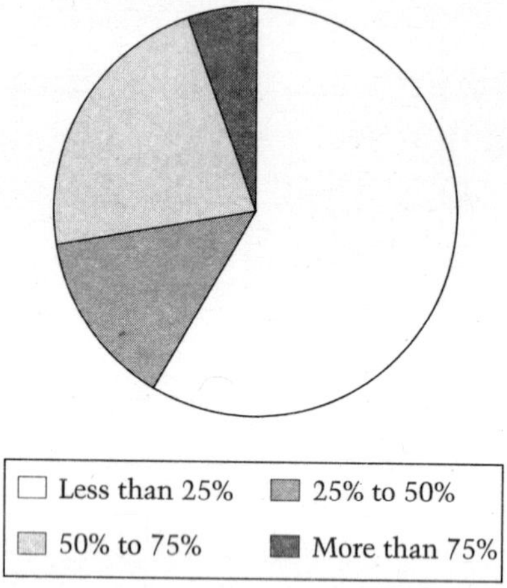

of the firms have more than 50 transactions and business and 39 per cent of the firms have 10-50 transactions in a year.

Current Hedging Scenario of the MSMEs

It has been found through the interview that only 11 out of 50 companies hedge for the FX risk. All the 11 companies (out of 50) use currency forward strategy to hedge the entire transaction amount against the FX risk.

The primary reasons for the companies not hedging are:

1. Lack of awareness about hedging.
2. Company's conservative approach.
3. Chance of losing extra profits during favourable market conditions.
4. The percentage of FX dealings is significantly low compared to the total business of the company.
5. The additional costs of hedging to be incurred by the company.

Figure 18.5

Number of SMEs Hedging for the Foreign Exchange Risk

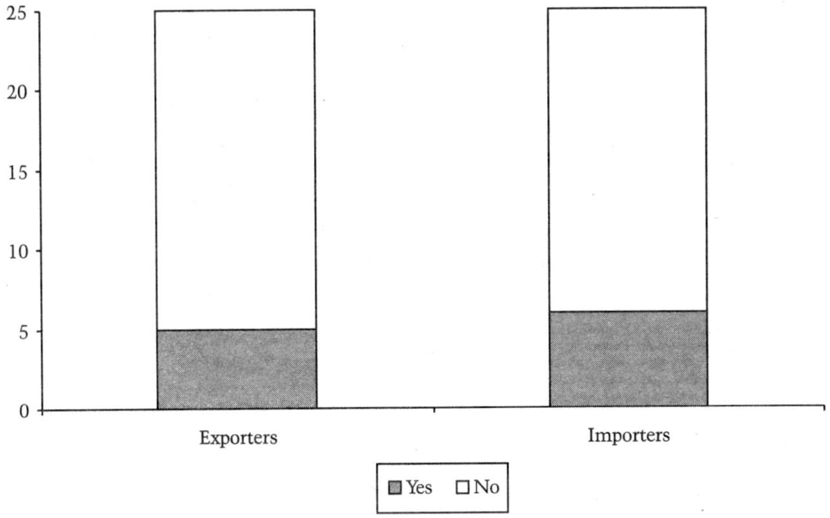

Impact of RBI Guidelines on the MSMEs

All 11 companies hedging though currency forwards have stated that the latest RBI guidelines have impacted up to 50 per cent of their business. Majority of the companies have opined that they would seldom or never hedge an anticipated FX transaction in current conditions. The primary reasons for the negative impact given by the respondents are:

a. Reduction in the hedging limits for importers.

b. Reduction in hedging anticipated contracts.

c. Reduction in speculation in the FX market.

Quick Facts

Price Determination

Exporters

Regarding price determination, 24 out of 25 exporters bill the customers in the foreign currency. Nineteen companies set the price by multiplying the rupee selling price by the foreign currency spot rate when

Figure 18.6

Impact of Latest RBI Guidelines on the Exporters

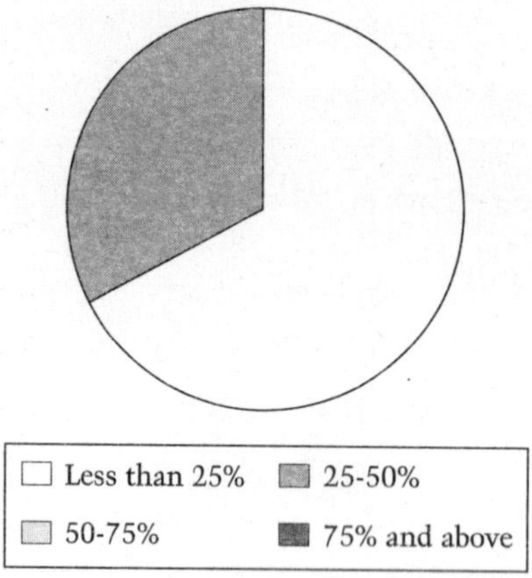

Figure 18.7

Impact of Latest RBI Guidelines on the Importers

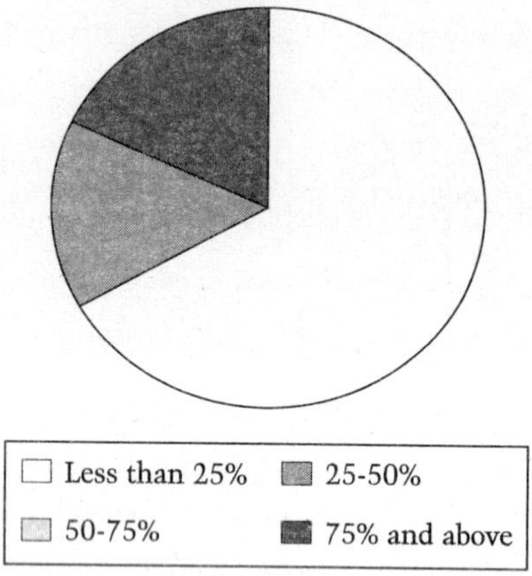

Figure 18.8

Willingness of the Company to Hedge Anticipated Foreign Exchange Transactions

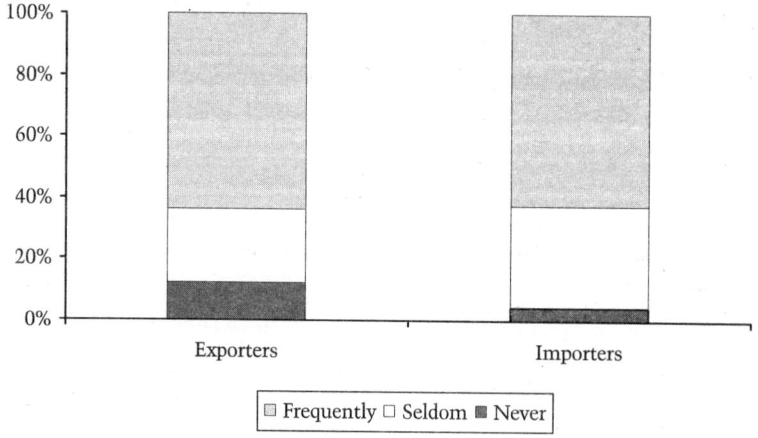

the sale is made. Six companies set the price by multiplying rupee selling price by the foreign currency forward rate when the payment date is due. The reason for the single company to bill in the Indian currency is the presence of a subsidiary company of the customer in India and the price is set by calculating the costs/prices in the local currency

Importers

All the importers are billed by the foreign suppliers in the foreign currency.

Future Prospects for Hedging

The companies where provided with the insight about hedging strategies, after which the response given on the willingness to hedge the foreign exchange risk is shown in Figure 18.9.

Figure 18.9

Willingness of the SMEs to Hedge the Foreign Exchange Risk

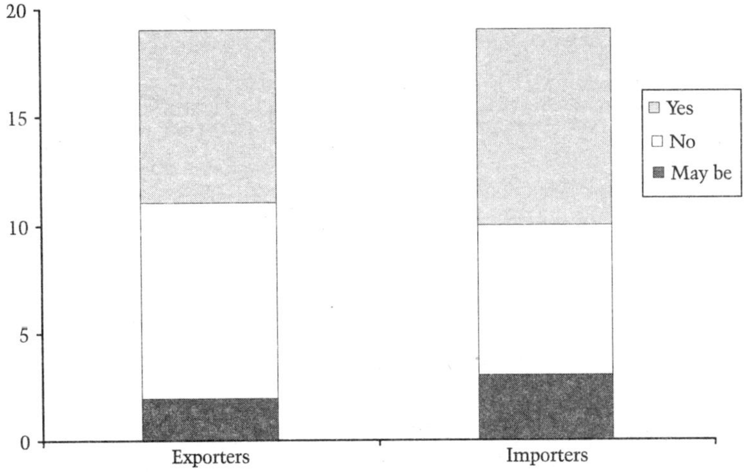

Comparative Analysis of Currency Forwards and Futures

It is clear from Figure 18.9 that the number of companies willing to hedge is very less. A large number of companies have responded in negative for the willingness to hedge and still many companies have said that they may hedge or are not sure.

Conclusion

Majority of the firms have been dealing in the FX market for more than 5 years with 40 per cent of them having less than 25 per cent of the business outside India. Sixty-three per cent of the SMEs have more than 10 FX transactions in a year. It is surprising that only 11 out of 50 SMEs hedge the FX risk through currency forward contracts. The primary reasons for the low percentage of hedging are due to the lack of awareness about existence of the hedging tools, the conservative approach of SMEs and the uncertainty of currency market. The SMEs hedging in the forwards contracts pointed out that there is up to 50 per cent reduction in the hedging activities due to the latest RBI guidelines as on December 15, 2011. They further opined that they would seldom or never hedge for an anticipated FX transaction beyond their regular contractual obligations.

Bibliography

Agri Exchange Directory.

Federation of Andhra Pradesh Chambers of Commerce & Industry (FAPCCI) – *Import and Export Directory*.

Froot, K., D. Scharfstein and J. Stein (1993). "Risk Management: Co-ordinating Investment and Financing Problems", *Journal of Finance* 48: 1629-58.

Gambhir, Neeraj and Manoj Goel (n.d.). "Foreign Exchange Derivatives Market in India: Status and Prospects". Available at: *http://www.iief.com/Research/CHAP10.PDF*

Hull, John C. (2006). *Options, Futures, and Other Derivatives* (6th edition). Upper Saddle River, NJ: Prentice-Hall.

Jorion, Philippe (1990). "The Exchange-Rate Exposure of U.S. Multinationals", *The Journal of Business* 63(3): 331-45. *http://rbidocs.rbi.org.in/rdocs/notification/PDFs/EAP58151211FL.pdf*

Singh, Devendra, Gaurav Aggarwal and Satinder Kaur (2011). "Role of Currency Potential in Indian Capital Market", *Journal of Applied Management & Computer Science* 3. Available on *http://cbsmohali.org/wp-content/downloads/n4e685095adc32.pdf*

Singh, Devendra, Gaurav Aggarwal and Satinder Kaur (2011). "Role of Currency Potential in Indian Capital Market", *BIZ n BYTES* 3: 1-14.

Singh, Nirvikar (2008). "Currency Future Trading in India", *Roubini Global Economics*, August.

Suresh, Padmalatha (2010). "Currency Futures: Heralding a New Dawn", *The Analyst*, March.

Talwar, Salil (September 2006). "Currency Hedging Strategies are Beneficial to Firms: A Study on the Developing Industries in India", University of Nottingham. Available on *http://edissertations.nottingham.ac.uk/723/1/06MAlixst14.pdf*

SECTION V

Non-Financial Institutions and Risk Management

19 A Study on Risks Faced by Non-Financial Corporations in Tamil Nadu

Thirumalvalavan and M. Padmavathi

Introduction

The word 'risk' is derived from the Italian word 'riscare,' which means 'to run into danger' (Douglas and Wildavsky, 1982). Generally, risk is considered to be synonymous with uncertainty. In the early 1920s, Frank Knight introduced an important distinction between the two concepts. He defines 'risk' as variability that can be quantified in terms of probabilities, while immeasurable variability is best thought of as 'uncertainty.' Collier and Agyei-Ampomah (2006) note risk as a hazard or threat (downside risk), this is what managers often mean when talking about risk. Risk management is defined as "Coordinated activities to direct and control an organisation with regard to risk" (ISO Guide 73 BS 31100).

At one time, risk management meant buying insurance and having enough fire extinguishers. But in the last 10 years, the scope and mission of corporate risk management have well expanded beyond and opportunistic hedging to include all kinds of corporate operating and strategic risks. Corporate risk management is no longer "just series of isolated transactions; it's a strategic activity that encompasses everything from operating changes to financial hedging to buying and selling of plants or new businesses anything that affect the level and variability of cash flowing forward." When viewed from this light, risk management is clearly a senior management responsibility, one that requires input from and coordination of the company at all operating levels. Together, they make risk an important board room issue. The factors driving the transformation of corporate risk management are increasing in the scale and varieties of uncertainties facing today's companies, everything from fluctuating commodity prices to threats of re-regulation and terrorist attacks. In late 1970s, finance scholars began to research for how Risk Management can increase corporate values.

Types of Risk

Understanding the different types of risk is important because tackling each risk requires different set of management skills. Classification is important because the risk management strategies are devised according to the type of risk faced by the companies. To obtain a general understanding of risk is not an easy task, as there are numerous definitions of risks of different types and on top of that, many different views on how risks ought to be classified. There are various types of risks faced by an organisation. The important types of risks faced by the companies are: credit risk, market risk, environmental risk, regulatory risk, reputational risk, industry risk, political risk, operational risk, strategic risk, human capital risk, natural hazard risk, information technology (IT) risk, treasury risk, economic risk and organisational risk.

Objectives of the Study

The following objectives were formulated:

1. To identify the types of risks faced by the organisations.
2. To measure the intensity of the risks faced by the organisations.
3. To find out the important risks faced by the non-financial corporations.

Scope of the Study

The present study seeks to measure the intensity of risks faced by non-financial corporations in Tamil Nadu. Fourteen types of risk mentioned above were considered.

Limitations of the Study

A few respondents were reluctant to respond, as they had the fear of disclosing information, in spite of the assurance given to them of maintaining the confidentiality. Data of such non-responding companies were one of the limitations. The survey was conducted only in Tamil Nadu. Hence, the results arrived from the study may or may not be applicable to other states. The study is based on primary data and hence some of the information is confidential to the management, and its non-availability also limited the scope of the study.

Review of Literature

Crouhy *et al.* (2006) in their book classified risk into eight types. These are: market risk, credit risk, liquidity risk, operational risk, legal and regulatory risk, business risk, strategic risk and reputational risk. Greene and Serbein in their book entitled "Risk Management: Text and Cases" have examined the risk under the following major headings: property risk and personnel risk, marketing risk, finance risk, personnel, production and environment risk. Terry Caroll *et al.* (2002) in their book on risk factor have given a typical list of business or organisational risks, based on their practical experience working with a variety of organisations in both the private and public sectors. A sample of risks quoted include: business risk, currency risk, environmental risk, financial risk, reputation and brand risk, treasury products risk, operational risk and interest rate risk.

Vedupuriswar in his book "Enterprise Risk Management" (Vol III) has discussed about a few types of risk faced by the organisation. The discussed risks are: strategic risk, financial risk, technology risk, political risk, environmental risk and legal risk. A few of the key types of risks facing companies highlighted by Andersen in his book "Managing Business Risk in the Information Age" include: market risk, competitive risk, technology risk, product risk, execution risk and capitalisation risk.

Miller (1998) in his article highlighted that the various risks faced by the corporations must be assessed and managed from an integrated perspective. The author has introduced a multivariate approach to assess the economic exposure. He has also addressed the implications of multivariate modelling for corporate risk management.

Ranga Swamy (2005) in his article discussed about the concept of risk. The main objective of risk management is to protect the property, earnings and personnel of the organisation against the losses and legal liabilities that may be incurred due to various risks. He has quoted various sources of business risk. The risk manager has to pinpoint the risk-sensitive area. As a head, he has to coordinate with all functional managers to make judicious use of the combined resources of the organisation and outside services to safeguard the objective of the organisation.

Abbasi *et al.* (2007) in their article highlighted on the profile of risk in large Jordanian manufacturing industries, their probabilities and impacts and the overall level of riskiness or significance. It has been found that the external risks have higher probabilities and scores than the internal ones. Companies with larger sizes, variety of products, good management systems, strong financial potentials and markets outside Jordan were found to have lower risk scores. The authors suggested such type of companies should provide a benchmark for developing countries, which have high-risk scores in adopting systematic risk management techniques necessary to reduce the risk levels in the industries.

Khan (2008) addressed that management of risks has become more and more an important issue. To manage risks, it is necessary to quantify them. Quantification of risk helps to improve business. He has also classified the risk into credit, market, liquidity and operational risks. The author has discussed the various methods in evaluating these risks.

Research Methodology

Sampling Technique, Size and Data Collection

Prowess database maintained by the Centre for Monitoring Indian Economy (CMIE) was used to draw the companies listed in Bombay Stock Exchange (BSE), with registered offices in Tamil Nadu. This yielded 312 companies. Service sector companies belonging to hotels and hospitals were eliminated because the risks faced, strategies and practices are different. After eliminating the service sector companies, the result comprised 302 companies.

Universal sampling method was used. The questionnaire was circulated to all the companies in the yielded list. After repeated remainders, continuous follow-ups and personal, mail and phone contacts, only 176 companies responded, which is nearly 58 per cent of the population. The accomplished response rate is satisfactory for statistical generalisation, because the companies which responded to the survey significantly belonged to the non-responded companies category and represented their views and opinions. In order to fulfill the objectives set, a questionnaire was devised to administer among the respondents. The use of survey questionnaires is common for risk management studies (Yazid *et al.*, 2008; Beasley *et al.*, 2006; Beasley and Frigo, 2007; Abbasi *et al.*, 2007; Liebenberg and Hoyt, 2003). The following techniques were adopted to collect data, because of the wide geographical area involved. (i) Personal contact (ii) Mailed the questionnaire. The questionnaire was hosted in the Web. The URL link to the questionnaire was given in the mail (iii) Posted the questionnaire with self-addressed return envelope.

Since the present study focuses on corporate risk management practices among different sectors, the 176 companies that responded belonged to various sectors like automotive, manufacturing, chemicals, fast-moving consumer goods (FMCG), resources, IT and technology, and construction. The secondary data related to the study was gathered from leading journals like: *Journal of Risk Finance, The Review of Financial Studies, Risk Management, Journal of Finance and Financial Analyst.*

Hypothesis Testing

The following hypotheses were formulated to accomplish the objectives formulated.

H_{01}: 'No difference exists between the average score of the likelihood of occurrence of risks and the mean level of all types of risks.'

H_{02}: 'No difference exists between the average score of the impact of occurrence of risks and mean level of all types of risks.'

H_{03}: 'No difference exists between the average risk score and the mean scores of all types of risks.'

H_{04}: 'No difference exists between the mean values of risk scores based on the nature of industry.'

Tools Used

Tools used in the present study were mean, standard deviation, analysis of variance (ANOVA) and one sample '*t*' test.

Analysis and Interpretation

Table 19.1 describes the basic profile of the respondents. The question pertaining to nature of industry reveals that seven industries are covered. Among the seven industries, most of the respondents reported that they belong to manufacturing sector (47.7%). The representations of other industries are IT and technology (17.0%), chemicals (12.5%), automotive (9.1%) and FMCG (5.1%). The least represented respondents hail from construction (4.5%) and resources (4.0%).

Table 19.1

Basic Profile of the Respondents

S. No.	*Factors*	*Column Title*	*Nos.*	*%*
1	Nature of Industry	Automotive	16	9.1
		Chemicals	22	12.5
		FMCG	9	5.1
		Manufacturing	84	47.7
		Resources	7	4.0
		IT and Technology	30	17.0
		Construction	8	4.5
2	Total		176	100

Mean and Standard Deviation for the Likelihood of Occurrence of Risk

To find out the variations of all the likelihood occurrences of risks, mean, standard deviation and coefficient of variation were computed, which is portrayed in Table 19.2.

Table 19.2 shows the overall mean and standard deviation of probabilities of each risk category. Weighted average means for each type of risks were calculated. The mean value ranges from 2.9716 to 3.7330. The overall weighted average mean score of the likelihood of occurrence of risks is found to be 3.28. The standard deviation represents how far it deviates from the mean value. The higher the standard deviation, the greater is the risk. It is noted that the maximum standard deviation value is for Political Risk (0.91275). The lowest value is for financing risk (0.67689). The natural hazard risk has the lowest mean value of 2.9716. It is interesting to note that environmental, operational and IT risks have the similar mean values (i.e., 3.1989). The mean values of all risk categories have been taken for further testing against the average score of the likelihood of occurrence of risks to find whether these risks have high or higher probability of occurrence.

Table 19.2

One Sample Statistics of Likelihood Occurrence of Risk

S.No.	Likelihood Occurrence of Risk	Weighted Average Mean	Std. Deviation
1	Credit	3.7330	0.77992
2	Financing	3.6818	0.67689
3	Market	3.6648	0.72199
4	Treasury	3.3807	0.73870
5	Regulatory	3.4034	0.80128
6	IT	3.1989	0.82129
7	Strategic	3.1648	0.73376
8	Environmental	3.1989	0.84866
9	Operational	3.1989	0.77105
10	Reputational	3.1307	0.84851
11	Political	3.0341	0.91275
12	Natural Hazard	2.9716	0.90981
13	Human Capital	3.0057	0.74448
14	Industry	3.1648	0.84252
15	Overall Weighted Average Mean Score	3.28	

Testing the Mean Value with a Hypothetical Value (One-Sample *t* Test)

One-sample *t* test was used to test statistically whether the likelihood of occurrence of different risk categories is around the scale mean of 3.28 at 0.05 level of significance. The scores range from 1 to 5. The calculated average score (3.28) is taken as test value for this analysis. Risks having probability means greater than 3.28 were considered to have high probabilities of occurrence.

H_{01}: 'No difference exists between the average score of the likelihood of occurrence of risks and the mean level of: (i) credit risk, (ii) financing risk, (iii) market risk, (iv) treasury risk, (v) regulatory risk, (vi) IT risk, (vii) strategic risk, (viii) environmental risk, (ix) operational risk,

(x) reputational risk, (xi) political risk, (xii) natural hazard risk, (xiii) human capital risk and (xiv) industry risk.'

Table 19.3

One-Sample Test Statistics for Likelihood of Occurrence of Risk

S.No.	*Likelihood of Occurrence of Risk*	*Test value = 3.28*		*Remarks*
		T	*p value*	*Level of significance*
1	Credit	7.705	0.000	0.05
2	Financing	7.875	0.000	0.05
3	Market	7.070	0.000	0.05
4	Treasury	1.808	0.072	Not significant
5	Regulatory	2.043	0.043	0.05
6	IT	-1.311	0.192	Not significant
7	Strategic	-2.083	0.039	0.05
8	Environmental	-1.268	0.206	Not significant
9	Operational	-1.396	0.164	Not significant
10	Reputational	-2.335	0.021	0.05
11	Political	-3.574	0.000	0.05
12	Natural Hazard	-4.497	0.000	0.05
13	Human Capital	-4.888	0.000	0.05
14	Industry	-1.814	0.071	Not significant

The results of one-sample *t* test portrayed in Table 19.3 show statistical significance for all types of risks except for treasury risk, IT risk, environmental risk, operational risk and industry risk. When the formulated hypothesis is rejected, the average score and the specific risk mean score is compared. When the overall probability means of different risk categories falls below 3.23, it indicates that their likelihood occurrence is low. When the overall probability means of different risk categories falls above 3.23, it indicates that their likelihood occurrence is high. It is noted from Table 19.3 the likelihood occurrences of credit risk, financing risk, market risk and regulatory risk were found to have high probability of occurrence. This may be due to the characteristic nature of the sampled industries. IT risk and strategic risk had overall probability means around the scale mean indicating that their likelihood occurrence is medium. Reputational risk, political risk, natural hazard risk and human capital risk were found to have low probability of occurrences.

Mean and Standard Deviation for the Impact of Occurrence of Risk

To find out the variations of all the impact of occurrences of risks, mean, standard deviation and coefficient of variation were computed, which is shown in Table 19.4. The mean, standard deviation and coefficient of variance for each risk probability were calculated. The table shows the overall mean and standard deviation of impact of occurrences of each risk category. Weighted average mean for each type of risk was calculated.

Table 19.4

One-Sample Statistics of Impact of Occurrence of Risk

S.No.	*Impact of Occurrence*	*Weighted Average Mean*	*Std. Deviation*
1	Credit	3.6080	0.82097
2	Financing	3.6591	0.70729
3	Market	3.6591	0.68262
4	Treasury	3.4602	0.76987
5	Regulatory	3.4261	0.73694
6	IT	3.2784	0.76104
7	Strategic	3.2500	0.78194
8	Environmental	3.2500	0.81766
9	Operational	3.3409	0.80550
10	Reputational	3.1534	0.82413
11	Political	3.1591	0.78393
12	Natural Hazard	3.1818	0.82178
13	Human Capital	3.2045	0.77325
14	Industry	3.2614	0.77819
15	Overall Weighted Average Mean Score	3.34	

The mean value ranges from 3.1534 to 3.6591. The overall weighted average mean score of the impact of occurrence of risks presented is found to be 3.34. The standard deviation represents how far it deviates from the mean value. The higher the standard deviation, the greater is the risk. It is noted that the maximum standard deviation value is for reputational risk (0.82413). The lowest value is for market risk (0.6826).

It is noted that both market risk and financing risk have a mean value of 3.6591, which is highest mean value among the different types of risks.

Reputational risk has the lowest mean value of 3.1534. The mean values of all risk categories have been taken for further testing against the average score of the impact of occurrence of risks to find whether these risks have high or higher impact of occurrence.

Testing the Mean Value with a Hypothetical Value (One-Sample t Test)

One-sample t test was used to test statistically whether the impact of occurrence of different risk categories is around the scale mean of 3.34 at 0.05 level of significance. The scores range from 1 to 5. The calculated average score (3.34) is taken as test value for this analysis. Risks having means greater than 3.34 were considered to have high impact of occurrence.

H_{02}: 'No difference exists between the average score of the impact of occurrence of risks and the mean level of: (i) credit risk, (ii) financing, (iii) market risk, (iv) treasury risk, (v) regulatory risk, (vi) IT risk, (vii) strategic risk, (viii) environmental risk, (ix) operational risk, (x) reputational risk, (xi) political risk, (xii) natural hazard risk, (xiii) human capital risk and (xiv) industry risk.'

It is noted from Table 19.5 that the impact of occurrence of credit risk, financing risk, market risk, treasury risk, reputational risk, political risk, natural hazard risk and human capital risk is found to be statistically significant. It is further noted from Table 19.5 the impact of occurrences of credit risk, financing risk, market risk, treasury risk was found to have high impact of occurrence. This may be due to the characteristic nature of the sampled industries. Political risk, reputational risk, natural hazard risk and human capital risk were found to have low impact of occurrences. This may be due to the characteristic nature of the sampled industries.

Table 19.5

One-Sample Test Statistics for Impact of Occurrence of Risk

S.No.	Impact of Occurrence	Test Value = 3.34		Remarks/Level of Significance
		T	p value	
1	Credit	4.330	0.000	0.05
2	Financing	5.985	0.000	0.05
3	Market	6.201	0.000	0.05
4	Treasury	2.072	0.040	0.05
5	Regulatory	1.551	0.123	Not significant
6	IT	-1.074	0.284	Not significant
7	Strategic	-1.527	0.129	Not significant
8	Environmental	-1.460	0.146	Not significant
9	Operational	0.015	0.988	Not significant
10	Reputational	-3.004	0.003	0.05
11	Political	-3.062	0.003	0.05
12	Natural Hazard	-2.554	0.012	0.05
13	Human Capital	-2.324	0.021	0.05
14	Industry	-1.341	0.182	Not significant

Testing the Mean Values of Risk Score

Risk Score

Risk score is the product of likelihood occurrence of risk and impact of occurrence of risk. For each type of risk, the below-mentioned formula was taken into account for calculation of risk score.

CRS = LOCR * IOCR (where CRS = Credit Risk Score, LOCR = likelihood occurrence of Credit Risk, IOCR = impact of occurrence of Credit Risk). FRS = LOFR * IOFR (where FRS=Financing Risk Score, LOFR = likelihood occurrence of Financing Risk, IOCR = impact of occurrence of Financing Risk). MRS = LOMR *IOMR (where MRS = Market Risk Score, LOMR = likelihood occurrence of Market Risk, IOMR = impact of occurrence of Market Risk). TRS = LOTR *IOTR (where TRS = Treasury Risk Score, LOTR = likelihood occurrence of Treasury Risk, IOTR = impact of occurrence of Treasury Risk). RRS = LORR *IORR (where RRS = Regulatory Risk Score, LORR = likelihood occurrence of Regulatory Risk,

IORR = impact of occurrence of Regulatory Risk). ITRS = LOITR * IOITR (where ITRS = IT Risk Score, LOITR = likelihood occurrence of IT Risk, IOITR = impact of occurrence of IT Risk). SRS = LOSR *IOSR (where SRS = Strategic Risk Score, LORR = likelihood occurrence of Strategic Risk, IORR = impact of occurrence of Strategic Risk). ERS = LOER *IOER (where ERS = Environmental Risk Score, LOER = likelihood occurrence of Environmental Risk, IOER = impact of occurrence of Environmental Risk). ORS = LOOR *IOOR (where ORS = Operational Risk Score, LOOR = likelihood occurrence of Operational Risk, IOOR = impact of occurrence of Operational Risk). RERS = LORER *IORER (where RERS = Reputational Risk Score, LORER = likelihood occurrence of Reputational Risk, IORER = impact of occurrence of Reputational Risk). PRS = LOPR *IOPR (where PRS = Political Risk Score, LOPR = likelihood occurrence of Political Risk, IOPR = impact of occurrence of Political Risk). NHRS = LONHR *IONHR (where NHRS = Natural Hazard Risk Score, LONHR = likelihood occurrence of Natural Hazard Risk, IONHR = impact of occurrence of Natural Hazard Risk). HCRS = LOHCR *IOHCR (where HCRS = Human Capital Risk Score, LOHCR = likelihood occurrence of Human Capital Risk, IOHCR = impact of occurrence of Human Capital Risk). IRS = LOIR *IOIR (where IRS = Industry Risk Score, LOIR = likelihood occurrence of Industry Risk, IOIR = impact of occurrence of Industry Risk.

Mean and Standard Deviation for Risk Scores

Table 19.6 shows the overall mean and standard deviation of each risk category. Weighted average mean for each type of risk was calculated. The mean value ranges from 9.755 to 13.83. The weighted average mean risk score is found to be 11.27. The standard deviation represents how far it deviates from the mean value. The higher the standard deviation, the greater is the risk. It is noted that the maximum standard deviation value is for credit risk (4.887). The lowest value is for natural hazard risk (3.8124). It is noted that credit risk mean value (13.83), is the highest mean value among the different types of risk. Natural hazard risk has the lowest mean value of 9.755. The mean values of all risk categories have been taken for further testing against the average risk score to find whether these risks have highest risk score.

Table 19.6

One-Sample Statistics for Risk Scores

S.No.	*Risk Score*	*Weighted Average Mean*	*Std. Deviation*
1	Credit	13.8295	4.88782
2	Financing	13.6875	3.82310
3	Market	13.5568	4.07742
4	Treasury	11.8977	4.14878
5	Regulatory	11.8295	4.16303
6	IT	10.7273	4.10499
7	Strategic	10.4489	3.81242
8	Environmental	10.7670	4.66442
9	Operational	11.0057	4.64696
10	Reputational	10.0511	4.02318
11	Political	9.8580	4.31704
12	Natural Hazard	9.7557	4.50174
13	Human Capital	9.8409	3.84079
14	Industry	10.6534	4.65732
15	Overall Weighted Average Mean Score	11.27	

Testing the Mean Value with a Hypothetical Value (One-Sample *t* Test)

One-sample *t* test was used to test statistically whether the risk score is around the scale mean of 11.27 at 0.05 level of significance. The scores range from 5 to 25. The calculated average score (11.27) is taken as test value for this analysis.

H_{03}: 'No difference exists between the average risk score and the mean level scores of: (i) credit risk, (ii) financing, (iii) market risk, (iv) treasury risk, (v) regulatory risk, (vi) IT risk, (vii) strategic risk, (viii) environmental risk, (ix) operational risk, (x) reputational risk, (xi) political risk, (xii) natural hazard risk, (xiii) human capital risk and (xiv) industry risk.'

Table 19.7

One Sample Test Statistics for Risk Score

S.No.	Risk Score	Test Value = 11.27		Remarks/Level of Significance
		T	p value	
1	Credit	6.947	0.000	0.05
2	Financing	8.389	0.000	0.05
3	Market	7.441	0.000	0.05
4	Treasury	2.007	0.046	0.05
5	Regulatory	1.783	0.076	Not significant
6	IT	-1.754	0.081	Not significant
7	Strategic	-2.857	0.005	0.05
8	Environmental	-1.430	0.154	Not significant
9	Operational	-0.755	0.452	Not significant
10	Reputational	-4.019	0.000	0.05
11	Political	-4.339	0.000	0.05
12	Natural Hazard	-4.463	0.000	0.05
13	Human Capital	-4.936	0.000	0.05
14	Industry	-1.756	0.081	Not significant

It is noted from Table 19.7 that credit risk, financing risk, market risk and treasury risk are located in high risk region. The likelihood of occurrence and impact of occurrence of credit risk, financing risk and market risk were also found to be high. Since the risk score is the product of likelihood occurrence of risk and impact of occurrence of risk, the overall risk score for credit risk, financing risk, market risk and treasury risk being high is justified. Reputational risk, political risk, natural hazard risk and human capital risk are found to be low. Even in these cases, the likelihood occurrence and impact of occurrence were found to be low. Therefore, the overall risk score for reputational risk, political risk, natural hazard risk and human capital risk being low is also justified.

Testing the Mean Score of Different Types of Risks Based on Nature of Industry

Nature of industry will have definite influence on the risk score and mean values of the risk. To test the above assumption, one-way ANOVA was used to test the following null hypothesis.

H_{04}: 'No difference exists among the mean scores of credit risk, financing risk, market risk, treasury risk, regulatory risk, IT risk, strategic risk, environmental risk, operational risk, reputational risk, political risk, natural hazard risk, human capital risk and industry risk on nature of industry.'

It is noted from Table 19.8 the risk score means of credit risk and human capital risk differs among industrial sectors at the 0.05 level of significance. Other risk categories had no significant differences in their risk score means among different sectors. It is worth mentioning that the same results were found when testing the likelihood and impact of occurrences of different risk categories among industries. The mean score of different risks across industries is plotted in Figure 19.1. From Figure 19.1 it is understood that construction industry faces high credit risk. Credit risk differs for different industries because of the characteristic nature of industry in terms of credit risk. Credit risk was highest for construction industry may be because of drop in announcement of new projects by private sector due to credit risk, land acquisition, etc. The same reasons were identified in similar case by Fei *et al.* (2010). Manufacturing industry has the lowest credit risk because of constituents of credit risk which includes counterparty risk, settlement risk and concentration risk affected leastly, due to high standardisation of credit policies. Figure 19.2 depicts the mean values of human capital across different sectors. From Figure 19.1, it is implicit that human capital risk is high in resources sector when compared to other sectors. This may be due to non-availability of experienced talent in our country which is a major challenge before resources sector. These findings coincides with the earlier study conducted by Dcsai (2010). The result that there is shortage of workers especially in the age group of 30-45 years coincides with the above. For the other types of risk, since the p value is higher than 0.05, the null hypothesis that there is no variation among the industries in terms of financing risk, market risk, treasury risk, regulatory risk, IT risk strategic risk, environmental risk, operational risk, reputational risk, political risk, natural hazard risk and industry risk is accepted.

Table 19.8

Comparing the Mean Value of Risk Scores based on Industries (ANOVA)

S.No.	Risk Score	F	p value	Remarks/Level of significance
1	Credit	3.039	0.008	0.05
2	Financing	0.711	0.641	Not significant
3	Market	1.112	0.357	Not significant
4	Treasury	0.740	0.618	Not significant
5	Regulatory	0.306	0.933	Not significant
6	IT	0.729	0.627	Not significant
7	Strategic	1.051	0.394	Not significant
8	Environmental	0.360	0.903	Not significant
9	Operational	0.558	0.763	Not significant
10	Reputational	0.853	0.531	Not significant
11	Political	0.559	0.763	Not significant
12	Natural Hazard	1.257	0.280	Not significant
13	Human Capital	2.878	0.011	0.05
14	Industry	0.542	0.776	Not significant

Figure 19.1

Mean Values of Credit Risk Score based on Nature of Industry

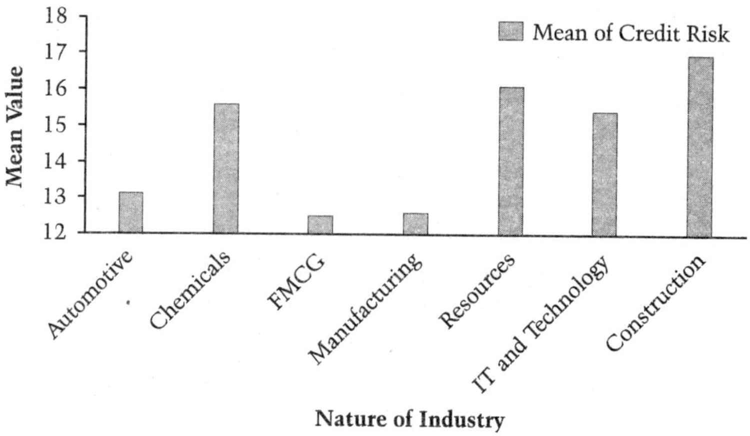

Figure 19.2

Mean Values of Human Capital Risk Score based on Nature of Industry

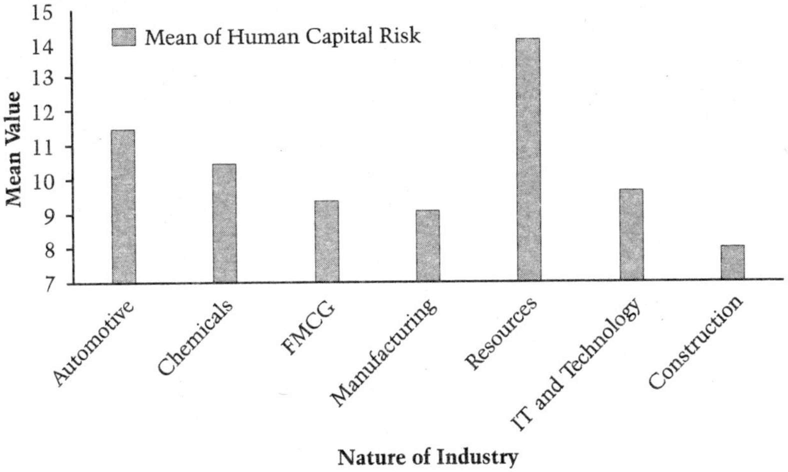

Findings and Suggestions

Findings

The mean and standard deviation of likelihood of occurrence of different categories of risks show that the credit risk has the highest probability of occurrence. It is divulged that the mean value of all risks falls in the range of 3 and above. Natural hazard has the lowest mean value among all the categories of risks. It is found from the one-sample test statistics that the likelihood occurrence of credit risk, financing risk, market risk, regulatory risk, strategic risk, reputational risk, political risk, natural hazard risk and human capital risk is statistically significant. The likelihood occurrences of credit risk, financing risk, market risk and regulatory risk were found to have high probability of occurrence. IT risk and strategic risk had overall probability mean around the scale mean indicating that their likelihood occurrence is medium. Reputational risk, political risk, natural hazard risk and human capital risk were found to have low probability of occurrences.

The impact of occurrence of credit risk, financing risk, market risk, treasury risk, reputational risk, political risk, natural hazard risk and human capital risk is found to be statistically significant. The impact of occurrence of credit risk, financing risk, market risk and treasury risk was found to have high probability of occurrence. Reputational risk, political risk, natural hazard risk and human capital risk were found to have low impact of occurrence. The risk score was calculated with the help of likelihood of occurrence of risks and impact of occurrence of risks. Risk score is the product of likelihood occurrence of risk and impact of occurrence of risk. Risk score was calculated for different categories of risk with help of the mentioned formula in the analysis section. Since the calculated risks score ranged from 5 to 25, the medium value was identified as 11.27. It is interesting to note that credit risk has the highest mean value. The lowest mean value is for natural hazard risk.

The one-sample *t* test results revealed that credit risk, financing risk, market risk and treasury risk are located in high-risk region. Reputational risk, political risk, natural hazard risk and human capital risk were found to be low.

The risk score means of credit risk and human capital risk differs among industrial sectors at the 0.05 level of significance. Credit risk is found to be high in construction sector and human capital risk is high in resources sector.

Suggestions

The analysis reveals that human capital risk is high in resources sector. Companies have to start thinking about being more innovative and creative in how they look at acquiring talent. A key person leaving the organisation may be a problem. Meeting employees regularly, listening to the problems will help towards building loyalty. Maintaining a smooth relationship shall ensure employee's long stay to deliver return. Best HR practices from other sectors should be incorporated. Not managing regulatory risk can cause headache to the company and it will damage the reputation of the firm. Therefore a culture of compliance, improving internal approaches to meet regulatory obligations, should be created. Well-trained employees to deal with compliance issue will help the companies to reduce regulatory risk. The senior managers can be made responsible for monitoring and analysing the changes in the regulatory environment. Credit risk is found to be high in construction sector. Legally sound credit documentation can play a vital role in managing credit risk. Credit rating will be a useful strategy for companies to mitigate their credit risk. Risk transfer in form of credit insurance will help the companies to shift their burden.

Conclusion

Risks are inherent in all business transactions. Complexity, uncertainty and change are prevalent within all business and business functions. The changing business environment has to be acknowledged and necessary steps have to be taken. The study undertaken on risk management revealed the important risks faced by the companies in Tamil Nadu. The present study revealed the risks faced by non-financial corporations in Tamil Nadu, which may help the companies to tackle these risks, by benchmarking the best practices adopted by other industries.

References

Abbasi, Ghaleb Y., N.A. Sandouqa, M.D. Al-Tahat and A.M. Mukattash (2007). "A Look into Jordan's Large Manufacturing Industries Risk", *Risk Management* 9(2): 108-17.

Adam, T. (2002). "Do Firms use Derivatives to Reduce their Dependence on External Capital Markets", *European Finance Review* 6: 163-87.

Allayannis, George and Eli Ofek (2001). "Exchange Rate Exposure, Hedging, and the Use of Foreign Currency Derivatives", *Journal of International Money and Finance* 20(2): 273-96.

Allen, Anne B. (1997). "Ghostly Tales of Opportunities for Change: A Legislative Carol", *Risk Management* 44: 66.

———. (1997). "Toward a Better Standard", *Risk Management* 44: 54.

Allen, J. and A. Touran (2005). "Risk Analysis in Transit Projects", Proceedings, *49th Annual Meeting of AACE International*, New Orleans, LA, June.

Anderson, J.C. and D.W. Gerbing (1988). "Structural Equation Modeling in Practice: A Review and Recommended Two-step Approach", *Psychological Bulletin* 103(3): 411–23.

Beasley, M.S., R. Clune and D.R. Hermanson (2006). "The impact of Enterprise Risk Management on the internal audit function". Available at: *http://erm.ncsu.edu/az/erm/i/chan/m-articles/documents/ERMJFAPaper21306.pdf*

Beasley, M.S. and M.L. Frigo (2007). "Strategic Risk Management: Creating and Protecting Value", *Strategic Finance*, 88 (11): 25-53.

Bodnar, Gordon M., Gregory S. Hayt and C. Richard Marston (1998). "1998 Wharton Survey of Financial Risk Management by US Non-Financial Firms", *Financial Management* 27(4): 70-91.

Bodnar, G., Abe de Jong and Victor Macrae (2003). "The Impact of Institutional Differences on Derivatives Usage: A Comparative Study of US and Dutch Firms", *European Financial Management* 9: 271-97.

Breedan, D. and S. Viswanath (1998). "Why Do Firms Hedge? An Asymmetric Information Model", *Working Paper*, Duke University.

Brookes, Andy, David Hargreaves, Carrick Lucas and Bruce White (2000). Can Hedging Insulate Firms from Exchange Rate Risk? *Reserve Bank of New Zealand Bulletin* 63(1): 21-34.

Brown, Gregory W., Peter R. Crabb and David Haushalter (2006). "Are Firms Successful at Selective Hedging?", *Journal of Business* 79(6): 2925-49.

Carneiro, L.A.F. and M. Sherris (2008). "Corporate Interest Rate Risk Management with Derivatives in Australia: Empirical Results", *Revista Contabilidade e Financas* 46: 86-107.

Carole Hicks (November 2002). "Risk Management in the Public Sector", *Booklet from Financial Management Accounting Committee of IFAC*: 57-60.

Collier, P.A., E. Davis, J. Coates, P. Colleger and S.G. Longden (1990). *Multinational Companies and the Management of Currency Risk*. Englewood Cliffs, NJ.: Prentice Hall.

Collier, P.M. and S. Agyei-Ampomah (2006). *Management Accounting: Risk and Control Strategy*. Oxford University Press.

Crouhy, M., D. Galai and R. Mark (2006). *The Essentials of Risk Management*. New Year: McGraw Hill.

Desai (2010). "A Report on Under Pressure: Natural Resource Human capital", Perspectives from TRANSEARCH International, available at *http://www.bedfordgroup.com/bedford/pdfs/under-pressure.pdf*

Doherty, Neil. A. (2000). *Integrated Risk Management: Techniques and Strategies for Reducing Risk*. McGraw Hill Press.

Douglas, M. and A. Wildavsky (1982). *Risk and Culture: An Essay on Selection of Technological and Environmental Dangers*. Berkeley: California University Press.

Khan, Gabriel (2008). *Risk Quantification*. Protiviti Publication.

Knight, Rony F. and Deborah J. Pretty (2001). "Philosophies of Risk Shareholder Value and the CEO", *Financial Time Mastering Risk* 1: 311-15.

Lam, James (2003). *Enterprise Risk Management: From Incentive to Controls*. New Jersey: John Wiley.

Liebenberg, A. and R. Hoyt (2003). "The Determinants of Enterprise Risk Management: Evidence from the Appointment of Chief Risk Officers", *Risk Management and Insurance Review*, 6(1): 37-52.

Malhotra, N.K. and D.F. Birk (2006). *Marketing Research: An Applied Approach*, Second European Edition. Harlow, U.K.: Financial Times/Prentice Hall.

Miller, K.D. (1998). "Economic Exposure and Integrated Risk Management", *Strategic Management Journal* 19(5): 497-514.

Miller, K.D. and Philip Bromiley (1990). "Strategic Risk and Corporate Performance: An Analysis of Alternative Risk Measures", *Academy of Management Journal* 33(4): 756-79.

Ranga Swamy, S (2005). "Risk Management in Industry—An Overview", *The Chartered Accountant* 54(4): 536-41.

Rogachev, Andrey Y. (2008). "Enterprise Risk Management in a Pharmaceutical Company", *Risk Management* 10: 76-84.

Sadgrov, Kit (2005). *The Complete Guide to Business Risk Management*, Second Edition, Gower Publishing Ltd.

Vedupuriswar, A.V. and Rajesh Kumar Singh (2004). *Enterprise Risk Management—Concepts and Cases* (Vol I-V), ICFAI Press.

———. (2008). *Enterprise Risk Management- Concepts and Cases* (Vol I-V), ICFAI Press.

Williams, C.A., Jr and R.M. Heins (1989). *Risk Management*. 6th edn. New York: McGraw-Hill.

Woods, Andrew (2010). "Risk Management and the Treasurer", *Risk Management* 57(12). Available at *www.rmmagazine.com*

Fei, Wang, Wang Shilei and Guo Yan (2010). "Countermeasures of Payment Risk in Construction Contract," E-Business and E-Government (ICEE), Proceeding ICEE 10 Proceedings of the 2010 *International Conference on E-Business and E-Government*: 5129-5131.

Yazid, A.S., M.R. Hussin and A.R. Razali (2008). "A Cross-Sectional Study on Foreign Exchange Risk Management by Malaysian Public Listed Companies", *International Business Management* 2(2): 28-32.

20 Information Technology Risks and Challenges

A.S. Kalyana Kumar

Business and Information Technology

Information technology (IT), as a technology with a rapid rate of development and application in all branches of business, requires adequate protection to provide high security. The aim of the safety analysis applied on an information system is to identify and evaluate threats, vulnerabilities and safety characteristics. IT assets are exposed to risk of damage or losses. IT security involves protecting information stored electronically. This protection implies data integrity, availability and confidentiality. Nowadays, there are many types of computer crimes: money theft 44 per cent, damage of software 16 per cent, theft of information 16 per cent, alteration of data 12 per cent, theft of services 10 per cent and trespass 2 per cent (Boran, 2003).

Information Technology Risks

Technology is a queer thing. It brings you great gifts on one side and it stabs you in the back on the other. As the technology advances, risk too advances. We the current generation need to create a balance between technology and man power in order to mitigate the risk from technology.

Risks and Categories

The 50 global risks in this report are divided into five categories: economic, environmental, geopolitical, societal and technological, as per the Perception data from the World Economic Forum's Global Risks Survey 2011.

Economic Risks: The economic category addresses those risks that are of greatest concern in terms of likelihood and impact in areas covering a range of macroeconomic concerns, from financial systems and infrastructure to price volatility and regulation.

1. Asset price collapse.
2. Extreme commodity price volatility.
3. Extreme consumer price volatility.
4. Extreme energy price volatility.
5. Fiscal crises.
6. Global imbalances and currency volatility.
7. Infrastructure fragility.
8. Liquidity/credit crunch.
9. Regulatory failures.
10. Retrenchment from globalisation.
11. Slowing Chinese economy (<6%).

Environmental Risks: The environmental category addresses environmental global risks of high concern, from natural disasters such as extreme weather and geomagnetic storms to man-made disasters such as irremediable pollution and species overexploitation. If realised, these risks have the potential to destabilise both economies and societies, trigger geopolitical conflict and devastate the earth's vital resources and its inhabitants.

1. Air pollution.
2. Biodiversity loss.
3. Climate change.
4. Earthquakes and volcanic eruptions.
5. Flooding.
6. Ocean governance.
7. Storms and cyclones.

Geopolitical Risks: The geopolitical category addresses risks that are of greatest concern in the areas of politics, diplomacy, conflict, crime and governance on a global scale. From diffusion of weapons of mass destruction to pervasive entrenched corruption, geopolitical risks are global risks of humanity's own making. The threats of geopolitical risks range from undermining socioeconomic progress to annihilating society and earth's resources.

1. Corruption.
2. Fragile states.
3. Geopolitical conflict.
4. Global governance failures.
5. Illicit trade.
6. Organised crime.
7. Space security.
8. Terrorism.
9. Weapons of mass destruction.

Societal Risks: The societal category addresses trends and uncertainties in population dynamics, social stability and human survival. Global risks in this category put into question the stability of modern civilisation and the continued well-being of populations.

1. Chronic diseases.
2. Demographic challenges.
3. Economic disparity.
4. Food security.
5. Infectious diseases.
6. Migration.
7. Water security.

Technological Risks: The technological category addresses risks that are of greatest concern in the area of current and emerging technology. Figure 20.2 shows a landscape of global technological risks as plotted by their perceived likelihood and potential impact over the next 10 years. Within the technology category, volatility and the inability to 'know the unknowns' are revealed by the large spread of impacts and likelihood of the risks. Technological risks range from cyber attacks, highlighted as having the highest likelihood and a high impact, to critical systems failure having the highest impact and lower likelihood, and to the unintended consequences of nanotechnology, which has a lower impact and lower likelihood.

1. Critical information infrastructure breakdown.
2. Online data and information security.
3. Threats from new technologies.

Figure 20.1

Overall Risk Ranking

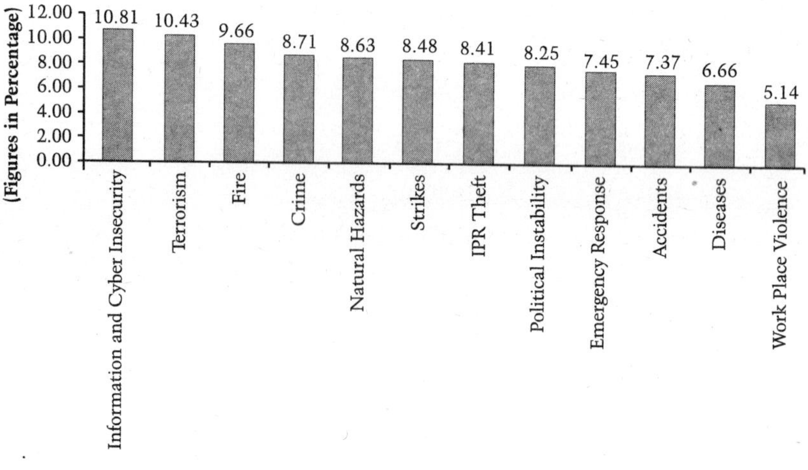

Source: World Economic Forum Survey 2011.

Five Risks to Watch

As per the IT risks concern, five risks have been designated as 'risks to watch,' as survey respondents assessed them with high levels of variance and low levels of confidence, while experts consider they may have severe, unexpected or underappreciated consequences:

1. *Cyber-security* issues ranging from the growing prevalence of cyber theft to the little-understood possibility of all-out cyber warfare.
2. *Demographic challenges* adding to fiscal pressures in advanced economies and creating severe risks to social stability in emerging economies.

3. *Resource security* issues causing extreme volatility and sustained increases over the long run in energy and commodity prices, if supply is no longer able to keep up with demand.
4. *Retrenchment from globalisation* through populist responses to economic disparities, if emerging economies do not take up a leadership role.
5. *Weapons of mass destruction*, especially the possibility of renewed nuclear proliferation between states. Effective risk response is not only about proactively reducing the downsides associated with global risks, it is also about seizing the opportunities for innovation and growth that may arise.

Information and cyber insecurity (information insecurity) has been identified as the most critical risk. The rationale lies in the enhanced use of computing and the burgeoning levels of digital crime. The risk of information security has figured in the top three risks for most of the sectors. Traditional risks of terrorism, fire and crime have been rated at number two, three and four respectively. Strikes and intellectual property rights (IPR) theft have been rated at number six and seven respectively. A very appealing verdict has been the rating of specific risks as per geographic regions and types of industrial sectors.

Figure 20.2

Risk in the Northern Region

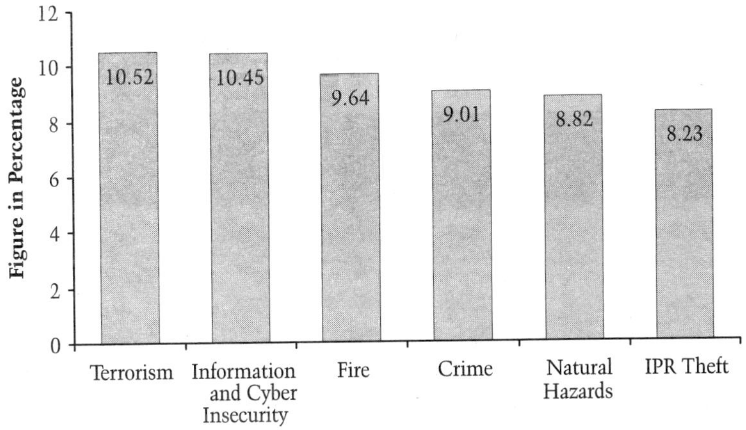

Source: *Indian Risk Survey (2012)*, FICCI and Pinkerton.

Figure 20.3

Risks in the Southern Region

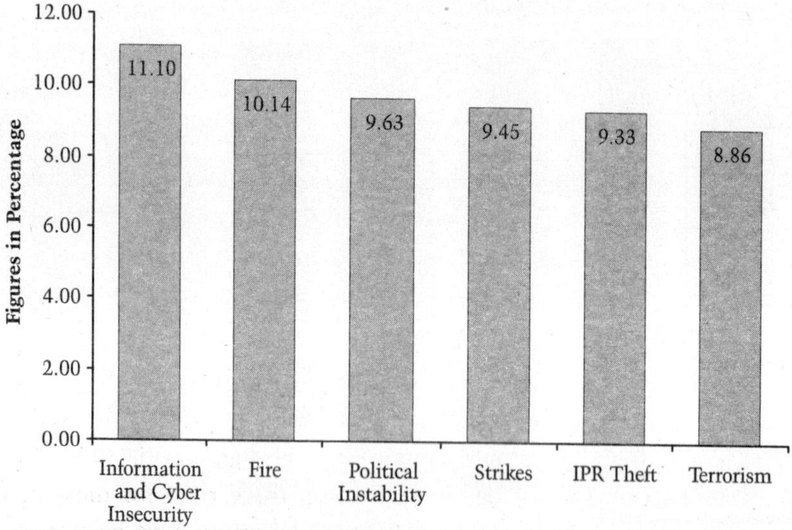

Source: Same as Figure 20.2.

While examining top six risks as per the geographic locations, the most remarkable result has been noticed when respondents from outside India placed terrorism as their fourth critical risk and have placed fire, information and cyber insecurity and strikes as major risks affecting their businesses.

Figure 20.4

Risks in the Eastern Region

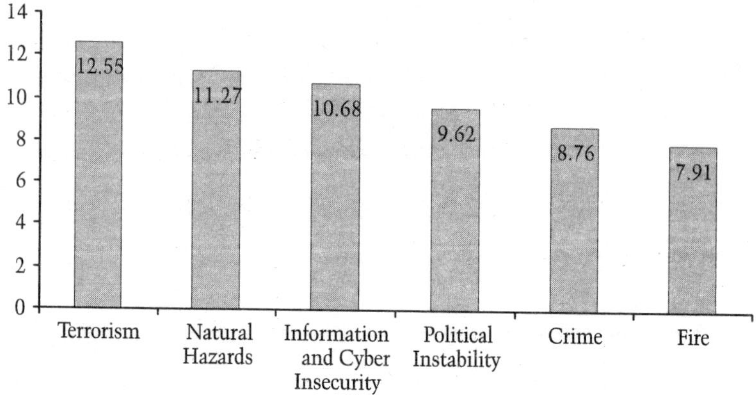

Source: Same as Figure 20.2.

Figure 20.5

Risks in the Western Region

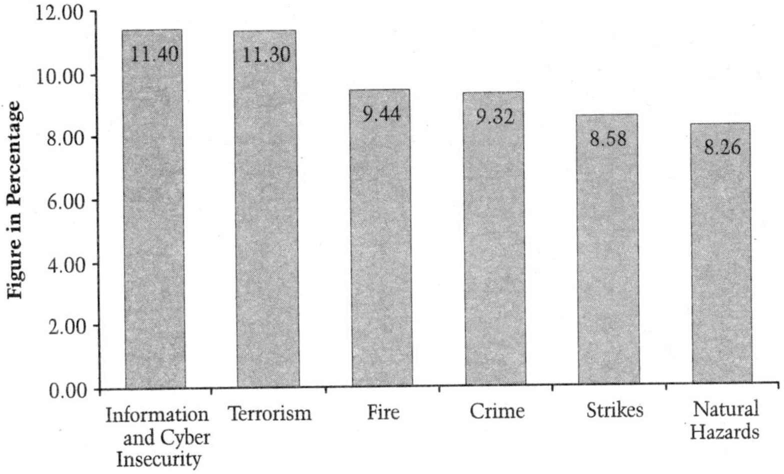

Source: Same as Figure 20.2.

Figure 20.6

Risks as Percieved from Outside India

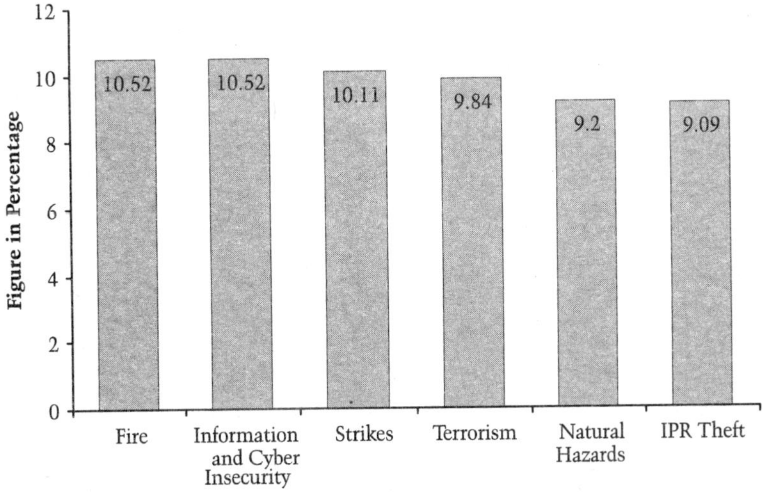

Source: Same as Figure 20.2.

The northern region did indicate terrorism as the top risk and also included crime and IPR theft in the list of top six risks. The frequent jolts from earthquakes and floods have made natural hazards as the number five risk in this region. The southern region with intense IT industry rated information and cyber insecurity as their prime concern. In the year 2010, the second largest number of cyber crime cases is reported from Andhra Pradesh. Recently, a large number of state government websites in Bangalore have also been attacked. The region rated political instability at the third rank among top risks. The focus on political instability may be because of movements such as Telangana and instability in some of the southern states. South India is the only region that has not categorised crime among the top six risks.

It is also interesting to note the eastern region of India preferred to nominate terrorism as their biggest risk but haven't mentioned strikes in the top six risks, though this region witnesses maximum number of strikes. The risk of natural hazards has been rated at number two due to losses suffered in the hands of cyclones and floods. With limited number of IT companies operating in the eastern region, the risk of information and cyber insecurity has been rated at number three.

The western region, in spite of being immensely affected by terrorism, has placed the risk of terrorism at number two and has kept information and cyber insecurity at number one. Though this region is known for higher degree of organised crime, the western region has rated crime at number four after the risk of fire.

IT/ITES Sector

With increasing incidents of cyber crime and terror attacks on websites, the information and technology sector has rated information and cyber insecurity and terrorism as risk number one and number two respectively. There has been a strategic shift in terrorist's target selection over the last decade and there have been intelligence alerts related to a possible attack on IT companies. In fact investigations did reveal that terrorists had carried out reconnaissance of three IT companies in Bangalore before carrying an attack on Indian Institute of Science (IISc), Bangalore, in 2005. The risk of fire being detrimental to life and business has been rated at number three.

Figure 20.7

Risks in IT/ITES

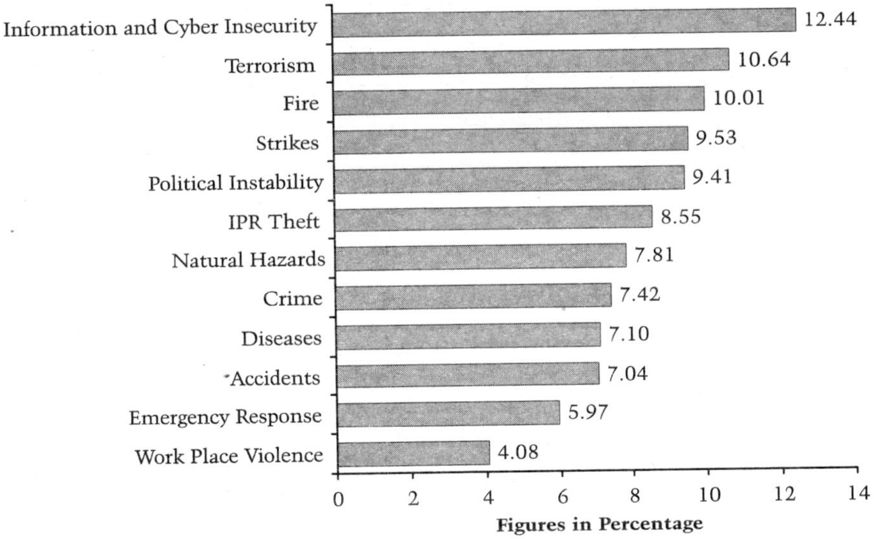

Source: Same as Figure 20.2.

Financial Services Sector

Financial services sector has been the victim of some major cyber financial frauds. This is the main reason why the financial services sector has rated information and cyber insecurity and crime as their top two risks. The number and magnitude of financial frauds have risen in the recent past. Unfortunately the sector is blamed for lacking preventive mechanisms to curb such incidences. There has been an effort to list fraudsters and defaulters in a single database and its implementation is likely to produce results in the near future. The risks of terrorism and IPR theft are rated at number three and four respectively.

Information and Cyber Insecurity

Information and cyber insecurity has been rated as the number one risk by most of the respondents during India Risk Survey 2012. Information espionage refers to obtaining secret or confidential information without the permission and knowledge of its holder. Cyber crime is a criminal activity, in which computers or computer networks are both a tool and the target.

Figure 20.8

Risks in Financial Services

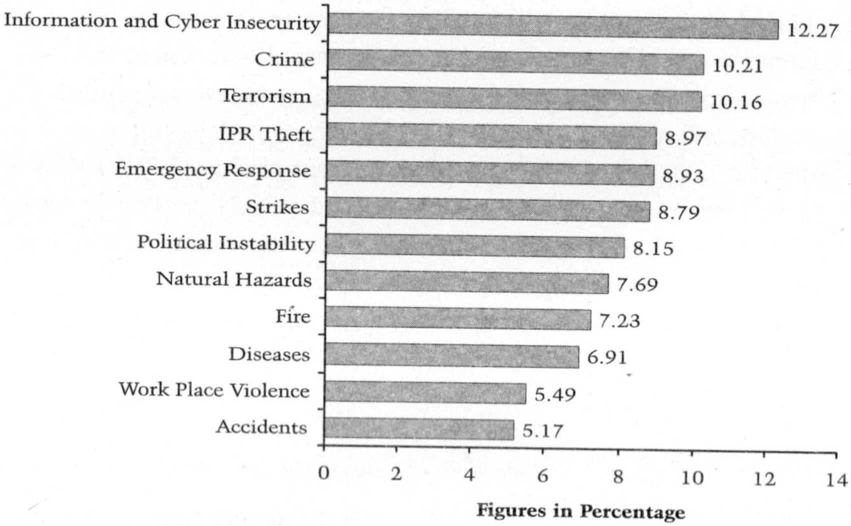

Source: Same as Figure 20.2.

Cyber crime includes everything from electronic cracking to hacking of websites to denial of online services. Considering the advantages of the cyber age and increasingly competitive corporate environment, cases of business information thefts are becoming more prominent. Norton's Cyber Crime Report 2011 reveals that India loses approximately ₹ 34,110 crore annually due to cyber-related crimes. Another major concern with cyber crimes is its low detection level and next to negligible prosecution. The monetary loss due to information theft is impossible to assess as it depends upon the nature of information stolen. However, such losses can neither be recovered through insurance coverage nor is the law able to protect from such incidents.

During the NASSCOM Global Leadership Awards, India's home minister revealed that India is ranked fifth in the number of cyber crimes. Every year, cyber crime in India is going up by 50 per cent and during the last five years, around 9,000 Indian websites including those of various government departments were hacked. Many government websites, some of them carrying sensitive information have become victims of cross-border hacking, mainly from Pakistan, Bangladesh, Nepal and China. Therefore, it is no wonder that the government has specifically rated information and cyber insecurity as the number two risk in this survey. Major cyber crimes reported in India are denial of services, defacement of websites, spam, computer viruses and worms, pornography, cyber squatting, cyber stalking and phishing. The Criminal Investigation Department Review for the year 2008 reveals that nearly 69 per cent of the information theft is carried out by current and ex-employees and only 31 per cent by hackers. In the present scenario, cyber terrorism and usage of cyber attacks to harm the enemy countries are the impending issues. Apart from many reported attacks on Indian military and intelligence agencies websites, there is a long list of failed attacks on Indian energy and infrastructure installations. This is a serious situation where lives of ordinary citizens are at risk, along with the losses caused to the economy. Despite the Information and Technology (Amendment) Act 2008, which is constituted to broaden several new provisions related to data protection, piracy and cyber terrorism, companies are still prone to the threat of information espionage, as the vulnerability has not been reduced due to the intangible nature of information stolen and because of the fact that in most cases, the accused are the employee or ex-employee of the organisation having access to the company database.

National Crime Record Bureau (NCRB) statistics indicate that from 2007 to 2010, police have recorded as many as 3,038 cases under the Information and Technology Act with only three convictions. Maharashtra recorded highest number of cyber crimes (104 cases) followed by Andhra Pradesh (66 cases) in the year 2010. The cases of data theft have been reported from almost every industrial and corporate hub of India. However, banking industry is found to be the most vulnerable to phishing attacks in India. There is a regular complaint from all the ensuing sectors about low understanding of technical skills by the law enforcement and judicial officials. In order to deal with such crimes, India has established Computer Emergency Response Teams (CERT) with an objective to coordinate and respond during major security threats. Bangalore has been credited with introducing one of the first cyber cells in India. As of now, there are only 18 cyber cells in major cities of India, but with increasing dependence on the internet, even smaller cities are registering a significant rise in the number of such cases.

The risk of cyber insecurity has been given the highest rating by industries across regions and sectors. Notwithstanding the perception of ordinary people who rate it below the category of physical crimes, incidences of cyber insecurity have affected every four out of five people using the internet. However, most cases go unreported in India. Lack of legal awareness related to cyber laws, dearth of cyber law experts, insufficient number of cyber cells across country, interdependence of cyber world and most importantly, rise of a net savvy generation are chiefly responsible for making this risk very critical.

IT Management and Challenges

In order to minimise losses, it is necessary to involve risk management and risk assessment in the areas of IT and operational risks. Risk management and risk assessment are the most important parts of Information Security Management. Most experts accept that risk management involves analysis, planning, implementation, control and monitoring of implemented measurements, and risk assessment as part of risk management.

It consists of several processes:

1. Risk identification.
2. Relevant risk analysis.
3. Risk evaluation.

Risk management recognises risk, accesses risk and takes measures to reduce risk, as well as measures for risk maintenance on an acceptable level. The main aim of risk assessment is to make a decision whether a system is acceptable and which measures would provide its acceptability. For every organisation using IT in its business process, it is significant to conduct the risk assessment. Numerous threats and vulnerabilities are presented and their identification, analysis and evaluation enable evaluation of risk impact, and proposing of suitable measures and controls for its mitigation on the acceptable level.

Common Global Risk Response Strategies

The focus of this report is on improving understanding of global risks, rather than analysing optimal risk response strategies—that is left to the ongoing discussions in the Forum's Risk Response Network and beyond. Nevertheless, a generic framework for risk response is helpful when contemplating risk. Figure 20.9 depicts five broad, non-exclusive strategies that might be employed by a government, corporation or individual to reduce overall risk exposure.

Figure 20.9

Generic Risk Response Strategies

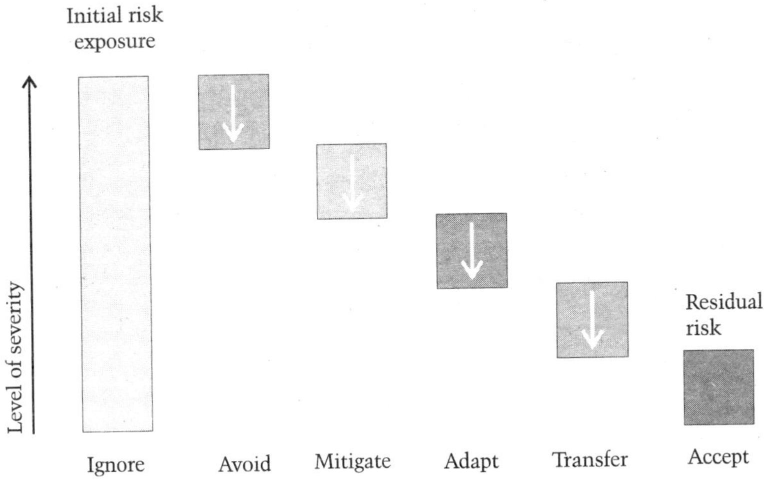

Source: Adapted from Cleary & Malleret's 'Resilience to Risk' and Vernon L Grose's 'Managing Risk.'

The first and most obvious option is to seek to avoid the risk wherever possible.

The second option is to mitigate the risk directly—to attempt to reduce the impact or likelihood of the risk at source. For example, a corporation facing climate-change-related risks could lobby internationally to reduce carbon emissions.

The third option is to adapt to the risk by preparing for its occurrence. Here, a corporation may strengthen buildings or prepare emergency response plans. Home owners residing in flood-prone areas could elevate their structures or collaborate to put drainage systems in place.

The fourth option involves transferring risk. For individuals and companies, risk could be transferred to a third party such as an insurer or through more sophisticated hedging strategies. The equivalent from a systemic perspective is to diffuse the risk, such that the second- and third-order impacts are reduced. For example, ensure that the collapse of a single bank does not cause the collapse of interbank lending.

These options can all reduce the resulting impact of the risk on an organisation or system. But the final step is also critically important—it involves accepting the residual risk, such that the organisation or individual is well aware of the potential impact and can hold reserves or make other provisions to deal with the possible consequences.

The NCRB data for cognisable crimes committed on yearly basis from 1953 to 2010 indicate a regular increase of crime rate in India. It is also to be noted that NCRB accounts only for the recorded criminal activities. The possibility of all criminal incidents not reaching police remains a reality. In addition, organised crime is on the rise in India. Theft accounts for approximately 14.8 per cent of the total recorded crime in India. Similarly the crime of kidnapping and abduction is rising which accounts for 1.7 per cent of the total crime.

India Ranked 11th

Share of malicious computer activity: 3 per cent

Malicious code rank: 3

Spam zombies rank: 11

Phishing website hosts rank: 22

Bot rank: 20

Attack origin rank: 19

Figure 20.10

Incidence of Total Cognisable Crime (IPC), 1953-2010

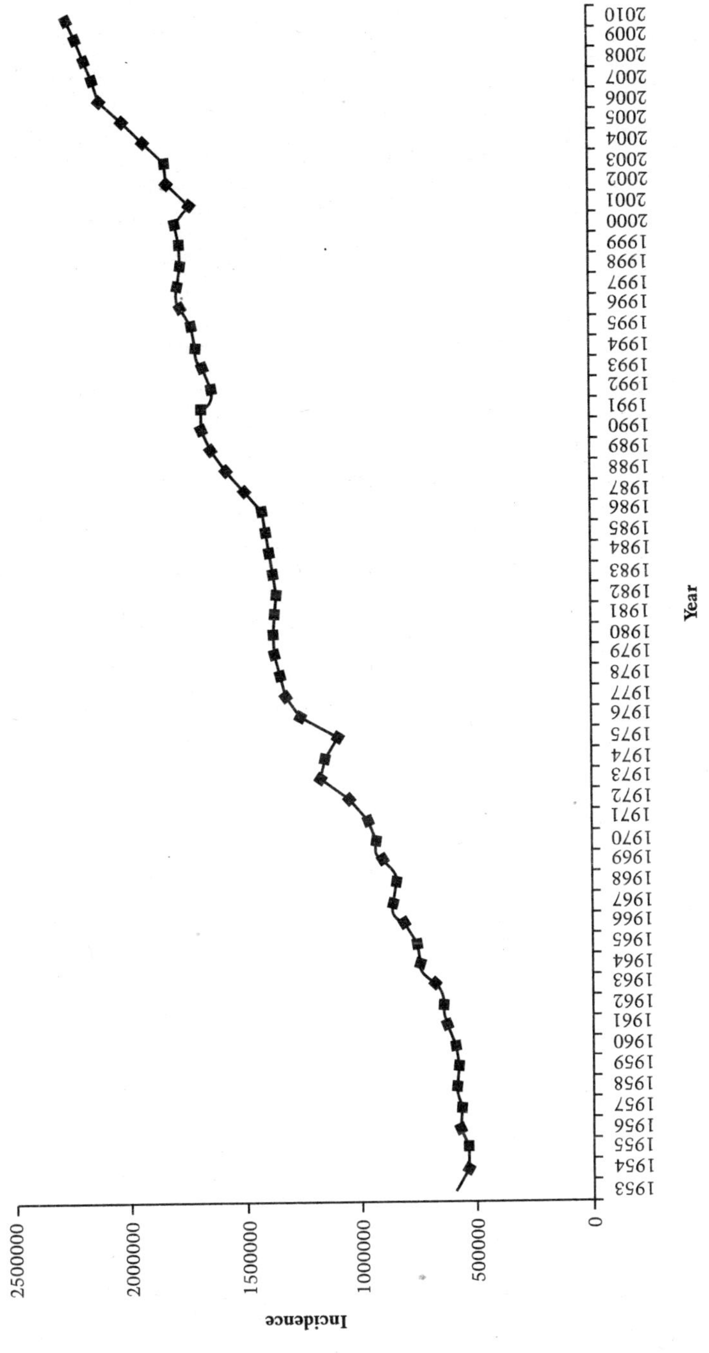

Source: Data on Recorded Crime in India, 1953-2010 (Source: National Crime Records Bureau, India).

Figure 20.11

List of Top 20 Countries with the Highest Rate of Cybercrime

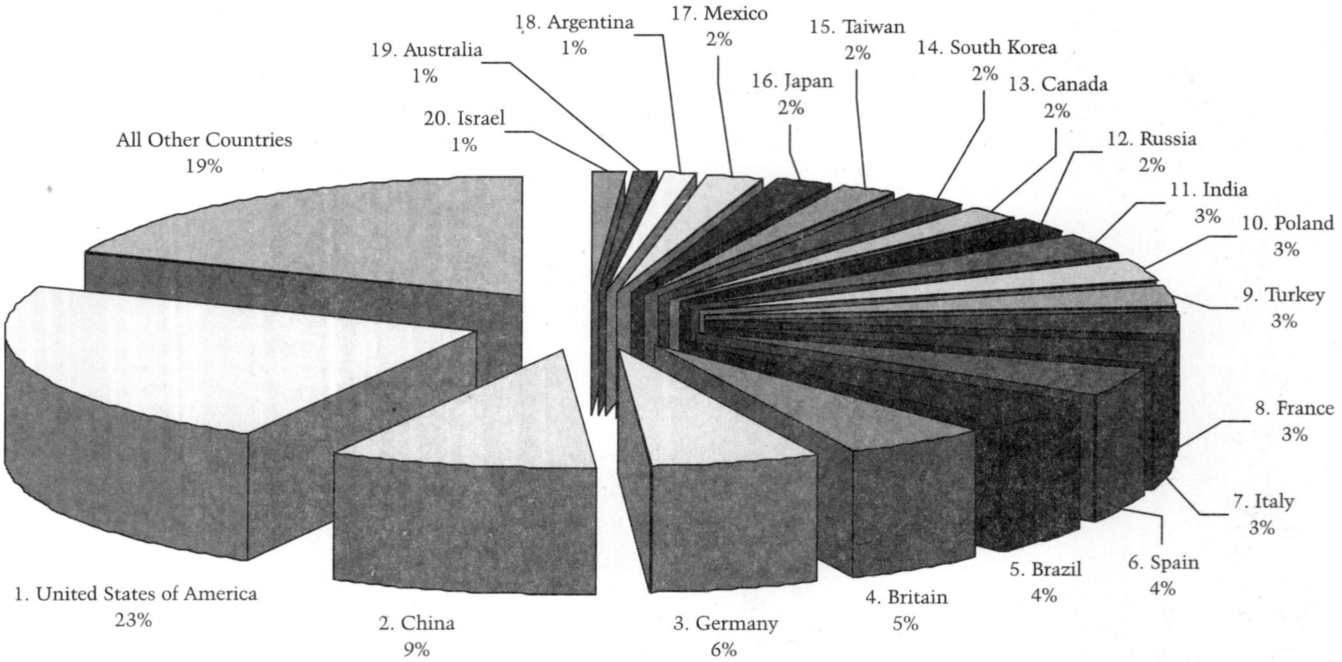

Source: BusinessWeek/Symantec.

Conclusion

IT risk management has become an area of increased focus over the last decade or so. Constant improvements in the information technologies make possible new IT applications that affect all areas of society, including the economy, households, government, and the research and development (R&D) enterprise. In the international ratings, India stood at 11th place in cyber crimes activities with 3 per cent. Continuous monitoring and updating our technology along with the other countries is needed at this movement.

Bibliography

Carroll, T., M. Webb and M. Griffith (2002). *The Risk Factor: How to make Risk Management Work for you in Strategic Planning and Enterprise*. Jaico Publishing House.

Cyber Security and Challenges Internal Report 2012.

Information Technology Management, Prof Bhel

IT Act 2001 Manual.

World Economic Survey 2010/2011/2012 Report.

Government of India Crime Report 2010.

21 M-Wallet: An Innovative Electronic Payment System

Savita S. Patil

Introduction

Electronic payment systems (Chen *et al.*, 1996) like credit and debit cards are an attractive alternative from the perspective of cost and convenience. However, the security of credit and debit cards depends upon the ability of the merchant to authenticate the card by comparing signatures and the ability and honesty of the merchant in protection of the sensitive information required for carrying out the transaction. The new trend in electronic payments is mobile payment schemes—those in which at least one part of the transaction is carried out using a mobile device.

The number of mobile phones in use far exceeds any other technical devices that could be used to market, sell, produce or deliver products and services to consumers.

Mobile commerce especially mobile banking is popular in countries where most of their population is unbanked. By 2012, it is estimated that there will be 1.7 billion people with a mobile phone but not a bank account (Consultative Group to Assist the Poor, n.d.). Mobile payment is being adopted all over the world in different ways. Combined market for all types of mobile payments is expected to reach more than $600 billion globally by 2013 (Wireless intelligence.com, 2008), which will be the double of the current figure (Wilcox, 2008a), while mobile payment market for goods and services excluding contact less near-field communication (NFC) transactions and money transfers is expected to exceed $300 billion globally by 2013 (Bonsoni.com, 2011). Some mobile payment solutions are also used in developing countries for micro payments (Wilcox, 2008b).

The current emerging mobile payment services are Google Wallet, Nokia's mobile money and the Interbank Mobile Payment Service (IMPS) with the latter two prevalent in India. Google Wallet works via NFC which means it requires an NFC-enabled phone in order to use the service. Nokia India Pvt. Ltd. has launched Mobile Money service in partnership with Union Bank of India and Yes Bank. But this service works only on handsets manufactured by Nokia. IMPS is a pilot service that allows transfer of money between bank accounts of registered users in the participating banks. But the transactions are carried out with simple personal identification number (PIN)-based security that can be easily defeated by replay attacks or mobile number spoofing (National Payments Corporation of India, 2011).

M-Wallet provides a mobile payment system that will be available on all mobile devices that support basic features like text messaging, yet be secure from spoofing of mobile numbers and replay attacks. M-Wallet transactions are totally based on text messages and provide mobile apps only for added convenience. A user-specified PIN allows only authorised access. Mobile number spoofing and replay attacks are eliminated as each transaction is protected with a unique one time key sent to the user's registered mobile number.

Headings

Entities

An M-Wallet mobile payment involves the participation of a consumer, merchant and the M-Wallet system. It also includes the provision of M-Wallet outlet for recharge transactions. In the payment scenario, the consumer intends to pay the merchant electronically through the M-Wallet system. In recharge transactions, the consumer wishes to add funds to his M-Wallet account by using the services of the M-Wallet outlet.

A consumer is a registered user of the M-Wallet system and intends to use it to pay for a service or product bought from a merchant. A merchant, depending on whether digital content or physical goods and services being purchased, is someone or some organisation that sells products to the consumer and is the intended recipient of the funds. The M-Wallet system is the entity responsible for the execution of the payment process.

It controls the flow of transaction between the mobile consumer and the merchant. The M-Wallet outlet is a point wherein a user can add funds to his/her virtual M-Wallet account by paying the required amount.

Registration

A user can register for this service by sending an SMS (short message service) to the M-Wallet system using his mobile number which is verified and this mobile number acts as a unique ID for the user. A unique PIN is generated and sent to the user which can be later changed by the user for additional security. The M-Wallet then creates a virtual account for the user with zero initial balance. According to the Reserve Bank of India (RBI) guidelines, an open prepaid payment instrument requires fulfillment of know your customer (KYC) norms. The account is fully activated only when the KYC documents are submitted at an M- Wallet outlet.

Transactions

The transactions that take place in the M-Wallet system are recharge, withdrawals, payments and recurring payments. A recharge transaction takes place when a user adds funds into his M-Wallet account through an outlet of the M-Wallet system or a bank using National Electronic Funds Transfer (NEFT). A user can withdraw funds from his M-Wallet account to his bank by sending a withdrawal request which is processed by the M-Wallet system through NEFT. Also withdrawal is available at M-Wallet outlets for users who cannot avail banking services. A payment transaction is consumer initiated. The payment process verifies the consumer and gathers details of the payment from the consumer and processes it accordingly. Recurring payments automate the process of payment transactions that have to be executed according to schedule.

Recharge

The virtual account needs to be recharged before it can be used for payments. The M-Wallet system supports two types of recharges. First one is recharge through participating outlets which can range from a pharmacy to a bakery. This is to facilitate consumers who do not have access to banking services. The outlet can recharge the accounts through their registered mobile devices by sending an SMS to the M-Wallet system containing the details of the recharge. The other mode is through a bank transfer which gives added convenience to those who have NEFT enabled bank accounts. The procedure is depicted in Figure 21.1.

Figure 21.1

Recharge using NEFT

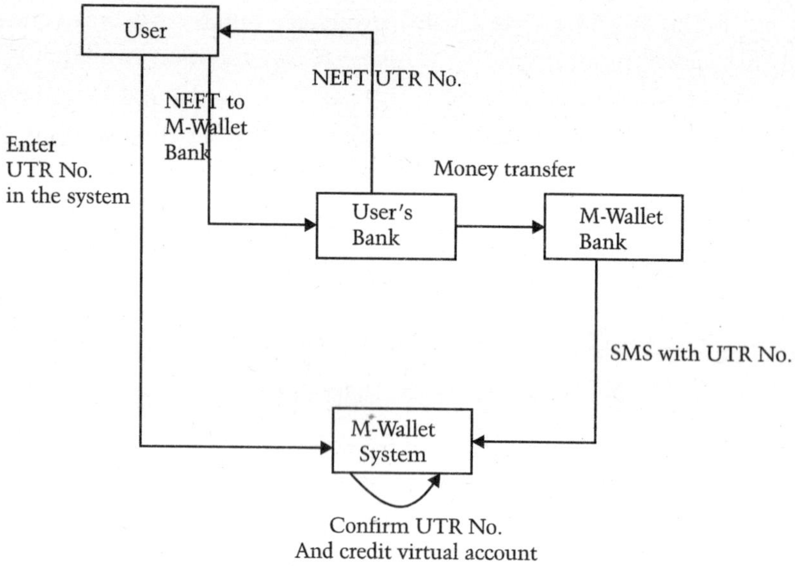

Payment

After the consumer has recharged his virtual account, he can use the funds in the account to make payment for various transactions. The payment process depicted in Figure 21.2 is initialised by sending an SMS to the M-Wallet system with the PIN for the authentication. The M-Wallet system generates a one-time random key for the next transaction with a timeout and sends it to the consumer. The consumer has to reply within the timeout with the key, payment details like the mobile number of the merchant, the amount to be paid to the merchant and an optional reference text that can be used by the merchant to identify the transaction. If successful, the consumer's M-Wallet account gets debited and merchant's M-Wallet account is credited with the specified amount and confirmations along with reference text is sent to both the consumer and the merchant.

The merchant is charged a percentage of the transaction amount as service fee which the merchant may pass on to the customer or bear it himself.

The merchant in payment transaction needs not be an M-Wallet user. A temporary M-Wallet account is created for the merchant if he is not an M-Wallet user and this account is maintained till the user registers for M-Wallet or decides to withdraw the funds in the temporary account. The account needs to be verified by using the mobile number as unique identity to withdraw the funds.

Figure 21.2

Payment Process

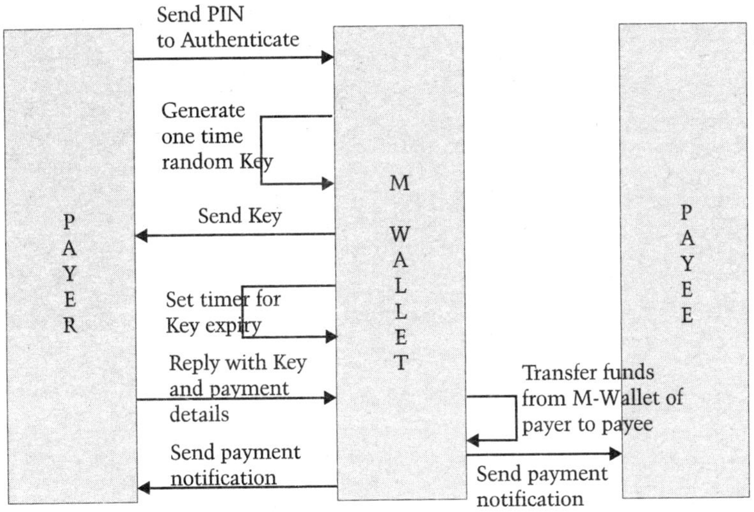

Redemption

The funds in the virtual account can be redeemed for money by direct bank transfer or redemption at an M-Wallet outlet. The user can request a bank withdrawal by sending an SMS to the system. The request will be processed and payment will be made to the bank account specified. The user can also use outlet redemption to redeem funds up to a certain maximum limit. A request needs to be made for outlet redemption in advance.

Miscellaneous Features

The M-Wallet system gives the user the facility of check his account balance by sending an SMS. Also the user can get details of all payments made and recurring payments scheduled over SMS. Flexibility in registration is provided to M-Wallet consumers wherein the consumer can update the existing M-Wallet account to the new subscriber identification module (SIM) number by registering the new number using the SIM of the old number and the PIN. If at any point an M-Wallet consumer believes that his account has been compromised, he can freeze his respective account via customer service or the M-Wallet web portal or sending an SMS.

Reserve Bank of India Rules and Regulations

M-Wallet falls into the category of Open System Prepaid Payment Instruments in the Reserve Bank of India's (RBI) draft for Draft Guidelines for issuance and operation of Prepaid Payment Instruments in India (RBI, 2009). These payment instruments can be used for purchase of goods and services and also permit cash withdrawal. According to the guidelines, a mobile prepaid system like M-Wallet can be implemented by any bank which has been permitted to provide Mobile Banking Transactions by the RBI. The guidelines on KYC/Anti-Money Laundering/Combating Financing of Terrorism guidelines issued by the Reserve Bank of India to banks, from time to time, also apply to prepaid payment instruments. Hence M-Wallet requires fulfillment of KYC norms. It also states that all prepaid payment instruments issuers shall disclose all important terms and conditions in clear and simple language. The outstanding balances of M-Wallet shall be part of the net demand and time liabilities of the bank for the purpose of maintenance of reserve requirements. This position will be computed on the basis of the balances appearing in the books of the bank as on the date of reporting.

Security

The popular standard used for mobile communication is Global System for Mobile communications (GSM; M-payment rides on the underlying infrastructure of GSM which is insecure as it does not have a provision for mutual authentication) which make a way for attacks like man-in-the-middle attack and replay attacks (Agarwal *et al.*, 2007). The default data format for SMS is plaintext. The only encryption involved during transmission is the encryption between the base transceiver station and the mobile station. End-to-end encryption is currently not available. The encryption algorithm used is A5 which is proven to be vulnerable. Therefore a more secure algorithm is needed. The SMS security mechanism relies on GSM/UMTS (Universal Mobile Telecommunications System) signaling plane security mechanism. SMS may be eavesdropped by the man-in-the-middle attack as no encryption is applied to SMS transmission.

The first step of a payment transaction in M-Wallet is authentication by sending a PIN by SMS. The PIN is sent in plaintext and also saved in user's sent items. This poses a security risk and hence the M-Wallet system provides an optional J2ME application that will encrypt the PIN before sending it to the M-Wallet system. The default java.util.Random has some weakness and hence cannot be used for generating encryption keys (Agarwal *et al.*, 2007). Hence java.security.SecureRandom is required for generating random keys. The IEEE paper on 'SSMS—A Secure SMS Messaging Protocol for the M-Payment Systems' (Toorani and Shirazi, 2008) provides an elliptic curve-based public key solution that uses public keys for the secret key establishment of a symmetric encryption. It also provides the attributes of public verification and forward secrecy. It efficiently makes the SMS messaging suitable for the m-payment applications where the security is of great concern. However J2ME may not be available on all devices and hence text SMS can also be used wherein the user is responsible for deleting his sent items. In this case, the GSM layer provides confidentiality.

The mobile number of the sender can also be spoofed if a direct connection to the short message service centre (SMSC) can be made. In order to eliminate this, the user is required to reply within a specified timeout period with a one-time random key. This one-time random key is sent to the user via SMS and hence will be received only by the authorised user on his mobile number.

Limitations

The M-Wallet system is vulnerable to SMS delays and loss. Loss of message will lead to a transaction failure while a delayed SMS may increase the time required for the transaction to complete. However, it is expected that this vulnerability will affect only a small number of transactions as studies indicate only 0.4 per cent of the SMS deliveries fail due to lack of resources (Meng *et al.*, 2007). Also the use of delivery reports will help track the delayed and lost messages.

Related Work

Safaricom, the leading mobile operator in Kenya, launched one of the most successful implementations of a mobile money transfer service, M-PESA. M-PESA is an SMS-based system that enables users to deposit, send and withdraw funds using their mobile phone. Safaricom accepts deposits of cash from customers with a Safaricom cell phone SIM card and who have registered as M-PESA users. Formally, in exchange for cash deposits, Safaricom issues a commodity known as 'e-float,' measured in the same units as money, which is held in an account under the user's name. This account is operated and managed by M-PESA, and records the quantity of e-float owned by a customer at a given time (International Finance Corporation, 2009).

The choice of bearer channel used to deliver mobile money transaction receipts in an important decision in the launch of the service since it impacts usability and security. Safaricom chose to use the SIM Toolkit (STK) with SMS delivery. With STK, the user has an application on the SIM card which is accessed from the phone's menu. This offers very high levels of security and usability. However, M-PESA is dependent on the Safaricom network and requires a SIM change as the M-PESA application is programmed using the STK.

Table 21.1

Comparison with Other E-payment Systems

Parameters	Credit and Debit Cards Online/Offline	Airtel Money/ Nokia Money	M-Wallet
Security	CVV and CCV	Relies on USSD which may be insecure	one-time random key
Convenience	Requires credit card terminal	Registration Required	No registration or device
Time	Less for offline and more for online	Fast since it uses USSD	Usually 15-20 seconds. Delays possible due to SMS
Verification process	Signature on the card	PIN	PIN and one-time key
Bank account	Required	Not Required/ Required	Not Required
Dependence on network provider/ bank/mobile manufacturer	Independent	Dependent	Independent
Ease of Use receiving or sending and	Easy/Not Easy	Easy	Easy, only SMS
Requirement	Card terminal/ merchant a/c, SSL	Registration	No requirement

Note: CVV: card verification value; CCV: card code verification; USSD: Unstructured Supplementary Service Date.

Conclusion

As the costs of mobile phone technology have fallen and as the technology has been adapted to support financial services, mobile banking innovations have begun to spread across and within poor countries. The low cost and the widespread unmet demand for financial services as captured by low rates of bank access mean that mobile banking has the potential to reach remote corners of the socioeconomic, as well as geographic spectrum.

This potential can be realised through M-Wallet, the SMS-based mobile payment system. M-Wallet is an innovation that clearly dominates its money-transfer predecessors on virtually all dimensions. It is faster, safer and network independent. It has been designed in adherence to all the guidelines laid down by the RBI.

In developing markets, M-Wallet will allow people to use financial services in a more efficient way and sometimes the only way—at more affordable costs, and can greatly improve standards of living. In developed markets, M-Wallet will be more of an extension of the existing payment infrastructure that allows people to deal with their financial needs in a timely and convenient way.

References

Agarwal, S., M. Khapra, B. Menezes and N. Uchat (2007). *Security Issues in Mobile Payment Systems.*

Bonsoni.com (2011). Research Shows Mobile Phone Payment Double by 2013.

Boran, S. (2003). *IT Security Cookbook*. Boran Consulting.

Consultative Group to Assist the Poor. Mobile Banking: *Overview* [Online]. Available at: *http://www.cgap.org/p/site/c/template.rc/1.11.14910/* [Accessed 06 February 12].

International Finance Corporation (2009, March). *M-Money Channel Distribution Case—Kenya.*

James F. Chen *et al.* (1996). "Electronic Payment System and Method". US Patent 5590197.

Meng, Xiaoqiao, Petros Zerfos, Vidyut Samanta, S.H.Y. Wong and S. Lu (2007). "Analysis of the Reliability of a Nationwide Short Message Service", *IEEE Infocom*, May.

National Payments Corporation of India (2011). *Interbank Mobile Payment Service*. [Online] Available at: *www.ncpi.org.in/impsVolumes.aspx*

Reserve Bank of India (2009). *Draft Guidelines for Issuance and Operation of Prepaid Payment Instruments in India.*

Toorani, M. and A.A.B. Shirazi (2008). "SSMS—A Secure SMS Messaging Protocol for the M-Payment Systems", Proceedings of the *13th IEEE Symposium on Computers and Communications* (ISC '08), pp.700-5.

Wilcox, Howard (2008a). *Press Release: Juniper Research Forecasts Total Mobile Payments to Grow Nearly Ten Fold* by 2013. Jupitor Research.

———. (2008b). *Press Release: Mobile Payment Transaction Values for Digital and Physical Goods to Exceed $300bn Globally Within 5 Years*. Juniper Research.

Wirelessintelligence.com (2008). Deployment Tracker\Mobile Money Live. [Online] Available at: *http://www.wirelessintelligence.com/mobile-money* [Accessed 06 February 12].

22 Hospitality Industry Credit Risk Evaluation Expert System

D.K. Sreekantha and R.V. Kulkarni

Introduction

Hotels today represent not only a home away from home for many people but is traveling office, a meeting place for learning and exchanging ideas, a place to enjoy, entertain and carrying out sporting activities and so forth. Many hotels have evolved into complex and multi-activity resorts within which traditional hospitality sits alongside a range of leisure and sport, conferences, conventions, gaming, retail and travel. Hotels have been classified into seven categories; these are five star deluxe, five star, four star, three star, two star and one star and heritage hotels.

India's recognition as an exciting place to visit is ever growing, the Reader's Travels Awards 2006, conducted by Conde Nast Traveller has recently placed India among the four must see countries in the world. Travel and tourism competitiveness report presented by the World Economic Forum has ranked India at the sixth place in tourism and hospitality industry. These factors boosted India's image as leisure travel destination. The Ministry of Tourism, Government of India (GoI), introduced a scheme called *Capital Investment Subsidy* in the year 2002, which was available during the tenth plan period till 2007, for setting up hotels in one, two, three stars category and heritage hotels with an objective to increase the supply of hotel rooms in the budget category in the country. The data collected show that 63 per cent units have availed loan from banks, followed by 29 per cent from state financial corporations and 8 per cent from development finance institutions (DFIs).

Credit risk is defined as the risk of debtors not repaying their financial obligations as agreed. A proactive management of these risks requires a serious and accurate calculation of probabilities of default, future exposures and recovers expectations. In today's turbulent economy, one of the major hazards faced by most financial and non-financial institutions is in the area of credit risk. Life insurance companies are among the largest financial institutions in the world. Life insurance companies have also played an important and varied role in hotel industry development by providing direct loans for development of hotel, catering and tourism (HCT) sector.

Present State of Hospitality Industry in India

India truly deserves to be a tourism haven, blessed with amazingly diverse natural bounty and tourism-related products catering to the tastes, preferences and budgets of tourists of varied backgrounds. International tourist arrivals to India have grown by 4.3 per cent between 1995 and 2008. Tourism and hospitality industry in India is the largest service industry providing 8.78 per cent of the total employment opportunities in India. World Travel and Tourism Council (WTTC) stated that India will definitely be one of the favourite tourist destinations from 2009 to 2018. At present, there are about 5.3 crore people employed in the hotel industry accounting for 9.24 per cent of total employment in the country. There were 6.29 million foreign tourist arrivals (FTAs) with foreign exchange earnings of US$ 11.394 billion last year. India has been ranked the "best country brand for value-for-money" in the Country Brand Index (CBI) survey conducted by Future Brand, a leading global brand consultancy.

India also claimed the second place in CBI's "Best country brand for history," as well as appears among the top five in the best country brand for authenticity and art and culture, and the fourth best new country for business. India made it to the list of 'rising stars' or the countries that are likely to become major tourist destinations in the next five years, led by the United Arab Emirates, China and Vietnam (*www.ibef.org/industry/tourismhospitality.aspx*). In India, medical tourism is a sunrise sector valued at more than US$ 310 million. Currently, India receives more than 100,000 foreign patients a year. The number of medical tourists is anticipated to grow at a compound annual growth rate (CAGR) of over 19 per cent during the forecast period to reach 1.3 million by 2013. India accounted for only about 0.6 per cent of the global tourist arrivals indicating a huge area of untapped opportunities in travel industry. Growth opportunities in travel and tourism cannot be realised without the development of the hospitality sector. UK, US and German tourists account for 55 per cent to 60 per cent of the business in most of the premium hotels in India. FTAs as well as domestic travel in 2010 suggest that the number of travelers have almost doubled since 2005.

Present State of Hospitality Industry across the World

The International Hotel & Restaurant Association (IH&RA) is the biggest association of the world with 2,00,000 hotels and 60,00,000 restaurants as its members. The Federation of Hotel & Restaurant Associations of India (FHRAI) has pointed out that by 2022, every 1 person out of 10 on this planet will be working for the travel and tourism industry. IH&RA forecasted that foreign exchange earnings will be ₹ 134,665 crores in 2016. The tourism and hospitality industry's direct contribution to the gross domestic product (GDP) in 2011 was estimated at US$ 32.7 billion. It has registered a CAGR of 13 per cent during 2006-2011. The total contribution increased to US$ 76.7 billion in 2011 from US$ 56.3 billion in 2009. The total contribution comprises direct, indirect and induced contribution to the GDP. Tourism is the first, second or third largest employer in 32 states. Hospitality is the world's fastest growing industry and will add one new job every 2.5 seconds.

China is one of the fastest growing outbound travel markets, benefiting from higher incomes, relaxed limitations on foreign travel, improved internal infrastructure and other investments. China's outbound travel grew annually by 22 per cent between the years 2000 and 2006 to 34.5 million in 2006. China's outbound travelers were 54 million in 2010, a 15 per cent increase from the 47 million in 2009. Islamic banks seem to be more comfortable in getting involved in hotel financing in countries such as Saudi Arabia where alcohol is not available which has proven to be a feasible and an attractive option for the banks.

Table 22.1 and Figure 22.1 show the international tourist arrivals from various regions like Europe, Asia, etc., in the years 1980-2009.

Table 22.1

International Tourist Arrivals by Region

Region	*2008 (in Millions)*	*2009 (in Millions)*	*Percentage of Share*
Europe	487.1	459.7	52.2
Asia and the Pacific	184.1	180.5	20.5
America	147.1	139.6	15.9
Africa	45.7	48.0	5.4
Middle East	55.6	52.5	6.0
Total World	920.0	880.0	100.0

Source: *2009 Arrivals*, United Nations World Tourism Organizations and World Tourism Barometer, January 2010.

Figure 22.1

Tourism Industry Facts and Figures

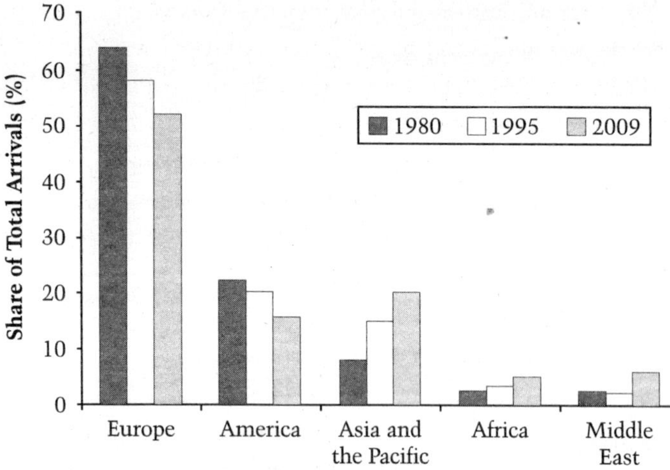

Source: *2009 Arrivals*, United Nations World Tourism Organizations and World Tourism Barometer, January 2010.

Investment Proposals in Hospitality Industry

The Indian hospitality industry is projected to grow at a rate of 8.8 per cent during 2007-2016 placing India as the second fastest growing tourism market in the world. Some of the major investments in this sector are from online travel firms; Yatra has acquired Travelguru from US-based Travelocity Global. It is proposed to invest ₹ 10 crore (US$ 1.8 million) in Travelguru for building up its brand and consumer presence according to Dhruv Shringi, co-founder and chief executive officer of Yatra.com. Berggruen Hotels, a mid-market business hotel chain funded by US-based Berggruen Holdings, plan to invest Rs 450 crore (US$ 80.56 million) in new projects across India. The company operates under the brand key hotels and aims to add 2,300 rooms over the next 18-24 months. Dutch pension fund (PF) manager of APG Group plans to invest ₹ 650 crore (US$ 116.36 million) to buy 6 per cent stake in Delhi-based mid-market hotel group, Lemon Tree Hotels. This group would form a joint venture with Lemon Tree to build 35 hotels in the country in four years. UK-based Eaton Smart Hotel has started its operations at Terminal 3 (T3) of the Delhi International Airport, making it the first transit hotel in India. Eaton, the 93-room property, is being managed by the Langham Hospitality group. India presently has an estimated 114,000 hotel rooms spread across various hotel categories. There is around 150,000 rooms short from what is required. While the opportunities are immense, there are also challenges associated with it.

Hotel, Catering and Tourism Industry Challenges

Universally hotel industry is sensitive to economic cycles and does face ups and downs based on the supply and demand for rooms at any point of time. The issues specific to India are poor infrastructure, high cost of land procurement, multiple licenses and levies which challenge the development. The commercial banks have historically played the most significant role in providing financing to the hotel industry. The bank provides 58 per cent of loans to hotel industry alone.

Credit Risk Concept

ISO (International Organization of Standardization) 31000 defines the risk as the effect of uncertainty on objectives, whether positive or negative. The first written document mentioning credit risk was issued in 1790 BC law code, as it was titled, is the first written law in recorded human history that stated that a failure to pay a debt is a crime (King, 2005).

Credit risk is the risk that one party bounded by a financial contract is unable or unwilling to fulfill his obligations in due time, causing a financial loss for the other part. Credit risk is inherent to banking activity. The rating agency Standards and Poor's defines a debtor as a defaulter who fails to fulfill his contractual obligations and to pay in due time, and a default as a failure to make required debt payments by or at the stipulated time.

Basel III an international regulatory framework was published on 16th December, 2010, which encompasses a set of reform measures agreed upon by the Basel committee on banking supervision. Those reforms aim at strengthening: (i) the regulation, to avoid or at least reduce systemic risks, (ii) the supervision of the banking sector by requiring more transparency and disclosures and (iii) the risk management and governance of the banking sector. The three major components of credit risk are the probability of default, the exposure at default and the loss given default. Credit risk can be expressed as a function of these parameters: credit risk = f(PD, EAD, LGD) where PD: probability of default, EAD: exposure at default and LGD: loss given default. The credit value at risk (VaR) is another key element of credit risk.

Survey of Literature

The author's present work comprises an exhaustive survey of relevant literature about hospitality industry from various sources. Some selected recent papers from this survey are discussed by way of illustration.

The GoI has launched the National Tourism Action Plan in 1992 and announced many subsidy schemes to promote this industry. Incredible India tourism promotion programme was launched by the Ministry of Tourism. Finance Corporation of India limited, New Delhi, has carried out an evaluation of the scheme incentives to accommode infrastructure in India.

The objective of the study is to assess and review the impact of capital subsidy scheme of the Ministry of Tourism. The Ministry of Tourism estimates that by the end of 2012, the foreign exchange earnings will cross US$ 12 billion.

Magan *et al.* (2001-02) has discussed about tax-exempt bonds, which are generally the least expensive form of hotel project financing and often require less equity to be contributed to a project than traditional sources of financing. Investors in tax-exempt bonds will accept a lower rate of interest because the interest received is exempt from federal income tax.

Hotels have traditionally been owned by private entities, and in general, private entities cannot get the benefit of tax-exempt financing. Tax-exempt bonds issued to finance hotel projects are typically structured on a non-recourse basis.

Tax-exempt bonds have limited obligations payable only from hotel revenues and any other specifically pledged revenues and assets. The proceeds of tax-exempt bonds may be used to finance the cost of land acquisition, design, demolition, site work, buildings, furniture, fixtures and equipment and/or related infrastructure for hotel projects, which may include the hotel rooms and guest registration area, convention and conference room space, restaurants, cocktail lounges, health spas, gift shops, parking and other facilities. The principal limitation on the types of hotel project assets that can be financed on a tax-exempt basis is that they must be owned by a local agency or non-profit corporation that is an eligible hotel owner.

Peric *et al.*'s (2010) papers outlines the role of International Financial Institutions (IFIs) in financing projects of tourism and hospitality industry in developing countries. Authors have conducted a study about how much has been invested in these countries, type of investments, effects of these investments on local economy and the results of these investments. The paper opens with background on the tourism sector in developing countries and its role in the economy. The demand for tourism services has increased among World Bank Group member countries and the World Bank technical assistance focused on attracting foreign direct investment (FDI) in the tourism sector. A survey shows that international visitors spend close to $900 billion on goods and services annually, with tourism-related inflows often the primary source of foreign exchange in many developing countries. Tourists spend more than $200 billion annually in emerging market nations. The International Finance Corporation (IFC) has invested over $2 billion in 220 hotel projects in more than 80 countries. Hotels play an important role in the development of many IFC client countries, as they catalyse tourism and business infrastructure. Hotels bring great potential for job creation, growth in tax revenues, improvements in foreign exchange earnings and opportunities for related smaller businesses.

Agarwal (2009) presented the necessary steps required to construct a world class hotels and resorts. The author discussed the advantages of

Udaipur or Jaipur of Rajasthan for establishing a world class hotels and resorts. The author projects Rajasthan as the safest state in India in terms of law and order and highlighted the advantages of investing in Rajasthan tourism sector.

Cristina Badenes (2006) discussed the condo hotels prospects and risks. The author finds that the market for condo hotels is booming, prospects are very positive and this sector has the support of industry experts. Mr. Starwood has taken very conservative approach for this type of hotels sector. A condo hotel is a property with different units that are centrally managed by an operator or one brand.

The condo hotel has the look of a hotel and rooms are similar to traditional hotel. Condo hotels are having a contract between unit owner and management company. The operator has to support for low cash investment with fully owning a hotel. Hoteliers who want to protect their brand should bring in the discipline to the process. Investors have to take the advantage of the hot market demand but with caution.

Raghavan (2005) has authored a paper on credit as well as credit risk management in banks. Credit portfolio is the real dynamic activity that requires close monitoring and constant management. The role of banks has changed from financial intermediately to risk intermediatory. An integrated and proactive approach is required for managing the credit risk. It is very much essential to conduct credit investigation before taking up a proposal for consideration. The preliminary study should lead to valuable information on borrower's integrity, honesty, reliability, credit worthiness, management competency, expertise, associate concern, guarantor, etc. A due diligence report shall invariably accompany the credit proposal evaluation. Banks have to strictly adhere to the KYC (know your customer) norms to ensure bonafide identification of borrows and should also follow the prescribed Fair Practice Code on lenders liability, by evolving their own best practices to be followed by the field functionaries, so as to avoid any complaints from customer at a later date. At present, due to lack of credit appraisal skill at the field level, manned by many generalist officials spread across the branch network, there is greater duplication of work at the sanctioning level at head office (HO) causing enormous and avoidable delay as papers pass through more than a dozen senior officials before they are placed before sanctioning authority. The author advised that banks should move from credit rating to credit risk rating and detailed discussion on cash flow generation should made a compulsory part of project proposal. Credit decision will not get better by how many people review it, but who review it are knowledgeable and how much experience they carry with them in credit portfolio.

Credit Risk Assessment Revisited: Methodological Issues and Practical Implications by Working Group on Risk Assessment (2007) discusses implementation methods and provide solutions to practical problems in credit risk measurement. In most of the papers, empirical examples are carried out from the special perspective of a central bank as most of the participants stem from such institutions. Two interesting papers provide empirical evidence on credit scoring and default prediction in central banks. The second paper on credit scoring was contributed by Ms Lauria Auria and Mr Moro. The authors discussed the advantages and disadvantages of support vector machines (SVMs) as a new promising non-linear, non-parametric classification technique, which can be used for credit scoring.

This paper proposes a simple mechanism for comparison of the performance of major rating agencies and other credit assessment systems. The aim is to provide a simple validation yardstick to help monitoring the performance of different credit assessment systems, more specifically those participating in the assessment of eligible collateral for Euro system's monetary policy operations.

Delamaire (2012) proposed implementation of credit risk management system based on innovative scoring techniques. Her thesis presents a credit scoring system which aims at setting credit lines and thus, controlling credit risk. It includes three types of models: application scorecards, early detection scorecards and behavioural scorecards. They have been built on real and recent data coming from a German credit card company. The models have been built with a training sample and validated accordingly, using logistic regression. Information value and validation charts have been used for comparing the models. In the scoring process described, the scorecards are used in a sequential order. The author shows that minimising losses might not be optimal in order to maximise profit. Finally, the author presents possible extensions to the research and hopes that the technique described in this thesis can play some part in preventing future financial crisis.

Lahsasna *et al.* (2010) have discussed credit scoring models using soft computing methods like neural networks, genetic algorithms and support vector machines. The authors claim that their methods are the most accurate methods as compared to other methods. The classification accuracy is the key determinant of the success in financial lending industry. Author's study has shown the benefits of using hybrid methods to overcome some limitations of single methods by using fuzzy system, artificial methods like neural networks and genetic algorithms. Hybridisation of fuzzy logic, neural networks and genetic algorithms has led to creation of a perspective scientific trend known as soft computing. Neural networks mimic the ability to adapt to circumstances and learn from past experiences. Fuzzy logic addresses the imprecision or vagueness in input and output. Genetic algorithms are inspired by biological evolution, can systemise random search and reach to optimum characteristics.

Sreekantha and Kulkarni (2010a) have discussed the expert system design model for credit risk evaluation using neuro fuzzy logic. They have used expert system builder (ESB) tool to demonstrate the workability of their expert system model. They have also authored an article The Survey of Credit Risk Assessment Techniques (Sreekantha and Kulkarni, 2010b). Sreekantha and Kulkarni (2008) have designed a credit rating framework for manufacturing sector of SSI (small-scale industries) by organising the five risk areas: technical feasibility, management commitment, commercial variability, financial analysis and economic analysis.

The authors have used fuzzy logic to capture the domain expert knowledge and assigned the standard weights to each of these risk parameters. The client's score is evaluated against these standard scores. This client score is used in determining the client risk rating, which ranges from AAA—Highest Safety to D—Default. The authors have described the process of computing the credit worthiness with a typical client example.

Problem Description and Analysis

Hotels are generally considered to be the most risky type of commercial property, clearly different from other sectors in that they provide services to short-term guests with revenues coming largely from room rents as well as such extras as restaurants and meeting rooms, especially at luxury hotels. Small increases in occupancy rates or room prices go a long way towards improving profitability because of considerable fixed costs. Yet unlike other income producing properties, hotels do have increased expenses as occupancy increases; therefore, maximising occupancy does not always equal maximising long-term profits.

The performance of hotels depends largely on the active management of operations; the rating agencies place particular emphasis on the quality of property management teams. Well-managed properties with competitive positions in their regions present attractive collateral for commercial mortgages.

Hospitality industry is indeed most vulnerable business which can be easily affected by internal as well as external factors. Risks from internal factors are management for business expansion, operations under hotel management contract, investment projects, hotel renovation projects and finance risk. The risks from external factors are competition, political situations, wars, epidemics, natural disasters, interest rate fluctuations and exchange rate fluctuations. Obtaining a hotel loan requires a profitable operating and occupancy history of the subject property. Getting a hotel loan for a new property is possible provided it has a well-known flag, is well located, and has strong management and sponsorship. A flagged hotel means that it is one of the major international hospitability brands such as Best Western, Hilton, Super8, etc.

The client who wants to set up a hotel should follow the following steps

1. Get experience in the hotel industry.
2. Check out hospitality programmes.
3. Conduct market research.
4. Choose your location for rent or purchase a building.
5. Apply for the required permits and partner with a hotel supply company.

The critical success factors for hotel industry are:

1. Project cost.
2. Visibility from national highway, airport, railway station and bus stations.
3. Customer focus.
4. Brand or corporate image.
5. Plan a grand opening.

Project Cost

Project cost for a hotel mainly depends upon three variables land cost, construction cost, and furniture and fittings. Out of these three, construction cost and furniture and fittings are generally comparable for a particular star category, but the main difference is observed in land cost. The land cost is around 30 per cent of the total project cost in case of mini-metros, as much as or even more than 50 per cent in case of metros. The cost per room varies among different star categories and also from project to project due to services and facilities like central air-conditioning, banquet hall, conference hall, business centre, restaurants and bar, cafeteria, recreation room, swimming pool and shopping mall provided within the hotels. These facilities mainly depend upon the location of the hotel, star category and the type of travelers visiting the hotel. The capacity of the borrower or the sufficiency of income from the property to service the debt depends on overall creditworthiness of the borrower; amount of equity invested by the borrower; and any forms of credit enhancement, including guaranties, mortgages, insurance and additional collateral. The four highest ratings categories—Triple A, Double A, Single A, and Triple B—represent what is referred to as 'investment grade' commercial, mortgage-backed securities (CMBS).

Credit Rating Framework (CRF) Design Process

A CRF is designed to measure all the objective and subjective parameters of credit decision environment. The CRF organises all the facts of the client in five levels depending on their nature and criticality.

Figure 22.2 shows the steps involved in the design of the credit rating.

Figure 22.2

Credit Rating Framework (CRF) Design Process

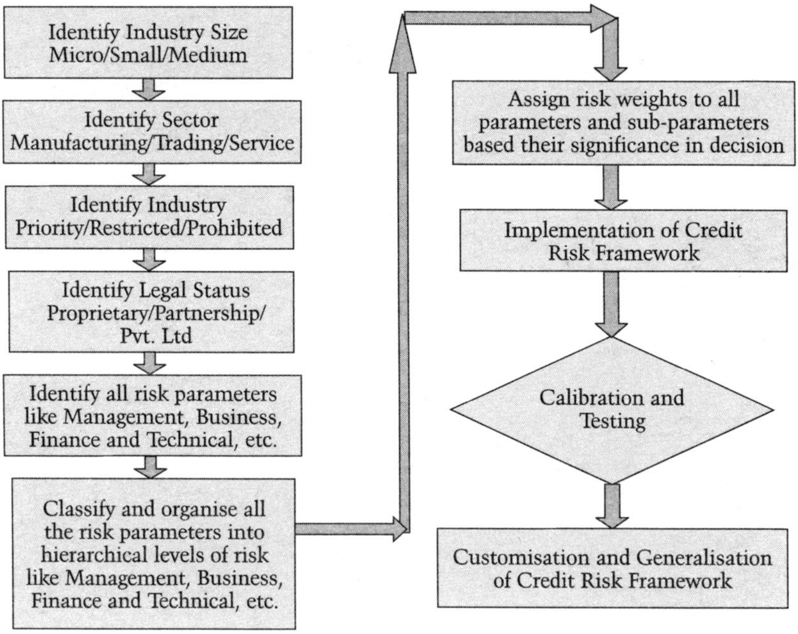

Table 22.2

Credit Rating Framework for Hotel Industry

Risk Code	*Risk Sub Code*	*Risk Parameter*	*Max Risk Score*	*Min Risk Score*	*Highest Safety 90%*	*High Safety 80%*	*Significant Safety 70%*	*Low Risk 60%*	*High Risk 50%*	*Highest Risk 40%*
1	Management Risk		100	40	90	80	70	60	50	40
	1.1	Integrity and Leadership	20	8	18	16	14	12	10	8
	1.2	Financial Resources	20	8	18	16	14	12	10	8
	1.3	Pursue long-term vision	10	4	9	8	7	6	5	4
	1.4	People risks/Key Personals	20	8	18	16	14	12	10	8
	1.5	Corporate Reputation Brand image	20	8	18	16	14	12	10	8
2	Property Risk		100	40	90	80	70	60	50	40
	2.1	Location and Visibility	20	8	18	16	14	12	10	8
	2.3	Property Condition and Characteristics	15	6	14	12	11	9	8	6
	2.4	Construction cost per room	15	6	14	12	11	9	8	6
	2.5	Access to Road, Rail, Air Port	20	8	18	16	14	12	10	8
	2.6	Parking Availability	10	4	9	8	7	6	5	4
	2.7	Catchment Area	20	8	18	16	14	12	10	8
3	Operational Risk		75	30	68	60	53	45	38	30
	3.1	Focus on Customer retention	15	6	14	12	11	9	8	6
	3.2	Offer superior services benefits	15	6	14	12	11	9	8	6
	3.3	Emphasise Exemplary customer service	10	4	9	8	7	6	5	4
	3.4	Food Safety	15	6	14	12	11	9	8	6
	3.5	Kitchen Safety	10	4	9	8	7	6	5	4
	3.6	IT and Communication	10	4	9	8	7	6	5	4
4	Financial Risk		125	50	113	100	88	75	63	50
	4.1	Project cost	30	12	27	24	21	18	15	12
	4,2	Means of Finance	20	8	18	16	14	12	10	8
	4.3	Projected Profitability	20	8	18	16	14	12	10	8
	4.4	Cash flow from Project	20	8	18	16	14	12	10	8
	4.5	Projected Financials	15	6	14	12	11	9	8	6
5	Market Risk		100	40	90	80	70	60	50	40
	5.1	Customer Behaviour	15	6	14	12	11	9	8	6
	5.2	Competition	20	8	18	16	14	12	10	8
	5.3	Demand/Industry Forecast	15	6	14	12	11	9	8	6
	5.4	Marketing Policy	10	4	9	8	7	6	5	4
	5.5	Cost/Pricing	15	6	14	12	11	9	8	6
		Total	500	200	450	400	350	300	250	200

Rulebase Design

A separate fuzzy rulebase has been developed for every major risk such as Management risk, Property risk, Finance risk, etc., in the credit rating framework to facilitate change of rules easily

Rule No. 1: Excellent Credit Proposal

IF (Property Risk Rating is Highest Safety) AND

(Management Risk Rating is Highest Safety) AND

(Operational Risk Rating is Highest Safety) AND

(Financial Risk Rating is Highest Safety) AND

(Market Risk Rating is Highest Safety)

THEN

Hotel Credit Proposal is Excellent, Risk Rating is Highest Safety

The Client Credit rating is AAA

Rule No. 2: Management Risk

IF (Integrity and Leadership Rating is Highest Safety) AND

(Financial Resources Rating is Highest Safety) AND

(Pursue long-term vision Rating is Highest Safety) AND

(People risks/Key Personnels Rating is Highest Safety) AND

(Corporate reputation/Brand image is Highest Safety)

THEN

Hotel Management Risk is negligible, Risk Rating is Highest Safety

The Client Credit rating is AAA

Rule No. 3: Property Risk

IF (Location and Visibility Rating is Highest Safety) AND

(Property Condition and Characteristics Rating is Highest Safety) AND

(Construction cost per room Rating is Highest Safety) AND

(Access to Road Rail Rating is Highest Safety) AND

(Parking Availability Rating is Highest Safety) AND

(Catchment Area Rating is Highest Safety)

THEN

Property Risk is Highest Safety

The Property Risk rating is AAA

Rule No. 4: Operational Risk

IF (Focus on customer retention Rating is Highest Safety) AND

(Offer superior products services benefits Rating is Highest Safety) AND

(Emphasise exemplary customer service Rating is Highest Safety) AND

(Food Safety Rating is Highest Safety) AND

(Kitchen Safety Rating is Highest Safety) AND

(IT and Communications Rating is Highest Safety)

THEN

Operational Risk is Highest Safety

The Operational Risk rating is AAA

Rule No. 5: Finance Risk

IF (Project cost Rating is Highest Safety) AND

(Means of Finance Rating is Highest Safety) AND

(Projected Profitability Rating is Highest Safety) AND

(Cash flow from Project Rating is Highest Safety) AND

(Projected Financial Position Rating is Highest Safety)

THEN

Finance Risk is Highest Safety

Finance Risk Rating is AAA

Rule No. 6: Market Risk

IF (Customer Behaviour Rating is Highest Safety) AND

(Competition Rating is Highest Safety) AND

(Demand/Industry Forecast Rating is Highest Safety) AND

(Marketing Policy Rating is Highest Safety) AND

(Cost/Price Structures Rating is Highest Safety)

THEN

Market Risk is Highest Safety

Market Risk Rating is AAA

Implementation

The authors have designed a web-based expert system software entittled Credit Risk Evaluation Expert System (CREES) using Java, Dream viewer and MySql server as backend. This software provides forms to enter all the credit data related to client business. The client data to be captured are designed by studying the business/industrial loan application forms from various banks and financial institutions.

Standard Credit Ratings

The clients are classified into various categories based on their credit worthiness. The client credit ratings are shown in Table 22.3. The most credit worthy client is rated as AAA and risk level is Highest Safety. The most risky client is rated as C. The client who is not creditworthy is classified as default.

Table 22.3

Standard Credit Ratings

Credit Rate	*Risk Level*	*Weight*	*Weight in %*
AAA	Highest Safety	WAAA	>=95<100
AA	High Safety	WAA	>=85< 95
A	Significant Safety	WA	>=80< 85
BB	Low Risk	WBBB	>=70< 79
B	High Risk	WBB	>=60< 70
C	Highest Risk	WB	>=50< 60
D	Default	WC	>=40< 50

Results Discussion

The authors have tested the expert system software using selected 500 real-time samples with different credit ratings from banks and results are tabulated as shown in Table 22.5. The results obtained from this CREES and the manual decisions are agreeing in many of the cases. The percentage of clients misjudged by the CREES is only (22/500)*100 = 4.4 per cent.

The following report is generated by CREES for a typical client:

Credit Risk Evaluation using Expert System

Hospitality Industry Client Credit Risk Assessment

Client Id : C000000001

Application Id : A000000001

Property risk percentage score is : 90/100 =90.0%, Percentage score is: 462/500 =92.4%

Property risk rating is highest safety, client credit risk rating is highest safety.

Table 22.4

Sample Client Score for Property Risk

Risk Parameter	*Score*
Management Risk Score	92
Property Risk Score	89
Operational Risk Score	72
Financial Risk Score	119
Market Risk Score	90
Total Score	462

Table 22.5

Sample Client Total Scores

Property Risk Parameter	*Score*
Location and Visibility Rating	18
Property Condition and Characteristics Rating	13
Construction Cost Per Room Rating	14
Access to Road Rail Rating	19
Parking Availability Rating	08
Catchment Area Rating	18
Total Score	90

Note: Client Name : ABC Paradise Hotels.

Table 22.6

Comparison of Results

Sl. No	*Client Risk Level*	*Manual Decisions*	*CREES Decisions*	*Relative Error %*	*No. of Clients Mis-classified*
1	Highest Safety	78	84	7.1	6
2	High Safety	70	74	5.4	4
3	Significant Safety	90	87	-3.4	3
4	Low Risk	91	94	3.1	3
5	High Risk	85	83	-2.4	2
	Highest Risk	86	82	-4.8	4
	Total	500	500	5	22

Figure 22.3

Comparison of Results

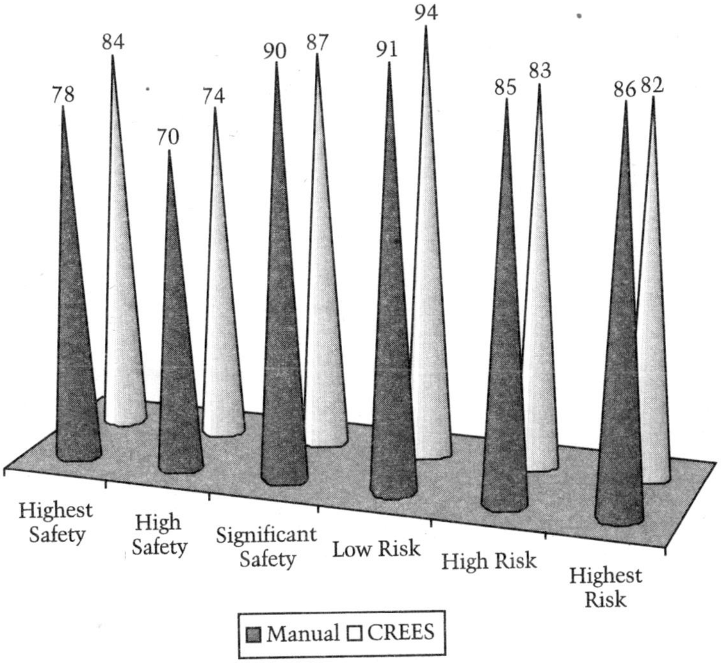

Extensions and Future Work

The authors are working on implementing the expert system model using Fuzzy Java Expert System Shell (FUZZYJESS) tool and encoding the rule base in FUZZYJESS. The CRF and the proposed expert system model are to be tested with two public credit data sets such as German Credit Data Set and Australian Credit Data Set, so that the method can be standardised internationally. The authors' main endeavour has been to achieve such a state. Building and maintaining the data warehouse of the industry-wise, business-wise knowledge base of CRFs demands lot of memory. Data mining techniques are needed to explore the hidden knowledge patterns in the data sets. The authors propose to develop a software using JOONE—Java Object Oriented Neural Networks—for upgrading the expert system solution to train the system.

References

Agarwal, Sneha (2009). "Project on Hotel and Resorts in the State of Rajasthan: A Case Study".

Badenes, Cristina (2006). "CONDO Hotels Great Prospects but Beware of Risks", Meridia Capital Issue 1. *cbadenes@meridiacapital.com*, December 2006.

Delamaire, Linda (2012). Implementing a Credit Risk Management System based on Innovative Scoring Techniques. Phd thesis. Department of Economics, University of Birmingham February 2012.

King, L.W. (2005). "The Code of Hammurabi". Available at: *http://www.yale.edu/lawweb/avalon/ medieval/hamframe.htm*

Lahsasna, Adel, Raja Noor Ainon and Teh Ying Wah (2010). "Credit Scoring Models Using Soft Computing Methods", *The International Arab Journal of Information Technology* 7(2): 115-23.

Magan, Jenna, Roger L. Davis, Parry E. Israel and Michael Liever (2001-2002). *Hotel Projects Financing with Tax Exempt Bonds*. San Francisco, CA: Orrick Herrington & Sutcliffe LLP Jože Peric.

Peric, Joze, Elvis Mujacevic and Mislav Simunic (2010). "International Financial Institution Investments in Tourism and Hospitality", *Journal of International Business and Cultural Studies* 4.

Raghavan, R.S. (2005). "Credit as well as Credit Risk Management in Banks", *The Chartered Accountant*: 996-1002.

Sreekantha, D.K. and R.V. Kulkarni (2008). "Industrial Loan Processing Using Neuro Fuzzy Logic", *International Journal of Intelligent Information Processing* 305-18.

Sreekantha, D.K. and R.V. Kulkarni (2010a). "Expert System Design for Credit Risk Evaluation Using Neuro-Fuzzy Logic", *Expert Systems* 29: 56-69.

———. (2010b). "The Survey of Credit Risk Assessment Techniques", *International Journal of Technology and Applied Sciences* 2(1).

Working Group on Risk Assessment (2007). *Credit Risk Assessment Revisited Methodological Issues and Practical Implications*. European Committee of Central Balance Sheet Data Offices.

23 An Overview of Project Risk Management

Vanarase Shilpa Satish

Introduction

Risk Concepts

Risk is a combination of the probability of a negative event and its consequences. If an event is inevitable but inconsequential, it does not represent a risk because it has no impact. Alternatively, an improbable event with significant consequences may not be a high risk. These two factors are combined in what we experience as the possibility of loss, failure, danger or peril:

Project Risk= Σ (Events*Probabilities*Consequences).

An easy way to reduce risk is to have less ambitious goals. After evaluating risks, one can choose a path of risk avoidance or risk mitigation and management. If we understand the risks on a project, we can decide which risks are acceptable and take actions to mitigate or forestall those risks. If our project risk assessment determines risks are excessive, we may want to consider restructuring the project within acceptable levels of risk.

Risks that do not offer the potential for gain/profit should be avoided. Risks associated with achieving challenging and worthwhile goals should be managed. One way to reduce risk is to gather information about relevant issues to lower the level of uncertainty. Then we can look for ways to reduce probabilities of failures or to reduce their consequences.

What may look like an unacceptable risk to one person might rightly appear as an attractive opportunity to another. The difference is vision.

Understanding Risk

To understand the risk better, it is important to classify risks. Broadly, there can be five types of risks that a project confronts.

1. *Governance Risk*: The governance risk arises out of the board and management performance with reference to ethics, leadership, reputation of the organisation, etc.
2. *Strategic Risk*: This risk arises out of an error in strategy adopted by organisation. For example, selection of technology that is not suitable to the organisation or choosing a strategy that can change the course of business drastically.
3. *Operational Risk*: This is a risk of having poor operational systems, poor implementation and process problems related to production and distribution.
4. *Market Risk*: The risk arising out of competition, fluctuations in foreign exchange rates, raw material suppliers, interest rates, credit and liquidity aspects, etc.
5. *Legal Risk*: This risk is a result of legal and regulatory obligations like contract risks and litigation suits filed against organisation.

Figure 23.1

Continuous Risk Management Principle Functions

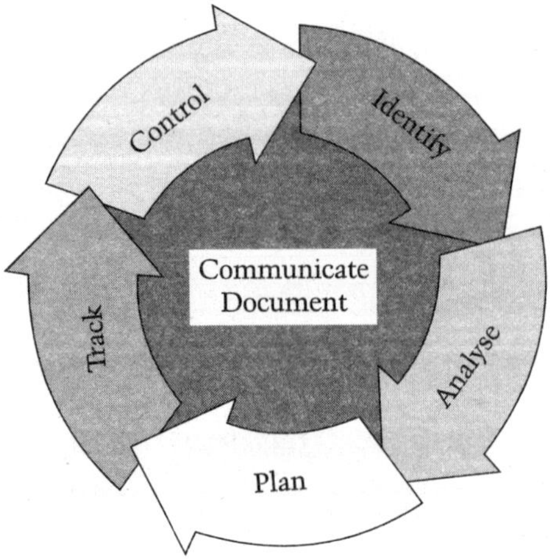

Functions of Continuous Risk Management

1. *Identify*: The purpose of identification is to consider risks before they become problems and to incorporate this information into the project management process. Anyone in a project can identify risks to the project. Each individual has particular knowledge about various parts of a project.

2. *Analyse*: The purpose of analysing is to convert the data into decision-making information. Analysis is a process of examining the risks in detail to determine the extent of the risks, how they relate to each other and which ones are the most important. Analysing risks has tree basic activities: evaluating the attributes of the risks (impact, probability and timeframe), classifying the risks and prioritising or ranking the risks.

3. *Plan*: Planning is the function of deciding what, if anything should be done about a risk or set of related risks. In this function, decisions and mitigation strategies are developed based on current knowledge of project risks.

4. *Track*: Tracking is the process by which risk status data are acquired, compiled and reported.

   The purpose of Track is to collect accurate, timely and relevant risk information and to present it in a clear and easily understood manner to the appropriate people/group.

5. *Control*: The purpose of the Control function is to make informed, timely and effective decisions regarding risks and their mitigation plans. It is the process that takes in tracking status information and decides exactly what to do based on the reported data. Controlling risks involves analysing the status reports, deciding how to proceed and then implementing those decisions.

6. *Communication and Documentation*: Communication and Documentation are essential to the success of all other functions within the paradigm and is critical for managing risk.

Project Risk Management Process

Project risk management (PRM) processes adopted by different project managers differ to some extent, the underlying concept or process remains the same. Basically it consists of five steps:

Step 1: Identify the risks in a project.

Step 2: Analyse the risks-potential impact on the project.

Step 3: Prioritise the risks in terms of magnitude and importance of attention and map the risks to the process.

Step 4: Resolve the risks-initiate appropriate actions to eliminate or minimise the impact of the risks on the project.

Step 5: Monitor the risks regularly to assess the effectiveness of the actions initiated and analyse the trends.

The process is summarised under five headings: Measure, Minimise, Mention, Monitor and Modify.

1. *Measure*: The project manager needs to measure, assess and understand:
   - the risk that the project will exceed the budget he is thinking of committing to,
   - the risk that the project will miss any dates he has in mind,
   - the risk that the project will fails to meet any other commitments he is about to make.
2. *Minimise*: The Project Manager has to do something about it, there's no point in assessing risks if you don't take action to reduce them.
3. *Mention*: The Project Sponsor owns the project risk; ultimately he is taking the risk. But many sponsors have no idea what the risk might be. Project managers have a duty to explain the risk to the sponsor before the sponsor gives the go ahead.
4. *Monitor*: Clearly we must make sure we monitor and manage risks during the project to make it less likely that they will happen and to minimise the impact if they do. Create a Risk Register,

which lists risks in priority order. For each risk, the register might include: risk number, description, consequence if risk happens, probability (high, medium or low), planned actions to mitigate the risk, contingency plan (what you'll do if the risk happens), Risk owner (a member of the project team), status (e.g., closed: no longer a risk)

5. *Modify*: At the end of each stage of your project hold a post-mortem. Look at the risks you identified at the outset. Record what you did successfully to deal with each risk, what you tried that did not work, and what you would do next time with the benefit of hindsight. These ways of addressing risks will be useful not only to you and your next project, but also to other project managers.

Principles of Risk Management

Every project manager and business leader need to be aware of the practices and principles of effective risk management. Understanding how to identify and treat risks to an organisation, a programme or a project can save unnecessary difficulties later on, and will prepare managers and team members for any unavoidable incidences or issues.

Tom Gilb explains 10 fundamental principles of risk management that help project managers to have better control on the project.

1. *Quantify requirements*: All critical performance and resource requirements must be identified and quantified numerically. Focus on achieving the maximum benefits within financial budget and time-scales rather than on attempting to eliminate all risk.
2. *Focus on financial budget and timescale:* Focus on achieving the maximum benefits within financial budget and timescale rather than on attempting to eliminate all risk.
3. *Design out unacceptable risk*: Unacceptable risk needs to be 'designed out' of a system consciously at all stages, at all levels, in all areas, e.g., architecture, purchasing, contracting, development, maintenance and human factors.

4. *Design in redundancy*: When planning and implementing projects, conscious backup redundancy for out-maneuvering risks is a necessary cost.

5. *Monitor reality*: Early, frequent and measurable feedback from reality must be planned into your development and maintenance process, to identify and assess risks before they become dangerous.

6. *Reduce risk exposure*: The total level of risk exposure at any one time should be consciously reduced to between 2 per cent and 5 per cent of total budgets.

7. *Communicate about risk*: There must be no unexpected results. If people have followed guidelines and are open about what work they have done, then others have the opportunity to comment constructively. Where there are risks, share the information.

8. *Reuse what you learn about risk*: Standards, rules and guidance must capture and assist good practice. Continuous process improvement is also needed.

9. *Delegate personal responsibility for risk*: People must be given personal responsibility in their sector for identification and mitigation of risk.

10. *Contract out risk*: Make vendors contractually responsible for risks, they will give you better advice and services as a result.

Strategies/Techniques of Project Risk Management

In order to be successful, companies must understand and use strategies for sound risk management. This can save them a lot of time, money and legal entanglements down the road. Depending on the situation and circumstances, there are specific techniques that companies can use to effectively manage risk:

1. *Avoid*: Strategies to eliminate the uncertainty confronted by the project. Knowing how and when to properly avoid unhealthy risk is an important technique when analysing a situation.

2. *Transfer*: Strategies that assist in transferring ownership of risk or risk liability to a third party and sharing of risk on mutually

Figure 23.2

Strategies/Techniques of Risk Management

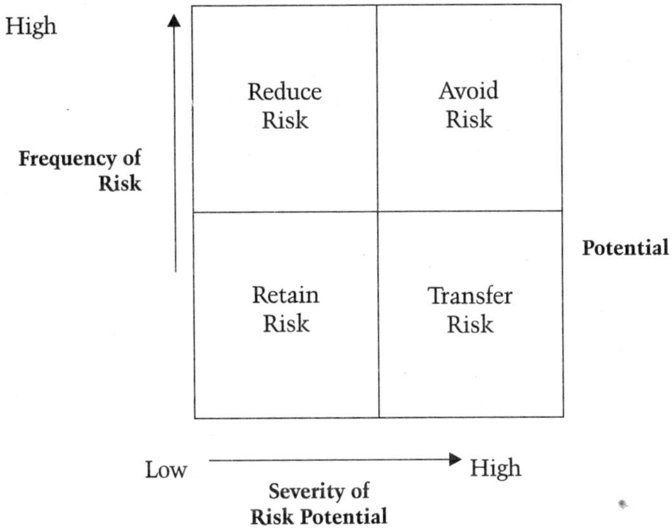

acceptable terms and conditions. This technique is often used when the risk being analysed can best be dealt with by a third party. It's important to know when to use the assistance of a third party when deciding how to handle risk.

3. *Mitigate/Reduce*: Strategies to reduce the magnitude of impact or risk exposure to an acceptable level or threshold. Mitigation is a risk management technique that is designed to lessen the negative impact of a certain risk. This technique is most often used when a risk cannot be avoided and efforts are focused on minimising damage or loss.

4. *Accept/Retain*: Strategies to manage residual risks to control and monitor them.

Project Management Responsibilities

The project manager's KEY responsibility has to be successfully delivering the objectives and benefits the sponsor expects of the project, or the project stage the project Manager is assigned to. All other day-to-day responsibilities feed into the **KEY** one. The following is a non-exhaustive list of responsibilities often referred to in a project manager's role and responsibility brief, ensure the following are carried out in accordance with the defined expectations:

1. *Progress:* deliverables are being completed within the baseline time scales.
2. *Cost*: deliverables are being completed within the baseline cost plan.
3. *Quality*: deliverables are being completed to defined expectations, first time.
4. *Performance (Value)*: progress is being earned for the expected cost.
5. *Cash flow*: net project cash flow is being achieved as the defined expectations.
6. *SHE*: the required Safety, Health and Environmental standards are being achieved.
7. *Regulatory*: all required statutory and regulatory conditions are being met.
8. *Reporting*: regular and timely reporting of project progress to the sponsors.
9. *Risk*: to proactively manage foreseen project risk, mitigating as necessary.
10. *Change*: managing changes to the project without unduly affecting the stated objectives and benefits.

The list can go on. However, it is worth noting that in addition to all the above, there are additional implied responsibilities that directly affect those stated above. For example: Positive Team management is an implied responsibility. If the Team is not led effectively, then progress, performance, quality, etc., will begin to suffer.

Project Management Duties

We understand duties as the tasks or activities a project manager must regularly carry out in order to meet the agreed responsibilities. Again, a list can be quite long and will be closely aligned with specific Terms of Reference, but could include the following duties:

1. Produce a progress report monthly
2. Review the risk register monthly
3. Weekly communication meetings with Team Principals
4. Review weekly progress reports of Team Principals
5. Approval of purchase order requisitions
6. Approval of supplier invoices for payment
7. Weekly telephone updates to the sponsor
8. Induct new Team members into the project
9. Market the project internally
10. Produce a monthly project newsletter
11. Maintain a project blog
12. And the list can go on...

Ten Golden Rules of Project Risk Management

Rule 1: Make Risk Management a Part of Your Project

The first rule is essential to the success of PRM. If you don't truly embed risk management in your project, you cannot reap the full benefits of this approach.

Rule 2: Identify Risks Early in Your Project

The first step in PRM is to identify the risks that are present in your project. This requires an open mindset that focuses on future scenarios that may occur.

Rule 3: Communicate about Risks

A good approach is to consistently include risk communication in the tasks you carry out.

Rule 4: Consider Both Threats and Opportunities

Project risks have a negative connotation: they are the 'bad guys' that can harm your project. However modern risk approaches also focus on positive risks, the project opportunities. These are the uncertain events that are beneficial to your project and organisation. These 'good guys' make your project faster, better and more profitable.

Rule 5: Clarify Ownership Issues

Some project managers think they are done once they have created a list with risks. However this is only a starting point. The next step is to make clear who is responsible for what risk. Someone has to feel the heat if a risk is not taken care of properly. Assign a risk owner for each risk that you have found. The risk owner is the person in your team who has the responsibility to optimise this risk for the project.

Rule 6: Prioritise Risks

Some risks have a higher impact than others. Therefore, you better spend your time on the risks that can cause the biggest losses and gains.

Rule 7: Analyse Risks

Understanding the nature of a risk is a precondition for a good response. Therefore take some time to have a closer look at individual risks and don't jump to conclusions without knowing what a risk is about.

Rule 8: Plan and Implement Risk Responses

Implementing a risk response is the activity that actually adds value to your project. You prevent a threat occurring or minimise negative effects. Execution is the key here. The other rules have helped you to map, prioritise and understand risks. This will help you to make a sound risk response plan that focuses on the big wins.

Rule 9: Register Project Risks

This rule is about book keeping. Maintaining a risk log enables you to view progress and make sure that you won't forget a risk or two. It is also a perfect communication tool that informs your team members and stakeholders what is going on (Rule 3).

Rule 10: Track Risks and Associated Tasks

The risk register you have created, as a result of Rule 9, will help you to track risks and their associated tasks. Tracking tasks is a day-to-day job for each project manager. Integrating risk tasks into that daily routine is the easiest solution. Risk tasks may be carried out to identify or analyse risks or to generate, select and implement responses.

The 10 golden risk rules above give you guidelines on how to implement risk management successfully in your project. However, keep in mind that you can always improve. Therefore, rule number 11 would be to use the Japanese Kaizen approach: measure the effects of your risk management efforts and continuously implement improvements to make it even better.

Benefit of Project Risk Management

There are many misperceptions about PRM. Some project managers have misgivings about doing it: "We don't have time for that," and some are uncertain what to do.

When applying properly, PRM activities normally cost much less than the recovery costs from project failures. The return on that investment is usually at least five to one, and may be much higher (Stump, 2000). In addition to its potential to save money, the typical benefits of PRM are:

1. Proactively address project risk factors.
2. Ensure risk management and crisis management plans are in place.
3. Promote rational, risk-informed thinking and risk awareness among project team.
4. Customer and job satisfaction.

Remember

Risk management has gained unprecedented significance in the recent past. As business environment has become more dynamic, projects have been exposed to more risks. With increasing risk exposures, project managers need to adopt various risk management tools and techniques to mitigate them.

1. A risk management process does not have to be complicated or time consuming to be effective. By following a simple, tested, and proven approach that involves five steps (section Project Risk Management Process) taken at the beginning of each project, the project team can prepare itself for whatever may occur. Of course there will always be changes and there may still be surprises, but the end result is that they are fewer, that the team feels prepared and that the project is not taken off course.

2. All risks are not bad.... Make sure you are managing the risks that are appropriate to the project and make related programmes and projects aware of them and you are most of the way there. Opportunities can be anywhere within a project space, but just remember to think about them as you go through the risks; it starts to make that risk review meeting far more meaningful.

3. Risk management is a proactive project management tool used to reduce the susceptibility to losses incurred during a course of action, which leaves an auditable trail of changes. The process focuses project resources on reducing vulnerability, providing early visibility of potential problem areas and creating mitigation actions.

   Good risk management should involve the entire project team, including design, engineering, business, contracts, finance, purchasing, estimating and project controls.

   The process is ongoing, a never-ending cycle and iterative process of identification, quantification, modelling, management and monitoring. The analysis can include identifying risks, estimate and schedule items, new risks, secondary risks, scope changes, change orders, and actual costs, so as to provide a graphic depiction of the changing nature of project risk over time.

4. These are just five skills that will help project manager to manage the project more effectively: be thorough, plan well, employ the right team members, set milestones and stay calm.

5. Risk assessment is a 'brain in gear' activity: it is not about failing in a checklist and forgetting it.

   Risk assessment doesn't reduce risks: you must do something to reduce them—if you don't attack the risks, the risks will attack you.

   Reduce risks at the start, but continue to reduce them throughout the project.

6. To summarise, identify your risks, grade them and decide what corrective actions you will take should the worst happen. Give most attention to the risks with a high likelihood and high/medium severity rating. Create an action plan to minimise the impact of these risks. Monitor and control your risks.

   At the end of the project, look back at the risks and record any lessons learned in your project closure report.

   Nobody likes to think about what may go wrong in a project, especially early on, but to overlook risk management means that you chance an unnecessary project failure.

Conclusion

There is no doubt that every project requires good management if it has to deliver what the customer is expecting and deliver it in an acceptable time frame and for an acceptable cost without any disasters along the way.

Even a team well-experienced in their individual roles needs direction and every project requires efficient use of its resources: time, people and money. The right sort of management will also ensure a team achieves to their full capacity and doesn't just trundle along in a low gear.

One must realise that PRM cannot predict when the next project failure would take place but it can allow project management to avoid making the wrong decision. The PRM is preventing project failure and increasing the likelihood of project success.

References

Chandra Sekhar, Y. (2001). "Project Risk Management: Understanding Basics". Projects and Profits, April.

Gilb, Tom (2003). "Managing Project Risks in Requirements, Design and Development using Planguage." Projects and Profits, July.

Roberts, Mike Harding (n.d.). "Risk Management in Software Development Projects—A Straightforward Approach to Project Risk Management". *www. Hraconsultingltd. co.uk*.

Rosenberg, Linda H., Theodore Hammer and Albert Gallo (n.d.). "Continuous Risk Management as NASA".

Stump, Evin J. (2000). *Project Risk Management: Perception and Reality*. Galorath Incorporated Internet.

Vesta, Ravindranath (2003). "Software Risk Management" Projects and Profits, March.